SHADOWS OF ETHICS   Criticism and the Just Society

Geoffrey Galt Harpham

Duke University Press   Durham and London 1999

© 1999 Duke University Press
All rights reserved
Printed in the United States of America on acid-free paper ♾
Typeset in Stone Serif by Tseng Information Systems, Inc.
Library of Congress Cataloging-in-Publication Data appear
on the last printed page of this book.

To four extraordinary teachers:
Jean Hagstrum, Erich Heller, John Espey,
Robert Martin Adams

Contents

Preface and Acknowledgments

The phrase "shadows of ethics" is an attempt to flag three traditional arguments that run through and, most intriguingly, cross and intersect throughout the following essays. According to the first, literature is overshadowed by the philosophical inquiry into the conditions of the good society, the good person, and the good life. Especially at their most pious or defensive, apologists for literature take cover in ethics, with its lengthy pedigree, prestige, and philosophical seriousness. Ethics, they contend, represents a hidden essence of literature, and speaks a kind of truth about literature that literature cannot speak about itself. For its part, literature represents the accessible form of ethical principles, which, like atoms, are invisible in themselves but cast a kind of "shadow." Making such arguments is part of the job description of criticism, which stands in an ambivalent mid-region between ethics and literature, with allegiances to both.

Criticism also, of course, registers the resistances of literature to the alien discourse of ethics—the sponsor, it is thought, of such sterile and singularly antiliterary qualities as rationality, regularity, universality, obligation. It is also the office of criticism to promote literature's immediacy, concreteness, vitality, and affective richness, and so to assert the claims of literature as a way of understanding human life that is superior to that of philosophy. Literature loves villains; but the ultimate villain in the literary universe might be the philosophical discourse of ethics itself. And so the second argument marked here concerns the ways in which criticism holds up literature as a representation of life unregulated by concepts, obligations, or abstract notions of virtue—the ways, that is, in which literature is said to make a home for itself in the dark, disorderly, and fertile spaces unilluminated by the klieg lights of ethics.

The third argument posits a more intimate and complex relation between ethics and literature, again as mediated by criticism. Literature, some say, does not provide obedient instances of ethical verities, nor does it roam wild and free in the hinterlands of ethics. Rather, literature actually exposes the shadowed, chiaroscuro character of ethics itself, which achieves a purified view of the ideal through methods that are themselves ethically dubious. One of the effects of literature, according to this argument, is to cultivate a generous and humane respect for life in all its striving and imperfection, a respect incompatible with the strict respect for the ethical law that some philosophers would urge. Delineating "fundamental human truths" or "enduring images of the human condition," literature tries, it is said, to develop an ethic *more ethical than ethics:* the "ethics of literature" both perfect and contradict the ethics of ethics.

Although each of these three arguments is interesting in itself, none is nearly so interesting as the mysterious fact that all seem intuitively true, a fact that leads directly to the large-scale claims that run through this book. These claims are actually indicated better by an unsuccessful candidate for the title, *Ethics and Its Others.* I liked this title despite its comparative flatness because it implied that ethics was locked into a relation with things—discourses, cognitive styles, ways of evaluating—that were alien to it, yet still its own. I see this intimate and dynamic engagement with otherness as the key to the kingdom of ethics: where such an engagement is, there is ethics. And this structure of engagement applies, as I argue throughout, at every level, beginning with the oppositions that define ethical discourse, as between inclination and law, freedom and necessity, "is" and "ought," and even "ethics" and "morality"; and proceeding to the inter-ethical wars waged among advocates of Aristotle, Kant, Hegel, Nietzsche, Rawls, Foucault, Lacan, Gilligan, and others; and, including, finally, all worldly circumstances in which something—a term, a principle, a discourse, a person, a group—is forced to discover some way between indifference and warfare of coexisting with an other that is adjacent to but distinct from it.

One largely repressed and underestimated instance of this ethical "structure of engagement" occurs within ethical discourse itself in the form of a struggle between questions and answers. Ethics offers to provide a way of thinking that produces solutions to problems as general as "How ought one live?" and as specific as "What should I tell my kids about sex?" If it does not do this, it does nothing; and yet, ethical discourse *en toto,* with its proliferating distinctions, refinements, and theoretical delicacies, can be seen as a stalling action, a deferral of the moment of decision that reflects—does it not?—a philosophical embarrassment at the imminence of a specific answer to a pressing worldly question. What is ethical discourse? A relentless drive toward the necessary answer, conjoined with the equally relentless generation of yet more preliminary questions.

The most monumental texts in the history of ethics confirm this fundamental ambivalence. Take for example that citadel of certainty, Kant. Very few ethical thinkers seem less congenial today than Kant, in part because he seems so assured in his absolutism. Any worthy act, Kant notes, can be done for the wrong reason, and so the burden of ethics must fall on the will, which is good only when it is altogether determined by one feeling, respect for the ethical law. The good will, according to Kant, has zero tolerance for self-love, self-interest, or self-ends of any kind. One can admire Kant's passionate purity of purpose and still wonder at his rationalist terrorism, his pre-Freudian obtuseness. Doesn't he know about the unconscious? In fact, he does. He proves it in a brief, rarely quoted, and apparently inessential passage from "Metaphysical Foundations of Morals," where he concedes that we can never determine with complete certainty why we act the way we do. "Sometimes," he says, "it happens that with the sharpest self-examination we can find nothing, besides the moral principle of duty, powerful enough to move us to this or that action and to such a great sacrifice; yet we cannot infer from this with certainty that it was not some really secret impulse of self-love, under the false appearance of [duty] that was the actual determining cause of the will" (155).

The inventor of modern philosophy, Kant seems at this moment to invent psychoanalysis as well, asserting the impossibility of self-knowledge, the ineradicability of a fugitive narcissism even at the core of our best intentions. The deeper point, however, is that these discoveries emerge in the environment not of an inquiry into the nature of the mind, but of the ethical question about the precise character of one's motivation. This question is both absolutely essential and, Kant says here, absolutely unanswerable. The point I want to insist on is that only the concept of a perfect respect for a universal ethical law based on reason alone, a categorical imperative, can provoke such a relentless and skeptical scrutiny of one's interior life. If we said, in a contemporary spirit, that our acts and motives are overdetermined, inflected by multiple contingencies, embedded in various contexts, the product of prevailing ideologies, invariably self-interested, we would be making perhaps accurate but definitely dull statements, simple descriptions of unfalsifiable fact. It is only when we begin with the speculative presumption that our motivations contain strands that are fundamentally different in kind that we are compelled to a genuine act of discrimination. And it is only when we add the possibility that one strand might actually be masked as the other that our self-interrogation becomes both merciless and endless.

A second example of the unexpected conceptual fertility of ethical discourse comes from Hegel. Few today would agree with Hegel's judgment in *The Philosophy of Law* that "the State is the march of God through the world, its ground is the power of reason realizing itself as will. . . . We must therefore worship the State as the manifestation of the divine on earth. . . .

The State, as the nation's spirit, is the law permeating . . . its ethical code" (443–44, 447, 449). To us, such pronouncements sound plainly fascist. But Hegel did not see it that way. For him, the state was both guarantor and concrete expression of the fundamental principle of "the whole modern world," "subjective freedom." Hegel's phrases are vague and dubiously lofty, but, as a kind of by-product, they provide a stringent test by which any state can be measured. A state apparatus failing to express the ethical consciousness of its people, in which the disconnect between the ideal of subjective freedom and civil realities cannot be denied, is by Hegelian definition illegitimate. And so popular protest, even uprising, may be driven and legitimated by the very account that had seemed to discourage dissent by enshrining the state as God on earth. Moreover, the very vagueness and loftiness of the terms provoke a communal self-interrogation concerning not just the practices and values of the state, but the nature of its own ethical consciousness.

This is good enough, but Hegel does not stop here. A state that rules by force and not by reasoned consent fails, he says, to accord with "public opinion," which contains "the eternal substantial principles of justice." These principles, he continues, provide the "inner character" of "sound common sense, which is a fundamental ethical principle winding its way through everything"—with "everything" referring to "the whole character of accidental opinion, with its ignorance and perversity, its false knowledge and incorrect judgment." How do we tell the true from the false when, as Hegel says with uncharacteristic epigrammatic facility, "all is false and true"? (459–60)

This is Hegel's version of Kant's dilemma, applied not to motivation but to expressions of popular consensus. Hegel's solution, which again prefigures a dark subsequent history, is to reserve this heroic feat of discrimination to "the great man." What excites me in this dangerous argument is not, however, the distant approach of the hero, but the extreme pressure applied to worldly institutions and public opinion by the presupposition of a luminous but often disguised ethical principle snaking through the compost heap of public life.

How fascinating the world becomes under this presupposition, especially when compared to a Nietzschean world, in which ethics is simply a strategic misnomer for interest, an index of power. Nietzsche details the prehistory of ethical ideas, but the conclusion he reaches forecloses on further analysis. After having thrown open the door to the torture chamber in which ethical ideals are forged, we can give things their proper names—and go home, because the analytical job is over. For all we know, Nietzsche's genealogy of morals may be as true as it is disturbing, but the inquiries to which it gives rise are short-lived. Kant and Hegel, those unapologetic believers, may well be wrong in many respects; but the questions they urge us to ask are important and enduring.

Arising in the environment of ethics, these questions are, it will be noticed, not all or exclusively "ethical." And this leads to my final point, that ethics exerts whatever force it does by virtue of its singular capacity to adhere to, affiliate with, bury itself in, provoke, or dislodge other discourses. Ethics, I argue throughout, realizes its full creative potentiality not in "itself," but as a kind of X-factor, a bracingly alien incitement to inquiry and discrimination.

Shadows of Ethics begins with more focused or concentrated studies; then turns out toward adjacent discourses of reason, aesthetics, and interpretation; and then pursues a series of studies of individual thinkers, not all of whom are explicitly concerned with ethics at all. The constant project in these chapters on Fredric Jameson, Noam Chomsky, Geoffrey Hartman, and Martha Nussbaum is to determine what functions in each case as an overriding law, what values determine critical judgments, what commands a necessary and automatic respect. Often, the kernel or germ at the center of a critical sensibility is something—a prejudice, an identification, a compelling image, a phobia—that has little claim to ethical credentials. Can the law hide within, or form a confederation with, the illicit? Can one pay an ethical respect to laws whose deepest appeal is unknown, or even unconscious? What is the proper form of the law; what kind of thing is it that commands us? Is *respect* the right term? These theoretical questions acquire, I hope, a human countenance in these chapters.

What's wrong with much contemporary criticism and theory, I argue in the last chapter, is its implicit but determined rejection of all of the above. In various ways, contemporary thinkers try to preserve their self-righteousness intact by remaining on the margins, in the uncritiquable position of critique, avoiding the disorder and equivocality that attend worldly agency. We must, I urge here, understand the desire for purity, consistency, and perfect validation as a species of potentially culpable passivity. Genuinely responsible thought entails more than mounting an effective and rigorous critique of something; it means "imagining the center," placing oneself in the position, both powerful and vulnerable, of the lawgiver, the policy maker, the judge, the executive. If a certain view of ethics as the site of a desire for a clean conscience can inform a species of irresponsibility, then, it is my hope, a richer and more productive account of ethics may encourage the opposite.

For most of the essays, I have kept the scholarly apparatus to a minimum. Chapters 5 and 7, however, were written not as essays but as scholarly articles, and retain their footnotes here. Earlier versions of the following chapters have been previously published: chapter 2, in *Critical Terms for Literary Study,* 2nd edition, edited by Frank Lentricchia and Thomas McLaughlin (University of Chicago Press, 1995); chapter 3, in *Southern Humanities Review,* vol. 23, no. 4 (fall 1989):343-55; chapter 4, in *Textual Practice,* vol. 5, no. 3 (winter 1991):383-98; chapter 5, in *Critical Inquiry* 20 (spring 1994):524-56; chapter 6, in *Raritan: A Quarterly Review,* vol. 14, no. 4 (spring 1995):88-114; chapter 7, in *Aesthetics and Ideology,* ed. George Levine (Rutgers University Press, 1994):124-52; chapter 9, in *Salmagundi,* no. 111 (summer, 1996):213-32; chapter 10, in *Salmagundi,* no. 121-122 (winter-spring, 1999):211-37; chapter 11, in *Raritan: A Quarterly Review,* vol. 18, no. 2 (fall, 1998):146-66. I am grateful for permission to republish, and would like to thank Richard Poirier, Dan Latimer, Dominic Rainsford, George Levine, and Alan Thomas for providing invaluable instigations and inducements; and Kristina Busse and Kevin Swanson for their technologically expert assistance. Chapters 1, 8, 12, and 13 have not appeared previously.

Shadows of Ethics

1 The Inertial Paradox: Thoughts Anterior to an Ethics of Literature

With an astonishing naiveté that sometimes, but not always, marks the truly first-rate thinker, Stephen Greenblatt wondered recently whether some positive relationship might be established between beauty and morality such that the love of Shakespeare might be the first step on the road to personal integrity. There is, he wrote, "something scandalously wrong in the cohabitation of viciousness and a delight in beauty," and the task for our times was therefore to "forge a more secure link between the love of art and human decency." Greenblatt is silent on how this link might be forged, and understands clearly that the job will be difficult. Standing in the path of its realization is, for example, the disturbingly recurrent figure of the artistically sensitive autocrat who conceives his task as the forcible crafting of the state, the purification of the race, the molding of the culture. I cannot see a clear path around this figure, or pursue the larger mystery to its black depths, but I would like to propose one or two ways of thinking about literature in particular that might enable us to get a purchase on the problem, and even to begin to articulate what it is about literature that might usefully be recognized and cultivated in pursuit of a broadly humanist agenda.

The first difficulty confronting Greenblatt is a traditional repugnance on the part of readers to moralizing texts and critics, who are held in wide contempt as roaches in the kitchen of art. I share this contempt, while recognizing that I must on occasion have earned it myself. The second difficulty, and the one that will really inaugurate the present argument, concerns the general problem of moving from one discursive order to another, in this case from the aesthetic to the moral. All efforts to move from art to somewhere else are inhibited, it seems to me, by what I will call the stillness, or rather, the peculiar kind of movement, distinctive to literature, the reading of literature, and theorizing about literature.

Picture the reader: seated, holding the text, only the eyes moving, but the imagination fully engaged. Think of the literary work itself, which begins in a kind of quivering stillness, an unrealized and gathering intentionality, as Edward Said noted of beginnings generally, that erupts into motion, pursues its surprising but necessary course, and then returns to stillness. And think of the literary text, which is in the world but not of it, existing in an ambiguously absented space, here but not here, in your hands but elsewhere, removed. And think, lastly, of textual representation generally, and the way in which, through the distribution of ink on a page, everything other than ink and paper is represented, so that what you see is never what you get.

These things need only to be remarked to be grasped. But we have just begun to assess the conceptual fertility of the paradox of stillness and movement, which I will posit as the key to the literary. If we were to be asked what it is about literature that we value so highly, we might respond that it moves us; or, as Tolstoi put it in his classic essay "What Is Art?," "The activity of art is based on the fact that a man receiving through his sense of hearing or sight another man's expression of feeling, is capable of experiencing the emotion which moved the man who expressed it" (709). Tolstoi had, of course, a pretty clear idea of the emotions he wanted his readers to receive; and most people today, even those who revere him as an artist, do not share his sense that literature united people with each other and with God through a kind of "infection." Still, we have our own pieties, among which are the sentiments that art "takes us out of ourselves," extending our horizons, broadening our sympathies, challenging our habits and prejudices, refining our sensibilities, etc. All these clichés—which are to be respected precisely because they are clichés, which means that many have felt the force of them—suggest that literature is valued as an anti-inertial force. Reading in that entranced way in which we lovers of literature specialize, with time, meals, responsibilities, identity, world, fading away, dissolving to fine mist before the mighty vaporizing force of the text, we find ourselves transported, removed, displaced. This removal is not simple, for it is imaginative and attitudinal only; it is an affair, as Tolstoi says, of emotion, which might also be called a-motion. One of the most intense experiences of my earnest undergraduate career was the night I sat up reading *Tess of the D'Urbervilles* in order to prepare for a class discussion the next morning. I finished half an hour before class, but found myself unable to leave my room. Instead, I simply sat there, staring out the window at the gently falling snowflakes. I was, as I told myself, too stunned by the final scenes, too awestruck before the powerful spectacle of human fortitude and frailty I had just witnessed, to submit my still-tender and palpitating feelings to the inevitable rough vulgarities of class discussion. A more succinct statement might have been that I was too moved to move. Stillness is moving, and endings, especially narrative endings, are conspicuously still. And so, gripped by the extraordinary stillness of Hardy's Stonehenge conclusion, I was hopelessly moved, and so stayed put. In the spell of the literary, I was both elsewhere, an occupant of Hardy's world and not my own, and immobilized, sitting exhausted and bleary-eyed on the floor of my frat-house room.

Literature, I am suggesting, has a more profound relation to inertia than we might have suspected, for it responds both to the tendency to remain at rest and the tendency to keep moving. It is not anti-inertial, but hyper-inertial in that it both liberates and immobilizes, paralyzes us and takes us away. An inert object that can only be taken in by an inert reader, the text is yet moving, and has the power to move. To put far too fine a point on it, we could say that literature is a moving but unmoved mover of those who, being moved, do not move. We could think of the reader's experience as a kind of oscillation, an outward movement of imagination and affect not just accompanied by immobility but positively determined by it, and crowned by it as its necessary backlash. Mikhail Bakhtin was thinking in these terms when, in his recently published first work, *Toward a Philosophy of the Act,* he noted that an "essential moment . . . in aesthetic contemplation is empathizing into an individual object of seeing—seeing it from inside in its own essence. This moment of empathizing," he added, "is always followed by the moment of objectification, that is, a placing *outside* oneself of the individuality understood through empathizing, a separating of it from oneself, a *return* into oneself" (14). Innocent of Bakhtin, and of much else, I experienced, in my post-*Tess* moment of quivering sublimity, something like this immobilizing return to myself after a flooding-out of emotion.

When we turn to the sociocultural work of literature, we find the same thralldom to the inertial paradoxes of literary movement. In one mode or moment, literature is a primary means by which a community situates itself in place. This function of literature is less prominent today than in ancient times, when, according to Georg Lukács's *The Theory of the Novel,* the epic served as the natural expression of a world protected by the starry firmament overhead and firmly rooted in the soil. Today, Lukács noted (1914), our unprotected ethos expresses itself in the confusion of the modern novel, the record of a world "abandoned by God"; but still, he insists, beneath the novel's anarchy is the unspoken and enduring effort to discover an unproblematic world, a world, we might say, in which human culture occupies consecrated, meaningful, stable space.

One could feel that our culture, unlike Lukács's, has no natural expressive literary form at all and still feel, as I do, the power of his argument concerning the archaic spatial function of literature. Simon Schama's recent book *Landscape and Memory* speaks with a magnificent eloquence of the way in which our most tenacious and inescapable obsessions take root in certain places—forests, rivers, and rocks whose full conceptual and affective richness is realized and celebrated in poems, epics, myths, stories, operas. One hypothesis emerging from his immense work is that, in the beginning, these places were what art was about, and that human characters are a late, if clamorous, arrival on the scene of literature; or perhaps we could say more specifically that with the decisive emergence of human characters, we move out of myth and into literature. In a sequence that recapitulates the speculative history of literature I am suggesting (in which James Michener would be the new Shakespeare, the central genius of the canon), Coleridge, after a bare nod in the direction of the human autocrat, begins "Kubla Khan" with the deep romantic chasm, the twice five miles of fertile ground, only gradually making his way back to Khan himself and the human world, the ancestral voices, the dulcimer damsel. Ovid is also interesting in this respect, for his *Metamorphoses* tell how, through an excess of passion, people can grade out of the human, becoming transformed by sheer extrahuman intensity of feeling into water, flowers, stars, and rocks. In Ovid's world, one can feel so much—by being raped, by discovering that one has eaten one's son, by raging lust—that the only thing left is to become a natural thing, but a thing that echoes silently with the passions that went into its making.

Ovid can be read as an allegorist of the cultural process by which nature came to be something more than just a deposit of mineral accidents or blind animal mating, but a site of feeling, a place in which human beings might make a home because they are, in disguised form, already there. In Ovid, literature invests place with meaning and feeling. And literature since Ovid has provided something of the same service. Fantasies of "this sceptred isle," *"la douce France,"* the "cathedral grove," or the American Eden serve, Schama points out, profound cultural needs for identifying with a particular place, which means seeing a place as having a certain identity that is already, if not one's own, at least animated, nearly humanized. The very word *culture,* as Geoffrey Hartman notes in *The Fateful Question of Culture,* evokes agriculture; it is a place-bound concept, suggesting the way of life of those who occupy a given plot or kind of ground. We know we belong to the land, as the inhabitants, soon to become citizens, of *Oklahoma!* sing, exalted by the thought that their own twice five miles is about to be transformed from mere sodden "territory" into a properly abstract and fully conceptualized "state." The notion that territories, pre-statehood plots of ground, are constructed in the first instance by human feeling that has exceeded its boundaries, its capacity to be expressed by a human—a merely human—being suggests that the most stable thing we can think of in a relative and decentered universe—earth—is not only moving but the product of motion, in the specifically literary form of emotion. If nations are imagined communities, the imagining typically begins, I would suggest, with such an extravagantly invested and post-Ovidian sense of place. I do not mean to suggest an exclusively spatial origin of nations, which can be imagined as religious, ethnic, political, or historical communities. But I do mean that however a community is imagined, there will very likely be a sense of moving stillness at the core, a "place," we could call it, that animates and grounds the imagination itself; and, moreover, that this moving stillness will, by a virtually necessary energy, take narrative form, such that stories of communities are virtually stories of places rather than persons: *Paradise Lost; Wuthering Heights; Winesburg, Ohio; Dubliners; Bleak House; Our Town;* "East Coker"; *Leaves of Grass; Spoon River Anthology; Swann's Way.*

In the cultivation of this communal ground, this moving place, literature is a primitive tool, something like the fixed-harness, horse-drawn plow. But plows move, and here we come upon the other side of the paradox of literary movement. For the essential thing about a text is that it is portable. Not only can it be carried, but it seems at a deeper level to be *made to carry,* to bear the word out from the culture of origin into the wide world, to speak to others. Just as literature integrates and filters group identity, it also constitutes a lesion in the bounded cultural self-imagination, a principle of communication that presupposes otherness, and others. The text itself "imagines" readers far away, who must in turn imagine the original world of the text as well as the possible community of other readers. "Why write?" Sartre asked, and concluded that one wrote not for oneself but for the other, as an act of self-transcendence. What else is a text for, but to speak to those who are not present at the cultic or priestly moment of enunciation, those who, through the contingencies of history and the market, may come into possession of this splintered mirror of the original community? And what does this speaking-to presuppose but some common ground, which is to say, some identity, however minimal, with the unimaginable other, and therefore some indistinctness in one's own identity?

How, to continue this series of questions, does this combination of un-contested self-assertion and communicative outreach work? What work does it do? Can we specify a single work for all literary texts? In answer to the third question, I would say, overcoming my admittedly feeble anti-totalizing scruples, yes, we can. The literary text, with its cultural, cultic, and agricultural roots, presumes, I will venture, that the culture represented in and by it is at least potentially normative for a plural world. If literature flourishes, as Bakhtin said, at crossroads and along trade routes, it still must come from somewhere, and that somewhere is, at a level of deep implication, presented to the world—a world of strangers and others—as paradigmatic. As a cultural export, literature offers a certain way of building, dwelling, and thinking that claims for itself the status not just of a folkway, an idiosyncrasy, but of a possible model for others, the expression of a human rather than a local essence. Each culture claims, through its literature, not just the right to distinctness and autonomy in a world of possibly hostile strangers, but also the right to consider itself as the truest, most authentic, and exemplary way of human being. F. R. Leavis offered as the underlying message of criticism the proposition, "This is so, isn't it?" He derived this message, I think, from the cultural message of literature itself, a message to which he was unusually responsive, at least in the case of English literature. Literature says to its readers, sunk in their local slumbers, "This story is true, isn't it? This is your story, isn't it?"

And *this* is true even in cases of diasporic literature, which still speaks from and of a place. Annie Proulx's *Accordion Crimes,* a brilliant example of the genre, tracks the fortunes of—what else?—an accordion, crafted in Italy and carried by its maker to New Orleans at the turn of the century, where it is lost and falls into the hands of a German, who, after many adventures, gambles it away to a Swede, etc. At the end, the battered and oft-reconstructed instrument, having passed through the hands of virtually every immigrant group to populate the United States, gives up the ghost by a country roadside, its bellows ripped open so that it scatters to the indifferent winds thousands of dollars that had been sewn in by one of its possessors, sowing wealth broadcast at the moment it is abandoned as worthless. Even in this text, which celebrates as few others the particularities of the cultures of the world, one senses a deep and solemn pride in the exuberant hospitality of American soil to so many and to so much, a capacity that enables this place to realize better than any other the manifold potentialities of humanity.

We have not yet exhausted the complications of this simple plow as it furrows the field of culture. Literature, I have contended, speaks from and of place; and it speaks in a way that suggests a movement outward into otherness, a certain kind of commonality with other places. I have suggested, too, that the literary text makes an implicit claim to normativity, an implied critique of the place-bound nativisms of other cultures, with their reek of the cultic and exclusive. But the really interesting fact is that this critique rebounds on the text itself, and the culture it represents. If literary representation defines and refines cultural identity, it also presents this identity in a way that makes everything, all the little ways and habits and presumptions and values of a culture, appear slightly odd, arbitrary, a little out of true, in the way that a mirror image gives you back yourself, indeed, but yourself framed, flattened, reversed, and self-observant. It is significant in this respect that so much of literature, but not myth, concerns itself with people who want to leave wherever they are, their place, their class, their condition. Is this intense longing for the abstract, the novel, the undefined and unrealized, this discontent with the habitual, this quickened interest in somewhere over the rainbow—is this integral to the literary? The Russian Formalists suggested that the essence of literature lay in an act of "defamiliarization"; and perhaps this amounts to the same thing. They generally confined this act to the agency of the word or figure; but it is more powerfully conceived as the necessary effect of textual representation, in which we can see a human world redoubled, alienated from itself into the text. It is often noted that literature as a genre seems especially committed to an exploration of outsiderhood. In *Exiles and Emigrés,* Terry Eagleton makes this claim of modern British fiction, which is, as it happens, written mostly by foreigners, including James, Conrad, Yeats, Shaw, Eliot, as well as by those such as Lawrence, Wells, or Woolf whose forms of exile, determined by class or sex, were subtler but no less decisive. But the estrangement in which modern literature specializes represents not an innovation or aberration, but simply a strong emphasis on the estrangement distinctive of literature.

All of these claims are, of course, speculative, but I am fortified by the ease with which they are supportable by reference to Shakespeare, inasmuch as all arguments at this level of generality ought to be subjected to this test. Often read as a monarchist laureate, Shakespeare also wrote one of the most explicitly antimonarchist lines ever penned—"A dog's obeyed in office"—and documents, with a genealogical relentlessness worthy of Nietzsche, the bloody and erratic means by which commoners become kings and kings commoners. As the national laureate, Shakespeare is the ultimate jingoist, setting a triumphant England against the Frances of the world; as the glory of "world literature," however, he speaks for civil and imaginative freedoms that any authority would feel threatened by. He represents, we might say, the maximal form of literary ambivalence, in which the highest possible degree of chauvinism makes a theoretically inconceivable common cause with the greatest possible measure of libertarianism. Or, to revisit our initial terms, we could say that Shakespeare epitomizes the ambivalence of the literary with respect to movement in that he makes a double investment in a rooted stillness, a sceptered *here,* and in a perspectival and often literal mobility (Denmark, Venice, Verona,

Prospero's island, Egypt, Rome, the forest of Arden), a critical *elsewhere* from which official England appears but one (small) place among many.

Oddly, but perhaps inevitably enough, this double investment in here and there determines the sociocultural profile of the profession, or semi-profession of literary criticism, which, at least in the United States, is notable for its rootlessness. When I arrived at UCLA in 1968, fresh from the wholesome Middle West and eager to begin a more hedonistic life, my graduate director asked me what had brought me across the country to his doctoral program in English. I replied—unbelievable, but true—that I wanted to travel, and I thought a degree in English would enable me to get a job anywhere I went. Tactfully suppressing his thought—"That's a fellowship wasted"—he replied amiably, "With a degree in English, the one thing you won't be able to get anywhere in the world is a job." That was bad news, but a bit inaccurate in my case. I have been employed, albeit sometimes in circumstances like those of a trapeze artist, spinning in mid-air, awaiting the arrival of the catcher, any catcher. I have moved, not always by choice but always, I think, for the best. But even if I hadn't, a life of literary study is a life of travel, a life in motion. My own career, which is not unusual in this respect, has taken the form of a geo-temporal tour, involving business travel in Paleolithic caves in the Dordogne, ancient and Renaissance Rome, Quattrocento Florence, the deserts of Egypt, late medieval Germany, Spain of the Inquisition, Yorkshire, Poland, Russia, and the sea, the sea.

Perhaps, in some tough-love evolutionary way, the notoriously unanchored lifestyle of the scholar-gypsy prepares critics for the kind of work they must do. Have you noticed a certain weightlessness of the academic-literary subject, a certain thinness of personhood, a lightness of being, like that of a woman in Poe? Does it seem to you plausible that this dessication might result from a constant engagement with others and othernesses, from a prolonged experience of permeability or porosity in the field of identity, an empathetic exposure to the outside that, in addition to being a professional qualification, actually becomes a distinctive kind of identity? It seems plausible to me that the kind of identity most conducive to professional success is not just flexible (and thus an effective mediator in seminar situations) but radically portable, disconnected from a founding place and free to assess, judge, and criticize from an unsituated "aesthetic" or "theoretical" point of view. In *Extraterritorial*, George Steiner, himself much-traveled, describes the writer as "unhoused," "a wanderer," "not thoroughly at home in the language of his production, but displaced or hesitant at the frontier"; and these metaphysical postulates are confirmed by the career narratives not just of writers such as Nabokov, Beckett, or

Heine, but of academic critics generally (3, 4). College or university teachers are hired guns rather than local color. I am not, or do not think I am, generally regarded as the sort of person one finds in New Orleans, a N'Awlins kind of professor. Professors are mobile: when they meet old friends from graduate school at conferences, they ask, "Where are you now?"

I think that our overdetermined disposition to mobility overdetermines our receptivity to theory and theory-building. What is theory? This question was not posed forcefully enough during the theoretical era, from the late sixties to the early eighties, and is still rarely heard today. We don't theorize about theory; we just do it. Sometimes, however, the question imposes itself so insistently that one can almost hear it, like Madeleine Usher wailing from within the tomb. I am thinking here of Edward Said's well-known essay from the early eighties, "Traveling Theory," in which he described the distortions that befall theoretical concepts when they move from one site to another. Said's example was Lukács's *History and Class Consciousness,* which emerged from the context of the Hungarian Soviet Republic of 1919 as an "act of political insurgency," a demonstration of how a fully developed class consciousness could overcome the reifications of a splintered capitalist object world. When Lukács's student Lucian Goldmann wrote his dissertation in exile in Paris, this theory was rephrased in a way that rendered the original context, already faint in Lukács's text, virtually invisible; and by the time that Goldmann introduced Raymond Williams to the mysteries of theory in Cambridge in 1970, the insurrectionary moment of 1919 was long forgotten. Said cautioned against a negative view of such traveling, which, he pointed out, often had the tonic effect of exposing defects in the original formulations, as it did when Williams probed the inherent conceptual limitations of Lukács's concept of reification, and the political dangers of promoting a totalizing movement of consciousness—limitations and dangers Lukács had not considered. Thus the new contexts in which the theory of reification and class consciousness found itself turned out to be productive for the theory in a way that could not have been anticipated. "Borrow we must," Said concluded, in part because if we don't borrow, then our theories do not transcend the conventions of our own context, and theory risks becoming "an ideological trap."

This is a characteristically powerful explanation that still, I think, misses one of its own deepest implications. What if we said that theory did not just profit from travel but was intrinsically a form of travel? This would not be a difficult hypothesis to prove in the case of Lukács, whose infernally abstract metaphysics are, as Said points out, best understood as displaced politics, politics at a distance. This distance from immediate political context, from the material circumstances of bourgeois life and from the power apparatus that supported that life, was in an almost literal sense what Lukács's "theory" of reification and class consciousness was all about. Without such traveling, Lukács might have produced many things, or nothing at all, but not theory.

The proposition that theory is travel helps explain the theoretical hyper-productivity of strangers in town. In the first blush of theory, in the early seventies, many in England and the United States were struck by its essential Frenchness. We eventually learned that de Man was Belgian, Derrida and Althusser were Algerians, Kristeva Bulgarian, and Levinas Lithuanian. And then, when we began to theorize on our own, "we" were led by such as the Palestinian-born Edward Said, the Manxman Frank Kermode, the Indian Gayatri Spivak, the son of Christian missionaries in China Fredric Jameson, the Jamaican Stuart Hall, and more recently the Slovenian Slavoj Žižek and the Parsee Homi Bhabha—all émigré-theorists. Even those who appear to be homegrown often betray some mark of difference, such as Terry Eagleton, a veteran of the Catholic Youth movement by the time he arrived at Cambridge to be educated by Williams, a working-class Welsh-man; or Judith Butler, whose meditations on gender and other issues reflect at a distance her own outsider's experience. The Hayden Whites of the world are far rarer than you might think; and even White might point to the aberrance of his Tennessee boyhood in the theorizing world of high academe. You can, if you are made like Foucault or Lacan or Irigaray, be a stranger even if you grew up in the town. And if you are, you are far more likely to theorize than if you are the vice-president of the Rotary Club, or the earnest soccer coach.

Now, perhaps, we can begin to understand how theory does what it does. The function of theory, as Williams said, is to develop a "general consciousness" within what is experienced as a "practical," often relatively isolated consciousness (*Marxism and Literature*). But it does not do this by promoting a dilated perspective in which universal laws are grasped in their pure and unchanging form. Rather, theory structures a difference and a distance between local instance and general rule, between material embodiment and abstract principle. Theory enables us to conceive of something not just as an isolated fact but as an example of something, and to grasp general formulations as precipitates of a host of otherwise unrelated phenomena. In short, theory generates a constant sense of movement, a perspectival shuttling from small to large, near to far, concrete to abstract; and it is this shuttling that generates the sense that one form of consciousness "develops within" another.

What is it that travels in order to produce theory? If we were to inquire into the genealogy of theory, we would, I believe, turn up, again and again, an unsettling fact, that the principles that regulate our practice, that stand as formulations of "general consciousness," began their careers on the shop floor as humble inferences or generalizations from practice—as foremen, perhaps, if not line workers. Take for example the primary instance of theory in literary study, Saussure's dicta that language is a systematic structure of differences without positive content, and that the relation between signifier and signified is "arbitrary." Empirical statements concerning signs and their moving parts, these became normative theoretical principles, but—and this is the most important part—they did so many decades later in a field far removed from their scene of origin, the emergent structuralist and poststructuralist discourse of literature and philosophy. There, they became prescriptions for the de-realizing and de-substantializing of discourse, an enterprise that fit right into a certain 1960s ethos that was highly receptive to destabilizations of official structures, thawings of the cold war fixing of discourses. People committed to this ethos recognized in Saussure's work a potential source of theory; and so, theory it became, and was ceded control of the ways in which many people thought about literature, philosophy, politics, and human life generally.

This is the way it goes: observations about the movement of smoke molecules are empirical in one domain, but become theory—"chaos theory"—when applied elsewhere, as, for example, to discussions of complex texts. Computers are known to work in a certain way; but that way becomes theoretical when definite knowledge about computers is applied as a template to the human mind. Foucault noted a series of facts about the construction of prisons at a certain point in time; but the theoretical potentiality of prison architecture was unrealized until mapped onto "modernity." The spandrels of the cathedral of San Marco were simply architectural leftovers until R. C. Lewontin and Stephen Jay Gould deployed them as figures for nonadaptive by-products of evolution. The point is that if a fact is to become theoretical, it must travel beyond its original context, suffering a decay or degradation in the process, losing something of its original context-specific solidity.

Let's take another example from linguistics. Noam Chomsky draws from the observation of language acquisition in early childhood the conclusion that a language faculty is innate, and is activated in a given linguistic climate. He notes that people constantly produce sentences they have never before heard, and infers that they are inherently "creative." It's difficult to argue with the original inference, or with the application of the term "creative," which he means as a descriptive rather than an honorific term. These statements are *not yet theoretical*. But when, in a different phase of his work, Chomsky began to think about political events, he did so from the base of his investigations into the language faculty, and so found himself compelled, out of theoretical necessity, to conclude that since human beings are innately oriented toward creativity, any political order that ignores this fact, or presumes otherwise, or seeks to regulate or circumscribe individual creativity, conflicts with a profound condition of human being, and violates not only the ethical but the genetic code. Although he is generally unwilling to put the matter in this way, Chomsky clearly believes that the basic truths about language lead directly to libertarian anarchism as a political philosophy. The autonomy of syntax determines the autonomy of subjects. In the discursive order of politics, descriptive-empirical insights into the language faculty become not just descriptive but normative and regulatory—in a word, theoretical.

Statements emerging from one order of discourse become theoretical by emigrating to another where their empirical adequacy is no longer debatable because the empirical field has dropped out of sight. Having traveled, such statements now function as fixture itself, governing the otherwise unregulated and dangerously mobile data of the new field. Now, we could contest Chomsky's view of language (or the "language faculty") as innate and creative by pitting it against Saussure's, which stresses rule-bound activity in accordance with arbitrary principles peculiar to each little linguistic group. But that is precisely the point: that while "language" can be defined in fundamentally different ways, any general account can, with a bit of luck and pluck, depart from its empirical home; it can arrive at foreign shores and present itself at court as the sole ambassador of the kingdom of "language," as long as no other general accounts are around to contradict its claims. Thus literary theory can base itself on Saussure and cultivate a system of differences without positivity, and a certain kind of political theory can base itself on Chomsky, cultivating inalienable human freedoms—and both can refer to the massive prestige of "language." And they can do this because the theory on which they draw—like all theory, I am contending—has traveled from its home and can no longer be challenged on empirical grounds, by reference to the facts.

As literary scholars, or, *a fortiori,* as literary theorists, we are specialists in the category of *the moving.* Always between houses, we constitute an entire class of Rushdies, to mention one more émigré-theorist. But, in a final permutation of the paradox of literary mobility, we have, built into our job description, the most ponderous and pretentious task imaginable: the preservation of the heritage, the guardianship of the tradition, the transmission of accumulated cultural wisdom, the tending of the flame.

The flame of what? Many today would, perhaps, answer, *culture.* But in the final movement of the argument, I would like to propose that we consider the claims of another term, one that reflects not the placing function of literature but rather its outreach function: *society*. This term, as Raymond Williams says in *Keywords*, began with a specific meaning of companionship or fellowship, a conscious organization or relationship, but has developed in addition to this a more general sense referring to the common life shared by all, unlike, for example, the "state," which refers to the apparatus of power. If we combine the two meanings that Williams so patiently and precisely disentangles, we have, in the form of a lamination, a virtually utopian image of a universal fellowship, a species-companionability.

Society so conceived makes a pointed contrast to *culture*, which is, Williams says, "one of the two or three most complicated words in the English language," with numerous conflicting meanings or implications crossing through it (*Keywords* 87). Early on, *culture* is, Williams says, always "a noun of process: the tending of something, basically crops or animals." *Culture* suggests, in other words, an effort of self-interested appropriation, of directed purpose, of modification of the natural course in pursuit of a certain goal. In the nineteenth century, Christopher Herbert has pointed out, the term stood as a site of resistance to the threats presented by an unregulated and destructive desire, a bulwark, in Matthew Arnold's formulation, against the "anarchy" of private interests and need-driven calculations of civil society. Perhaps as a consequence of these emphases on acquisition and coherent purpose, the term acquired during this time implications of exclusivity or elitism that remain today—the Ministry of Culture; to be "cultured" or "cultivated" (by going to symphonies, ballets, and operas); a specific "culture" as distinct from, and probably superior to, others. And *culture* splinters easily, as into "high culture," "middle-brow culture," and "popular culture." We think of "cultural attainments," but not of social ones. *Culture* is a far more material concept than society, and more mystical as well; especially compared to what the Romantics conceived as a mechanistic, inorganic civil *society, culture* forms a kind of harmonic tone with *cult*.

Culture's associations tend, we can see, toward the hyper-refined and the primitive. Yeats's prayer that his daughter might grow "like some green laurel / Rooted in one dear perpetual place" reflects a cultural rather than a social desire, and collates with his nationalist-fascist political sympathies. A univocity that I cannot help regarding as sinister (recall the mesmerized, quasi-coital, panting Oklahomans—*Okla! Homa! Okla! Homa!*—after the death of Jud Frye) infects the notion of culture at its fringes. The associations of society, by contrast, are benign, relatively passive with respect to individual members, and largely inclusive. "High society" suggests the harmless, if profligate, ways in which the wealthy enjoy and think well of themselves; "high culture" implies a certain arrogance, even aggressivity. Culture, I am arguing, is rooted like the corn in Oklahoma, or like Yeats's daughter; perhaps, in fact, it suggests a fantasy of rootedness, a fantasy that is powerfully attractive to highly cultured but nomadic academics. The symmetrical social fantasy is an unreal mobility, a perfect emancipation from the ancestral home, the ancient ways.

In some respects, culture and society do indeed appear as symmetrical fantasies: on the one hand, an entrenchment, a hardening, a delusional solidarity consecrated in space and deep time; and on the other, an airiness, a delusional sense of freedom and unencumberment. But they are not precisely symmetrical. The fantasies of culture include, as Geoffrey Hartman points out, the racist nationalism of the *Kulturkampf* whose most extreme expression was the Holocaust. A history of evil fantasy stains the very concept of culture, which has been, Hartman acknowledges, structurally vulnerable to political manipulation, especially in projects of identity-purification. A Nubian poet recently defended the opening of a Nubia museum by saying, "We are afraid of being swallowed by Egyptian culture." He did not say that he was threatened by Egyptian society. In fact, *society* does not swallow; it includes. And perhaps this is why I think that universities are essentially social, rather than cultural institutions—volitional, hospitable to innovation and to new members, differentiated but companionable. Students of the humanities in particular are implicitly committed, as Frances Ferguson has recently said, to what I think of as the eminently social project of "scrutinizing texts in such a way as to enable one to recognize views that one doesn't hold." "Recognition" means here not simply "taking in," but "according recognition to," apprehending something with a presumption of respect. The kind of nonhierarchical encounters by which literature is always fascinated, as between the great Macbeth and a trio of filthy witches, or Lear and his Fool, or Black Elk and Queen Victoria, or Jaggers and Pip, or St. George and the dragon—or in which writers seem to figure with some regularity, as when Marianne Moore teaches Jim Thorpe at the Carlisle Indian School, or Freud sits in the audience to hear Mark Twain lecture ("The First Watermelon I Ever Stole"), or Gabriel García Márquez swaps fish recipes with Fidel Castro, or Joyce Carol Oates interviews Mike Tyson at his workplace, or Truman Capote huddles with Gary Gilmore in prison—such encounters, the sort of thing that can occur in an aggregation conceived as a permeable and plural unity, suggest the unusual access writers have to the fluidity of society, often at the expense of their original cultural identities.

Classical humanist accounts of literature, for which I will return to my two sages, have stressed what I am describing as its social determinants. Sartre conceives of the others for whom one writes as "interposed persons" whom you do not and cannot know in advance, but must regard as sufficiently like yourself to communicate with, and even to feel responsibility for. Tolstoi, too, sees the social bond between unlike people, rather than the cultural bond of identity, as the precondition and constant effect of art. If one yawns and others yawn, or laughs and makes others laugh, Tolstoi says, that is not art. Art begins when "one person with the object of joining another or others to himself in one and the same feeling, expresses that feeling by certain external indications"—words, sounds, stone, pigments. The material "externality" of the medium dictates a humane distance between creator and audience that enables the distinctively free communication that marks the aesthetic. This externality can take the form, Tolstoi says, of a gift, as when the artist "hands onto others feelings he has lived through," so that they can live them too, if they choose. Thus, if we ask, with Tolstoi, "What is Art?" we conclude that art is a kind of sympathetic infection that ignores, if it does not overcome, barriers of race, class, religion, age, sex, ethnicity; it is "a means of union among men joining them together in the same feelings, and indispensable for the life and progress toward well-being of individuals and of humanity" (709-10).

It is, perhaps, the conspicuously good conscience with which we retail grand pronouncements such as these that truly defines the professionalized student of literature. But if we feel a dubious ease tossing off generalizations about the mission of art, the history of Western metaphysics, the laws of global capitalism, the nature of language, the constitution of gender—things we know, really, very little about—it is, I think, because we understand that the very insubstantiality of our discussion exerts on whatever audience we can gather a gentle but not an overpowering or oppressive force—the force, I submit, of the social rather than the cultural. We operate by suggestion—this is so, isn't it?—not by performative proclamations of the law; and so we can say, if not exactly anything, at least far more than our mere credentials would seem to authorize. And that is another way of saying that we operate in the thinner air of the social rather than the thick miasma of culture.

Literature departments are and ought to be central to the university inasmuch as literature, with its roots plunged into the space of culture and the past, branches out—like a laurel, perhaps—and achieves itself in the air of the unprogrammed future, sowing seeds broadcast to germinate where and how they will. Hartman urges us not to neglect aesthetic education, by which he means a constant tutelage in sympathy, an interest in the widening and intensification of feelings for others unlike one-self or views one doesn't hold, a hospitality to those strangers we meet, converse, and associate with, who are exemplified by the wanderers who populate Wordsworth's poetry, Cervantes's prose, Shakespeare's drama, even Dante's Christian epic in which the poet himself is the wanderer—the numberless invaluable men from Porlock who arrive to disturb our self-enraptured and uncreative trances. A world without strangers would be like the furious enclosure of *Wuthering Heights,* whose singularity in the literary history of Britain may be that it is, for most of its wild course, an unusually pure expression of culture: even the alien Heathcliff seems un-cannily to belong to the land. Still, the book does not sustain this mode, becoming social by fierce necessity in the third generation when Cathy teaches Hareton to read, enabling him, and the two of them together, to leave the ancient burdens behind them, to cross the moors, and to enter the lighter and more properly social ethos of Thrushcross Grange. In fact, I think that this is one way of describing the essential movement of literary plots: from culture to society. Do any narrative literary plots go backwards in this respect? Or do they, in general, recapitulate the movement sug-gested by Joyce's *Portrait,* or by Lawrence's great double novel, *The Rainbow* —which begins with an image of agriculture, the land tended by immemo-rial generations of Brangwen men—and *Women in Love,* which concludes with fully individuated and urbanized Brangwen women? Are there ex-ceptions? *Gatsby?* I don't think so: the return to culture after the failure of society happens, really, *after* the conclusion of the narrative, and falls any-way under the shadow of the dictum that you can't go home again, or that if you do, you won't (as Nick will shortly discover) find yourself accepted as a proper member of the culture from which your narrative was launched.

I do not mean to suggest that we can ever truly leave the culture of home, or even that we ought to try. Hartman conceives of aesthetic education as an indispensable function of culture, and the best weapon, he stubbornly insists, against the perversions of the idea of culture. And culture is nec-essary in any event as a check on the social fantasy of perfect mobility, which is even on its own terms far from utopian. We cannot either achieve a purely social, nor abandon a purely cultural, condition. Beneath the vari-ous uses to which the idea of culture may be put lies a hard necessity: we live, as a matter of fact, in the double, self-canceling and mutually sustain-ing fantasies of culture and of society. Literature serves the ends of both. But the directionality of literature runs from culture and toward society. I would even be willing to argue that this is on balance a good thing, and that *society* is a good word, perhaps the best word, for the human aggre-gation implied by a serious program in literary study. If the passage from

Hamlet to human decency is never finally accomplished, this is neither a mystery nor a failure, but a necessary consequence of the constant but inconclusive *streaming* of literature from one principle of human association to another. Those eager to solicit literature for lessons in living might, at least, learn from this streaming the general direction in which we ought to be — and are already, and must be — going.

Ethics in Our Time

For most of the Theoretical Era (c. 1968–87), ethics, the discourse of "re-spect for the law," had no respect. All the critical schools that arose or re-defined themselves during this era—semiotics, deconstruction, feminism, Marxism, and psychoanalysis, to name the most prominent—took as their founding premise the radical inadequacy of such Enlightenment leftovers as "the universal subject," the "subject of humanism," the "sovereign sub-ject," the "traditional concept of the self"; and in the assessment of the various crimes and misdemeanors committed by or on behalf of this sub-ject, ethics was seen to be heavily implicated. For it was in the discourse of ethics—was it not?—that the subject, grossly flourishing in all its pre-theoretical arrogance, claimed an undisturbed mastery over itself and in-deed the entire world by claiming to base its judgments and actions on the dictates of universal law. According to this account, whenever some-one claimed to be acting on "the ethical imperative" or "the moral law," they were in fact rendering mystical and grand their own private interests or desires. Making claims of this sort, one might even persuade oneself that one's interests were somehow globally necessary: ethics could be the particular way in which people preserved a good conscience while over-riding or delegitimating the claims of others. Ethics thus became for many the proper name of power, hypocrisy, and unreality. As the Marxist critic Fredric Jameson charged, it was "ethics itself" that had arranged the binary oppositions such as self and other, good and evil, to which the Western mind had become so disastrously attached; and ethics itself that served as "the ideological vehicle and the legitimation of concrete structures of power and domination."

Others echoed and varied this charge. "Women, stop trying," Luce Iri-garay wrote; "Do what comes to mind, do what you like: without 'rea-sons,' without 'valid motives,' without 'justification.' You don't have to raise your impulses to the lofty status of categorical imperatives" (*Specu-lum of the Other Woman* 203). Irigaray and others denounced one specific conceptual form of the "concrete structures of power and domination" that Jameson noted, the way in which the presumably unsexed subject of morality, the subject who was subject to categorical imperatives, was tacitly assumed to be male. As when one (male) philosopher, arguing for a liberal pluralism, stated that "there are many different ends that men may seek, and still be fully rational, fully men" (Berlin, "On the Pursuit of the Ideal" 14); or when another contended that the "classic tradition" he would like to revive involves "one central functional concept, the concept of *man* understood as having an essential nature and an essential purpose or function" (MacIntyre 56); or when a third reflected on "that sense of freedom which men take to be peculiar to themselves," and proceeded to meditate on "the intrinsic character of thought," which is "self-correcting, when thinking reaches a first stage of complexity, as it does in adult men" (Hampshire 78, 54). Somehow, ethical discourse, which ought to concern itself exclusively with Reason, Freedom, Value, or the Good, still insistently constructs a particular sexual scenario, casting "man" in all the lead roles: the Hero of Duty, the Prince of Reflection, the Knight of Temptation, the Sovereign of Freedom, the General Exemplum of Humanity.

Such sinister and silent collusion between particular, concrete arrangements of power and an abstract and "universal" style of representation seemed to many to be the peculiar specialty of ethics, and provoked the accusation that, in its worldly work, ethics was predicated not on "respect" but rather on what Jacques Derrida called "nonrespect," and not just for women. The mighty complex of ideas and prejudices that Derrida titled "logocentrism" works tirelessly to neutralize or marginalize the qualities of "absence, dissimulation, detour, différance, writing," and gets ethics to do the dirty work; or rather, does its dirty work and calls it ethics. The bias in favor of "presence" that Derrida says characterizes all Western thought works by holding up speech rather than writing as the more natural, fundamental, primary—in a word, ethical—form of language. "The ethic of the living word," Derrida wrote in *Of Grammatology*, "would be as respectable as respect itself if it did not live on a delusion and a nonrespect for its own condition of origin, if it did not dream in speech of a presence to writing, denied by writing. The ethic of speech is the *delusion* of a presence mastered" (139). Like Jameson and Irigaray, Derrida warned that a discourse that encouraged submission to a general or universal law lent itself to projects of mastery whose agendas were not universal, just unvoiced or unacknowledged. In ethical discourse, it was widely believed, values and practices with no special claim to worthiness became normative.

Thus, virtually all the leading voices of the Theoretical Era (an era conspicuous for its deification of "leading voices") organized their critiques of humanism as exposés of ethics, revelations of the transgressive, rebellious, or subversive energies that ethics had effectively masked and suppressed. And virtually all joined Derrida in seeing ethics as a combination of mastery *and* delusion. For Jameson, the focus of ethics on the individual confronting a moment of moral choice obscured the deep currents of collective, historical life; for Jacques Lacan, the Kantian ethic of rational self-legislation masked the desire that ultimately aligned ethics with masochistic enjoyment, and Kant with de Sade; for Paul de Man, ethics had "nothing to do with the will (thwarted or free) of a subject," and was best considered a "language aporia," a "linguistic confusion," a "discursive mode among others" (*Allegories of Reading* 206); for Michel Foucault, ethics was a typical humanistic soap bubble whose hard kernel of reality was the relentlessly productive force of various discursive and disciplinary regimes. For all of them, the truth of ethics was announced by Nietzsche: "a mere fabrication for purposes of gulling: at best, an artistic fiction; at worst, an outrageous imposture" (*On the Genealogy of Morals* 10).

Then, something happened.

On or about December 1, 1987, the nature of literary theory changed. When the *New York Times* reported the discovery of a large number of articles written by the young Paul de Man for a Belgian collaborationist newspaper in 1941–42, virtually everything about literary theory and criticism as practiced in the United States underwent a transformation as violent and radical as that which had been wrought a generation earlier by the advent of "theory" itself. A profession that had just accustomed itself to the tenuring of theoreticians was subjected to the spectacle of their dethroning; heated but still decorous debates about the nature of literary language, the role of metaphor in the discourses of rationality, the functioning of discursive regimes, the relevance of philosophy to literary study, or the dominance of "Western metaphysics" abruptly gave way to charges of personal immorality, collaboration in the Holocaust, opportunism, and deception. The stakes and temperature of critical discourse rose appreciably. And as the great Durante used to say, everybody wanted to get into the act. In the wild controversy that ensued, every possible position, it seemed, was attacked or defended by somebody. By his enemies, de Man was bluntly accused of complicity in Nazi savagery, while his friends and allies claimed to discern even in the most incriminating of the newly discovered articles signs that a rhetorically hypersubtle de Man was only appearing to collaborate while actually resisting. The later work also came in for reassessment. Some saw in the "impersonal" austerity of his literary criticism a mere continuation of his youthful enthusiasms; but to others, the stress de Man placed in his last years on linguistic "inhumanity" seemed a heroic attempt to imagine a language unstained by human criminality, as well as a warning to others of the errors into which he had fallen as a young man. Deconstructionists, who had been attempting to outlast and outpublish the feminist, Marxist, and historicist scholars who had been attacking them for their indifference to history, the material base, justice, and value, suffered even more heavily, it could be argued, than they had when de Man had died in 1983. Deconstruction's dominance had discouraged any ethical evaluation of the author; but now that that dominance was rapidly proving to be delusory, the repressed was returning in force, and the American academy gave itself over to a glut of judgment. Many antitheorists seemed simply astonished at their good fortune in finding de Man and deconstruction vulnerable on ethical grounds just when they had nearly given up hope of victory on other grounds. When the last incontrovertible point was made, one thing, and perhaps only one, was clear: ethics was on the agenda.

The effect on deconstruction was traumatic. De Man's work suddenly switched genres, being read now not as literary criticism but as a coded testimony. The template of the wartime journalism disclosed in de Man's often curious and impacted phrasings patterns of obsessive worry about exposure, proleptic self-defense, reflections on the uselessness of confession, signals for help, as when he introduced, in the last year of his life, a second edition of his first book, *Blindness and Insight*, by noting, "I am not given to retrospective self-examination and mercifully forget what I have written with the same alacrity I forget bad movies—although, as with bad movies, certain scenes or phrases return at times to embarrass and haunt me like a guilty conscience" (xii). The timing of the discovery had an unfortunate effect on J. Hillis Miller's 1986 book *The Ethics of Reading*, which had placed de Man in the succession of Kant: whereas Kant had evacuated the ethical subject of every feeling but "respect for the law," de Man had, according to Miller, erased from the reading subject every concern but respect for the text. A properly respectful or ethical reading, Miller had argued, lingered in the apprehension of textual "undecidability"; and now, when the response to the wartime journalism began to assume threatening proportions, Miller charged de Man's enemies with a failure to *read*. It was noted by some that, measured against the virtually infinite prolongation Miller had envisioned, any definite judgment could seem premature, or "unethical." Although mounted with considerable energy and commitment, the argument that de Man's ethics could only be judged in de Man's terms was not universally persuasive.

Perhaps the most complex and productive effect of the de Man affair was on the work of Derrida. Painful though it was, the controversy seems actually to have stimulated Derrida not only to expand and deepen a meditation on ethics that was, as we have seen, present in his work from the very beginning, but to move his general critique in a new direction, his formidable style becoming in the process much more flexible and accessible. His long and deeply personal essay "Like the Sound of the Sea Deep within a Shell: Paul de Man's War" proceeded through the newly discovered texts according to reading procedures he had established twenty years earlier, citing evidence for (on the one hand) active collaboration in the anti-Semitic project of the Reich, and (on the other hand) for an elusive, indeed fugitive critique of what de Man had referred to in one piece as "vulgar anti-Semitism," and, possibly, of all anti-Semitism inasmuch as it was vulgar. With excruciating attention to textual detail—an attention that, by itself, seemed to some violently inappropriate considering the context—Derrida "read" de Man, registering both the full, appalling force of the shock and, with a grim fidelity to principle, the scant but, he insisted, definite possibility that things were not as bad as they seemed— an argument that, to those persuaded otherwise, was reminiscent of Mark Twain's comment that Wagner's music was not as bad as it sounded. Derrida's essay drew the fire of those who wanted from him for once an unambivalent statement; they got what they wanted, but in the form of an unequivocally scathing criticism of themselves in a text that was at once Derrida's most intimate and most violent, a freeswinging diatribe entitled "Biodegradables."

This, clearly, was not Derrida's chosen battlefield. Unlike many other eminent philosophers or academics, Derrida never sought to use his position to make pronouncements, ethical or otherwise. But the crisis of the moment tested the strength of his principles and methods, and perhaps fortified him to undertake a general defense of deconstruction on ethical grounds. He reiterated arguments to the effect that, far from representing a principle of frivolity, deconstruction actually entailed a higher level of readerly and political responsibility by identifying the fissures and instabilities in what had seemed to be thoroughly grounded structures. And he systematized the ethical commitments of deconstruction in a 1988 essay, "Afterword: Toward an Ethic of Discussion," where he outlined a normative process of deconstructive reading in which a "layer or moment" of "doubling commentary" establishing the "minimal consensus" on the "relatively stable" meaning of a text and its relevant contexts was to be followed by a second, "productive" layer or moment of "interpretation." Derrida seemed to envision a structural relationship between these aspects of reading and what Kant defined as the antinomies of pure practical reason, necessity and freedom. Stating that deconstruction began with the humble and disinterested reproduction of fact, Derrida was also claiming that the interpretive "freeplay" of his own texts constituted the full realization of traditional scholarship, the ripened completion of critical understanding. Far from licensing indifference or neutrality, Derrida said, he was trying to determine the conditions under which a reading became truly responsible by identifying a phase of undecidability through which reading must pass, a phase in which conclusions that had been taken for granted become subject to disinterested questioning. Why, Derrida asked at the end of this essay, "have I always hesitated to characterize [the unconditionality that prescribes deconstruction] in Kantian terms . . . when that would have been so easy and would have enabled me to avoid so much criticism, itself all too facile as well? Because such characterizations seemed to me essentially associated with philosophemes that themselves call for deconstructive questions" (153). The difference between Kant's discourse and his own was not that one is ethical and the other critical, for Derrida claimed ethical value for deconstructive criticism. It was that Kant still believed in the subject and related "philosophemes," and so must be deconstructed—according to the ethical imperative that he himself glimpsed, but only glimpsed.

While Kant's particular formulations can be deconstructed, the imperative to deconstruct has become categorical, that is, Kantian and ethical. At the same time (the late eighties), Derrida was turning to such concepts as law, justice, and responsibility, solidifying the image of deconstruction as a discourse of what might be called imperativity in general. Even "the subject" reappears in an interview in which Derrida speaks of the linking of "the ego" to an inhuman other, "and above all to the law, as subject subjected to the law, subject to the law in its very autonomy, to ethical or juridical law, to political law or power, to order (symbolic or not)" ("Eating Well" 99). The subject can "return" on the condition that it be transformed and modernized—no longer the self-identical, self-regulating subject of humanism, but rather a subject inmixed with otherness. This otherness, Derrida said, would consist not only of the obligation that all people owe to other people, but also of the iron laws, the internal otherness, which we, as speaking animals, harbor within our living consciousness: "the mark in general," "the trace," "iterability," "*différance*," othernesses that "*are themselves not only human*" (116).

I have dwelt at some length on Derrida's account of the terms on which a return of the subject might be admissible or conceivable because it marks both a decisive emphasis in his recent work and a consensus emerging within various schools of thought about the role of such factors as necessity, law, and obligation in the formation of a subject—a subject that must be ethical. In fact, the date of December 1, 1987, does not mark the moment when ethics abruptly returned from its exile in a predeconstructive wilderness, but rather the approximate time when the large fact that all sorts of thinkers had for some time been heavily invested in ethics became inescapable. For it was not only Derrida who could claim to have been ethical all along. As North American readers now began to realize, a persistent strain of ethical concern had for some time troubled the margins of critical discourse, even in the work of those who had been thought to be most rigorously antihumanistic.

Marx, for example, was taken by Jameson as the authority for an antiethical campaign to "[transcend] the 'ethical' in the direction of the political and the collective" (*Political Unconscious* 60). But Philip J. Kain's *Marx and Ethics* argued that Marx himself rejected ethics only for a brief period in the mid-1840s and was a decisively ethical thinker both before and after. Similarly, psychoanalytic criticism had for the most part sustained Freud's dismissive attitude toward any claims to ethical transcendence or grounding; but a 1986 volume called *Pragmatism's Freud: The Moral Disposition of Psychoanalysis* awakened suspicions that Freud might have underestimated or failed to appreciate his own ethical commitments (Kerrigan). In the same year, Jacques Lacan's 1959–60 seminar *Ethique de la psychanalyse* appeared, crystallizing the complex and unorthodox ethics that had hitherto appeared in his work primarily in the form of cryptic comments such as "The status of the unconscious is ethical." If Lacan had been perceived by readers of *Écrits* and *The Four Fundamental Concepts of Psychoanalysis* as a debunker of ethics, he now emerged as an ethical thinker in his own right with the claim that psychoanalysis did in fact have a law, if only one: that one must not "give way as to one's desire." Moreover, the psychoanalytically informed French feminists who, in one mood, rejected the very idea of ethics often proposed as a replacement another ethic. In an early article, Julia Kristeva, for example, noted the dominance in linguistics of the concept of structure, and thus of a regularity and systematicity that were, she claimed, drawn from "social contract" ethics. As a corrective, Kristeva sought to restore to its rightful place the notion of language as a signifying practice with revolutionary potential, in which the speaking subject was allowed to sense the "rhythm of the body as well as the upheavals of history." This was not an antiethics at all, but an ethics plain and simple. "Linguistic ethics," she wrote in *Desire in Language*, "consists in following the resurgence of an 'I'" (34). And Irigaray, whom we last saw denouncing Kantian ethics, argued that feminine difference compelled not a rejection of ethics *tout court,* but rather a different ethic, an ethic of difference, or, as she put it in her 1984 book, *An Ethics of Sexual Difference.*

Even the theory of postmodernism, which originally defined itself in opposition to such aspects of "modernity" as Jürgen Habermas's neo-Kantian "discourse ethics," subsequently advanced its own ethic. While Habermas and Jean-François Lyotard, postmodernism's leading theoretician, disagreed on many issues, they held one key position in common— that the emphasis on language so central to contemporary self-understanding yielded a positive ethic. For Habermas, this ethic embraced the values implicit in transparent, undistorted, and open communication, a normative equality that was "counterfactually" immanent in all utterances whatsoever, no matter how duplicitous, inept, or mendacious. Lyotard, who had seemed to many readers an opponent of all norms, ideals, regulations, and even—given the density and obscurity of some of his texts—of transparent communication, argued against Habermas by defining a counterethic specific to postmodernity. Lyotard praised Levinas for completing the work Kant had begun, absolutely severing "the language game of prescription" from any connection with the "ontological discourse" cultivated by the knowledge-obsessed Greeks, and creating a perfect "emptiness" of the commandment to obey. "Obligation without normativity"—this was an ethic consistent with postmodernity's emphasis on heterodoxy and dissemination and also, interestingly enough, with the secret essence of modernity itself, which was beginning to be understood by Lacanians, Derrideans, and Foucauldians as the ethos of ungrounded commands, of necessity "suspended over an abyss."

It was, however, the late work of Foucault that represented the most decisive marker of the emergence of ethics. In the second and third volumes of the History of Sexuality series, and in a number of late essays and interviews—all of which appeared in translation in the mid-1980s—Foucault attempted a complicated series of rapprochements with the Enlightenment, with antiquity, with the asceticism of early Christianity, with the notion of self-fashioning—in a word, with ethics. The title of one of his several "final interviews," "The Ethic of Care for the Self as a Practice of Freedom," indicates the direction of his thinking in the last few years of his life, and suggests, too, the new clarity or "innocence" of his last style. Having flamboyantly announced the obliteration of Man in his earlier work, Foucault now, by a logic that continues to excite wonder, underwent a conversion to ethical humanism.

The massive and general consequence of (1) the de Man controversy, (2) the rapidly accumulating evidence of a powerful interest in ethics among "literary" theoreticians (theoreticians whose work influenced students of literature), and (3) the appearance of several notable philosophical texts on ethics that drew heavily on the formal and conceptual resources of literature—among which were Alasdair MacIntyre's *After Virtue* (1981),

Martha Nussbaum's *The Fragility of Goodness* (1986), and Richard Rorty's *Contingency, Irony, and Solidarity* (1989)—was a fundamental reorientation of literary theory through a convergence on the question, the issue, the problem, the status of ethics.

Ethics Itself

What might have escaped notice in this convergence was the curious fact that ethics had been clearly understood in radically antithetical ways, as the agent of repression *and* as the repressed itself, as the essence of classical humanism *and* of postmodern antihumanism, as the discourse of the integrated and self-mastering subject *and* of the fissured or overdetermined subject, as the locus of forthright worthiness *and* of self-disguising power. Such a paradox compels the fundamental question: What is ethics?

The answers to this simple inquiry are complexity itself, for they take us straight to the decentered center of ethics, its concern for "the other." Ethics is the arena in which the claims of otherness—the moral law, the human other, cultural norms, the good-in-itself, etc.—are articulated and negotiated. In the domain of ethics, "selfish" or "narrow" considerations are subjected to cancellation, negation, crossing by principles represented as "deeper," "higher," or "more fundamental." Ethics is the ultimate trump card; to say, as did the President's Commission on Medical Ethics in 1983, that "ending a patient's life intentionally is absolutely forbidden on moral grounds" is to attempt to end the life of that particular dispute, for no claim can be advanced that would properly override the moral one. The elementary fact that ethics stands over and against other kinds of claims only begins, however, to indicate the role of otherness in ethical discourse. Considered as a Foucauldian "discursive regime," ethical discourse betrays an extraordinary regularity owing to its structural obsession with the relations between apparently opposed terms. In the field of ethics, philosophers consider questions of self and other, interest and principle, fact and value, "is" and "ought," the "hypothetical" and the "categorical," *Moralität* and *Sittlichkeit,* rules and cultural norms, virtues and principles, the "view from nowhere" and the contingent position of the subject, meta-ethics and normative ethics. And the history of ethics is a history of debates: Hume v. Kant, Kant v. Hegel, Kant v. Nietzsche, emotivism v. rationalism, phallocentrism v. feminism, universalism v. communitarianism, deontology v. consequentialism. The real paradox of ethics is that a discourse that seems to promise answers is so obsessed with questions.

Moreover, the two questions that dominate ethical inquiry—How ought one live? and What ought I to do?—suggest sharply incommensurable points of view. The first reflects the distanced perspective of some deindividualized and ideal being free to consider laws and norms as such; the second, the particular perspective of a real person confronting an actual situation. The consequence of this incommensurability has escaped the attention of many philosophers: it is that the controversies that structure the history of ethics can never be settled, for obedience to one kind of imperative alone would be—unethical. To consider only the point of view of "one," for example, would be to make oneself inhuman, a brain in a vat; while the absolute refusal to consider that point of view, to think only through the "I," would suggest a personality almost inconceivably self-absorbed and even mentally handicapped, powerless to generalize. Thus, despite the incoherence that would seem to be entailed by the overdetermination of action by different principles, both are necessary; for each, by itself, is radically unworthy if not simply impossible. The contentious history of ethics itself constitutes powerful evidence that ethics can never hope to resolve its internal difficulties and offer itself to the world as a guide to the perplexed. Articulating perplexity, rather than guiding, is what ethics is all about.

What makes the fact of overdetermination truly interesting is that ethical reasoning powerfully appears to be, in Stuart Hampshire's phrase, "underdetermined by the arguments," predicated on norms and ideals that stand beyond reasons and must simply be accepted or rejected (*Morality and Conflict*). This feature of ethical thinking structures the one indispensable word in ethics, *ought*. Ethical discourse zeroes in on the *ought* by depriving it of any support in the form of appeals to fears, desires, or immediate interests that might distract from its peculiar force. The ethical *ought* is the *ought* in and of itself, reduced to its tautological essence: you ought to because you ought to. And yet, the stark *ought* of ethics is not empty; rather, it constitutes a compromise formation, proclaiming the law to a creature who is presumed to be free to follow it or not. If human beings were not free, there would be no need for urging because their acquiescence would be irrelevant; but if they were not in fact bound by the law so that the right or worthy represents, in effect, a prior commitment, no urging would succeed. In the structure of the *ought,* we see, then, the style or strategy of ethical reasoning generally—apparently underdetermined but actually overdetermined.

While the apparent underdetermination of the *ought* suggests that we can simply choose right over wrong, its actual overdetermination confirms a gathering suspicion that can now be stated directly, that ethical choice is never a matter of selecting the right over the wrong, the good over the evil, and that a choice is "ethical" insofar as *both* options available for choosing embody principles that can be considered worthy. In other words, an ethical choice to do X rather than Y—to poison one's tormentor rather than permitting him to ruin one's life, to vote for Democrats on principle, to cut the kid some slack, to shoot doctors who perform abortions, etc.—is never merely a decision to act on principle rather than just acting any way one pleases. An ethical choice of actions follows a prior, often silent and even unacknowledged *choice of principles*. "To end a patient's life intentionally" may be absolutely forbidden on moral grounds, but the same could be said about "exposing a patient and his family to pointless suffering," and we will choose what to do based on which principle we think overrides the other. Do we decide to parole the convicted rapist? We can say we have chosen an "ethic of mercy" over an "ethic of retribution." Do we bomb the abortion clinic? The judge may differ, but we can tell our children that our choice was not "to bomb or not to bomb" but rather to pursue "an ethic of life" as opposed to other, less caring alternatives. In October 1997, Nelson Mandela threw many people, including ethical philosophers, into confusion when he traveled to Libya to express support for Moammar Gadhafi as a "brother leader." Protesting UN sanctions against Libya for its role in the 1988 bombing of a Pan Am jet over Lockerbie, Scotland, Mandela embraced Gadhafi and cloaked himself in the higher rhetoric of ethics, proclaiming that "those who object . . . have no morals, and I will not join them because I have morals" (El-Dakhakhny). This was followed by the statement that "Gadhafi is my friend, he helped us at a time when we were alone," a comment that seems virtually a confession that he has chosen his principle out of political-utilitarian rather than strictly ethical considerations, but which reveals with brilliant efficiency what I have described as the actual overdetermination of all ethical principles generally.

But while ethical choice is always a choice between ethics, the apparent underdetermination of the *ought* actively discourages an inquiry into this prior choice. The fact that the poor, bare, forked *ought* of ethics stands alone, without reasons, effectively masks the complicated interior determinations and weightings, the "feel" for the situation that eventually issues in decisions and acts. The discourse of practical ethics makes a fetish of a choice that is in some respects no choice at all, the (non)decision to act according to principle, according to a law that is given rather than invented for the occasion or crafted to rationalize our pursuit of self-interest. For since either option could be represented as exemplary of some principle or other, we could not have failed to act on principle; this is in fact one sense in which the imperative to act on principle could be "categorical." Practical ethical discourse thus misses the mark—and misses it, as it were, purposely—insofar as it focuses on the decision to "act ethically" or "obey the ethical law." Representing our actions in this way virtually invites some aggressive skeptic to come along and perform a triumphant "genealogy of morals," demonstrating how our choice was in fact driven by motives of interest, power, pleasure, self-aggrandizement, motives of which we might not even have been conscious. Skeptical genealogies can be performed with considerable guarantee of success because, in a terminal paradox, the fact that any choice can be reconciled with "principle" also means that any choice can also be shown to be incompatible with principle or unethical because it violates some other, entirely credible principle. Thus every "ethical" decision violates some law or other, and violates it precisely because it is "ethical."

So ethics includes within its internal structure a "nonethical" element. The traditional name for this transgressive element is "morality." In *Ethics and the Limits of Philosophy,* Bernard Williams defines morality as the bad cop in the ethical system; it stresses the idea of blame, overrates the importance of individual agency, and draws an implausibly bright line between right and wrong—and still enjoys a nearly synonymic relation with ethics. In the history of ethical discourse, the precise content of the terms *ethics* and *morality* varies, sometimes indicating the general field of inquiry as opposed to the particular rules one must follow, or right action itself as opposed to right action for the right motive, or cultural norms as opposed to the iron law of reason. But the gesture of drawing a kind of dotted line between phases or aspects of ethics remains remarkably constant.

Wishing to preserve the intuition behind this gesture, I would suggest that we extend Williams's distinction, but try to overcome his fastidious distaste for morality's violence and crudity. Morality represents, I would argue, a particular moment of ethics, when all but one of the available alternatives are excluded, chosen against, regardless of their claims. At the moment of morality, the circumstance of choice that defines and is defined by ethics is closed off by a decision that crushes all opposition in its drive to self-actualization. The injunction not to decide on a final interpretation of a text may qualify as an "ethics of reading," but it is definitely not a morality; morality does not shrink from such tasks but welcomes them as its proper responsibility. Morality is the "rigor" of ethical thought, where the rubber of a definite principle meets the road of reality. Ethics constitutes a general and categorical imperative to "act on principle"; morality constitutes a further imperative nested within the ethical that commands us to act now and on the right principle, that is, the one we want to stand *as* principle.

If morality is stigmatized in the eyes of some who would prefer beveled to sharp edges, it is because moral decision is on easy terms with desire and force, two factors that embarrass those whose thought runs to piety. Also, as the moment when thought ceases, morality has little defense against the suspicion that it stands for nothing more than the fatigue, the impatience, the indifference, the complacency, the death drive of ethical thought. The moral moment is necessary and inescapable, however, not just because decisions must be made, but also because mere choice has, by itself, no ethical value whatsoever; without decision, ethics would be condemned to dithering. It is morality that realizes ethics, making it ethical.

At the same time, however, morality negates ethics, and needs ethics in order to be moral. Decisions achieved without a passage through what Derrida would call undecidability and what a more traditional account would call the circumstance of free choice represent mere blindness and brutality. Ethics places imperatives, principles, alternatives on a balanced scale, sustaining an august reticence, a principled irresolution to which, nevertheless, the limited and precise prescriptions of morality must refer for their authority. So while, once again, neither ethics nor morality has any claim on our respect, their incoherent union is respect itself.

To illustrate some of the ways in which this network of othernesses might work in a particular case, we can track the argument of a recent book, Virginia Held's *Feminist Morality: Transforming Culture, Society, and Politics* (1993). Held is one of those who, in the wake of Carol Gilligan's claim for the specificity of female moral development, are seeking social "transformation" by renovating rather than rejecting ethics. The target is not ethics as such, but rather, as with Kristeva, "social contract" or "rational choice" theory, in which those kinds of activities in which men have, in advanced cultures, been historically dominant are advanced as universal norms. In contrast to Kristeva, however, Held argues not for anarchic upheaval but for the quieter virtues of "being" over those of "doing," family relations over contractual relations, and affect over abstract reason. A male-dominated society has, she contends, contrived to define the virtues and the principles of obligation in such a way as to distribute most of the rewards to men while representing women as submoral specialists in the "natural." Held argues in response that "feminist" values and practices such as relationships, shared values, mothering, and trust are matters of genuinely ethical import. Held thus offers a critique and a remedy. She seeks to provide a deepened historical understanding of the strategic uses of ethics in a phallocentric society by disclosing the free choices, and therefore purposive agency, at work in determining a human norm in a certain way. And she suggests that equally free choices can now be made to define, as Held puts it, "our own moral concerns as women."

So far so good. But the rule is that every (moral) choice in an ethical situation chooses against other alternatives with comparable claims. In this case, the unselected alternatives include not only Kristeva's ethic of upheaval but also what might be called an ethic of equality. Many women may well wish to refuse any attribution of ethical "difference" as a losing game, dignify it how you will. They may be troubled by a self-proclaimed "feminist morality" that displays a residual attachment to traditional roles that they might feel constitute not genuine endowments but rather historical damage. And they may be unimpressed by an "ethic" invented, as it were, for the occasion, to meet the self-esteem needs of a certain group. Absent the strict neutrality of Kantian formulations (act only on universalizable maxims; people should be treated as ends and not only as means; etc.), a group-specific ethic may actually undermine the ethical credentials of ethics itself. With its promotion of "more intimate forms of interaction" based on "idealized models of the family and friendship groups," Held's ethic in particular is vulnerable to the charge that it merely reinscribes the original problem. The family is, after all, the defining institution of the patriarchy; and some of the worst abuses in the public sphere, from a feminist perspective, have been committed by men acting as if they were members not of a society of law but of a "friendship group," that is, an old-boy network, a team, a fraternity, a secret club. And even the argument that the family might be a more proper locus of ethical concern than the corporation might simply confirm, for some, the prejudice that women ought not to be allowed into business at any level higher than the secretarial.

Held seems partly aware of the problems created by the attempt to define a group-friendly set of principles, an ethic that is substantial rather than "abstract" and "formal." For the sketchiest and most tentative part of her book is the brief section at the end where she offers a "satisfactorily worked-out feminist and moral point of view." The new emphases she would promote include "different" "levels of caring and trust," common access to "universal emotions" and "universally shared concerns," a commitment to governmental help in "meeting needs," concern for the welfare of children, "changes in prevailing relationships between 'man' and 'nature,'" closer interpersonal relations, "an openness to new possibilities, and a deep sense of responsibility for living children, future generations, and global well-being." Such a list—drawn, it seems, from some Toastmaster's Guide to Ethical Bromides—says so little because it tries to say so much, to include every possible desideratum as a way of warding off the accusation of special pleading.

Because it posits an "overriding" imperative, ethics is a grievous offense to those who are overridden, and a mighty temptation to those who wish to override. But ethics, the general injunction to act on principle, cannot plausibly be advanced as the warrant for particular values or practices. The extreme generality of Held's ethic reflects, perhaps, her distant apprehension of the fact that the very notion of ethics cuts against the grain of feminism as a political movement with certain definite goals and projects. Still, not even the most abstract ethic can altogether get quit of the charge that it merely fronts for such goals and projects. Kant's very formalism has been seen as a natural expression of his own class (those with the leisure to think of themselves and the world from the formal point of view), a notion that would undoubtedly have astonished him. What we are beginning to understand is that ethics has, or is, two general and incommensurable functions. An ethical critique consists of an analysis of the free choices made by certain groups in the constitution of a given norm. All ethical systems can be shown by determined critics to be driven by a machinery of interest, and those who wish to transform culture, society, and politics often approach their project as Held does, through a critique of ethics, a project whose motto is: "Where monolithic necessity was, there shall freedom be." The revelation of freedom can be used to encourage both skepticism toward some norms and optimism about the prospects for achieving the second function of ethics, articulating and defending different norms. But here's the rub: the demonstration that a particular ethical system is politically, economically, or otherwise determined makes ethics in general look bad, and this makes it hard to propose an alternative ethic without exciting the same suspicions about its origins. The motto of properly ethical norms is "Where freedom was, there shall necessity be." Such norms just are, and those who follow them accept constraint as a law of their being, not as a mere preference. So while ethical critique must debunk the very notion of ethics as a precondition of its effectiveness, ethical norms, if they are to function as norms, must "forget" or "repress" their own genealogy. Held's dilemma—that her ethic is both too feminist and not feminist enough; or to put it another way, that it is too feminist to be ethical and too ethical to be feminist—exemplifies the general circumstance of ethics, that it is critical above all of itself.

Ethics and Literature

Ethics has traditionally been a powerful critical instrument for literary study. Literature, especially narrative, is said to "be ethical" in a number of ways. As a representation of life in which we are not directly engaged, literature lends itself well to the indispensable pedagogical activity of asking the classical philosophical questions: What obligations do I owe my fellow creature? What are the chief virtues and how should they be ranked? How can I negotiate conflicting claims? How can one know the good?

Ethics also provides the general format for obligatory pedagogical questions: What insights does Quentin Compson achieve about the nature of historical responsibility? How does Huck mature over the course of the book? Was it right for Dorothea Brooke to marry Casaubon? Should Hamlet have killed Claudius immediately? Literature contributes to "ethical" understanding by showing motivations, revealing the ends of action, holding the mirror up to the community and the individual so they can judge themselves, promoting explanatory models that help make sense of the diversity of life, and imaging the "unity" that might be desirable in a human life. Such questions and concerns, typical of plot- and character-centered analysis, enjoy a codependency relationship with traditional humanism. For this reason, the ethical approach to literature, which is "theoretical" in the sense of being a kind of rehearsal or model of life, has been set in opposition to theory itself by MacIntyre, Rorty, Nussbaum, Iris Murdoch, and others. When such critics use the term *theory,* they mean theory of two kinds, ethical theory exemplified by Kant, and literary theory exemplified by Derrida and deconstruction. With its referential specificity, human voice, and uncertain form, narrative—the argument goes—subverts both kinds of theory. As Eve Kosofsky Sedgwick writes in *The Epistemology of the Closet,* narrative, especially "of a directly personal sort," has the righteous power to "disarm the categorical imperative that seems to do so much to promote cant and mystification about motives in the world of politically correct academia" (60). Martha Nussbaum reports that in Derrida's work, "the ethical vanishes more or less altogether," leaving her with "a certain hunger for blood," a craving she satisfies by blowing the dust off volumes by Aristotle and Henry James (*Love's Knowledge* 170, 171). For many critics, the ethical approach to literature represents a highly effective "resistance to theory."

This is a bad mistake.

Ethics is, rather, the point at which literature intersects with theory, the point at which literature becomes conceptually interesting and theory becomes humanized. Within ethical theory, narrative serves as the necessary "example," with all the possibilities of servility, deflection, deformation, and insubordination that role implies. Take the moment when Kant defends his statement that all lies violate the categorical imperative against the objection that in certain cases one has a "right to lie" to protect others. In a little essay, "On a Supposed Right to Lie Because of Philanthropic Concerns," Kant repeats his argument that lies erode the force of statements and contracts in general, thus vitiating "the very source of right"; but, aware that theory cannot defend itself without seeming dogmatic, he utters the inevitable words "for example." For example, if a man plotting a murder asks you whether his intended victim is in a certain house, you are still obligated to tell the truth, because—but let's allow Kant, a vastly underrated raconteur, to tell the story:

> It is indeed possible that after you have honestly answered Yes to the murderer's question . . . the [intended victim] went out unobserved and thus eluded the murderer, so that the deed would not have come about. However, if you told a lie and said that the intended victim was not in the house, and he has actually (though unbeknownst to you) gone out, with the result that by so doing he has been met by the murderer and thus the deed has been perpetrated, then in this case you may be justly accused as having caused his death. For if you had told the truth as best you knew it, then the murderer might perhaps have been caught by neighbors who came running while he was searching the house for his intended victim, and thus the deed might have been prevented. ("On a Supposed Right to Lie" 65)

Lying does not necessarily solve the man's problem, and may well create problems for you as well as for "mankind in general"; but if you tell the truth, then, as Kant says, "public justice cannot lay a hand on you." The point in the present context is that the example, though necessary, creates certain problems for Kant. For while a strict formalism in theory might give the impression of an admirable rigor, the same formalist approach to an emergency in real life seems repugnant and inhuman. While public justice may be unable to punish you, your other friends, the murdered man's family, and the community in general may well choose to regard you as a pious monster, zealously protecting your own morality even at the expense of other people's lives. The point is that theory requires examples, but the difference in kind between theory and example will always create an opportunity for the unpredictable subversion of the theory by the example enlisted to support it.

Narrative does not just exemplify (or fail to exemplify) theory; it excites it. William Styron's *Sophie's Choice* has stimulated a considerable amount of philosophical rumination because its central incident seems to provide a challenge to the theory of distributive justice. An officer in a German concentration camp demands that Sophie choose which of her two children will be sent to the gas chamber, threatening that if she refuses to choose, both will be sent. Sophie's choice causes a kind of theoretical nausea among those who believe, with John Rawls and others, that a non-contingent justice should prevail over any utilitarian determination of the good. While utilitarian logic might tell us that it is rational to put some innocent people to death so that others may be spared, those holding the anti-utilitarian liberal standpoint would defend the right of the individual not to be wronged. But as Slavoj Žižek explains it, in Sophie's choice, "nobody is less harmed if she refuses the choice: in this case, both of the children die." Even the sacrificed child would have to accept the sacrifice, since he loses nothing by it that he had not already lost. So Sophie must choose, since choosing is preferable to not choosing on both utilitarian and anti-utilitarian grounds; yet, Žižek notes, "our ethical intuition tells us unmistakably that there is something wrong with it," and Sophie eventually commits suicide (*Enjoy Your Symptom* 72).

In both instances, Kant's and Styron's, narrative engages with theory in a process of reciprocal probing and stressing that tests the capacity of theory to comprehend and regulate practice, and the power of "actual life" —albeit in a highly exotic, speculative, and theoretical form—to elude or deform theory. Beginning with a dispute in philosophy, we find ourselves suddenly in a city full of intrigue and violence, with murderers stalking the streets, victims leaving home without a care in the world, neighbors rushing to the rescue, public tribunals, grieving families, whispering citizens; and from the appalling choice faced by a mother in a concentration camp, we move immediately to arguments about distributive justice, rationality, utilitarianism, political liberalism. The name for this mutual stimulation of theory and example, this fundamental instance of the relation of consciousness to life, is ethics: it is "in ethics" that theory becomes literary and literature becomes theoretical.

One of the most obdurate problems in literary theory is narrative form, the study of which seems to have stalled since Aristotle's statement that the plot of tragedy proceeds toward a moment of reversal, followed by recognition, and ending in a dénouement. The Russian formalists, the Chicago School of neo-Aristotelian formalism, and the more recent discipline of structural narratology have chosen to emphasize other aspects of narrative—its "grammar," "functions," "motifs," "logic," "indices," as well as its handling of temporality, point of view, narration, and so forth. But the attempt to define further the basic form of narrative has been virtually abandoned, defeated by the apparent shapelessness and singularity of extended narratives. Efforts such as those by Gerald Prince to define the "minimal story"—a state of affairs, followed by an action that brings about a new state that is the inverse of the first—have been criticized for being both too minimal, that is, reductive, and not minimal enough in that it contains numerous elements. As Wallace Martin wrote a decade ago in *Recent Theories of Narrative*, "there is little hope of discovering an underlying set of structural principles in texts that so obviously confute our zeal for regularity," and so "the quest for a rigorous theory of narrative must end without closure" (83, 106). But lamentation or celebration may be premature. Perhaps theoretical closure can be achieved if we think of narrative in ethical terms. For one general but nonreductive way of characterizing all narratives from the simplest to the most complex is to remind ourselves of the antinomies of pure practical reason.

We can, for example, conceive of narrative form in a way that builds on Prince's basic insight by thinking of narrative as a representational structure that negotiates the relation, cultivated by ethical philosophers since Hume, of *is* and *ought*. Philosophers want to decide the question one way or the other, arguing either that there can be no determinate relation between the two kinds of propositions, or that there are (in such special cases as promises or contracts) various ways in which the two are bound together. But narrative has its own way of addressing the question, through plot. The most general and adequate conception of a narrative plot is that it moves from an unstable inaugural condition, a condition that *is* but *ought not*—a severance of the two—through a process of sifting and exploration in search of an unknown but retrospectively inevitable condition that *is* and truly *ought-to-be*. Narrative cannot posit a static *is;* this function, according to Gérard Genette, is allocated to "description," which inhabits narrative like a cyst. Nor can it prescribe an unresisted *ought:* this is the business of sermons. What it can—indeed what it must—do is to figure a process of rejecting disjunction in favor of ultimate union. Narrative plot thus provides what philosophy cannot, a principle of formal necessity immanent in recognizable worldly and contingent events that governs a movement toward the eventual identity of *is* and *ought*.

Another antinomy can be enlisted to address not the logic but the location of narrative form. As students of the scholarship on narrative form know, the concept of plot underwent a mighty shift during the 1970s, mutating from a formal property of the text to a kind of readerly phantasm or construction. The shift is virtually visible in the work of Peter Brooks, who oscillates in his important book *Reading for the Plot* between "plot" and "plotting"; and in that of Paul Ricoeur, who moved from a rigorously formalist position in an article on "narrative time" in 1980 to a far more readerly position in *Time and Narrative,* published a few years later. "To make up a plot," Ricoeur says in the later text, "is already to make the intelligible spring from the accidental, the universal from the singular" (1:41). Through a sustained rhetorical indecision, Ricoeur leaves open the question of whose "making"—the text's, the author's, or the reader's—is involved. Both Brooks and Ricoeur register the pressure exerted on formalism during this period, but neither is willing to surrender the idea of plot as formal feature. To hand the plot over to an all-licensed, plotting reader would be to make a dog's breakfast of narrative theory, which could no longer count on even the most minimal understanding of its central component. The text would be permanently disheveled, deprived of the structure that secured its coherence. Empirical study would lie vanquished while the feckless reader frolicked.

Enter ethics, whose specialty is articulating the relation between freedom and necessity, desire and the law. An "ethical" approach to the dilemma of narrative theory would begin by conceding the strength of both formalist and reader-centered positions, and making of these apparently incompatible claims the cornerstone of its understanding. Plot is a construction of a particular narrative that uses only materials in that text. In one sense external to the narrative, plot is also deeply internal. In a word, plot is the law of the narrative, arising from within and yet not precisely as its own, since the narrative is regulated by the plot. Interestingly, this account also describes the reader. The reader is free and autonomous, and responsible for his or her construction of the text; but in order to make a plot at all, readers must believe that they "perceive" it; they must submit to the text and try to understand it "on its own terms." Readers thus construct the law of the text freely but construct it as the law *of* the text. The text binds the reader, who binds the text. Where, then, is the law? In both, that is, in the relation between the two: the relation of reader to narrative text provides a compelling instance of the free submission of the subject to the law. Understanding the plot of a narrative, we enter into ethics.

How to think of ethics? *Can* one think of ethics? As the locus of otherness, ethics seems to lack integrity "in itself," and perhaps ought to be considered a matrix, a hub from which various discourses, concepts, terms, energies, fan out and at which they meet, crossing out of themselves to encounter the other, all the others. Ethics is where thought itself experiences an obligation to form a relation with its other—not only other thoughts, but other-*than*-thought. Ethics is the *ought* in thought. And if the battles of literary theory are won on the playing fields of ethics, this is because literary theory, as a kind of oxymoron, has always already accepted the responsibility of otherness, just as literature itself bears the burden of managing the encounter between language and the world. Ethics will always be at the flashpoint of conflicts and struggles because such encounters never run smooth; that is what otherness is all about. No matter what settlement is reached with some other or other, there will always be some *other* other demanding our attention. Ethics does not solve problems, it structures them. And yet the durability of ethics, the fact that we continue to have what Žižek calls "ethical intuitions," suggests an ongoing commitment to the task that does not wait for our conscious assent, a commitment that is barely, but fairly, begun by the double project of thinking through literature from the ethical, and ethics from the literary, point of view.

3 Ethics and the Double Standard of Criticism

Referring to Jean-François Lyotard's 1979 book *Just Gaming*, Terry Eagleton says that Lyotard seems to have rediscovered America in the form of "a rigorous duality between descriptive and prescriptive statements." Eagleton has this much right: the entire argument of *Just Gaming* is founded on the impossibility of bridging the differences between these two kinds of "language games." Since we cannot infer prescriptions from descriptions, the good from the true, value from fact, *ought* from *is,* then there are no true principles, and we must, Lyotard asserts with barely contained enthusiasm, resign ourselves to a "pagan" practice of judging "without criteria," on a "case by case" basis. "The most amusing feature of his argument," Eagleton writes, "is that, having apparently not read David Hume, he spontaneously reinvents his notorious dichotomy of 'fact' and 'value,' without, it would seem, the slightest awareness of the hammering to which this case has been submitted. . . . Hume's coupling of positivism and idealism, the most banal gesture of bourgeois ideology . . . is uncritically reproduced in rather different political conditions by the 'anti-bourgeois' Lyotard. It is as though an English philosopher blissfully unaware of Descartes was to announce triumphantly, at the conclusion of some contorted argument, 'I think, therefore I am!' " ("Two Approaches in the Sociology of Literature" 471).

It's a pity that Eagleton can't be right as well as amusing, or that he can't be amusing at Lyotard's expense without also being amusing at his own. But this passage suggests that while Eagleton has indeed heard of Hume, he is as innocent of the text as Lyotard, and, for that matter, as a great many other philosophers who credit Hume with inventing the "rigorous dichotomy" between fact and value. In fact, the first to hammer such a distinction was Hume himself. True, Hume did complain at the end of book 3, part 1, section 1 of the *Treatise of Human Nature* of the dubious and "vulgar" argumentative strategies of "every system of morality which I have hitherto met with," in which he observed an "imperceptible" yet fateful passage from *is* to *ought.* This complaint is Hume's legacy to ethics:

No Ought from an Is. The standard line of commentary on Hume affirms this rule, especially as it applies to fact and value, which Robert Nozick describes as a "chasm" that "despite determined efforts no one has been able to leap across or bridge" (*Philosophical Explanations* 535). But someone has—Hume himself, who concedes that *ought* was deduced from *is* in every system he had met with. Nor is Hume in principle opposed to the deduction; rather, he is simply amazed by it. "'Tis necessary," he says, "that it shou'd be observ'd and explain'd; and at the same time that a reason should be given, for what seems altogether inconceivable, how this new relation can be a deduction from others, which are entirely different from it" (*Treatise on Human Nature* 196). The distinction between *is* and *ought* is further weakened by being linked, in a casual slippage, to the distinction between fact and value which, in the previous paragraph, had been collapsed altogether. Here, Hume had concluded his argument that morality does not consist merely in facts or in reason, but rather in the moral sentiments of approbation or revulsion with which we regard certain acts, by saying, "Here is a matter of fact; but 'tis the object of feeling, not of reason. It lies in yourself, not in the object" (195). Far from distinguishing between facts and values, Hume insists that, in the realm of morality, evaluative feelings *are* facts. In the case of *is* and *ought,* then, Hume makes the distinction but, *contra* Eagleton, fails to make it "rigorous"; while in the related but not perfectly synonymous case of fact and value, he fails to make it at all. (For probing accounts of Hume and others on the problem of *is* and *ought,* see Mackie and Hudson). Actually, Eagleton may suffer from a Humean ambivalence himself, as he puts the issue in terms of a "rigorous dichotomy" in one sentence, and a "coupling" in the next. "Rigor" in distinctions may, in fact, be what Hume means by "vulgarity": maintaining distinctions so rigidly that the move from one set of terms to another cannot be explained.

The standard view of Hume as a proponent of rigorous distinctions is so dominant, so standard, that I am sometimes given to wondering whether I'm reading into this passage something that just isn't there, reading him not the way he is, but the way I think he ought to be, the way he must be if he wants to earn my approbation. When I feel this way I fortify myself by reading Hume on the necessary and inescapable unity of fact and value. The danger of this second reading of Hume is, of course, that we might come to confuse cognition with evaluation, concluding that since one simply is the other, then as long as we are sincere in our feelings, we must be right. For that reason alone, perhaps we ought to read Hume as endorsing a fact-value distinction.

Indeed, such a distinction has many advantages. Within ethics itself, it has been enormously useful, suggesting, as in the "decisionism" of R. M. Hare, that once the labor of fact-finding on a given issue has been exhausted, then the work of "pure evaluation"—pure because unburdened by uncertainty as to facts—may begin. If, for Hare, Hume's distinction opens up the possibility of decision and responsibility, for Bernard Williams it serves as a reassurance that "we cannot be forced by the world to accept one set of values rather than another" (128). Sartrean existential "commitment" may also trace its genealogy back to Hume. All three philosophers suggest that ethical matters are independent of the tyranny of fact—an argument that can, of course, only be plausible if the "rigorous duality" of fact and value has already been established.

As Alasdair MacIntyre argues in his highly influential *After Virtue,* the dualism that ethical philosophers have found so useful was originally an import from science. The modern notion of the isolated object of critical investigation, the value-free fact, dates, MacIntyre points out, from the period of the Royal Society, when a new principle of representation emerged that bore no traceable connection to human beliefs, desires, antipathies, or agency. As MacIntyre traces the succession, the principle of evaluative neutrality descended to Weber, whose ideas about technocratic or managerial expertise inform our notions of bureaucracy. Logical positivism as developed by Tarski, Carnap, and Russell begins by distinguishing the purely referential, verifiable terms of science from the "meaningless," emotive, and nonverifiable terms of, say, poetry. The same basic dualism, with some more recent modifications, defines the aspiration to neutrality that, no matter how theoretically discredited it may be, continues to define the very notion of "knowledge" in many fields today.

So powerful are the forces whose interest this distinction serves that we could say that if Hume had never made it, it would have been invented anyway—pretty much the argument I am in fact making. But Hume—the counter-Hume I am constructing—has powerful allies in his resistance to making this case, too. The most powerful hammering to which the fact-value distinction has been put has come from the "philosopher with a sledge hammer," Nietzsche. In the first essay of *On the Genealogy of Morals,* Nietzsche portrays a prehistoric world in which "the strong" impose values—*their* values—on "the weak," and on the world, which is henceforth knowable only under the terms assigned to it by the strong. A fact under these conditions is merely the tombstone or memory of power, a sedimented and highly "successful" instance of evaluation. According to Nietzsche, at least at this moment of this text, every *is* memorializes and legitimates a struggle between unequal forces. The cultural and philosophical tradition whose most representative figures are the scientist and the bureaucrat holds, then, that fact precedes and remains distinct from evaluation. But the Nietzschean tradition holds that from the start, value defines and determines fact.

Stark as the alternatives seem, they can, under a bit of pressure, reverse themselves with alarming indifference to their own integrity. Many of those who hold to the fact-value dichotomy believe that there *ought* to be an *is* separate from the *ought* as a way of sheltering the fact: what is valuable, they insist, are the value-neutral facts. And many contemporary Nietzscheans contend that the fact is that facts just are values. Thus we see, on the one hand, those committed to the idea of fact defending their evaluative predispositions with an extraordinary bluntness. It was, after all, T. S. Eliot, self-proclaimed Tory, classicist, and Anglo-Catholic, who declared that the first requirement for a critic was a highly developed sense of fact. And Matthew Arnold himself formulated the notion of critical disinterestedness in an essay filled with complaints about the vulgarity of Philistine chauvinism, the spiritual superiority of the French to the English Revolution, the monetary system, the divorce laws, and the ugliness of English names—Higginbottom, Stiggins, Bugg! And on the other hand, the neo-Nietzscheans today whose genealogical inquiries invariably discover power struggles and evaluations are invariably exacting and meticulous devotees of the archive as the repository of fact.

This reversibility is precisely what Hume's passage concedes. Moreover —and here I elaborate on Hume—ethics is the typical site of such reversals. In ethics, fact is conjoined with feeling, overturning the definition of each, but establishing a certain definition of ethics. We might, with some Humean authority, regard the characteristic form of ethics not as a dichotomy, but rather as a lamination in which the terms are joined without losing their identity. Both are essential: without the bracing *is,* the *ought* becomes vacuous and unmotivated; and without the animating *ought,* the *is* becomes dull, inert, and useless. In the realm of ethics, fact and value are not opposed, but rather distinguished—an identity with a difference, which I have elsewhere called *resistance.* We are in the presence of the ethical when something is represented as both a fact and a value. This new definition of ethics itself jeopardizes other distinctions, for both the realists of truth and the realists of power contrast their master terms to ethics. But if ethics is the conceptual space of a fact-value resistance, then both these resistances to ethics could, albeit over their dead bodies, be reconceived as specialized forms of ethical discourse rather than oppositions to it.

Robert Nozick, whose comment on the unbridgeability of the fact-value split I quoted earlier, has (within several pages of that comment) attempted the feat himself, and done so in a way that enables us to bridge the gap between ethics and aesthetics. According to Nozick, value is not a fact in the Enlightenment sense of the term, but rather a choice, a "reflexive imputation of the existence of value" (*Philosophical Explanations* 563). Against, for example, the state of depression in which there is no value, we choose that there be value, a quality external to ourselves and discoverable in things (hence worth hooking up with), and yet one that does not humble or coerce us, does not compromise our freedom. What kind of things possess this delicate quality? The kind, Nozick continues, that have "organic unity," a fact about things that renders them valuable. Not only does the object of value possess organic unity within itself, but it also enters into a state of organic unity with the value-choosing subject. With this move, Nozick becomes the Evel Knievel of ethics, leaping the fact-value chasm by defining value in terms both of subjective choice and objective attributes: the subject is brought into a certain kind of relation with the valuable object, whose value he does not create but rather chooses, seeks, and finds. On this point, Nozick is much clearer than Hume, for he enables us to see how, within the object of value, fact implies value, since any "fact" has some measure of formal integrity; and how, too, value inescapably suggests fact, since there is no free-floating or subjective value, only valuable things. For Nozick, both fact and value condense in themselves the fact-value distinction, or, as I prefer, the single complex entity, the fact-value resistance.

The entire issue might seem by this point to consist of the parochial cultivation of a few boringly similar logical knots or tricks. But the most familiar scene of the reversals and laminations I have been discussing is nothing less than that global form of discursive self-fashioning and world making, narrative. Consider only the Aristotelian description of the beginning, middle, and end of a plot. The beginning undergoes a series of complicating actions, rising to a climax in which occurs a reversal, swiftly followed by a recognition, which gives to the dénouement the quality of being, no matter how initially surprising or improbable, fitting after all. The whole sequence can be accommodated to our distinction. Plot, as I suggested in the previous chapter, begins with a movement out of a static condition of *is:* (restless all afternoon,) the Marquise goes out at five o'clock. The dynamism of this initial condition suggests that it suffers from a failure of formal integrity: its center cannot hold, it repels value; it *ought not to be.* The movement of the plot constitutes a process of discovery of what *ought to be,* a process of winnowing and selection that culminates in closure, wherein the narrative achieves formal integrity and the regained *is* truly *ought to be.* Narrative tracks along the issue defined with a generous ambiguity by Hume, but displays something that ethical choices, being underdetermined by the arguments, do not: a formal principle of necessity that works through resistance to bring the two together.

I take this to be the most general description of the ethics of narrative as well as the best indication that it is nothing other than ethics that provides what Hayden White has called "the content of the form." If we see narrative as a passage from an is-but-ought-not to an is-and-ought, we can get a new purchase, too, on one of the difficult dicta in White's famous essay "The Value of Narrativity in the Representation of Reality." There, White describes closure as a *"passage* from one moral order to another" (26). The difficulty, as one of White's critics has pointed out, lies in the apparent suggestion that there are as many moral orders as there are narratives. But if we define closure in the way I have suggested, we can see that closure achieves a moral order that is "other" to that which preceded it, an other to whatever it is in the narrative that *is* but *ought not to be.* There are an infinite number of narratives but only one closural moral order, which is other not to other narratives but to the incessant questing of all narrative for formal closure. Insofar as our aesthetic education acclimates us to narrative, then, it instructs us in ethics. For narrative teaches us that however fact and value may be sundered, they can and should struggle toward reconciliation.

This teaching of narratives suggests further that ethics and aesthetics, often held to be opposed and just as often to be united, might also struggle toward a resistant reconciliation of the sort achieved by fact and value in narrative. I will leave this suggestion like a baby on a doorstep, hoping that someone else will take it in and nurture it to maturity, and will turn instead to the relation of ethics to literary criticism. Recurrent efforts to encourage criticism to promote desirable values, to think more seriously about ethical issues raised in texts, to critique the value judgments implicit in the author's point of view or construction of plot, or to acknowledge more candidly its own ethical agendas seem to me doubly impoverished: first, because they presume that "ethics" should be confined to the activity of conscious evaluation; and second, because they reduce literature to a primitive realism, with the critic judging either the author or the characters as though they were people, producing criticism that is mushy and arbitrary, confusing its proper textual object for something else. This is why nearly every school of criticism to emerge in this century—formalism, reader-response criticism, structuralism, deconstruction, the New Historicism, psychoanalytic criticism, and especially Marxism—has defined itself against ethics. But the recurrence of the summons to ethics suggests an institutional disquiet with this self-definition of criticism, a suspicion that criticism somehow already runs and indeed ought to run the risk of ethical mushiness. (This is the central point of Christopher Clausen's elaborate demonstration in "Moral Inversion and Critical Argument" that "evaluative moral criticism is recognizably similar in its modes of argument to other genres of critical thinking" [22]). If criticism already "risks" ethics, then we do not need new versions of criticism or ethics, but rather a new account of this risk. This account should begin with the premise that the ethics of criticism reside in precisely the lamination of fact and value that we have already seen conceded in ethical, and enacted in narrative, discourse. I am not suggesting any ethical obligation on the part of critics to pay attention to facts and transmit worthy values, nor do I even want to focus attention on particular critical statements as such. I prefer to focus on the relation that criticism establishes with its "other," the aesthetic text; for it is in this relation that criticism, regardless of kind, orientation, or subject, invariably reconstitutes the fact/value dyad. This argument itself entails two premises: first, that criticism always operates under a realist account of its own activities; and, second, that criticism always depicts its object as a network of forces, contingencies, and intentions that can most efficiently and comprehensively be described as "evaluations."

One of the most remarkable facts to emerge from the history of literary criticism is that while critics in this century have, with almost no exceptions, been bent on a single project, the destruction of the Romantic notion that literature speaks a timeless truth—with some schools arguing against the timelessness and others against the truthfulness—virtually all schools of criticism have presumed and often explicitly claimed such truthfulness for themselves. That is, in terms of the self-conception of criticism, an utterance is "critical" insofar as it is demanded, determined, or authorized by the text, not simply produced by the need, interest, or desire of the critic.

I infer such a self-conception from the consistent appeal, made by each new critical movement in its turn, to the object as in itself it really is. No Arnoldians, the Russian formalists broke with their predecessors by turning, as Eichenbaum says in his history of the formalist movement, "to the facts," not because they wanted to but because "literature demanded it." When Bakhtin repudiated formalism, he did so in the name of different facts, but facts just the same—the facts about the ideological factors that formalism excluded from consideration. When the New Criticism reinvented formalism, it did so by turning—where else?—to the facts— that is, to the poem as "an object of specifically critical attention" of the sort that would yield the "objective criticism of works of art as such" (see Wimsatt and Beardsley). Refusing the task of interpretation, Jonathan Culler argued, in his reader-response phase, that criticism should turn to the reader, whose interpretations should become the new "facts to be explained" (*Structuralist Poetics* 123). When Stanley Fish repudiated formalism he also referred to the reader, and to "what is objectively true" in the reading experience ("Literature in the Reader" 44). When Stephen Knapp and Walter Benn Michaels subsequently charged that Fish implies that one can speak about beliefs without having any, they clinched their argument by constructing "a true account of belief" ("Against Theory" 28). Rejecting the appeal to the reader as well as all forms of pragmatism, Paul de Man described a proper "reading" as an epistemological necessity that goes "against the grain of what one would want to happen in the name of what has to happen" ("Foreword" xi).

This list could be extended indefinitely, but the point would not remain the same: that all critical statements are constituted as statements of fact, determined by the way things are, ideally independent of psychological, economic, cultural, or professional contingencies. So unyielding is this principle that it structures even arguments that set out to prove the opposite. Take for example this claim in Eagleton's *Literary Theory: An Introduction:* "All of our descriptive statements move within an often invisible network of value-categories, and indeed without such categories we would have nothing to say to each other at all. . . . Interests are constitutive of our knowledge, not merely prejudices which imperil it" (14). If this passage seems rather limp, it is not only because it expresses a truism for our times, a postmodern tautology, but because in its manifestly "factual" and descriptive neutrality, it enacts a convention of criticism itself, in this time and in all others.

As a richer example, consider Susan Stewart's essay "The Marquis de Meese," which compares the Meese Commission's report on pornography to the Marquis de Sade's *The 120 Days of Sodom.* The essay begins with a reminder of "the impossibility of describing desire without generating desire . . . and, most important, the impossibility of constructing a metadiscourse of pornography once we recognize the interested nature of all discursive practices" (163). But having made, and in a sense inoculated herself against, this recognition, Stewart proceeds as though she were writing just such a metadiscourse, plowing through the morass of misogyny, paranoia, "horror of viscosity," and the oddly excited body-phobia displayed by the Meese Commission "researchers" and "witnesses," bearing witness through her research to the facts. She concludes with an evaluatively denuded retroactive assessment of her aim in which she says that she has not been arguing for or against anything, but has merely been trying "to point to the impossibility of mounting a critique of pornography within . . . forms of rationality, to assert thereby the identity of the Meese Commission's *Report* with the tradition of the Sadean project, and to broadly position the pornographic gesture within the state and the rationality of the state" (188–89). Is all rational discourse about pornography pornographic? No, only the Meese *Report;* "The Marquis de Meese" is PG. As it turns out, she is more right at the beginning than even she knows. In the context of her clever exposé of the *Report*'s compulsive and unconscious repetition of pornographic gestures through buried metaphors, her conclusion itself reveals to the jaded eye a winking principle of pornography: she *points* to the impossibility of *mounting* an argument, *ass*erts an identity, *broadly* positions something *within* something else.

This is not to criticize Stewart, whose resistance to criticism in the name of facticity simply repeats the founding premise of criticism, that it is determined by an other: the abjection of criticism before its object. This self-conception is displayed by bluntly evaluative criticism such as that practiced by F. R. Leavis, and by the indirectly evaluative criticism of the New Critics, and deconstruction, and by the New Historicism, all of which refer their conclusions to "the words on the page." Critics can be described, with I hope just the right combination of irony and pity, as those who value the facts more than values, who are more interested in the truth than in interests, who desire to know more than they desire to desire.

A discourse operating under this self-description virtually brings into being a certain kind of object, a "primary" text constituted by intentional acts, choices, and evaluations. The facts that criticism discovers reflect the evaluation processes that constitute that object. Formalism discovers not just devices, but "motivated" devices; not just defamiliarization, but a strategy for overcoming habituation and convention so that we may perceive afresh. New Criticism discloses the ways in which the poem links the reader to "the world's body," in Ransom's phrase, and the ways in which poetry overcomes disharmony, tension, and ambiguity, ways that are not neutral, but connected to larger social, religious, or political projects. Marxism, feminism, the New Historicism, all present accounts of the object as determined by evaluative acts informed by class, gender, ideological or economic interests, taking as their task the saying of what the text does not say, the unearthing of the text's "political unconscious," as Marxism would have it. Marxism in particular is unusually candid on this score. According to Althusser, Marxist theory "always works on 'generalized material' even when the latter takes on the form of a 'fact.' . . . It always works on preexistent concepts, on 'Vorstellungen.' . . . It does not 'work' on some pure and objective 'datum' which would be that of pure and absolute 'facts.' On the contrary, its business consists in *elaborating its own scientific facts* by means of the critique of *ideological 'facts'* elaborated by the more properly ideological practice that has preceded it" (187). In other words, a Marxist "science" will attack precisely where facticity is claimed, revealing the facts in question to be impure, non-neutral, ideological; at the same time, it will claim that its own procedures, because they are "more properly" or candidly ideological, produce the truth. For another Marxist example, we could consider Raymond Williams's description of the task of criticism: "What we are actively seeking," Williams writes, "is the true practice which has been alienated to an object, and the true conditions of practice . . . which have been alienated to components or mere background" ("Base and Superstructure" 216). If we seek, we shall surely find the "true practice" and the "true conditions of practice"; and, it goes without saying, we shall find them in "alienated" forms whose alienation reflects ideological distortion and contradictions.

Deconstruction is also instructive in this respect, for the covert unbalancing of binaries, the slippages and oppositional elements displayed by the most apparently stable terms, the rhetorical "literariness" evidenced even by "scientific" (e.g., Freud, Saussure, Husserl) or philosophical discourses—all this would be a trivial and even incoherent matter if it were not possible to connect these discursive features to larger and unspoken strategies and interests, in short to values and evaluations. This is not the occasion for a full demonstration of deconstruction's strategies, but interested and ambitious readers may refer to Derrida's *The Post Card,* in which Derrida exposes Freud's treatment of pleasure in *Beyond the Pleasure Principle* as itself a function—despite Freud's explicit and energetic denials— of the pleasure principle, and Freud's scientific posture a function of his "artistic" rhetoric. At this point, Freud is exposed, but critical objectivity itself is in fine shape, as Derrida reveals the truth about pleasure.

The most condensed example comes from Roland Barthes, writing on criticism's pretension to facticity: "How could we believe, in fact, that the work is an object exterior to the psyche and history of the man who interrogates it?" (83). Even when it is criticism that is in question, "the work" is constituted as the end result of subjective evaluative processes, while the critical text—Barthes'—establishes the facts.

I am not claiming that criticism either really or ideally is nonevaluative. I agree with Stewart that all discourse is interested, and that our ideas about how the world is are tangled up with our views on how the world should be. Who could doubt that New Critics, for example, felt not only that poetry *was* full of tension, irony, and ambiguity, but that it *ought to be* as well? Or that such terms as *différance, undecidability, heterotopia, power, textuality, paganism, history,* or *feminism* all gather around themselves not only bodies of fact but bundles of ethical and political interests? And the circumstances and character of the critic are everywhere on display and everywhere instrumental in determining the power and interest of the criticism. But this "display" actually leads to my final point. What we value most highly in criticism is the spectacle of the powerful mind confronting the powerful text: Johnson on Shakespeare, Freud on Michelangelo, Frye on Blake, Derrida on Rousseau. These confrontations are not free, but predetermined, assuming a ritual form, in which the critic always, in one sense—the critical sense—loses. See, for example, the way in which Cynthia Chase begins a recent article with a confession. "My work on this paper," she says, "led me eventually, I must say only very gradually, to re-*reading* Lacan"; and this re-reading has, to her professed surprise, made it "difficult to sustain the argument I originally thought I could make" (990). Power grows under weight, and one way to claim power, critical power, is to profess that one is not doing what one wanted, that one is following the imperative of the text. Criticism represents itself as bound, as *not* making significant choices, as being commanded against the will of its author. The more general claim I'm making is that criticism, in a gesture at once routine and obligatory, attributes evaluation and, necessarily, such concepts as freedom, choice, and desire to its object; and it reserves necessity, obligation, and facticity to itself. I am not speaking here of conscious critical decisions made by individuals, but of the rhetorical requirements of the discursive mode itself. Criticism entails a formal suppression of the *ought* in favor of the *is* in itself, and a corresponding elevation of the *ought* and depression of the *is* in its object. Statements such as Eagleton's and Stewart's to the effect that all descriptions really are evaluative go down so easily with other critics because they represent at once the paradigmatic and most general form of critical statements as such: a bound and "objective" representation of a free and "subjective" other—statuses achieved not in fact, not in ontology, but in the very relationship with their others. A discourse that fails to establish such a relationship between its own discourse and the discourse of its object, as does Barthesian *écriture* that makes no distinction between the analytic and the literary, is simply not "critical."

Part of criticism's passivity may reflect the fact that its objects are all stuck in the past, with no possibility of reformation. Additionally, there may, in certain individuals, lurk some timidity, failure of nerve, naiveté, or unworldliness. And there are, too, principled reasons for considering the *ought* alien to criticism. But our principles should not keep us from recognizing that the formal suppression of the *ought* produces a prescriptive power that is far stronger than it could be if the prescription were overt. Stewart's scrupulous refusal to prescribe, for example, ensures that the arguments against the Marquis de Sade, against the Meese Commission, against pornography and its customers will be made—indeed, that they will seem to issue forth from rationality itself. The moral force of the essay derives from its refusal to make a moral case. The essay constitutes a "critical moment" in the career of evaluation, a moment of reversal/recognition in a narrative implied by the act of criticism. From a free but marginal fictiveness in the aesthetic text, evaluation undergoes a mortification into fact in the critical text, emerging into the world through the readers of criticism as valuable information, that is, a kind of value capable of being set to definite work in the world. In order for an antipornographic case to be made, the critic must first persuade people that there is such a thing as pornography, and that it has certain attributes; and this can only be done by a "factual" representation of the effects of the system of desires and needs—the evaluations—that constitute pornography. Criticism becomes factual-verifiable only in relation to its other, the discourse it constitutes as nonverifiable. The critical conversion of evaluation into ontology provides what I have called the "spectacle" of criticism, the emergent image of desire acknowledged but mastered by obligation, of value chosen and discovered. This spectacle becomes valuable as a model not just for the antipornography forces but for those who would act ethically on behalf of anything at all. Neither criticism as truth, then, nor criticism as evaluation, but rather criticism as spectacle. That is not only the way it is, but, I need hardly add, the way it ought to be as well.

Over thirty years since Derrida's rapid ascent to international academic fame, his work, if no longer violently controversial, still harbors undiscovered pockets of unrealized theoretical potential on subjects with which he is scarcely associated, the ethics and politics of criticism. For many—those for whom the very name "Derrida" signifies amorality itself—this statement must seem astonishing. For them, Derrida's eminence was one of the weirder by-products of a post-sixties ethos of Spockian indulgence, countercultural "free speech," and omnidirectional protest, not to mention the death of God, Man, and everything else worth giving a damn about. From the beginning, Derrida's work had met an "ethical" counterforce so entrenched and dogmatic that one must infer that he was widely regarded as heralding a paradigm shift which, if it were to become general, would spell the end of long cherished practices in literary criticism, linguistics, philosophy, and other fields. The very prestige of the Kuhnian notion of the paradigm shift may in fact explain some of the more extreme features of the reaction to Derrida; for what Kuhn describes as a periodic occurrence in science is an upheaval so total that everything within a practice is changed, nothing can proceed as before, the old crowd is suddenly made redundant. The new paradigm finally wins, Kuhn says, not because everybody is convinced but because the partisans of the old gradually die off. Thus the subtext of the typical anti-Derridean reaction was: *I am not dead.*

In defense of their own vitality, and of such terms as "real life" or "lived experience," some anti-Derrideans even in recent years, when clarity should have replaced the initial violence and confusion, apparently feel they can say anything. They can, for example, insist that it is the opponent who is dead, as when Roger Scruton warns that any who are "tempted" by the *"fata Morgana* of deconstruction" will "wander from their purpose, in a desert of unmeaning, and dwindle into parched unwholesome remnants of themselves" ("Modern Philosophy and the Neglect of Aesthetics" 617). Or they can simply pronounce Derrida "wrong," as in: "Derrida is a great philosopher whose views are mostly wrong" (Gorman 205). In an article that dealt only briefly with Derrida, Frederick Crews provided a kind of inventory of the ritual charges. Derrida would, he argues, ban all recourse to "such flagrantly bourgeois concepts" as "social contracts and laws of human nature"; his work is characterized by "a willingness to settle issues by theoretical decree, without even a pretense of evidential appeal"; he is a "cognitive minimalist" trafficking in "unsupported contentions"; his judgment that " 'there is nothing outside the text' automatically precludes recourse to evidence"; accordingly, "he has no way of arriving at more fruitful ideas than the inherited ones he has doomed himself to deconstruct *ad infinitum* and thus to remain in a limbo of combined attention and nonassertion"; he is "an intellectual nihilist"; he "and his followers think nothing of appropriating . . . propositions from systems of thought whose premises they have already rejected"; his work is an affair of "monotony and hermeticism" ("In the Big House of Theory" passim.).

The last charge especially makes one blink. The fact that Derrida has produced a vast quantity of extraordinarily influential work not only in the field of philosophy (virtually all periods of Western philosophy from the Greeks onward) but also in anthropology, linguistics, theology, art, aesthetics, psychoanalytic discourse, and literature; the fact that he has written on such subjects as the Declaration of Independence as an instance of the discourse of the origins of democratic power, the logic of nuclear deterrence, Nazism with respect to Heidegger and to de Man, spectrality in Marx, the history and structure of the university, racism, the concepts of law, genre, invention, femininity, friendship, mourning, friendship, and framing; the fact that he may well have accumulated more frequent-flier miles than any other scholar in our time, exposing his ideas to constant scrutiny, testing, and criticism, in the process doing *more* than anybody else to bridge the gap between Continental and Anglo-American academic cultures, as well as between disciplines within the humanities; the fact that his work has helped greatly to encourage and legitimate whatever philosophical and linguistic sophistication that literary theory and criticism have been able to accomplish in the last twenty years (the work of Paul de Man, for example, would have been striking and powerful in any event, but the connection with Derrida helped make it *important* as well); the fact that his ideas have been as fertile and provocative to architects, photographers, and artists as they have been to literary critics, philosophers, linguists, psychoanalysts, and others; the fact that he has also been an active administrator, participating in GREPH and serving as director of the International College of Philosophy, a communal venture devoted to the promotion of nonstandard forms of research; the fact that his active sponsorship of a number of liberal causes is sufficiently well known and sufficiently effective to get him arrested and interrogated in Czechoslovakia in 1982—none of this seems to be enough to persuade those who haven't done a fraction as much or a fraction as well that Derrida has yet risen to the threshold of being interesting, or that he believes in reality. Go figure.

Like many of Derrida's more recent critics, Crews attributes technical or procedural characteristics of Derrida's work to an ethical deficiency that could be called, broadly, narcissism. Hence the charge that Derrida just says whatever he likes with no respect for evidence. It is the same charge made in canonical form by Crews's Berkeley colleague John R. Searle in the notorious exchange conducted in the pages of *Glyph* in the mid-1970s. As it unfolded, the debate had defined the terms and the terrain in and on which the battle of deconstruction and Anglo-American analytic philosophy would be fought. Extended commentaries were written by Jonathan Culler, Mary Louise Pratt, Samuel Weber, Stanley Fish, Jürgen Habermas, Barbara Johnson, and Gayatri Spivak. Even today, one's view of who won is a marking as immediate and unmistakable as a regimental flag. For Searle and his supporters, it was an Agincourt, with the French routed by virtue and plain common sense. But for the always-already band of Derrideans, it was more like a Hastings. The republication by Northwestern University Press of Derrida's 1971 and 1977 contributions to this debate, along with his "Afterword" written in 1988, a response to questions put by Gerald Graff in which Derrida generalizes his outrage at Searle's criticisms into a general statement on ethics, created an intriguing opportunity to review the debate, to assess Anglo-American hostility to Derrida's work generally, and to ask what contribution had finally been made to an understanding of what Derrida calls the "ethics of discussion."

The origin of the Searle-Derrida debate has a kind of Sarajevo improbability to it, with the already-dead Oxford philosopher J. L. Austin standing in for the Archduke. In an essay he would later drily refer to as *Sec* ("Signature event context"), Derrida discussed Austin's *How to Do Things with Words* in terms of the critique of writing he had already elaborated in a number of texts. Insisting, modestly enough, on "the possibility of disengagement and citational graft" in every mark or sign—that is, on the structural possibility that any sign can break with any given context, that it can be "cited" in or "grafted" onto an infinite number of contexts—Derrida argues that this "iterability" or "citationality" is most manifestly characteristic of the written sign, and so the extension of the principle makes of every sign "a grapheme in general," a "nonpresent *remainder* of a differential mark cut off from its origin" (*Limited Inc* 10). Derrida never asserts that there is no stabilization of meaning, no original context; he only argues that these forms of primordiality are broken by a "dehiscence" or a "cleft" that joins them to their opposite, the possibility of infinite grafting onto other contexts, in which they acquire other meanings. While nobody has claimed that words can have only one meaning in one context, some theoreticians of language, including Austin and Searle, have taken a relative determinability within a given context—such as that often attributed to particular spoken utterances—as evidence of the absolute ideal determinability of linguistic meaning in "normal" circumstances, from which such a relative stability in fact differs radically, even absolutely.

Derrida discovers in Austin's text a repeated gesture of exclusion that describes as "marginal" or "parasitic" a whole host of acted, fictive, joking, sarcastic, or ironic utterances which are contrasted with the "central" instances of serious, literal speech. This banishment of the non-standard presented as a neutral and "temporary" maneuver, an expeditious "research strategy," reflects, Derrida says, the same self-blinding logic as the consignment by traditional philosophy of writing to a "ditch of perdition." But what especially fascinates Derrida are the occasional concessions in Austin that various "kinds of ill" can "infect *all* utterances" and that "features of this [marginal] sort can and do constantly obtrude into any case we are discussing." The force of Derrida's critique is that Austin should have taken his own insights more seriously and proceeded to the consideration of the possibility that what he excludes as nonserious anomaly reflects a general principle of "iterability," without which there could be no successful performative utterance in the first place. This strategy is familiar to all readers of Derrida.

Humble as it was, merely proposing the amplification and extension of certain elements within Austin, Derrida's essay provoked a pugnacious and indignant response from Searle, Austin's self-appointed intellectual heir, who had several years before published a book called *Speech Acts: An Essay in the Philosophy of Language.* Searle's "Reply" reiterated a number of differences—between the true Austin and Derrida's version of Austin; between speech-act theory and Derridean grammatology; and above all between all the things that speech-act theory, or at least Searle's more rigid and systematizing speech-act theory, was concerned to distinguish between—use and mention, standard and nonstandard, literal and nonliteral, performative and constative, serious and nonserious, illocutionary and perlocutionary. Such distinctions, Searle insisted, were not only necessary for theoretical purposes but claimed the fundamental legitimacy of common sense.

Confident that the misreadings were Searle's—both of Austin and of his own text—Derrida might simply have let the matter drop. Instead, he produced one of the most exhaustive and detailed refutations of a philosophical argument ever written, the eighty-page "Limited Inc a b c . . . ," a merciless word-by-word (or *a b c*) shredding that exposes Searle's essay as a product of inattention and a bad attitude, of violence, meanness, resentment, and even incompetence. Derrida's object here is not merely to defend his original essay but absolutely to demolish, or, to adapt Mike Tyson, to deconstruct and destroy; and, just as important, to do so by using the methods and values Searle had claimed to stand for: rigor, precision, order, even common sense. Searle, Derrida tried to demonstrate, simply did not play by the rules he so dogmatically defended.

Many thought Searle had survived, whether in an outright victory or in a no-decision. Richard Rorty commented in *Critical Inquiry* that Derrida "didn't lay a glove on Searle" ("Deconstruction and Circumvention" 2). Searle himself literally did not know what hit him, for he published a comparably pugnacious and self-assured attack on deconstruction in the form of a 1983 review of Jonathan Culler's *On Deconstruction* in the *New York Review of Books* (mentioned by Crews as a "decisive rebuttal"). Why didn't "Limited Inc" take? The explanation readiest to hand is that neither the sense nor the force of Derrida's arguments was well understood. Derrida is often thought to be a "difficult" writer, and he himself mentions the "difficulty" of *Sec*. But the difficulty does not really lie with his "style"; it lies rather with the kind of logic Derrida employs and especially with the kind of entity he envisions as the object under interrogation. It would appear that Searle is committed to a binary logic according to which a thing either is or isn't something—serious or nonserious, standard or nonstandard, central or parasitic, literal or metaphorical. Through patient and exacting readings of "classical" texts, Derrida does not propose as much as expose another logic in addition to the binary, a "supplementary complication" which, he argues, is embedded in and, in small but crucial ways throughout, conceded by this classical logic. Blindness to the supplement thus constitutes a repression both *in* and *of* that logic. As Derrida tells Graff in the "Afterword," "One shouldn't complicate things for the pleasure of complicating, but one should also never simplify or pretend to be sure of such simplicity where there is none. If things were simple, word would have gotten around, as you say in English" (119).

For some reason, many feel that if news spread of this other logic, though it is derived from scrupulous readings of canonical texts, massive automatic sell programs would be triggered, causing everybody to dump their stock in Western Thought Consolidated. The blank refusal to understand the logic of the supplement, the insistence on reading it as a simple reversal that still preserves binary logic, and worst of all the presumption that Derrida's conclusions are just "views" or "opinions" or "premises" lead Searle and many of Derrida's other hostile readers to argue that if one doesn't believe in all the claims traditionally made on behalf of the serious, the literal, the obvious, or whatever, then one must necessarily believe the opposite claims. If one can say that Derrida "believes" in rhetoric *over* logic, or metaphor *over* reference, iterability *over* intention, or the nonserious *over* the serious, then one can slide along to the conclusion that Derrida's arguments themselves are merely "rhetorical," illogical, nonserious, and in a word—Searle's—"obviously false." And, incidentally, that the values motivating such wild notions are essentially those attributed to the French in *Henry V*—irresolution, disorganization, vanity, nonseriousness, effeminacy, perhaps also "cognitive minimalism" and "intellectual nihilism," I'll have to check.

One resonant way of characterizing the entire dispute is through the idea of temptation. A leitmotif running through the discourse not only of Austin but also of Derrida and Searle, the notion of temptation, the most fundamental and straightforward idea of traditional ethics, provides one way of approaching the entire discussion. In one view of temptation, the view generally foregrounded in official discourse, especially discourse directed at a popular audience, temptation occurs when some external agency arrives to disturb one's tranquillity, one's integrity, one's oneness. A person's duty, a Searlean moralist might say, is to resist, to exclude, to maintain the center. But in another, equally ancient though typically unstressed view of the tempted subject, temptations arise from within a transgressive force residing in some weak or receptive layer of even the most resolute will. In this scenario, any external agency simply repeats, externalizes, and represents the internal flaw. This conception is often underplayed because it suggests a more problematic idea of resistance in which one's will resists itself, not as a matter of fortitude but structurally and necessarily, and this conception affords no comforting sense of a clean resistance, a decisive gesture that secures internal purity. The idea of temptation, we can see, efficiently condenses into itself both a "traditional" position, involving clean distinctions, effective and strategic exclusions, and essential purity; and the deconstructive "complication" of that position.

Derrida's "Afterword: Toward an Ethic of Discussion," brings such issues into the open. For Derrida not only repeats the charge that Searle has failed to read him, but raises the larger ethical and political issues of "violence," "brutality," and the dereliction of "duty" signaled by such a failure. The "Afterword" is most illuminating on the kind of political and ethical responsibility Derrida envisions as proper to deconstruction. Although the "practical analysis of the parasite" on which deconstruction is based "translates necessarily into a politics," that politics cannot be defined in traditional terms, for it is not "inherently either conservative or revolutionary, or determinable within the code of such oppositions." ("That," Derrida notes, "is precisely what gets on everyone's nerves" [141]).

This practical analysis is based on the idea of duty, the "theoretical duty" which is "also an 'ethical-political duty,'" first to what Derrida called in *Of Grammatology* a "doubling commentary," a lucid, exact, and minute description that paradoxically but necessarily takes the form both of a faithful account of the primary discourse, including its acts of exclusion and marginalization, and a defiance of that discourse, a refusal to collaborate in its suppressions, an insistence on repeating it all (135). For Derrida, questions may be "undecidable" but never "undeterminable," for even—especially—the undecidable can, must be, and is in fact determined. The principle is the mirror image of Kant's *ought* implies *can:* if something *can* be said, then it *ought* to be said. The first "layer or moment" of deconstruction is thus the establishment, using all the traditional resources of the scholar, including knowledge of the "literary, philosophical, rhetorical traditions, the history of [the] language, society, history," of a "minimal consensus" determining the "relatively stable" meaning of a text, without which no research is possible within a community, for one could "just say anything at all" (143–44). For Derrida, Searle and others who accuse deconstruction of hostility to truth or evidence simply get it wrong: "this definition of the deconstructionist is *false* (that's right: false, not true) and feeble; it supposes a bad (that's right: bad, not good) and feeble reading" (146).

Derrida does not pretend that commentary reflects without distortion an uninterpreted object; he simply acknowledges that within a community a relative consensus in fact prevails, and that consensus must be noted and respected, because it enables whatever meaning the text has. (This is why, Derrida says in a brief passage that yanks the rug out from under a small army of flat-earthers, the notorious statement that there is nothing outside the text really means there is nothing outside context. Any "text" implies "all the structures called 'real,' 'economic,' 'historical,' socio-institutional, in short: all possible referents" [148]). But although it is a repetition, the commentary is never a repetition of the same, for it obeys what Derrida calls the "logic that ties repetition to alterity." Citation of the original, as Derrida's subversive citation of Searle had established all by itself—he quotes virtually all of Searle's "Reply" in the course of destroying it—makes the original different from itself in the very act of establishing what the original is. Thus, although doubling commentary is a principle of rigor, it cannot be rigorously separated from its other, which Derrida calls "interpretation." The most passive commentary is thus necessarily already a "productive" or "inventive" recontextualizing. This second layer or moment accomplishes the grafting of which the original text had always been theoretically capable. In the second layer, the possibilities for destabilization opened up by the disclosure of the text's strategies that had occurred in the first layer are realized in some particular way, and pushed as far as evidence will permit.

I must confess that I am greatly impressed with the depth of passion Derrida brings to the articulation of the first layer or moment, that of doubling commentary. For in his account, I find the greatest respect for not just certain traditions of scholarship but also for the contemporary community he seeks to address. However, I am sufficiently impressed that I grow suspicious of my own reaction. For upon reflection, it becomes clear that the values Derrida espouses and the practices that in his account work to secure them have never been brought seriously into question. The scholarly community maintains a systematic and principled preference for necessity, as dictated by the text, over desire, the whim of the individual. So entrenched is this preference, in fact, that it seems impervious to questioning, and this imperviousness makes one wonder whether it can be considered a preference at all. Are not the procedures of commentary simply the elements of a general definition of analysis itself? One may, of course, carry out these practices well or poorly, but if one does not carry them out at all, one has simply not performed an act of analysis. The issue then becomes whether we can describe as an ethical-political duty what is in fact simply a value-neutral qualification, more like an ante than a winning hand. Ought we to praise an act of repetition that has the character of a compulsion?

What Derrida means to do by isolating as an "ethical-political duty," a first "layer or moment" of analysis, is to define a formal category of obligation, to determine the source of what he considers to be Searle's bad faith and professional irresponsibility. Searle, he charges, simply has not read *Sec* carefully; he has overleaped the epistemological moment of faithful repetition and proceeded straight through to an undisciplined and intuitive "interpretation." But the deconstructive "complication" complicates deconstruction itself; for in order to make such a case, Derrida has had to do precisely what he did not want to do, to distinguish sharply, as between different layers or moments, between operations based on "sameness" and those based on "difference." The impossibility of such a rigorous distinction was, after all, the lesson of "iterability," on whose ambivalence Derrida had insisted against Searle. Now, trying to show exactly where Searle has failed, Derrida has had to forget or repress, if only for a moment, iterability itself.

This forgetting, no matter how temporary or strategic, produces a streak of drollery in the debate. As we have just seen, Derrida puts himself in the position of having to propose as a duty what is in fact a compulsion, to hold up as a value what is merely a fact. But even more curiously, he has had to revert to Searle's strategy of insisting on precise categories in language. Thus a queer reversibility takes hold, which becomes even queerer in light of Derrida's repeated insistence throughout "Limited Inc" that it is Searle who has adopted Derrida's position by repeatedly, and apparently unconsciously, borrowing arguments from *Sec* in order to attack *Sec*. The most striking example is Searle's statement that iterability "is not as Derrida seems to think something in conflict with the intentionality of linguistic acts . . . it is the necessary presupposition of the forms which that intentionality takes"; to which Derrida responds, "Precisely the thesis of *Sec,* if there is one!" (105). Indeed, Derrida suggests that, in his defense of rigorous distinctions, Searle is "ultimately more continental and Parisian than I am." Over and over again, Derrida shows, Searle employs a "discourse from/to-*Sec,*" in which, through a kind of unheimlich maneuver, Derrida's own arguments are uncannily recontextualized, claimed as Searle's, and turned back against Derrida. It is as if Searle had somehow been persuaded both that *Sec*'s arguments were false and that they were his own.

As we have already seen, Derrida is not immune to the oddly contaminatory effects of commentary, as he himself testifies in a startling moment in "Limited Inc," where he insists that Searle has falsified the issue: "I note here that I seem to have become infected by [Searle's] style: this is the first time, I believe, that I have ever accused anyone of deception, or of being deceived" (86). Derrida openly courts the "logic that ties repetition to alterity" while Searle repudiates it; but, at least at this point, it is Searle who appears to profit and Derrida who appears to suffer. From a longer point of view, the effects of this logic on Derrida seem even more dramatic, for while he criticizes Austin and Searle for allowing "ethical" concerns to determine their analyses, Derrida has proceeded in his three texts from what he calls an "academic and 'micrological'" discussion of the effects of signature, context, speech-act theory, to a passionate and "serious" denunciation of falsehood and error, and finally to an exhortation to ethical responsibility, justice, reason, and truth. From this longer point of view, Searle—or at least his "position"—seems decisively to have won.

What Derrida gives us, then, is not only a formal account of the ethical principles of discussion, but also a spectacle, a dramatization, of the limits and difficulties of any formal account of ethics. The difficulty is on display in Derrida's concession that Searle has in fact performed the "ethical-political duty" of repetition; and it is intensified when Derrida is forced to acknowledge that Searle's borrowings demonstrate that he understands *Sec* "quite well, even if everything is done to create the contrary impression, one which, it must be admitted, often seems very convincing"; and it is taken to its (il)logical conclusion when Derrida says that Searle's "actively defensive attitude" shows that Searle stands in "a more certain and more vital relationship" to "what is in effect at stake" in deconstruction than do some "avowed 'deconstructionists'" (140). Derrida is really conceding here not that Searle has done something right, but that his own categories are inadequate and that Searle's are necessary. He is saying that while Searle has repeated, and while he has even understood, he has not done either intentionally or consciously, and so his analysis cannot be principled. Derrida is forced to represent the difference between himself and Searle as a difference between conscious and unconscious repetition, with Derrida standing for the principle of purposive consciousness—the very principle on which speech-act theory is based, the very principle Derrida has criticized.

Irony is not the word for a state of affairs in which the only way Derrida can claim victory is through the reassertion of Searle's notions, including the idea of intention in its crudest form possible, speculation about what the author consciously knew when he was writing. Even Searle, who in one respect gains from this return of the unrepressed, might agree that consciousness is cloven and divided against itself if his own arguments proved to be the most, indeed the only, effective weapons Derrida had against him. But even Derrida, who gains in another respect, might be troubled by the cost of victory, by the necessary submission of ethics to primitivism and vulgarity.

Two morals emerge from this morality play (whose title is "Morality and Play"). First, no value based on principle can be determined without strict and rigorous categories. Only through such categories as "doubling commentary," for example—categories whose apparent neutrality indicates that they are a duty for everyone without exception—can a true obligation be conceived. Second, there are no such categories. There is no formal, categorical way of representing a practice that will on all occasions produce a positive moral value. A gap, such as that which separates *is* from *ought,* will always remain, to be bridged by a value-determined "decision." Any claims about the superiority of one practice to another must be based not just on a categorical, but also on what Kant called a hypothetical determination. If I judge Derrida to have won the debate, as I do, I must concede that my judgment is not based solely on Derrida's having performed the ritual of doubling commentary, or even on Derrida's superior understanding; for as Derrida himself concedes, Searle repeats and understands.

My judgment must also be based on such factors as my preference for what Derrida says, and my admiration for Derrida's brilliance, style, wit, persistence, directness, and a host of other qualities l find missing in Searle. These preferences and admirations are not strictly categorical determinations either, however; for they are in turn tangled up with my disposition to praise certain things by calling them "brilliant," "witty," and so forth. My inclination to value wit and brilliance must figure in, too; and my very perception of "things" or "qualities" is confused with other, noncategorical factors. There is no shelter from commitment and principle, no strictly formal test of value, any more than there can be principle without forms and categories. Even the categorical imperative must confront and respect its other. "Ethics," the name we might give to this entire situation, is not only a concept of fairness, but a fair concept: it offers to one's opponents a sword just as long and sharp as that which it claims for itself.

Let us turn now to politics. One of Crews's most damning criticisms of Derrida is that deconstruction's "combination of attention and nonassertion" leads to political ineffectuality or evasiveness. This does not square very well with another of Crews's contentions, that Derrida settles issues by peremptory "theoretical decree." But even more troubling, it implies a rejection by Crews of the most traditional and essential values of scholarly inquiry, which are, as we have already seen, based on precisely such a combination. While it is unclear what task Crews might be imagining for the scholarly community, the connection between his charge of political ineffectuality and Searle's defense of the literal, serious, and central is apparent. For "politics" here stands not for campaigns, elections, advertisements, money-raising, propaganda, inauthentic rage or dismay, inflated jubilation, tracking polls, media hype, or deal-cutting, but for *the serious in general*. Crews seems to imply that Derrida and his gullible readers are so bewitched by textual curlicues and gewgaws that they are incapable of engaging with the real world that is represented by the term *politics*.

If Derrida were to be confronted directly with such an argument, he could, I contend, make no more effective response than to recall the principle of citationality. It is a curious but indisputable fact that statements that do not grow out of a reading of some text, that are not in some way cited, have little value or force. Take as examples the following declarations: that "the self is the place where the abyss opens up, where the whole trembles, where the ground gives way"; or that "ethics is bent on dispersing power clusters . . . which grind us all under"; or that "Finally, we come up against the . . . unencompassable depth in both things and our (non)selves. . . . That it seems to me is where hermeneutics leads us: not to a conclusion which gives comfort but to a thunderstorm." All these quotations, while representative of an entire species of contemporary cliché, are taken from John D. Caputo's *Radical Hermeneutics,* a book that promises a specifically "Derridean" inquiry, but which repeatedly indulges in the kind of general pronouncements Derrida himself refuses to make. The world—I believe wisely—does not care if I or anyone else says that the self is a place where the ground gives way, or that the world is an abyss, or that power grinds us all under, or that hermeneutics leads to thunderstorms (a statement that the city of New Orleans, soaked with thunderstorms but bone-dry, hermeneutics-wise, would seem to disprove). These statements are simply not interesting, much less scary; indeed, in this bald form, they are virtually unprofessional because they are not supported by evidence, nor do they serve as evidence for anything worth knowing. But if somebody else, especially some canonical writer, said them, they would assume a kind of value that would increase when they were quoted by others; then they would become both evidentiary and forceful. Spoken or written by a canonical writer, they would be "supported" at least by the writer's reputation, and could serve as evidence that, for example, Freud or Foucault or Nietzsche (whose reputations would in turn depend upon how often and in what contexts their words were cited) believed they were true. Quoted by critics or commentators, the statements would become evidence not merely about the author, but about those who have thought the statement worth quoting. Evidence and political force—both Crews fetishes—grow with citationality. And the more a given utterance is cited, the more energetically it is weaned from its original context, the greater is its value, for value, too, increases with citationality.

Even more counterintuitively, value and power increase dramatically if an utterance suggests a consciousness that is ambivalent or undecided. Once again, the idea of evidence plays the crucial role. If an utterance can be shown to indicate that the self is the place where the ground gives way, in the course of an argument that the self is firmly grounded, then the value of that part of the utterance soars. In analyzing such an argument, a very precise form of "internal" textual evidence can be advanced to show that the author really believes the opposite of what is apparently said even though he or she was not aware of, or did not want to admit to, believing it. The emergence of the buried belief can then be attributed to the pressure of reality exerting itself against prejudice or denial, creating, perhaps, a guilty conscience that half-intentionally betrays its own suppressions. Intimately linked to its history of citation, the worldly force of an utterance increases with the abundance and precision of the evidence that is connected to it; moreover, that evidence becomes *more evidentiary* insofar as it can be shown to conflict with an apparent or manifest intention. Those who criticize Derrida for political softness or inattention to evidence have to contend with the fact that value, weightiness, and evidence are deeply implicated in such "Derridean" concepts as citationality and divided consciousness.

Take as an example of the worldly power of citation a moment in the opening section, called "Provocations," of Frank Lentricchia's *Criticism and Social Change,* a text that has contributed greatly to Lentricchia's reputation as a tough-minded, politically serious opponent of the "abstract," "formalist," and "ahistorical" practice of deconstruction, and also, as Crews says elsewhere, "arguably the most influential of academic critic-theorists" in the United States ("Parting of the Twains"). Calling on the literary intellectual to "work for social change" even through the indirect means of literary analysis in a classroom setting, Lentricchia quotes Marx and Engels: "The philosophers have only *interpreted* the world, in various ways; the point is to *change* it." Who can doubt that the power of the sentence would have been greatly diminished if it were Lentricchia's own? The fact that the sentence comes from Marx and Engels—who proposed it not exactly as *their* own but as the eleventh of their "Theses on Feuerbach" —and that it has been quoted thousands of times in thousands of contexts, works to erase the element of individual psychology that accompanies any "original" utterance. The sentence's extraordinary history of citation gives it a certain factual status and also enables it to serve as evidence, not just about Marx and Engels's interpretation of Feuerbach, but also about the interpretations of those who have acted to "change the world" on the basis of that interpretation, and hence about the world itself. By the time Lentricchia gets to it, the sentence has accumulated a fantastic assemblage of citational barnacles that have formed themselves into the shape of a ship that is eminently seaworthy, with a very considerable displacement. This solidity—relative, not absolute, but massive and determined—is the very essence of the sentence's force, a force that by itself deconstructs the opposition the sentence posits between interpretation and change.

The point is not that interpretations can change the world, but that both interpretation and worldly change are darkly connected to iterability and citationality. In a book devoted to an attack on deconstruction (with Kenneth Burke triumphing over Paul de Man), Lentricchia provides a virtual illustration of Derrida's case in "Limited Inc." Lentricchia begins with a sentence Searle would applaud as serious, literal speech in which there is no space at all between the speaker's intentions and his words. The subject of the sentence is in fact those intentions, the speaker's inner state, communicated directly to a competent listener. Here it is: "I can tell you what my book is about, at its polemical core, by citing a distinction of John Dewey's that I first encountered in the amazing meditative labyrinth Kenneth Burke called *Attitudes Toward History*" (1). The assurances of "I" and "you," of "polemical" directness, of free and undistorted communication, are both secured by and ensnarled in a network of meditations from which suddenly emerges a nested citation of Dewey, through Burke, through Lentricchia, or through their texts and far more labyrinthine contexts. All these are invoked but dismissed, as though, through an immediate and radical reduction, they could be made to serve as a simple letter of introduction of "me" to "you." And of course they can, but only at the cost of implicating the author and the reader in those "amazing" labyrinths, that unmasterable play of texts and contexts—the nonseriousness of which is the object of Lentricchia's polemic.

Without discussing fully Lentricchia's often admirable text, both its "polemical core" and the rest, one can at least make a few comments regarding its opening strategies. "Provocations" begins with stick-figure sketches of "the radical," "the conservative," "the reactionary," and "the liberal," concluding that "we are left with two political choices: conservatism or radicalism," the latter being favored. Favored despite the disquieting recognitions that the two cannot be decisively distinguished, as the reactionary is simply a "radical in reverse gear"; or that the radical Lentricchia finds himself in agreement with some positions of the religious far right; or that the radical and the reactionary share fundamental beliefs "that society should be a function of education," and that "our society is mainly unreasonable." This disquiet is put aside, unrecognized, unattended to, unheard, marginalized beyond hope of return, as the text proceeds to the further specification of "what my book is about," a phrase that is repeated a number of times in "Provocations," each time with a more private and more conservative determination. "My book is about" the distinction of Dewey's; about "culture, intellectuals, the authority and power of intellectuals"; about "literary intellectuals," especially the "university humanist." Finally, in the last paragraph, "you" learn that "this book is not about Kenneth Burke and Paul de Man. It is about my work, what I do, and what I would do as a literary intellectual" (20).

Given this progression, it can be no surprise that in the end the "radical literary intellectual" is actually encouraged to take as his or her essential and "most powerful" political act the teaching of "expository writing or American fiction," that is, encouraged to remain not merely on campus but in the classroom. Nor can it be accidental that an "oppositional criticism" that says it champions "the marginalized voices of the ruled, exploited, oppressed, and excluded" takes as its central "point," articulated in the very last sentence of "Provocations," "to work where we are without at the same time regretting that those who struggle elsewhere may never hear our voice" (20). Or we theirs: teaching English is never having to say you're sorry.

One reason why a deconstructive politics that is not "inherently either conservative or revolutionary, or determinable within the code of such oppositions" might get on Lentricchia's nerves is that such a politics threatens the binary ease of the *soi-disant* radical. Crews's charge that Derrida has "no way of arriving at more fruitful ideas than the inherited ones he has doomed himself to deconstruct" is, once again, by some uncanny but by this time predictable logic, grossly misapplied to Derrida but richly deserved by his opponents. If the radical cannot but repeat the gestures of the reactionary, discovering in these very gestures not only the comforts of home but also the self-applauding machismo of the outlaw, then clearly the impulse to specific change, change that is not self-canceled, is going to have to come from elsewhere. It is here that the procedures of deconstruction outlined by Derrida in the "Afterword," based on the resistance to any assertion that comes at the expense of attention, and on the commitment to repeating and amplifying the voices of the marginalized and to doing so in contexts other than those in which they have been determined as marginal—it is here that the procedures of deconstruction emerge as the basis of a politics. Failing—and failing without regret—to repeat or even to hear the "voices of those who struggle elsewhere" (but hey, it's his book), Lentricchia must repeat instead the rancid oppositions whose corrupt inadequacy even he recognizes. He puts his considerable energy into an attack on deconstruction for translating politically into "that passive form of conservatism called quietism," using as his example a single 1969 essay by de Man that nowhere mentions the word *deconstruction,* rather than exposing himself to the practice of Derrida or even of the later de Man, a practice that might have taught him what is worth repeating and what is not (51).

It would be altogether beside the point to praise "the politics of deconstruction." But the example of Derrida can inculcate among those who read him a salutary reverence for the facts and an uncompromising commitment to see them otherwise. He does not trade in the undefined pseudo-concept of Foucauldian "power." Nor does he permit himself the use of academic tough-guy slang, as in Lentricchia's definition of criticism as "the production of knowledge to the ends of power and, maybe, of social change" (11). (What *are* "knowledge," "power," "social change"; and hence, what is "criticism"?) Derrida remains committed to the more properly Nietzschean category of "difference" as the indispensable precondition for any determination of "power," and as the particular point of attack for any specifically political intervention. Moreover, Derrida seems to understand what he is, a philosopher who speaks and writes about texts. Nowhere in his work can one find any trace of a simple confusion between such activity and political action per se, which remain, as they do not in Lentricchia, related but resistant categories. Claiming that the literary humanist is an agent for "social change," Lentricchia seems unaware of the fact that society changes all the time, that things do not stay put, that change itself is neutral. Nothing in "Provocations" discourages the inference that he believes that "ruling culture" is unfailingly repressive and that all change is therefore desirable. "The activist intellectual," he writes, "needs a theory of reading that will instigate a culturally suspicious, trouble-making readership" (11). Only a "radical," that is, one still thinking in "inherited" oppositions, would regard the "ruling culture" as entirely "repressive" and all "trouble" as good; and only a "radical," that is, a person who looks a lot like a reactionary, would define the current need as "a theory of reading."

If "politics" indicates anything, it indicates a certain proximity, a causal link, between action and specific desired effects in a particular setting. It is hard to accord political seriousness to a proposal to adopt an undefined theory that might inspire a practice that may one day produce effects that would perhaps be desirable in a realm that could be called social. And if "ethics" indicates anything, it indicates action undertaken in strict accordance with principle, regardless of desire, interest, or context. The two, linked by Derrida in the phrase "ethical-political duty," are not always mutually reinforcing. I have tried to indicate that Derrida is potentially far *more* radical than Lentricchia. I will conclude with the claim that the force of Derrida's politics derives from his refusal to follow an "inherently" radical or leftist program of reading. His politics are forceful and effective only to the extent to which he subordinates—that is, convincingly appears to subordinate—his own political purposes to an ethical imperative to read in a particular way.

It is often difficult to gauge the extent to which this subordination has occurred, and this is why the emphasis must be placed on "convincing" as a textual effect rather than on any psychological cause. My example will be controversial, but the difficulty of the case itself argues on behalf of this emphasis on convincing. I refer to Derrida's reading of the wartime journalism of Paul de Man, which I take to be a powerful and poignant demonstration of personal cost, the possibility of which is implied by the very concept of ethics. Reading through his tears, with an anguished sense of the inexcusable complicity of de Man in the Holocaust, Derrida writes his response according to his own exacting principles, exquisitely sensitive not only to the shocking evidence of collaboration but also to the traces of a possible fugitive counter-energy, an admittedly marginal, suppressed argument critical of "vulgar" anti-Semitism that runs through de Man's texts. Derrida writes, I am convinced, in full awareness of the wild inappropriateness of such a delicate reading of this counter-argument in the "original context" of publication. And he does so in full and excruciating knowledge that his very sensitivity, although "principled"—and just because it is principled, and sets aside all pragmatic or self-interested objections to principle—will be excoriated not only by his enemies but by honorable people, including those who may have been his allies and defenders and even friends, for honorable reasons. He writes knowing that both he and the memory of de Man will suffer, that his response will be taken as a "sophisticated" justification for unpardonable crime, and a suggestion that de Man himself was "sophisticated" in just this way. With the exception of Jonathan Culler's, the responses to this article printed in *Critical Inquiry* are as venomous as their authors could make them. In the *Times Literary Supplement,* Terry Eagleton suggested that Derrida might wish that he had not written this article. It would surely be more accurate to say that he must wish he did not have to write it, that it had not been possible to write it. But it was, he did, and the principle of an ethical, rather than a politically desirable, reading—that *can* implies *ought,* that if the evidence makes it possible to say something then one has a duty to say it—prevails. Having earlier criticized Derrida for his formalism, I now want to praise him for his refusal to compromise his principles, his insistence on forms.

In this incident we can see how difficult is the task Derrida has set himself. When deconstruction passes from the scene of practice and controversy, it will not be because it has been disproven or exposed by a triumphant "traditionalism," "historicism," or "culturalism," but for other reasons. The world must turn, paradigms must shift, society must change, battles must be fought, people must die; and in any event, the number of writers, never large, who can do anything at all like what Derrida does may well fall below a critical mass. In the next millennium, it is, however, to be hoped that something at least of his practice will linger as a kind of graphematic "remainder," which, even if not permanent, might nevertheless preserve for a while the principles of attention and nonassertion. For it is in these principles, insofar as they are maintained and powerfully extended no matter what the cost, that lies whatever hope the marginalized and dominated might permit themselves to nurture.

5 So . . . What *Is* Enlightenment?
An Inquisition into Modernity

Germs and Shells: Countering the Enlightenment

When in 1983 Michel Foucault invited a small group of friends and colleagues—Richard Rorty, Hubert Dreyfus, Charles Taylor, and Jürgen Habermas—to consider a private colloquium to be held at Berkeley on the subject of Kant's essay "An Answer to the Question: 'What Is Enlightenment?'" he was nearing the end of one of the most remarkable and, to many, incomprehensible "turns" in recent intellectual history. Throughout his career, Foucault had been at pains to reject in the most uncompromising terms Kant's account of the conditions of knowledge, the autonomy of the subject, and the universalizing rule of reason—all of which could be taken as historical errors, metaphysical masks worn by "discourse" or "disciplinary regimes." But having established himself securely in a philosophical genealogy that extended from Nietzsche and Heidegger to Lacan, Lyotard, Deleuze, Derrida, and other thinkers of the "counter-Enlightenment," Foucault sought not just to rehabilitate the chronically "incomplete project" of the Enlightenment as a subject of contemporary discussion but also to establish some positive relation of his own to that fissile and complex movement by reopening the question to which Kant had provided "An Answer." "What is modern philosophy?" Foucault asked a Berkeley audience that came to hear him lecture in the fall of 1983; "perhaps we could respond with an echo: modern philosophy is the philosophy that is attempting to answer the question raised so imprudently two centuries ago: *Was ist Aufklärung?*" ("What Is Enlightenment?" 32; hereafter abbreviated WIE).[1] Not all were persuaded that Foucault's conversion

1. James Miller draws attention to a lecture given by Foucault at the Sorbonne in May 1978 called "Qu'est-ce que la critique?" that served as a point of departure for "a series of subsequent talks and texts" on Kant, including the inaugural lecture in his last series of lectures at the Collège de France in winter 1983 ("The Art of Telling the Truth"), and culminating in "What Is Enlightenment?" See Miller, *The Passion of Michel Foucault;* hereafter abbreviated *PMF.* Each time Foucault returned to Kant's call to have courage to use your own reason,

was sincere. Indeed, in an acrimonious public exchange with Foucault just a few months earlier, the historian Lawrence Stone asserted that Foucault's works constituted "a denial of the Enlightenment as an advance in human understanding and sensibility, and a causal linkage of it to the sexual fantasies of domination, violation, and torture which obsessed the mind of Sade" (43). According to one powerful school of thought, the only quality that Foucault and the Enlightenment held in common was imprudence.

If, as Christopher Norris argues, this jagged and complex lecture—which Foucault called "What Is Enlightenment?" and placed at the very beginning of *The Foucault Reader* being prepared by his Berkeley colleague Paul Rabinow—marks a genuine appreciation of Enlightenment thinking, many of the old antipathies remain. Foucault consistently represents Kant as both indispensable and unacceptable. He is especially hostile to Kant's anxious concern for freedom of conscience in religious matters. Religion stands as the historical locus of every mystification that Foucault sought to unmask or subvert by emphasizing the local, the material, the historically specific, the apparently discontinuous or haphazard. Religious thinking is in fact the implied target of an archeological-genealogical method that sought, according to Foucault, to place "within a process of development everything considered immortal in man" ("Nietzsche, Genealogy, History" 87). In a late interview, Foucault had noted that the Greeks managed to find their distinctive "style of existence" "only within the framework of a religious style," so that "all of antiquity seems to me to have been a 'profound error' [Laughter]" ("The Return of Morality" 244). Nor, Foucault argues in his lecture, is Kant persuasive as an analyst of contemporary conditions; indeed, he seems systematically to have missed the point on most issues. "No historian," Foucault writes, "could be satisfied with [Kant's analysis] of the social, political, and cultural transformations that occurred at the end of the eighteenth century" (WIE 37).

But for Foucault the most bewilderingly unsatisfactory moment in Kant's essay is the famous and fateful distinction between the realm of obedience and the realm of reason. One can argue about the system of taxation, Kant argued, but one must pay one's taxes; or one can maintain

---

Miller says, "he revealed still another aspect of his puzzlement about himself, usually in the guise of some convoluted and gnomic question" (*PMF* 332). For some sense of the extraordinary diversity of the thought that now goes under the rubric of Enlightenment, see *The Enlightenment: A Comprehensive Anthology*, ed. Peter Gay and *What Is Enlightenment? Eighteenth-Century Answers and Twentieth-Century Questions*, ed. James Schmidt. For a mass of documents dealing with the "Enlightenment" understanding of race, see *Race and the Enlightenment: A Reader*, ed. Emmanuel Chukwudi Eze.

reservations about some points of religious belief, but if one is a religious official, one should, for the good of the congregation, preach the approved doctrine. The result, as Foucault paraphrases Kant, is that reason "must be free in its public use, and must be submissive in its private use. Which is," he notes with some vexation, "term for term, the opposite of what is ordinarily called freedom of conscience" (WIE 36).

It does appear that, in this founding text, Kant has for some reason simply given things the wrong names, for what he calls the public use of reason, which "alone can bring about enlightenment among men," actually consists of private thoughts, discoveries, research, and reflections that happen to have the advantage of print publication: "By the public use of one's own reason I mean that use which anyone may make of it *as a man of learning* addressing the entire *reading public.*" The chilling consequence is that, for Kant, most people simply do not have access to the public sphere; for them, the public exists only in the diluted and distorted form of aftereffects. Moreover, the private, which today we might think of as a realm of introspection, self-knowledge, affective movements, or one's relations with one's friends and family, is, for Kant, similarly restricted not to scholars but to men in some position of public responsibility, "a particular *civil* post or office with which he is entrusted" ("An Answer to the Question, 'What Is Enlightenment?'" 55; hereafter AQ). Kant's private realm seems, to a modern liberal sensibility, simply a specialized form of the public, a form from which, once again, all but a few are excluded. The whole epochal challenge, the entire management of "the age," is effectively reserved for scholars and public officials. This creates what Foucault describes as a "political problem," an elitism that seems sharply at variance with the universalism of Enlightenment itself—which has, Foucault notes, found itself from the beginning "struggling with attitudes of 'countermodernity'" (WIE 39).

Skeptical about Kant's analysis and dismissive of his politics, Foucault asks bluntly "how the use of reason can take the public form that it requires, how the audacity to know can be exercised in broad daylight, while individuals are obeying as scrupulously as possible" (WIE 37). With this final complaint, he abruptly takes leave of Kant—"Let us leave Kant's text here"—and veers off into a highly un-Kantian discussion of Enlightenment as he understands it, focusing on Baudelaire's dandyism as a form of ascetic self-invention that responds to "the essential, permanent, obsessive relation that our age entertains with death" and concluding on an anarchic note with a call to "the undefined work of freedom" (WIE 37, 40, 46).

Foucault died in June 1984, the bicentennial of Kant's essay, before the planned colloquium could take place. But his essay has stimulated further conversation among a group of scholars that includes Dreyfus and Rabinow, Habermas, and, more recently, Norris, men of learning who have published their reflections for the *"reading public."* [2] In fact, the very idea of such a conversation goes straight to the heart of the Enlightenment legacy, suggesting a colloquy of rational, self-determining subjects sharing their insights with other similar beings. Conversation so conceived constitutes the public exercise of enlightened maturity. Indeed, the philosophical establishment of unencumbered public conversation, answerable to the truth but not to prince, church, or nation, could be said to be an Enlightenment invention, perhaps even the defining Enlightenment invention, a social instance of Kant's distinctions between private and public, reason and interest, freedom and coercion.

But such conversation also points up the fragility of those very distinctions. For scholarly exchanges not only reflect the Enlightenment distinctions but mediate and in many ways confound them. As eminent professors of philosophy, all those just named enjoy the support of institutions whose sponsorship makes them public functionaries operating in a regime where, according to Kant, reason should be submissive "for the good of the congregation." And perhaps it *is* submissive, as unencumbered as it may appear to be. For all these earnest, heavily footnoted essays on Enlightenment do little to disturb the status quo and even, in their unresponsiveness to those deep and specific circumstances such as race, class, religion, nation, ethnicity, and so on, make a powerful claim for the value and privilege of the tenured philosophical life. Conversation, as Foucault would have seen, is not unimplicated with what he called power, which is reflected, produced, and reproduced by even the freest acts of conscience. A conference on Kant's view of Enlightenment would not just determine what Kant really said or meant but would help to shape a scholarly consensus on a philosophical and cultural heritage and thus to fashion a contemporary self-conception, from which point the happy few could determine, with a freedom issuing from a new account of history, the course of the future.[3] This course might entail war, anarchy, suppression of dissidence,

2. See Jürgen Habermas, "Taking Aim at the Heart of the Present: On Foucault's Lecture on Kant's *What Is Enlightenment?*" See also Christopher Norris, "What Is Enlightenment? Foucault on Kant," in *The Truth about Postmodernism;* and Hubert Dreyfus and Paul Rabinow, "What Is Maturity? Habermas and Foucault on 'What Is Enlightenment?'"

3. In his own essay, Foucault may have been trying to bend Kant's essay in the direction of Jean-François Lyotard's 1979 postscript to *The Postmodern Condition,* which urges a rejection of Enlightenment "metanarratives" in favor of the kind of local microlegitimations that Foucault himself was promoting. See Lyotard, "Answering the Question: What Is Postmodernism?"

beheading the sovereign, a middle-class tax credit—anything, including a continuance of the current arrangement.

So scholarly conversation, the characteristic Enlightenment form of inquiry, turns out to be thoroughly compatible with submission in some senses and authoritarianism in others. Indeed, each may hide behind the other. The appearance of bustle and contentiousness at a scholarly gathering may mask indolent timidity; or, contrariwise, the harmless aspect of a group of agitated intellectuals may conceal real work. Perhaps it was this understanding of the possibly subversive undecipherability of scholarly conversation that led Kant to enter, as Foucault notes with obvious disappointment, into his notorious nonaggression pact with Frederick the Great, committing himself to applauding the sovereign's suppression of politically subversive acts in exchange for his own intellectual liberty. A subtle, daring, and psychologically penetrating Kant may have enticed a sovereign hungry for a reputation not just for overmastering puissance but also for wisdom into an agreement in which the sovereign obliged himself to permit freedoms that the philosopher well knew might be radical in their ultimate, if not their immediate, effects. Perhaps—a generous heart might argue—this is why Kant's argument conveys a powerful sense of *lulling:*

> I have portrayed *matters of religion* as the focal point of enlightenment, i.e. of man's emergence from his self-incurred immaturity. This is firstly because our rulers have no interest in assuming the role of guardians over their subjects so far as the arts and sciences are concerned, and secondly because religious immaturity is the most pernicious and dishonourable variety of all. But the attitude of mind of a head of state who favours freedom in the arts and sciences extends even further, for he realises that there is no danger even to his *legislation* if he allows his subjects to make public use of their own reason and to put before the *public* their thoughts on better ways of drawing up laws, even if this entails forthright criticism of the current legislation. We have before us a brilliant example of this kind, in which no monarch has yet surpassed the one to whom we now pay tribute.
>
> But only a ruler who is himself enlightened and has no fear of phantoms, yet who likewise has at hand a well-disciplined and numerous army to guarantee public security, may say what no republic would dare to say: *Argue as much as you like and about whatever you like, but obey!* (AQ 59)

What could this bizarre injunction mean? From a perspective formed both by Lacan and by decades of life in "really existing socialism," the

Slovenian philosopher Slavoj Žižek sees in these words the precise definition of *cynicism,* a prescription for lip service.[4] Beneath this "political problem," however, Žižek discovers the psychological problem presented by a law determined from the outset as given, "traumatic," unfounded, nonsensical. "In the traditional, pre-enlightened universe," Žižek writes, "the authority of the Law is . . . always illuminated by the charismatic power of fascination. Only to the already enlightened view does the universe of social customs and rules appear as a nonsensical 'machine' that must be accepted as such" (*Sublime Object of Ideology* 80; hereafter *SO*). Only a law that, like the categorical imperative itself, does not pretend to rational justification can free us for theoretical reflection and enable us to "enjoy" our obedience. This hidden dimension of Kantian obedience anticipates not liberal democracy but totalitarianism. If we ask now, What is "An Answer to the Question: 'What Is Enlightenment?'" the possible answers might be: (1) a piece of flattery thrown off by a tame intellectual; (2) a shrewd effort to circumscribe the sovereign's recognized appetite for the suppression of (especially religious) dissent; and (3) a prescient disclosure of the (totalitarian) obscenity of Enlightenment itself. Whatever it was, it did not work. When Kant published *Religion within the Limits of Reason Alone* nine years later, he was rebuked by the official censor and forced to apologize. This exercise of old-style power in the very heart of the Aufklärung raises once again the initial question: What is Enlightenment?

Enlightenment may be lurking in Kant's very next sentences:

> This reveals to us a strange and unexpected pattern in human affairs (such as we shall always find if we consider them in the widest sense, in which nearly everything is paradoxical). A high degree of civil freedom seems advantageous to a people's *intellectual* freedom, yet it also sets up insuperable barriers to it. Conversely, a lesser degree of civil freedom gives intellectual freedom enough room to expand to its fullest extent. Thus once the germ on which nature has lavished most care—man's inclination and vocation to *think freely*—has developed within this hard shell, it gradually reacts upon the mentality of the people, who thus gradually become increasingly able to *act freely.* (AQ 59)

---

4. Slavoj Žižek, *Enjoy Your Symptom! Jacques Lacan in Hollywood and Out,* x. Tzvetan Todorov makes a related observation. "I came to know evil during the first part of my life, when I lived in a country under Stalinist rule," Todorov writes. "I was never a direct victim of the regime, since my reaction . . . was not to protest or challenge it, but to take on two distinct personalities: one public and submissive, the other private and independent." *On Human Diversity: Nationalism, Racism, and Exoticism in French Thought* vii.

It is paradox itself, naturalized by the figure of the germ within the hard shell, that lies deeply and productively encased within the hard shell of an argument that otherwise may appear confused (as Foucault says), cynical, or obscene (Žižek). For paradoxes only appear to conflict with themselves; they answer equally to at least two competing accounts—as Kant says things inevitably do when considered "in the widest sense," the sense cultivated by enlightened thought. One of the paradoxes confronted by the *Berlinische Monatsschrift*, the newspaper that had posed to its readers the original question about Enlightenment, concerned the perpetual crisis represented by substantial numbers of prosperous Jews existing as empowered outsiders, or marginalized insiders, within a dominant Christian culture. As Foucault points out, Moses Mendelssohn had responded some months earlier to the same question as Kant; and although Kant had not seen that essay when he wrote his own, what amounted to a joint contribution to a question of public moment may have appeared to be a public affirmation by the two authors, and by the newspaper itself, of a common history, a common destiny.[5] This common destiny had been sorely tested by other forms of the Enlightenment, especially by the virulently anti-Semitic Voltaire (one of whose nicknames was, weirdly enough, Goebbels). In this context, Kant's emphasis on freedom of religion may have been understood by his readers, his publishers, and perhaps even by Kant himself as a way of heading off threats not to his own security but to Jews, whose precarious existence within the hard shells of various nation states provided a telling measure of the enlightenment each culture had attained. Indeed, since "World Jewry" was, unlike the Hapsburg empire or the French crown, centered nowhere, governed according to no local or place-bound set of interests, Jewish culture existed more purely "in the widest sense" than any regime, no matter how vast its territories or enlightened its sovereign. Jews thus constitute the missing term of an Enlightenment syllogism: the army is to intellectual freedom as Christian nations are to Jews.

The form of paradox is stamped on everything in the Enlightenment. Kant's critical philosophy as a whole could be seen as a mighty effort

---

5. "Who is Kant?" Derrida asks in a lecture published in 1991. "He is the holiest saint of the German spirit, the deepest, innermost inner sanctum of the German spirit . . . but he is also the one who represents the innermost affinity . . . with Judaism." See "Interpretations at War: Kant, the Jew, the German" 58. As a counterexample still within the Enlightenment, however, we may cite Fichte, the most aggressively pro-Robespierre of all contemporary German philosophers—and also the most anti-Semitic. For a discussion of Mendelssohn's contribution, see Altmann 660–65.

to articulate the paradoxes appurtenant to the widest sense of things, in which—somehow—theoretical reason, practical reason, judgment, and all their internal moving parts (reflective and determinant judgment, laws of nature and freedom, the antinomies of pure reason, and so on) collaborate in ongoing cognitive projects. In an even broader sense, the Enlightenment as a whole can be seen as devoted at once to particularity and distinctions *and* to an overarching reason, which dispels contradictions or paradoxes by discovering, "in the widest sense," a principle of compatibility between apparently opposed terms such as armies and consciences.[6] Ultimately, however, and most paradoxically of all, the triumphant overcoming of paradoxes concludes by affiliating the Enlightenment itself with its other. As Martin Jay comments, "The familiar linkage of Kant with the French Revolution is thus perhaps justified not only because the antidogmatic 'terrorism' of his critical method may have surpassed that of Robespierre, as Heine once observed, but also because Kant shared many of the hopes that fed the Revolution" (*MT* 47–48).[7] From serene thoughts of reason it is but a short step to critical terrorism in the service of revolutionary fantasies of the essential unity of mankind, fantasies that coordinate nicely with the Marxist notion of totality—which "seems on the surface foreign to the Enlightenment" but nevertheless "can be said to have emerged in its interstices" (*MT* 30).

The edifice of Enlightenment has so many interstices that it can be considered, in the manner of Adorno and Horkheimer, not as a "project" but as a "dialectic," an oscillation between ideals of political emancipation,

6. As Martin Jay comments, the Enlightenment is "a movement whose major intellectual impulses were critical, analytic, scientific, mechanistic and anti-metaphysical. Epistemologically, the Enlightenment is normally seen as sensationalist and associationist, with a straight line running from Locke to the outright skepticism of Hume. The deductive reasoning characteristic of seventeenth-century metaphysicians like Spinoza and Leibniz was replaced by empiricist deduction. Politically, the Enlightenment is usually associated with social contract theory, individualism, natural right theory, and the pursuit of self-interest, rather than the search for community or the justification of hierarchy." Jay, *Marxism and Totality: The Adventures of a Concept from Lukács to Habermas;* hereafter abbreviated *MT.* But this partitioning occurred, as Ernst Cassirer points out, within the domain of reason, which "cannot stop with the dispersed parts, it has to build from them a new structure, a true whole. . . . Reason understands this structure because it can reproduce it in its totality and in the ordered sequence of individual elements." Cassirer 191; quoted in *MT* 30–31.

7. Heinrich Heine, *Concerning the History of Religion and Philosophy in Germany* 369. See also two books by Frederick C. Beiser, *The Fate of Reason: German Philosophy from Kant to Fichte;* and *Enlightenment, Revolution, and Romanticism: The Genesis of Modern German Political Thought, 1790–1800,* for discussions of the ways in which the French Revolution transformed and politicized German philosophy and its central concern with the authority and limits of reason.

universal rights, the autonomous subject, and the reign of reason, on one hand, and their dark familiars—statist or nationalist repression, the administered society, the disseminated subject, cynicism, and mass culture—on the other. Adorno and Horkheimer argue their case as though it were a new discovery, a radical overturning of received wisdom about Enlightenment, but in fact they merely retrieve Kant's figure of the "germ" or "seed." Enlightenment, they write, is not only indispensable for "social freedom" but also "already contains the seed of the reversal universally apparent today," in 1944, when the well-disciplined and numerous armies Kant prized had secured "hierarchical," even "totalitarian" structures in both thought and social organization.[8] Thus while the only cure for the mutilations of the Enlightenment is more Enlightenment, the cure only inflicts more wounds. The result is that within the regime of Enlightenment, certain things must—again, as Kant seemed to intuit—be misnamed, an imperative Adorno and Horkheimer follow by bluntly describing Enlightenment itself as "mass deception" (DE 120).

We are now in a better position to understand why Foucault came to a quickened if belated appreciation of Kant's accomplishment. Foucault was evidently beginning to understand that Kant could be appropriated for his own (counter-Enlightenment) arguments through what has been called the Fourth Critique, Kant's less portentous and systematic writings about history and politics, including the essay on Enlightenment and "The Contest of the Faculties." While in his three great Critiques Kant poses the "question of the conditions in which true knowledge is possible," in the fourth, Foucault writes, he is concerned with "an ontology of the present, an ontology of ourselves."[9] The discovery of a second Kantian tradition perpetrates a series of recognitions startling above all in that Foucault does

8. Theodor W. Adorno and Max Horkheimer, *Dialectic of Enlightenment* xiii; hereafter abbreviated *DE*. Žižek, who in some senses represents the furthest reach so far of the counter-Enlightenment, betrays an Enlightenment germ by his own use of this figure: "The Lacanian thesis is, on the contrary, that there is always a hard kernel, a leftover which persists and cannot be reduced to a universal play of illusory mirroring" (*SO* 47); "is not this effort to historicize the family triangle precisely an attempt to elude the 'hard kernel' which announces itself through the 'patriarchal family'—the Real of the Law, the rock of castration?" (*SO* 50); "the symptom as a 'return of the repressed' is precisely such an effect which precedes its cause (its hidden kernel, its meaning)" (*SO* 56); "what lies beyond [the pleasure principle] is not the symbolic order but a real kernel, a traumatic core" (*SO* 132); the Lacanian Real "is usually conceived as a hard kernel resisting symbolization" (*SO* 161). The cause of this figure has been significantly advanced by the appearance of Karl Abraham and Maria Torok, *The Shell and the Kernel,* a translation of *L'Écorce et le noyau* (Paris, 1978), a collection of psychoanalytic, literary, and philosophical essays.
9. Foucault, "The Art of Telling the Truth" 95.

not seem startled by them. "What Is Enlightenment?" tracks a ragged line of descent from Kant to all of Foucault's own themes: "a mode of relationship that has to be established with oneself" (WIE 41), "what the Greeks called an ethos" (WIE 39), "a desperate eagerness to imagine [the present] otherwise than it is, and to transform it" (WIE 41)—all these, Foucault asserts, are firmly "rooted in the Enlightenment" (WIE 42). So much has been made of Foucault's late "turn to antiquity" that it takes a certain effort to see that Foucault was simultaneously turning, or perhaps twisting, to Kant. No longer seeking simply to negate the Enlightenment, he was discovering in the Enlightenment a congenial principle of self-negation. Marking the critical distinctions between himself and Kant, Foucault draws a line . . . in the sand (see WIE 47).

The counter-Enlightenment seems as incapable of scraping the primordial mud of Enlightenment off its boots as the Enlightenment had been of suppressing its own perverted other. In a round world, Foucault—like Lyotard, Lacan, and Derrida—comes back to Kant.[10] Ian Hacking has identified a "Kantian side of Foucault's ethics" in the renewed emphasis on the autonomous human "construction" of the moral law, an emphasis Foucault retained while rejecting the imperative role of reason. "Foucault's historicism combined with that notion of constructing morality leads one away from the letter and the law of Kant," Hacking comments, "but curiously preserves Kant's spirit" ("Self-Improvement" 239). What we can now begin to see is that any preservation of "Kant's spirit" will be "curious," because curiosity is rooted in the "letter and law" itself. For both Kant and his disciple Foucault, Enlightenment inspires a compulsion to contradiction, to self-division, to paradox. If one cannot simply accept or reject the Enlightenment, the reason is not simply that Enlightenment dominates our thinking so utterly that it contains all the thoughts we are likely to think, but also that no matter what one thinks about it, Enlightenment is always otherwise.

Still, it is possible to distinguish between a characteristically "Kantian" (Enlightenment) and a characteristically "Foucauldian" (counter-Enlightenment) habit of mind, on the following basis. Anchored by his fundamental distinctions, Kant insistently abstracts the issues in order to see them in their widest sense, in which contraries coexist and all things are paradoxical, a sense in which things held to be separate, such as armies and free consciences, are revealed to be compatible but resistant parts of a

10. See Lyotard and Jean-Loup Thébaud, *Just Gaming;* Lyotard, *The Differend: Phrases in Dispute;* Lacan, "Kant avec Sade"; and Derrida, "Afterword: Toward an Ethic of Discussion," in *Limited Inc,* esp. 152–53.

single complex whole. Kant's thinking seeks to achieve a level of generalization on which the apprehension of, and critical purchase on, specificities is risked. Not the Revolution but the "enthusiasm" for the Revolution as a paradoxical testament—paradoxical given the actual, terroristic Revolution—to an elemental human destiny of freedom enlists Kant's admiration (see Kant, "Contest of Faculties").

Foucault, by soft contrast, begins with a conviction of undifferentiation or identity. I am referring here not only to the ideologically imposed totalities he analyzed but also to his analysis itself, which characteristically takes the form of a counterintuitive insistence on a *general continuum.* From within the conviction of continuity overriding apparent distinctions, Foucault works toward a level of particularity on which discrete things emerge bristling with detail, a level on which the critical purchase on general structures is risked. Thus Foucault can treat prisons as, in Michael Walzer's words, "only one small part of a highly articulated, mutually reinforcing carceral continuum extending across society, in which all of us are implicated, and not only as captives or victims" ("Politics of Michel Foucault" 60). And thus knowledge itself can be seen, as Arnold I. Davidson puts it, as "linked in a circular relation with systems of power which produce and sustain it, and to effects of power which it induces and which extend it" ("Archeology, Genealogy, Ethics" 221).[11] Davidson admires Foucault's methods, while Walzer charges him with a "confusion" to which "the language of all his books" is "a perpetual incitement" ("Politics of Michel Foucault" 62). Illuminating though it may be to grasp concealed connections, the form of Foucault's analysis makes it impossible to celebrate or critique any particular event, institution, or practice by referring to its relation to an elemental destiny of freedom.

If in the "Kantian" method one is always moving toward a paradoxical totality in which what is critiqued is the general structure, in the "Foucauldian" method one is always moving toward the particular instance, which cannot be evaluated with reference to a general structure because the general structures are all co-implicated; one is not intrinsically better than another because when properly seen it *is* the other. The figure of the germ or seed within the hard shell encapsulates each method, and both together. For the coexistence of germ and shell is paradoxical but also continuous, because the germ is part of the same organism as the shell and will one day produce shells and germs alike.

11. Interestingly, the sense of a continuum is anticipated in Adorno and Horkheimer's *Dialectic of Enlightenment,* written in the 1940s, which begins with the blunt statement: "Power and knowledge are synonymous" (4).

Christopher Norris and the Critical Difference

The recurrent charge against counter-Enlightenment thinkers such as Foucault, Lyotard, Lacan, and Derrida is "confusion": they betray the Enlightenment by confusing everything, by being confused, by sowing confusion. One of the most passionate and plainspoken defenders of Enlightenment against postmodern confusion is Christopher Norris, whose recent *Uncritical Theory: Postmodernism, Intellectuals, and the Gulf War* (1992) refines arguments he has been making for several years. According to Norris, Foucault stands for the "postmodern sophisticates" who have taken a deplorable turn to the right by renouncing the crucial Enlightenment distinctions (for example, between power and knowledge) and abandoning "that tradition of critical and social-emancipatory thought whose earliest manifesto was Kant's polemical essay 'What Is Enlightenment?'" (*Uncritical Theory* 144; hereafter *UT*). In the climate of postmodernism, Norris charges, truth has been reduced to little more than the current consensus, to an uncritical orthodoxy that is, as pragmatists like Richard Rorty say, "'good in the way of belief'" (*UT* 145). The intellectual no longer claims to speak for the true, much less the good, but is content with a micrological analysis whose subtlety reflects political timidity. Contemporary thinkers have, Norris argues, simply played themselves off the field, defining themselves and their mission in terms so restrictive, unambitious, and ornamental that they could have no impact, certainly no productively critical impact, on a controversial public event such as the Gulf War.

Norris was provoked to write the book by the principled passivity in the face of this war displayed by intellectuals such as Jean Baudrillard, who had actually predicted that the conflict would not "take place"—and then, after the war, argued that it had not "taken place" because the images representing it had been not just arranged but created by the media. In the Foucauldian mind-set, Norris charges, everything becomes aestheticized or, more specifically, sublimated, with the sublime operating not as it does in Kant as an analogy for a moral law that surpasses our powers of representation and cognition but rather as "pretty much *coextensive or synonymous* with the realm of practical reason." As a result, ethical judgments operate within a general premise of undecidability and become powerless to refer themselves to real-world facts. "For poststructuralists and those of a kindred persuasion—notably Foucault," Norris writes, the sublime has become an ultimately privileged category, dictating—as it does not in Kant—a critical paralysis, an inability to lay hold of, much less to correct, a world become all fiction (*UT* 94). Compared to the "sheer moral courage" exemplified by Noam Chomsky's opposition to the Gulf War, the belief of the post-structuralists—"Foucault in particular"—that the "delusive Enlightenment creed" was now badly outdated seems a cowardly retreat, a perverse renunciation of reformist power (*UT* 102,103).

In assessing Norris's commanding argument, three points of instability —two external and one internal—must be noted. First, much of the argument's force depends on a contrast with such Enlightenment standard-bearers as Chomsky and, especially, Habermas. But this dog won't hunt. In "Taking Aim at the Heart of the Present," his own essay on Foucault's 1983 Collège de France lecture on Kant's essay on Enlightenment, Habermas finds little to criticize.[12] To be sure, Habermas is writing something like a memorial shortly after Foucault's death; still, it is remarkable how respectful Habermas is of Foucault as "a thinker in the tradition of the Enlightenment." Habermas clearly understands that what is at stake in Foucault's account of Enlightenment is Habermas's own cherished hope that modernity could progress through a careful cultivation of Enlightenment values and practices toward a condition of greater justice and emancipation. He understands, too, however, that Enlightenment is no stranger to force. Under its dispensation, the subject must draw its norms and ideals from within itself, a project that seems to "demand infinite power." In one frame of mind, Habermas might have criticized Foucault for confusion, for asserting that a "will to knowledge" deformed all cognition, yet claiming to perceive actual structures and true meanings. But here Habermas concedes that the contradictions in Foucault's project are "productive" and "instructive" precisely because they mirror and continue fundamental Enlightenment contradictions. Foucault "warns us," Habermas says— and by "us," he may mean himself—"against the pious attitude of those who are intent only on preserving the remains of the Enlightenment," the "thinkers of order" anachronistically seeking universal conditions of validity ("Taking Aim at the Heart of the Present" 177-78). Habermas seems, in short, unable to get quit of the suspicion that his own commitments are merely pious and that, of the two of them, Foucault is the true heir of Kant.

The second external source of instability in Norris's attack on Foucault as an Enlightenment traitor is provided by Norris's own even more recent text on Foucault as a reader of Kant, a chapter in *The Truth about Postmodernism*. Here, in an admittedly "tortuous commentary," Norris contrasts Foucault to the very postmodernism he was held to exemplify in *Uncritical Theory*, portraying Foucault as a trenchant critic, but in the end a faithful representative, of Enlightenment premises, especially the emphasis on freedom (75). For Foucault, Norris notes, the essence of freedom lay in "a space of individual autonomy—created in the margins or interstices of an

---

12. For a more critical assessment of Foucault by Habermas, see *The Philosophical Discourse of Modernity* 238-93.

otherwise ubiquitous will-to-power whose watch words are 'reason,' 'enlightenment,' and 'truth'" (59). Foucault did not resolve the issues raised by Kant, Norris acknowledges, but rather oscillated, with faltering commitments all around, between "the twin poles of a determinism pushed to the utmost extreme—where the 'subject' is nothing more than a transient construction out of various discursive registers—and a doctrine of autonomy (or private self-invention) that leans right over into an anarchist ethics and politics" (51). While striking anti-Kantian poses, Foucault was actually exploring serially the Kantian antinomies of pure reason: necessity and freedom. Tracking, in this text, Foucault's wary but consistent Kantianism, Norris also marks his own ambivalence with respect to Foucault.

The third source of wobble in Norris's case against Foucault in *Uncritical Theory* is internal, and so even more unsettling than the first two, for it is embedded in the very distinction between truth and ideology. Norris rehearses with approval Edward Said's contention that the West has constructed itself as the home of reason and the "Orient" as the space of barbarism, despotism, shiftlessness, "the embodiment of everything supposedly left behind in the ascent of Western rationality and truth" (*UT* 142). Norris agrees with Said that the Enlightenment has been historically implicated in a practice of imperial/colonial world mapping, a moral crusade with racist overtones undertaken by a privileged hegemonic culture with the power to impose its own values and beliefs on a well-nigh global scale. Still, he advances as "the basic principles of rational thought" the decidedly Enlightenment-based "criteria of adequate grounds, of evidential warrant and respect for the standards of logic, consistency, and truth" (*UT* 142). The problem Norris confronts, and suffers, is this: how to criticize one's opponents—imperialist scholars, warmongers, rival candidates, industrial polluters, whatever—without accusing them of being blind to reason and determined by mere ideology or self-interest, thereby reinvesting in the racist/moral project of the West? The emergent answer in Norris's work is that one just does, by insisting on "the crucial premise: that there is a difference between truth and falsehood in these matters, and that scholarship, criticism, and reasoned argument . . . are the disciplines best equipped to maintain a due sense of that distinction" (*UT* 141); or by clinging to the "critical difference" between "beliefs brought about by some determinate set of ideological interests and beliefs arrived at through the exercise of reasoned or truth-seeking inquiry" (*UT* 145). As Norris concludes, there is, with heroes such as Chomsky and Habermas, "never any question" of collapsing "the difference—the critical difference—between pragmatist thinking in the Fish-Rorty style and the interests of a 'transcendental pragmatics' that would criticize consensus-values from the standpoint of a genuine (if admittedly 'ideal') speech-situation" (*UT* 144).

One would like to know why, given all the concessions, there could *never* be any question of surrendering the "crucial premise" or "the critical difference." Within the Enlightenment ethos, isn't questioning, especially of the most crucial or critical presumptions, always legitimate? Isn't such questioning the only way of ensuring that Enlightenment will prevail over barbarism, despotism, and shiftlessness, and against its own worst hegemonic tendencies? Isn't this precisely Norris's point?[13] Without questioning fundamental premises, how can we ensure that the protocols and institutions of rationality deserve respect as something other than ethnocentric prejudices, the implements of ideological domination; how can we know whether what Norris calls "the history of western practical reason" is not rather too Western, too historical, too practical to represent reason itself? And specifically how can one register, as Norris does, the full force of Foucault's various deformations, radical adjustments, translations of the Enlightenment project, and still proclaim in the end the untroubled dominance of autonomous practical reason, adequate self-reflection, "suprasensible" ideas, principled choices made on universally valid grounds, factual understanding, veridical warrant for statements, and so on?

The answer, I believe, is that we *cannot* be certain that Enlightenment reason is not an ethnocentric prejudice, a local growth like kudzu that is peculiarly suited for dominance wherever it finds itself. Žižek tells a little story that illuminates the difficulty of opposing "truth" to "ideology": "Let us take a typical individual in Germany in the late 1930s. He is bombarded by anti-Semitic propaganda depicting the Jew as a monstrous incarnation of Evil, the great wire-puller, and so on. But when he returns home he encounters Mr. Stern, his neighbour; a good man to chat with in the evenings, whose children play with his. Does not this everyday experience offer an irreducible resistance to the ideological construction?" (*SO* 49). No, it does not. When ideology is really working, the gap between fact and ideological deformation simply disappears, and "our poor German" says, " 'You see how dangerous they really are? It is difficult to recognize their real nature. They hide it behind the mask of everyday appearance—and

---

13. It is certainly Habermas's point. In developing his discourse ethics, he cites R. Alexy's "rules of discourse," including "(3.2) a. Everyone is allowed to question any assertion whatever." Later in the same essay, he argues that to those participating in "a discourse," "the normativity of existing institutions seems just as open to question as the objectivity of things and events." Habermas, *Moral Consciousness and Communicative Action* 89, 107.

it is exactly this hiding of one's real nature, this duplicity, that is a basic feature of the Jewish nature.' " On which Žižek comments, "An ideology really succeeds when even the facts which at first sight contradict it start to function as arguments in its favour" (*SO* 49).

What Norris really demonstrates in his sustained insistence on the critical differences crucial to a universalistic critical philosophy is a "philosophical" resistance to taking account of one's own ethnocentrism. Sometimes so provocatively and deliberately "unsophisticated," Norris's work exemplifies both the ruthlessness of the Enlightenment tradition in bringing reason to bear on the most obdurately reactionary, unenlightened, or entrenched political and social formations *and also* the sheer presumption of Enlightenment thought in assuming a dominance that it decries in political terms, a comfort level with the power of positive thinking more readily associated with the counter-Enlightenment than with its "official" or "original" version. If, to recall an earlier formulation, Enlightenment thought posits a contradiction—between truth-seeking inquiry and interest, armies and consciences, freedom and obligation, domination and reason—at the expense of an irrational circularity or commonality that cannot be recognized, that must be denied, then Norris is an Enlightenment thinker—as his sometime distinction between Foucault and Kant confirms. But if counter-Enlightenment thought characteristically posits a continuum or circularity at the expense of a systematically denied contradiction (for example, that prisons and universities, domination and reason, and so on are unlike rather than like), then Norris belongs equally to this alternate tradition—as his recuperation of Foucault as loyal neo-Kantian confirms.[14]

Power/Knowledge in Spain

There can be no possible exercise of power without a certain economy of discourses of truth which operates through and on the basis of this association. We are subjected to the production of truth through power and we cannot exercise power except through the production of truth. . . . We are forced to produce the truth of power that our society demands, of which it has need, in order to function: we

14. Derrida, about whom Norris has written at length, sustains the same ambivalence with respect to Enlightenment. While he has, in more recent work, tried to insist on critical differences in a Kantian spirit (see "Afterword: Toward an Ethics of Discussion," *Limited Inc*), the defining gesture of his early work was the putting-into-question of difference, as in his treating as "suspect . . . the difference between signified and signifier," as well as that between writing and speech, literal and figurative, and so on. See Derrida, *Of Grammatology* 14.

must speak the truth; we are constrained or condemned to confess to or discover the truth. Power never ceases its interrogation, its inquisition, its registration of truth; it institutionalises, professionalises and rewards its pursuit. In the last analysis, we must produce truth as we must produce wealth. —Michel Foucault, lecture, 14 January 1976

The test, for Kant, of the private/public distinction was not just freedom of opinion but freedom of specifically religious opinion. As I have already speculated, Kant may have been thinking of the always-precarious situation of the Jews in Prussia, or he may have been trying to secure a guarantee of liberty for himself and others who sought, in the name of reason, to question certain tenets of traditional revealed religion. Or he may have been referring Frederick to the garish counter-instance presented by the Spanish Inquisition, which was nearing the end of its more than three centuries of activity, a perpetual reminder of what the Enlightenment was not.

For not only did the Inquisition seek to root out freedom of conscience by prosecuting heresy, it also worked to establish Catholic Spanish hegemony over what had been the most thoroughly multicultural society in Europe by imposing an unprecedentedly rigid orthodoxy over all of Spain, including its Moorish and Jewish populations. The Inquisition has had a bad press (a phenomenon it would have known how to deal with), having been held responsible for exceptional cruelties, including torture and public burning, inflicted upon hundreds of thousands of victims to whom due process was denied; the suppression of learning, the arts, and the free expression of ideas; and the grisly spectacle of a nation degraded by fear of a secret and unaccountable institution that violated all the principles on which the Enlightenment was staked. In its later years, the Inquisition was openly hostile to the Enlightenment, as it had been to the Reformation before that. In sum, the Inquisition was, as a nineteenth-century detractor argues, one of "the aberrations of human reason," proof of "the capability of our nature, when under the influence of fanaticism, to inflict, with systematic indifference, death, torture, misery, anxiety, and infamy, on the guilty and the innocent" (Llorente, *Critical History of the Inquisition of Spain* v; hereafter *CHI*). Worst of all was the Inquisition's utter disregard for privacy: "In the present state of knowledge," wrote one historian in 1837, "we look with disgust on the pretensions of any human being, however exalted, to invade the sacred rights of conscience, inalienably possessed by every man" (William Hickling Prescott; quoted in Kamen 250). By every modern criterion the Inquisition seems a vast abomination, vicious in principle and procedures—something Foucault might have called, without laughing, "a profound error."

Many of the most notorious procedures of the Inquisition display the fundamental principle of counter-Enlightenment thought, that of circularity. Two forms of circularity were presumed, both of which Kant explicitly repudiated. According to the first, private convictions *ought* to be continuous with public orthodoxy, and, according to the second, public expressions *were in fact* continuous with private convictions. There was no question of "arguing as much as one liked" and no question of a right to reserve one's private judgment while mouthing the party line, or of nodding agreement to a blasphemous statement while inwardly preserving one's faith intact. The very processes of inquisition themselves suggest circularity. As D. Juan Antonio Llorente, a secretary of the Madrid Inquisition in the late eighteenth century, reports, if one were summoned to denounce, one really could not help denouncing. Witnesses were not informed of the subject of depositions they were supposed to give but were "asked in general terms, *if they had ever seen or heard anything which was, or appeared, contrary to the Catholic faith, or the rights of the Inquisition.* Personal experience has shown me," Llorente writes, "that the witnesses who were ignorant of the cause of their citation often recollected circumstances entirely foreign to the subject . . . and were then interrogated as if their examination had no other object; this accidental deposition served instead of a denunciation, and a new process was commenced" (*CHI* 60). Moreover, as Henry Kamen writes, "fear of denunciation alone became the spur to confession and counter-denunciation. . . . The chain reaction set in process by this was highly effective in uprooting heresy" (164). The Inquisition guaranteed its effectiveness by simply presuming that accusations were true. Unproved accusations were "semiproofs"; once accused, one was labeled either a *formal* (that is, fully proven) *heretic, violently suspected,* or *slightly suspected.* As A. S. Turberville puts it, "The question which inquisitors decided was not 'Guilty or Not Guilty?' but 'How far Guilty?'" (Turberville 234). (In defense of this procedure, it might be argued that the Inquisition was such a fearsome and oppressive institution that it would have been difficult to find anybody who had not harbored a thought that ran "contrary to the . . . rights of the Inquisition.") Through denials that became self-accusations, persecutions that bred the anti-Catholicism that was suspected, and strategies of survival that compelled confession, the Inquisition invariably discovered what it sought, fostering a juridical circumstance in which, as Foucault says in a counter-Enlightenment mood, "we are forced to produce the truth of power that our society demands."

Even more offensive to modern sensibilities than the Inquisition itself, however, are those occasional apologists who try to justify it. It is distressing even to contemplate the possibility of, for example, a common

Enlightenment-Inquisition investment in the practice—introduced by Foucault as the "ignoble" origin of the "sciences of man" and thus as a mark of modernity—of examination and documentation (*Discipline and Punish* 191). According to Foucault, "the examination," in various realms including the military, the medical, and the academic, became established in the eighteenth century as the instrument of a new form of "disciplinary power" that, in contrast to spectacle-oriented traditional power, was "exercised through its invisibility; at the same time it imposes on those whom it subjects a principle of compulsory visibility" (187). Within the new regime, documentary records or "files" constitute the individual "as a describable, analysable object . . . in order to . . . maintain him in his individual features, in his particular evolution, in his own aptitudes or abilities, under the gaze of a permanent corpus of knowledge" (190).

Foucault is not speaking here of the Inquisition, but he might well be, and even perhaps ought to have been. The Inquisition innovated in the practice of power precisely by eschewing display during its often extended procedures, operating out of public view until execution of the sentence—the grand, public auto-da-fé. Intended to shield accusers from accused, this secrecy required an unprecedented level of documentation. The Inquisition set down in exhaustive detail not only its own elaborate internal procedures but also the details of denunciations, interrogations, confiscations, expenses, tortures, precedents, confessions, executions, and so forth. As Kamen writes, "The administrative and secretarial apparatus of the tribunal took care to set down on paper even the most trifling business. Thanks to this, the Spanish Inquisition is one of the few institutions of its era about whose organization and procedures an enormous amount of documentation is available" (Kamen 169; see 161–77). Even records of torture are scrupulous. "On being given these [turns on the rack] he said first, 'Oh God!' and then, 'There's no mercy'; after the turns he was admonished, and he said, 'I don't know what to say, oh dear God!' Then three more turns of the cord were ordered to be given, and after two of them he said, 'Oh God, oh God, there's no mercy, oh God help me, help me!' " (177). Despite the charismatic spectacle of power at the moment of execution, then, Kamen at least has no hesitation describing the Inquisition as an "early modern" institution, no doubt in part because of its introduction, through documentation, of a decisively "modern," that is, "ignoble" play of coercion over bodies, gestures, and behavior.

Is it possible that this nascent modernity has extorted a certain respect for the Inquisition from historians grateful for a rich archival record? The evidence for such respect is abundant. Presenting a "balanced interpretation," Edward Burman argues that while torture and massive injustice did occur, "it must not be forgotten that Spain enjoyed her greatest moment of power and prestige during the centuries in which the Inquisition was at full spate. The colonies were established, literature, music and painting flourished . . . and modern Spain was created" (155). The current scholarly consensus seems to be that the Spanish Inquisition was incomparably fairer and even more lenient not only than the medieval Inquisition but also than contemporary secular courts in terms of the number of people burned, the use of torture, and the prosecution of witchcraft.[15] In this last respect, Kamen reports that "for most of the sixteenth century the Inquisition maintained an enlightened record" (212) and did so, William Monter points out, through its "enlightened" instructions to prosecutors (262).

An "enlightened" judiciary is autonomous, independent of both church and state, an institution unto itself. By this criterion, the Inquisition was indeed an "early modern" institution. Although it was financially dependent on the crown and served the crown's purposes in prosecuting Jews, Moriscoes, and Protestants, its powers, Kamen reports, were deliberately

---

15. It has been determined that only a tiny fraction of those brought before the Inquisition were actually burned. Virtually all of the rest were either absolved, penanced, or reconciled. Kamen concludes that, after the first twenty years, in which the Inquisition killed nearly three-quarters of all those it would kill in its three centuries of activity, the Inquisition was by no means a "juggernaut of death either in intention or in capability." Indeed, he writes that "during the sixteenth and seventeenth centuries less than three people a year were executed by the Inquisition in the whole of the Spanish monarchy from Sicily to Peru—possibly a lower rate than in any provincial court of justice" (189). Torture, although employed, was exceptional and tightly circumscribed by procedural restrictions: "At a time when the use of torture was universal in European criminal courts, the Spanish Inquisition followed a policy of circumspection which makes it compare favourably with other institutions." Moreover, "confessions gained under torture were never accepted as valid because they had obviously been obtained under pressure. It was therefore essential for the accused to ratify his confession the day after the ordeal" (Kamen 174). William Monter describes tales of hyperrefined and ferocious Inquisitorial torture as "hoary myths" and "fables." "The truth," Monter writes, "is that the Spanish Inquisition, like any self-respecting legal system in continental Europe, employed torture and sometimes wrung important confessions from prisoners under torture"; but "when the Holy Office was at its most severe point, it rarely tortured anyone." Indeed, "Inquisitorial skepticism about the efficacy of torture apparently increased over time," and its use continually declined (74, 75). Thus it is precisely in the use of torture that modern historians might discover not only a modern impulse to documentation but also a rudimentary sense of the difference between free and coerced statements, and even something like penal reform. Moreover, the Inquisition generally held itself aloof from the witch-hunts endemic to the secular courts of the sixteenth and seventeenth centuries, emphasizing judicial skepticism and, in the event of conviction, reeducation and other lesser penalties rather than burning. In fact, in the early sixteenth century, the Inquisition actually, if not wholly effectively, discouraged witch-hunts.

ill-defined, secular as well as ecclesiastical: it could take refuge from secular attacks in the papal bulls it had been granted, but it could also circumvent attempts to limit its authority to religious matters by insisting that it was a secular tribunal exercising power delegated by the crown. The fact that it was ambiguously independent of both church and state gave the Inquisition "unlimited authority in both ecclesiastical and secular matters" (Kamen 241).[16] The best proof of autonomy was the roll of its targets. Only an independent court could prosecute emperors (Charles V), kings (Henri IV of France), queens, duchesses, dukes, archbishops, bishops, and even saints. (The Inquisition heard charges of "illuminism" against Ignatius of Loyola and Teresa of Avila, and did not license her *Life* for publication until after her death.) In fact, the Inquisition was so independent, and so resilient, that it had to be put to death twice, both times by offended powers: first in 1808 by Napoleon, who feared its encroachment on royal power, and then, after a brief restoration following the return of Ferdinand to the throne of Spain in 1814, by the pope in 1817, who justified his act by appealing, spuriously, to "the progress of reason" (*CHI* 573).[17]

The Inquisition asserted and maintained its autonomy through its absolute dedication to procedural regularity. The first (postmedieval) Inquisition, in 1484, was given a set of twenty-eight instructions that codified a severe but scrupulous set of procedures for determining heresy. These were shortly supplemented by eleven new articles; in 1488 by fifteen more, in an effort, as even the hostile Llorente says, "to prevent abuses" (*CHI* 50); and then in 1498 by sixteen more. All these were renewed in 1561 with the publication of eighty-one articles that reflected long experience of conducting tribunals. As the preamble written by the Inquisitor General states, "we inform you, venerable apostolical inquisitors, that we understand, that although it has been provided by the ordinances of the holy office, that the same manner of proceeding should be exactly followed in all the Inquisitions, there are, nevertheless, some tribunals where this measure has not been, and is not well observed" (*CHI* 227–28). The elaborately detailed articles that follow constitute an early modern monument to legal formalism, stipulating procedures of impartiality and even of "mercy,"

16. The initial motivation on the part of the crown for establishing the Inquisition appears to be not wholly irreligious, for Ferdinand was fully aware in 1486 that the Inquisition might well produce "harm and ill" and could even "hit our taxes and revenue. But because our firm intention and concern is to prefer the service of God to our own, we wish the Inquisition to be established regardless, putting all other interests aside" (quoted in Kamen 46).

17. In fact, the Inquisition, showing remarkable postmortem vitality, did not receive the final blow until 1834.

such as a readiness to hear recantations.[18] Above all, they institutional-
ize the imperative to absolute specificity, an uncompromising rejection of
all generalizations in describing incidents, comments, acts, and persons.
This mania for detail did not, to be sure, always work in favor of the accused. Llorente details how individual charges could be multiplied by the
number of minute variations in the telling that occurred during the denunciation and made to appear as many, on hearing which the accused
would respond to each, with the minor variations in his denials constituting "contradictions"—since they referred, after all, to the same event—
that would then form the basis of fresh accusations of "concealment" and
"denial" (*CHI* 63–64).

As modern historians have established, "abuses" occurred. But these do
not, as their work takes pains to establish, proceed from an inherently
unjust set of procedures. Trials were slow, and victims could languish for
years in prison without even being charged; but the Inquisition was rarely
accused of being sloppy, indifferent, or inept. The advantage lay with the
prosecution, as the accused was not informed of the charges against him
or her before the actual trial itself; but a lengthy period of preparation, it
was argued, only enabled the accused to prepare an alibi, a practice not
unknown in modern courtrooms. The accused did not, it is true, enjoy
the opportunity to confront his accuser; but by this precaution those who
acted on behalf of the truth were protected from recriminations and in-
timidation, eliminating the need for a witness protection program, with
its inevitable imperfections. The accused could not have an attorney see
the evidence in advance and prepare the case; but this, too, discouraged
fabrication and ensured the secrecy on which the safety of the denouncers
depended. True, the Inquisition derived its income largely from confiscations, and thus there was a powerful motive to convict; but the potential
for a state of affairs in which inquisitors "cannot eat unless they burn"
was recognized as deplorable, and measures were taken to defend against
it (Kamen 150). And though the secrecy of the proceedings would be deplored today, it guaranteed a kind of leveling in which the rich were tried
on an equal basis with the poor, the eminent with the anonymous—a
condition of equality that few modern courts have achieved. In fact, some
of the condemnations of the Inquisition sound, to enlightened ears, like
antidemocratic whining: "It placed," Turberville complains, "the distin-

18. The sixteenth article of those issued in 1561, for example, reads: "It is proper that the
inquisitors should always suspect that they have been deceived by the witnesses, and that
they shall be so by the accused, and that they should not take either side" (quoted in *CHI*
231–32).

guished at the mercy of the common-place, the courageous at the mercy of the craven, the noble-hearted at the mercy of the malicious" (233).

The Inquisition qualifies, then, as an incident in the early modern History of Western Practical Reason, with many of its subsequent contradictions writ large, and in blood. Devoted to the individual in all his or her particularity as an incomparable singularity, the Inquisition was yet a totalizing movement. Through strictly legal, formal, and rational methods, it sought to expunge all elements that could not be fully assimilated to the zeitgeist, to realize in society the "unity of mankind" subsequently articulated by the Enlightenment.

Still—the voice of modernity protests—this enlightening of the Inquisition, however warranted, must reach a limit when the crimes typically prosecuted are considered. For *we* do not prosecute heresy (or races, sexual orientations, or witches); *we* cherish our freedoms, including the freedom of worship, the freedom of conscience, even the freedom not to worship if conscience so dictates; *we* envision a holism of reason rather than of legislated faith; *we* protect rather than punish the private convictions of the individual and hold them distinct from the questions of justice that occupy the social realm.

Perhaps. Having grown accustomed to arguing as much as we like, we prefer the enlightened regimes of modernity and the freedoms they afford, or at least promise. But the question is, does Enlightenment represent a superior understanding of the private-public distinction on which that freedom is based? I believe that it does not.

The fact is that the Inquisition was highly sensitive to facts of which Kant seems blithely unaware. The widespread public cynicism that Kant seems to commend as a political attitude was held by the Inquisition to be not simply a crime but criminality itself. The largest category of crimes prosecuted by the Inquisition involved "propositions," or verbal offenses. As the body of doctrine was so intricate, these offenses were sometimes difficult to identify, especially by the semieducated "qualifiers" who gave the initial and often decisive pronouncements on the evidence; sometimes even doctrines held by the fathers of the church were held to be heretical (*CHI* 61). But the Inquisitors were, Kamen notes, "concerned less with the words than with the intention behind them and with the implicit danger to faith and morals" (Kamen 201–2). Stated doubts about the nature of the eucharist, the moral status of fornication, and the efficacy of confession, as well as oaths during games of dice and barroom discourses, all drew the Inquisition's interest. After the Reconquest and the expulsion of the Jews, Spain was Catholic; and if Catholicism was truly to flourish, it could not be eroded from within by hypocrisy, nor could the marketplace or the home be permitted to operate under different protocols than those that prevailed in church or at the court. While for Kant "the private" was rather quixotically exemplified by the published ruminations of the man of learning, the Inquisition held a more realistic and recognizable conception of the private, one that focused on conversations and small gatherings. Most significantly, the Inquisition understood that conversations and thoughts were not exempt from the pressures, conflicts, and demands of the total social context.

What strikes a modern eye most forcibly is the soundness of the political rationale for the Inquisition as compared to fatuous Enlightenment assertions of a free private realm secured by submission in a public realm by which it is magically untouched. The Inquisition's rationale can be clarified by referring to the vigorous defense made by Joseph de Maistre, a Sardinian aristocrat serving as minister at the Russian court in 1815, when he wrote *Letters on the Spanish Inquisition* to an imaginary correspondent. De Maistre makes two interrelated arguments that are especially pertinent in the present context. The first is that religious doctrine has consequences: "The seeds of the misnamed REFORMATION, as sown by the base apostate Luther, had produced a thirty years' war in Germany, which thus became an immense Golgotha. . . . Catholic Switzerland, France, and the Netherlands, were immolated upon the altar of remorseless Calvinism. Once happy England, enlightened, hospitable, Catholic Ireland and the once Catholic Scotland, were converted into one vast 'field of blood' " (9-10). "Well, indeed, does it become you," he writes sarcastically, "to blame our Spanish kings for having foreseen and prevented all this. Tell us not that the Inquisition has been guilty of various abuses at various times; such is not the question; for the real, the only, object of the inquiry is, to know whether, for the last three centuries, the Inquisition has insured more peace and happiness in Spain than were in all the countries of Europe put together" (93-94). De Maistre points out not only that the record of tortures, burnings, and arbitrary imprisonments compiled by the Inquisition was consistent with that of secular courts elsewhere in Europe but also that the Inquisition had found one way of resolving a thorny problem. Jews in Spain had, by the late fifteenth century, become so numerous at the upper levels of society as to be "a nation contained within another" (22). Social divisions based on nearly exclusive Jewish control of money had given rise to increasing civil unrest, including riots, insurrections, and even slaughters. The Inquisition brought these to an end. To prefer private freedoms to public order is, de Maistre suggests, to prefer sectarian massacres to harmony and peace. The sedentary theorizing of the elderly Kant blandly promoting the "enthusiasm" generated by the Revolution, his retirement defended by numerous and well-disciplined armies, seems in this context cavalier, an unfeeling dismissal of the (French) victims of the Revolution. Indeed, Kant may be the vulnerable target of a sentence in which de Maistre derides the "modern sophist who *vapors* in his study, and writes as he pleases" (60).

De Maistre's second argument is even more telling when pitched against the likely rebuttals from the Enlightenment. Indeed, the same argument is advanced by Christopher Norris in his attack on the theoretically undiscriminating and morally flaccid versions of postmodernity that acknowledge no limit to the domain of the imagination, no check to the powers of fictionalizing. "*Truth,*" de Maistre writes, "is in its very nature *intolerant*" (114). He contrasts the "intolerance" of Spain, which "admits religion alone, and rejects each Babel sect" (110–11), with the no less violent tolerance of England, which permits every sect but "cannot associate with any *positive* faith" and so proscribes—with incarcerations, tortures, burnings, and so on—the one true religion (108). Indifferent to religion in fact, England, de Maistre charges, arrogantly presumes to "pass sentence upon such nations as view this indifference as the most pregnant source of misery and crime!" (114). From a religious point of view—which is Kant's as well as de Maistre's—error can be pardoned but not tolerated. In a curious and controversial passage, Kant himself actually seems to argue against tolerance: "A prince who does not regard it as beneath him to say that he considers it his duty, in religious matters, not to prescribe anything to his people, but to allow them complete freedom, a prince who thus even declines to accept the presumptuous title of *tolerant,* is himself enlightened" (AQ 58).

The "political problem" we are now confronting is this: manifestly the "other" of the Enlightenment, the Inquisition is in many respects founded on principles the Enlightenment claimed as its own, and where it is not, the advantage in terms of realism and coherence seems to lie with the Inquisition. The Inquisition is, perhaps, Enlightenment without denial, its "counter" elements displayed in full view. If Enlightenment consists, as Žižek says, of obedience to "nonsensical" and ungrounded rules, then the Inquisition, as a prominent historical home of such rules that lay, as it were, adjacent to the Enlightenment, might represent a clarified form of the "traumatic kernel" of Enlightenment itself.

But surely, it might be objected, even the most cynical of analysts must respect the human "instinct for freedom"? And, just as surely, the place to look for this instinct would be among the victims of the Inquisition, the persecuted Jews of Spain. Surely; but the problem is that after 1492, when the Jews who had not taken the opportunity to convert were expelled, there were, as a point of law, *no more Jews*. Thus the Inquisition, though undoubtedly anti-Semitic, cannot be properly compared to, for example, the Holocaust, in which Jews were slaughtered just for being Jews. The Inquisition prosecuted, especially in its first half-century or so of activity, not Jews but "New Christians," *conversos*, potential hypocrites or "judaizers" whose conversions were suspected of being insincere, as in many cases they doubtless were.

The *conversos* are truly interesting. Living, as Kamen writes, "neither in one law nor the other," they were scorned by Jews for their apostasy and despised by "Old Christians for their race" (27). Indeed, they must have been problematic even to themselves. For how, exactly, could they determine whether their conversions were sincere? A rigorous examination of the most piously "sincere" conversion could scarcely have failed to discover traces of opportunism and hypocrisy. On the other hand, however, the most "insincere" conversions must have had elements of sincerity. The Catholic faith was, after all, an impressive edifice: the cathedrals, the Latin mass, the ceremony, the crowds of believers, the collateral fact that Catholicism was the state religion—all these strongly encouraged a certain receptivity, laying the foundation of "belief." And then, too, *conversos* must have experienced "sincere" desires to avoid the uncertainties (as well as the certainties) of expulsion, to remain in the place of one's birth and ancestry, to live in one's house, to practice and prosper in one's trade, to wear traditional clothing, to follow traditional practices, to be oneself in familiar surroundings—all the myriad forms of residual Judaism documented by the Inquisition with characteristic thoroughness—which may also have helped to induce a confused but still voluntary profession of faith.

Foucault distinguishes modern, all-around power from a premodern power based on spectacle. Žižek contributes to this distinction the observation that modern power is ideological, the essence of ideology being apparently free action whose determined essence is "unconscious." It is, however, difficult to locate the *conversos* on this map, or this time line, for the undecidability between sincerity and insincerity meant that they lived simultaneously inside and outside ideology. Insofar as their belief in their new faith was freely chosen and sincere—a possibility the Inquisition was willing to grant[19]—it was *their faith*, all bound up with their inmost sources

19. Although modern Jewish historiography does not. According to Kamen, the Inquisition's suspicion of New Christians is largely confirmed by Jewish historians, who argue "that the Inquisition was right and that all conversos were aspiring Jews"—a position that contradicts a mass of testimony by contemporary *conversos* to the effect that they were Jews neither in belief nor in practice (27).

of identity and their deepest convictions about the universe. They lived within ideology. But insofar as their conversions were insincere, that is, merely a practical response to the Inquisition's panoptic gaze, they stood in the position of cynical ideological outsiders—looking on at a spectacle in which they were not participating. Another way to put this is to say that the *conversos* lived simultaneously inside and outside enlightened modernity, operating *both* by distinctions whose continuities they repressed (You say you're Jewish, but here you are, in Spain) and by continuities whose internal distinctions they repressed (How could you, a Jew, pretend to be Christian?). In the case of the *conversos,* there seems to be little functional difference between modern and premodern forms of power.

The *conversos* bear the full historical burden of the co-implication of Enlightenment and its other, the burden of structural undecidability concerning their religion, their race, their culture, their personal identity. It would be too easy to say they chose their (Christian) religion whereas their (Jewish) identity was given. In Spain, Christianity was not an option but a necessity, while Jewishness for the *converso* was not a necessity but a choice. The Inquisition did not prosecute people for *feeling* Jewish but for saying prayers, attending meetings, keeping dietary laws—in general exposing themselves to denunciation. The *conversos* did not need Derrida, Lacan, Ricoeur, or Levinas to teach them that identity is achieved "through the other," and they might have been skeptical that it could be "achieved" at all. But the ease with which they can be assimilated to contemporary theories of identity raises anew the suspicion that the end of the Inquisition through the triumph of the Enlightenment might not, after all, have eradicated, but simply continued by other means, the poignantly specific dilemma of the *converso.*

Behold, Then, a Beautiful Theory

The poignance increases, of course, with the specificity. At the level of the anecdote, issues of necessity and choice, private and public, identity and the other, Enlightenment and Inquisition can achieve a virtually transhistorical clarity precisely by being so painfully particular.

Consider, for example, Melchior Hernandez, a New Christian merchant of Toledo who, in 1565, found himself accused of having some years earlier attended a clandestine synagogue, a charge he denied. As Llorente tells the story, the witnesses contradicted each other and were known to be his enemies. Under duress, he admitted that he "remembered being in a house in 1553" where others spoke of "the law of Moses." Four days later he declared that everything said in that house "was spoken in jest" and then, some days later, that he had not heard what had been said, and that he said he had heard only because other witnesses "had deposed to that effect." He was "declared to be a Jewish heretic, guilty of concealment in his confession, and condemned to *relaxation* [*relajado;* a heretic handed over to the secular authorities to be burned], as a false penitent and obstinate heretic." On the eve of his scheduled burning, he confessed with greater specificity, naming others and denouncing their doctrines. In vain, however; his sentence was not itself relaxed. When, however, he added that he really believed in what was preached in the house that night twelve years earlier, he was not relaxed, but taken back to prison. His confession earned him consideration as a cooperative and honest man; but it did not set him free. After two weeks of confinement, he provided a more nuanced account to the effect that although the Jewish Scriptures were read in the assembly, he had only "believed part of what he heard." Moreover, after consulting a priest who told him that the Jewish Scriptures "ought to be held in contempt," he had subsequently held them so. This seemed to confuse the inquisitors, who on a split vote allowed him to be reconciled but then, on review, voted three to two to relax. On arriving at the auto-da-fé, however, Melchior named more houses and people, and his execution was once again suspended. But by this time, because his various confessions did not agree with each other, he had accumulated abundant evidence of concealment, and on this basis he was once again sentenced to be burned. At the place of his third scheduled execution, he again poured forth a long string of houses and persons but was accused of concealing the names of still others. At this, he lost his composure, declared everything he had formerly said about others to be false, and demanded to be burned immediately. He was, instead, invited to make a complete confession. But he had had enough and simply restated his initial defense, *"that he knew nothing of the subject on which he was examined."* Then why, he was asked, did he declare against himself? "I did not think it would be injurious to me," he replied; "on the contrary, I expected to derive great advantages from it, because I saw that if I did not confess anything, I should be considered as impenitent, and the truth would lead me to the scaffold" (*CHI* 260–68). As a final act of mercy—the Inquisition prided itself on its mercy—the royal judge ordered him to be strangled before finally being relaxed.

What is truth? The guiding premise of the Inquisition appears to be that truth is a property of relations between propositions and states of affairs. Melchior is charged with Judaizing, and he is expected to confirm or disconfirm the charge by making verifiably true statements. From a point of view more deeply situated within the dynamic of inquisition itself, however, a very different notion of truth emerges, one more consistent with what Heidegger called "unconcealment." Richard Campbell has recently argued for this more pragmatic and processual notion, contending that truth "happens" when something becomes apparent as that which it really is. This second account of truth describes more accurately the experience of inquisition for both Melchior and his inquisitors. But the point to be stressed is that the two kinds of truth collaborate. If truth were not held to be assertorial, a function of the relation between statement and referent, then Melchior would not be able to prolong his life by his strategically progressive disclosures. The limit to his maneuvering is reached, however, not when his statements are proven to be either true or false, but when they can be shown to conflict with each other, a circumstance that furnishes its own internal proof of "concealment." At that point, truth is "unconcealed"; it "happens." And one is "relaxed."

Having received the judgment and the criminal, the secular authorities were, Kamen states, "obliged to carry out the sentence of blood which the Holy Office was forbidden to carry out" (184). The church could not shed blood, but the crown could not burn without an Inquisition to determine heresy—a condition of general deniability, or autonomy, that fills the Inquisition's apologists with a glowing satisfaction. De Maistre writes to his imaginary correspondent, "Behold then, sir, a beautiful theory" (32). What theory might that be? How might this practice be stated in theoretical terms? During his most anti-Enlightenment period, Foucault might have responded that relaxation, the verdict translated into flames, constitutes the moment when knowledge demonstrates its continuity with power. Defenders of the Enlightenment distinctions might, on the contrary, portray relaxation as a corruption of knowledge itself. But the "theory" exemplified by relaxation leads, I believe, to a more fertile and complex understanding of the relation of knowledge to power than that proposed either by Foucault or by his opponents.

In Enlightenment orthodoxy, an untransgressable margin divides power and knowledge, whereas in the Foucauldian or counter-Enlightenment ethos, the two are virtually identified. What neither wishes to acknowledge is what relaxation and the Inquisition in general suggest most forcefully: that power and knowledge are both distinct from *and* determined by each other. As a paradigmatic instance of power-knowledge, relaxation suggests that the claims of each depend upon the repression of the other. According to the law of relaxation, power becomes knowledge, and knowledge power—but only elsewhere, or later. That is, although each is determined by the other, the inadmissibility of this fact is built into the definition of both terms, which present themselves—*must* present themselves—as undetermined by the other. While power, for example, is informed *by* knowledge and effects itself ultimately *as* knowledge, power is power by virtue of its not *being* knowledge. The relation is one of *transgressable distinctions*. Power and knowledge are, we may say, each other's unconscious, a "germ" or "kernel" secreted in the "shell" of the other, though figured as the other's prehistory, telos, or opposite.[20]

On the way to death—the end of distinctions, but also the ultimate distinction—relaxation takes us through the experience of pain. In a counter-Enlightenment tradition extending from Nietzsche to Foucault, pain represents the irreducible reality underlying all idealizations; indeed, from a certain perspective, the counter-Enlightenment as a whole argues for the reality and authenticity of pain, especially the pain of cruelty or punishment, over and against the illusory Enlightenment advocacy of self-regulating rationality. But we must not overlook the particular form of pain cultivated by the Enlightenment. In the Enlightenment ethos, truth is achieved by Kantian men of learning who undertake patient, exacting, scholarly work in a spirit of free inquiry—free, that is, of coercive external pressures or distracting desires. For the "modern age," Hans Blumenberg asserts, an "absolutist" truth is achieved through "a renunciation that lies in the separation between cognitive achievement and the production of happiness" (404). The critical and radical difference, defenders of Enlightenment might say, lies in the fact that Enlightenment pain represents a voluntary submission of the self to the truth, a willed surrender of pleasure in the interests of principle, a self-determined obligation to a necessity strictly impersonal and therefore noncoercive.

The truly critical fact, however, may be that even in the Enlightenment regime, truth is constructed as the overwhelming of the private subject, of the subject *in his or her privacy,* by a principle hostile to interest, pleasure, or desire. The most extreme possible form of this overwhelming, according to Elaine Scarry, is torture, in which truth is sought in the deepest interiorities of the subject, in the spaces between joints, fingers and nails, skin and muscle, where the private is reduced to consciousness of pain. Hardly an enlightened mode of determining the truth, one would think—at least

---

20. Something like this formula is urged by Stephen Greenblatt in the course of taking issue with Marxist and postmodernist accounts of the effects of capitalism. For Fredric Jameson, Greenblatt notes, the law of social life under capitalism ruthlessly demarcates and differentiates between discursive, social, and psychological realms, especially between the public and the private. For Lyotard, on the other hand, capitalism works, as Greenblatt paraphrases him, "not to demarcate discursive domains but, quite the opposite, to make such domains untenable." Arguing in the end for seeing life under capitalism as "an unsettling circulation of materials and discourses," a restless oscillation between the impulse to differentiation and the impulse to totalization, Greenblatt splits, or relaxes, the difference between Jamesonian Enlightenment and Lyotardian counter-Enlightenment. Greenblatt, "Towards a Poetics of Culture" 4, 13.

before reading Page duBois's *Torture and Truth,* which argues for a disquieting "resonance" between torture and the "forced approach to truth" exemplified, for example, in Plato's allegory of enlightenment, in which a person freed from his fetters in the cave is "compelled to look at the light itself," an experience painful and involuntary. "Of course," duBois says, "the compulsion here is directed toward enlightenment, toward the achieving of a recognition of what truly is"; yet the means are barbaric: the truth "must be rooted out, extracted and dominated, in the process of torture" (121, 150).

To her credit, duBois deplores torture but honors truth, and so feels uneasy with her own arguments. "I have had," she writes, "to resist lyricizing the tortured body, offering a baroque description of the body on the rack, of the pains of the slave. I have resisted the perverse pleasures associated with sado-masochism and torture, resisted even naming those pleasures as pertaining to the logics of democracy and torture. I have not wanted to sensationalize and exoticize and create desire for torture, to make this text any sort of celebration of torture, a philosophical lure, an antique" (141). She has, in short, tried to be enlightened even while exploring "the determining instance of ancient Greek culture, to prove that our civilization is based on barbarism" (143). Torture may be the truth about truth, duBois implies, but as for me, I am—as my diligent research, my respectful citations of authority, my tightly drawn inferences, my scrupulous normality (Oh, God, there is no mercy!) all testify—unequivocally opposed to torture. Just as torture can be desired, the renunciation of torture can be torture once again, the species of torture distinctive of the post-Enlightenment regime.

The effort to get beyond pain does not, then, get very far. A psychopathology of scholarship would have to interrogate the numerous ways in which "researchers," "critics," and "scholars" seek to secure the truth of their "findings," "conclusions," and "results" by representing them as the issue of a suffering that is both genuinely painful and eagerly desired.[21] Scholarship and criticism seem to be subject to a misnaming that permits the enlightened a double ambivalence, renouncing *and* embracing *both* pain and pleasure. The transgressability of the distinctions qualifies the protocols of modern truth as post-Inquisitorial practices of relaxation. With this possibility shimmering in the air, we return to the dance—an exceptionally long, slow dance—of Enlightenment with its counter, that is, with something that is at once *its* other and its *other.*

There are those who insist that Enlightenment is philosophically and

21. As preliminary studies in this area, see Harpham, *Getting It Right: Language, Literature, and Ethics* 106–56; and *The Ascetic Imperative in Culture and Criticism* 237–70.

politically indispensable and must be defended against its enemies, and those who say that it is not only eminently dispensable but philosophically and politically indefensible. Perhaps the truth does not lie in its classic position—in between—but rather all around. Incoherent as such a statement seems, the example of Foucault suggests that it is not exactly impossible to sustain both views at once. As James Miller shows in *The Passion of Michel Foucault,* the philosopher was enacting his belated rapprochement with Kant, puzzling out the contemporary significance of Enlightenment, at the very time he was exploring with accelerating enthusiasm the San Francisco S/M scene. What Foucault referred to as the "limit-experiences" available on Folsom Street corresponded to his long-standing theoretical interest in torture as a form of truth that "happens," a truth "inscribed in the body," a truth "that scientific practice has step-by-step discredited, covered up, and driven out" ("La Maison des fous"). While dreaming during the day of a convocation of philosophers discoursing on Kant, a leather-clad Foucault was exploring, with the aid of certain "instruments," the imbrication of ecstasy and excruciating pain at night. Enlightenment, he told his students in 1983, "may be characterized as a *limit-attitude,*" a "practical critique that takes the form of a possible transgression" (WIE 45); it is a "historico-practical test of the limits that we may go beyond, and thus as work carried out by ourselves as free beings" (WIE 47). Foucault may well have felt that he was engaged in a complex adventure whose components were as co-implicated as theory and practice and yet as different as day and night. Inevitably, his efforts to go "beyond" what had become an untenable opposition between Enlightenment and counter-Enlightenment took him back as well. In a book published in the year of Foucault's death from AIDS, Jean-Paul Aron, a former friend who was himself to die of AIDS in a few years, wrote that "this critic of controls aspired to control [the world] in its essence." He was, Aron concludes, "a born inquisitor" (88; trans. in James Miller, *PMF* 396).

Once every century at about this time, it seems, Goya is vindicated as reason goes to sleep and produces monsters. The eighteenth century produced revolution and Romanticism; the nineteenth, aestheticism, mysticism, and decadence. The *fin* of our own explosive *siècle* is second to none in this respect, exhibiting an unprecedented variety of derangements, phantasmatic formations, and deformations both benign and malignant. These monstrosities do not, however, simply take over the stage; they share it with purified, highly aggressive forms of reason that also emerge at century's end: Kantian, Weberian, and—shall we call it Gatesian, to indicate the collaboration between computer technology and global capitalism? At these chronological junctures, the concordat of reason breaks down and its constituent parts become visible: not "Yugoslavia," but Bosnia-Herzegovina, Croatia, Serbia, Montenegro, Slovenia. But also emerging at these moments are the ligatures, now badly stretched, that bind part to part. What has been called the "terrorism" of Kant's critical method aligns it decisively with the Revolution he praised. The waning of the Victorian age disclosed a general interest, among managers and aesthetes alike, in maximizing the fleeting moment, and a general indifference to evaluating the moral ends of action. Postmodern culture, empowered by a technology that demands, promotes, and rewards hyper-rationalism, is haunted not by a psychic or a political, but rather by a "technological unconscious." Interestingly, many of the behaviors that define the irrationality of the present answer, from a distance, to certain philosophical accounts of rationalism. Squeezing the syringe or the trigger, assuming large amounts of debt, developing nuclear weapons, slaughtering a rival clan, one may be contributing to the stock of the world's irrationality, but may still be (rationally) pursuing one's own ends, securing an expanding horizon of desires, realizing one's principles, furthering one's own interests, maximizing one's position.

The question at this century's end, as at others, is the relation between the distilled forms of reason and unreason. Should "monsters" be likened to the rats that play when the cat's away, or asleep? Or is irrationality the dream of reason, reason's unconscious? When reason sleeps, does it liberate monsters or become monstrous?

Although my intentions in doing so will only gradually become apparent, I would place in this lofty and speculative context the disorderly recent quarrel between Robert Nozick and Ian Hacking in the *London Review of Books* over Hacking's review of Nozick's 1993 book, *The Nature of Rationality*. Considering the dauntingly technical character of the book, the discussion was remarkably meaty. "This is an ideological book," Hacking wrote in his review, "concluding with evolutionary premises implying a complacent vision in which something like our present social order rose out of biological facts" ("What's Best"). By representing rationality as a "product of evolution," something that "defines and symbolizes the distance we have come from mere animality," Nozick has, according to Hacking, implied that those who are less rational are hanging back with the primates. The higher forms of rationality become in Nozick's account not a human universal but something like "skin pigment," a phenomenon existing in different levels and degrees, and concentrated chiefly in "Western societies," where it has been able to take root, become instinctual, and "extend its sway," a Greater Serbia of the mind. As Hacking finishes the argument, the dominance of rationality *in* the West enables the domination of other societies *by* the West. Thus Nozick confronts us with two unsettling possibilities. The first is that rationality now constitutes what Hacking calls "a hypostasised entity" that is "out there 'extending its sway' "; and the second is that rational people have attained to a "biologically ordained mastery of the universe and its denizens."

In a long letter to the *London Review*, Nozick recorded his displeasure: "I do not assert these propositions, I do not believe them, I find them repugnant and I think they can be shown to be false." "Am I mistaken," he asked, or is this talk about biologically ordained mastery "Nazi-like rhetoric"? If rationality flourishes in certain individuals and cultural conditions, and does not flourish in others, it is, he contended, no different in this respect from any other trait that distinguishes humans from animals or indeed any animal species from any other. Some birds can fly and some can't; but all have wings, and penguins are no less avian than hawks. Responding to the comment about "skin pigment," Nozick declared that "racism is an abomination, a plague humanity has inflicted upon itself. It leads to horrors, it is false, and it morally corrupts those who see the world through its distorted lens." Nor does his high respect for rationality entail a comparable appreciation for the forms of capitalism that take rationality to the streets, producing world markets, subjugating previous modes of production, calculating, measuring, estimating probabilities and equivalencies, replacing precapitalist local institutions with the life forms appropriate to a deracinated capital. Nor, he insisted, does he believe that rationality is autonomous: "When I say that rationality changes the world, I, of course, mean that it is the continuing rational actions of individuals, and the ensuing institutional effects, that produce these changes, not some hypostasised entity." In short, Hacking has proceeded in a "bizarre and irresponsible fashion," producing a "slanderous distortion" of his book. "It is loathsome," Nozick concluded, "that he fabricates, and seeks to attribute to me, theses which I condemn utterly." Trying to remain a philosopher, Hacking said little in reply other than, "I welcome his clarifications."

But several things remain, or have become, unclear. Is Hacking simply dead wrong or is he wrong in the way that, for example, the unconscious is "wrong"? What—other than the experience of one's own unconscious held up to the light of day—accounts for the element of nausea in Nozick's reply? Why does Nozick seem so convulsed; why has he found it necessary to abandon his position as an analyst of rules, principles, paradoxes, and hard cases to announce his passionate opposition to injustice, the excesses of capitalism, the perversions of racism? Most important, has Hacking been disproven or merely shouted down? Does Nozick maintain that his claim that rationality is an evolved trait could not be deployed in the service of subrational enthusiasms and phobias, including racism? How would Nozick explain Frantz Fanon's description of a "racism that aspires to be rational, individual, genotypically and phenotypically determined" (110)? Or Adorno's isolation of the element of unreason in modern rationality? Does Nozick have any comment on Foucault's linkage of the "flamboyant rationality" of social Darwinism and Nazism; can we conceive of some "Nozism" that mediates between rationality and fascism? Does Nozick deny, or even have an opinion on, the argument made by feminists and postcolonial scholars that, in the words of Veena Das, "the rationally controlled individual who exercises a constant and alert control over himself in the interest of transforming the world becomes the measure [so that all] other forms of being—whether of nonwestern man or western woman—are understood in terms of a lack, a deflection from the ideal typical action represented by the paradigm of rational action" (312)? What does Nozick mean by "mere animality," which rationality has supposedly enabled us to transcend? Does he have a worked-out view of the difference between humans and animals? Is "animality" constant from the paramecium to the dolphin? Why does Nozick begin his book by describing rationality as "one among other animal traits"? Is it an animal trait or an expression of discontent with animality? Can an animal trait enable, and even compel animals to transcend their animality? Is human rationality hardwired or voluntary? And what *are* the political implications of describing rationality in terms that few human animals can hope to comprehend? Ashis Nandy argues that "in every system of organized oppression the true antonyms are . . . not the past versus the present but either of them versus the rationality which turns them into co-victims" (99). And Nozick? Failing to raise, much less answer such questions, he seems not confused but unaware of his confusion, and of the potential for confusion he has created.

Nor does Nozick provide knock-down arguments against the charge that he makes rationality into an "hypostasised entity" with designs on conquest. No one could deny the intimate relation between rationality and power, certainly not after reading Dominique Janicaud's 1994 *Powers of the Rational: Science, Technology, and the Future of Thought.* But Nozick goes further, describing rationality as an exceptionally powerful instrument that "provides us with the . . . power to investigate and discover anything and everything," a weapon with a "sharp cutting edge," and even a "bold venturesomeness" comparable to "the very greatest chess champions" (xi, 175). More interestingly, Nozick presents rationality as an agent endowed with something like consciousness, "imagination," and even self-awareness. "It is part of rationality," Nozick writes in this vein, "to be intent on noticing biases, including its own, and controlling and correcting these" (xii). But it doesn't stop there. Through its cumulative and self-multiplying effects, rationality ratchets, making the world "inhospitable to lesser degrees of rationality":

> Rationality first was able to extend its sway by bringing benefits to other traits too, but the other traits became more dependent upon rationality and rationality became more powerful and subject to fewer constraints. Rationality is proceeding now to remake the world to suit itself, altering not only its own environment but also that in which all other traits find themselves, extending the environment in which only it can fully flourish. . . . This presents a challenge to rationality's compassion and to its imagination and ingenuity: can it devise a system in which those with other traits can live comfortably and flourish —with the opportunity to develop their rationality if they choose— and will it? (180)

By this point in the book, we have become long accustomed to thinking of rationality as capable of planning, emoting, imagining, feeling qualms of conscience about its own amazing success, providing for those less well off, possessing a rich inner life all its own. And accustomed, too, to thinking that only rationality could possibly muster the resources now needed to check its own tendency to homogeneity, to resist it in the name of a justice that only it could define. Reading Nozick, it becomes increasingly difficult to think of rationality without thinking that it is all of thinking worth thinking about.

In the professional discourse on the subject, the issue of whether something can be called rational assumes great importance, for "rational" is virtually a synonym for good, right, valuable, worthy. According to an argument often encountered in this discourse, one can behave amorally, viciously, or deceitfully, but if one is unable to *provide an account* of how this behavior can be accommodated to the necessary commitment to honesty that, after all, enables one to lie successfully in the first place, then one must *surrender the claim* that one is acting rationally. The presumption is that this would be an unbearably heavy loss, in the face of which one would experience a considerable pressure to straighten up and fly right. The presumption, in other words, is that rationality rules by universal consensus, that its domination extends deep into the mind, even deeper than the value-commitments specific to ethics.

Is there any limit to rationality, anything it can't do? A curious sentence from the same passage suggests at least that it needs no help to do what it does. "Rationality," Nozick comments, "has brought many benefits and thus enabled rationality to extend its domain further" (180). With awkward precision, Nozick has implied that rationality doesn't wait for you or me to extend its domain—it proceeds on its own, enabling itself to extend itself, producing effects that beget more effects, distinctions that engender further distinctions. The question arises as to who's in charge, a question usefully if unintentionally aggravated by the circularity of Nozick's formulation. A host of ungainly questions throng in here that Nozick never considers. When people act rationally, are they truly pursuing their "own" goals and projects? Can rationality's sway be extended by irrational people, by irrational means, for irrational reasons? Can we pursue irrational goals through rational means and still be rational? When we are behaving semirationally, is rationality itself compromised in us, or does it simply meet a counterforce capable of deflecting it from its true path? Does rationality invariably seek to dominate whatever else it confronts in the mind?

The only way, it seems, of managing such questions is quietly to assume a kind of homunculus, an imp that arises almost naturally from the very dilemmas, paradoxes, hypotheses, and formulae that seem designed to eliminate the human or pseudohuman. These include such keyboard-challenging Nozickian artifacts as the following:

$$\text{Measure}(h_1/e) = \cfrac{\text{prob}(h_1 \to e) \times \text{prob}(h_1)}{\displaystyle\sum_{(i==1)}^{n} \text{prob}(hi\ e) \times \text{prob}(hi) + \text{prob}(Ce)}$$

(83)

Such formulae are presented as the final state of precision, rules rather than approximations, the real stuff. Still, a kind of personality emerges in the interstices, and it isn't pretty: an inhuman will to mastery, a positive taste for abstraction, and an aggressive arrogance toward other modes of thought or representation, which it must regard as sub-, non-, pre-, or ir-. Rationality (or is it rational people?) can approve only of itself.

Nozick's analytical style, which presumably represents his version of rationality in action, yields a number of other clues about rationality's personality, especially its dislikes. It appears, for example, to be in the "nature of rationality" to be indifferent to history. The argument for evolution notwithstanding, this rational book says nothing about how rationality came to be, perhaps because the necessarily narrative record of history would be itself irrational. A lively genealogical curiosity would distract rationality, or *rat* (a neologism I introduce as a way of suspending the question of whether we are dealing with rationality itself or with rational minds, a way of bracketing the crisis in cognitive agency represented by rationality), from focusing on the present as a problem to be solved by the brisk application of appropriate rules. In a rational approach, history exists in the past perfect tense: the town having been taken. Rationality having evolved, we can now study its nature.

In its stricter formulations, *rat* is also famously indifferent to ends. The model might be the military mind, which is rational in its obedience to orders, no matter what they may be. Not for the highly trained bombardier to decide on the wisdom, moral status, or even strategic necessity of his orders to destroy Dresden, London, Cambodia, Afghanistan, or Iraq's Highway 1; those orders are issued by loftier intelligences charged with realizing certain ends they determine—by means other than strictly rational—to be worthy. Like Aladdin's genie, *rat* is effective without full agency, a perfect instrumentality, a servant with more power than you could possibly possess yourself, but powerless to direct his power. And despite having what Nozick calls "*intrinsic* value," *rat* resembles a perfect butler—say, Anthony Hopkins in *The Remains of the Day*—in its unwillingness to make an independent assessment of value. It is rational for your butler to regard you as a führer, even if it is irrational for you to regard the Führer as a führer, not being the Führer's butler.

Nor, in the most general sense, does *rat* busy itself with people, their particularity, their contingencies, their bodiliness, their hopes and fears, except as these impinge on *rat*'s "own" interests or advantages. Nozick discusses the well-known logical exercise known as "the prisoner's dilemma" as an instance of the calculation of probabilities, but omits any mention of fear, claustrophobia, isolation, bad food, boredom, insomnia, hatred, or anything about prison life that might inflect such a calculation. It is a prisoner's dilemma without the prison and indeed without the prisoner.

Rationality seems to be what is left when personhood, community, conventions, sensibility, and context in general are subtracted, a disintoxicated dream of thought that imagines itself plunked down in the world, unburdened by a past or an unconscious, and all this unused disk space, as it were, to set about calculating with. Not quite inhuman, not quite identical with pure abstract logic, *rat* seems curiously autonomous and alone, a prisoner in solitary confinement; to the extent that people are rational, they are as if incarcerated, confronting their dilemmas in the solitude of their cells. Take for example the classic formulation of that great philosophical myth, John Rawls's "original position," a hypothetical initial circumstance of equality the rationality of which consists in the fact that nobody knows anything about themselves or the others they find themselves dealing with. They exist, Rawls says in *A Theory of Justice,* behind a "veil of ignorance," knowing that they possess "some rational plan of life" but not what the details of that plan might be or what ends it might serve. They are rational "in the ordinary sense" insofar as they are exempt from envy, jealousy, discontent, all of which can, "for the present," be set aside. The "assumption of mutually disinterested rationality" between "theoretically defined individuals" comes to this: that persons in the original position try to "win for themselves the highest index of primary social goods, since this enables them to promote their conception of the good most effectively whatever it turns out to be. . . . The assumption only says that the parties have a capacity for justice in a purely formal sense" (*Theory of Justice* 144, 145). Purely formal; that is, absent any motivation that one might have for doing anything other than *rat*'s appetite for self-extension. In the original position, *rat* reigns. But the entire point is that we do not live our lives in the original position, and that justice can only be served by leaving it and committing ourselves to some particular "conception of the good."

Here we have arrived at one edge of rationality's mystery. What I referred to as the "strict formulation" represents the hard kernel of rationality, an understanding of pure instrumental self-interest comparable to, say, Bentham at his most caricaturally Benthamite. In the "rational choice" model of decision making, economists have traditionally taken into account mainly material incentives, preferences for material goods, and the desire for an immediate payoff. As James Fallows argues in the December 1993 issue of the *Atlantic,* however, behavior modeled on this paradigm eventually becomes self-destructive. "The standard illustration," he writes, "involves pollution. If the law allows factories to dump pollutants into the air or water, then every factory will do so. Otherwise, their competitors will have lower costs and will squeeze them out. This 'rational' behavior will leave everyone worse off. The answer to such a market failure is for the society—that is, the government—to set standards that all factories must obey" (64). In other words, a "higher" rationality will dictate that constraints be put on "strict-formulation" rationality so that we don't all choke to death in our own profits. In a gesture both self-augmenting and self-negating, *rat* will incorporate into itself new principles, rules, and components that seem to run against the grain of rationality. Recognizing this, more recent rational choice theorists have argued for the relevance of other preferences in addition to the material, other ways of calculating interests than the most immediate or narrowly conceived, other kinds of utility.

From this perspective, rationality is not a single, identifiable quality with a determined "nature," but a relational term, a comparative assessment. A rational decision, we might say, is one that maximizes value or interest better than some other decision might have done. But this means that a third decision that produced even better results would render the first decision relatively or comparatively irrational. Nozick attempts to rescue the notion of a "nature" of rationality by arguing that this capacity to transcend or critique itself testifies to a variousness, a capaciousness, a flexibility that is easily missed. In its quest for primary social and individual goods, he argues, a kinder, gentler *rat* responds sensitively to context, appearances, interests, others, incorporating into itself certain qualities or traits such as "imagination" or "compassion" that are, or appear to be, less strictly rational than rationality itself. Max Weber speaks of "the complexity of the only superficially simple concept of the rational," and Henry Sidgwick of the "fissure in reason," but it is Nozick who, with a kind of inspired Quaylesque serendipity, captures the true complexity of the issue in a nutshell: "Rationality . . . is not the whole of our rationality" (Weber 194; Sidgwick 499; Nozick, *Nature of Rationality* 138).

Let's see how this works in a real-world situation. Say I want to impress this woman, but find the going rough. She sees through my tacky stratagems and phony moves and decides that someone so aggressively needy, someone who views her as a "theoretically defined individual" or a military objective (a town to be taken), is not for her. The problem seems to be that I am altogether too rational to be a desirable acquaintance, much less a lover. At this point *rat* swings into action, recalculating probabilities, contexts, new facts, the fit between ends and means. If this woman, this primary social good, is to be mine, I must factor in the utility of certain acts that will have evidentiary force, and will express a human character this woman might admire, which is to say, a human character that does not constantly calculate probabilities and seek to maximize advantages. Like Eisenhower feigning an assault on one beach only to land the body of his force at another, I pretend a deep absorption in people other than her, emotions other than love, activities other than pursuit, and—the pinnacle of perspicacity—even display attributes other than desirability. Drawn to my attractive self-sufficiency, she asks me for my e-mail address. *Rat* has won.

Or, as Nozick puts it in his colorful way,

> In certain contexts, certain things are taken for granted [the erotic undesirability of unchecked rationality]. These things set the framework within which a person is acting or choosing, within which he attempts to maximize some function or have his action exhibit a certain property [erotic desirability]. For a person to take some statement q ["rationalists need not apply"] for granted in context C is for him to stand upon it in C as he attempts to maximize some function. He is not doing calculations to get to q; he is attempting to travel *from* q to reach somewhere else [her good graces]. In context C we take q for granted, and in this context we arrive at belief r [I should not seem so rational], and we now can take *it* for granted, but only in contexts like C in which it is appropriate to take q for granted. Because q was tied to C, r does not float free of what was taken for granted in C in order to reach r [So: out of her sight, I can calculate to my heart's content]. (98)

The glosses raise, in the midst of a passage stressing rationality's dependence on context, the question of motive. It is precisely because *rat* not only can but must, in pursuing its own interests, dissimulate itself in ordinary cognition that it can so easily be suspected of pulling the strings whenever it is not plainly visible, as if, like that great rationalist Richard III, it knew that its effectiveness depended upon concealment.

Rat can also accomplish its objectives by rationalization, which conceals not calculation but rather the desire that calculation serves. The veil of ignorance is a serviceable villain in this respect. Contemplating the unequal distribution of goods and resources, those unwilling to redistribute their own property but guilty about their unwillingness might find it useful to step, for a few moments, behind this veil. From this position they might be able to entertain a belief in the tangible reality of a circumstance in which people—no matter how illiberal, malicious, confused, and desperate they might be—could act on what Rawls calls "principles that they would acknowledge under conditions that best express their nature as free and equal rational beings" (515). Such a belief might well produce the desirable (rationalizing) consequence of lessening the pressure, born of the guilt-inducing spectacle of unfreedom and inequality, to take radical remedial action, even though the possibility of such action constitutes the basic premise of "justice as fairness."

In these instances, *rat* pursues its objectives by indirection without ceasing to be rational or dominant. But Nozick argues a more radical case that *rat* can actually, not just apparently, yield the floor to something other than itself, surrendering power to emotion, passion, and spontaneity when the context renders these more appropriate: "Even decision-theoretic rationality can recommend henceforth making many decisions without thought or calculation, if the process of doing this is more valuable than the losses that might be incurred by these less-reflective decisions, or if the process of calculation itself would interfere with the nature of other valued relationships, such as love and trust. . . . Rationality can be modest and choose to step aside sometimes" (106). The prisoner's dilemma is in fact a case in which the exercise of individual rationality would prevent people from achieving a better solution that required cooperative rather than dominant reasoning. The question Nozick here finesses, however, is whether, in stepping aside, *rat* actually stops calculating, or rather simply perfects its calculations in the manner of the *Star Trek* character Data, who occasionally does something "irrational," such as giving someone a kiss, explaining later that "it seems that the natives on this planet place a high value on such gestures." This question, which reaches into the "unconscious" of rationality, is crucially undecidable. For it is clear that the natives of *this* planet fear and distrust an all-licensed rationality, and so *rat* is compelled on occasion to step aside and surrender its dominance. Doing so may seem a fair-minded, generous, or even an endearing gesture on *rat*'s part. But if it is taken that way, and *rat*'s standing improves as a consequence, it will thereby also qualify as a shrewd and effective one. When *rat* calculates, it calculates; and when it doesn't calculate, it might as well be calculating because the result is identical if not superior to the one that would have been attained by calculation. *Rat* is unable really to acquit itself of the charge that it dreams of a state in which everything that is not rational is either secretly rational or exists only with rationality's permission, in which the distinction between it and other cognitive modes fades, leaving not some liberal parliament of faculties, but simply a regnant *rat* that has only one function, but that almighty—extending its sway.

The question of motive replays a similar feature of liberal political thought. Liberalism envisions a split-level political consciousness in which parties presumed to be self-interested and homogeneous are enjoined not to abandon or moderate their inward-turning identities, but to consider as well that they are participating with other similarly self-centered groups in a large "conversation" that requires from all parties a kind of macro-commitment to a fair and open exchange in which no position enjoys an *a priori* advantage. At some point, certain people take upon themselves the necessary task of maintaining the openness of the conversation. They define their interest as disinterest, taking as their bedrock commitment— since all groups must have some such commitment—the preservation of the "open" form of the conversation itself. These are "liberals." As the only group without interests of its own, liberals might seem to be uniquely altruistic, having given up everything just so others can contend fairly. But as the only group whose selfish interests are identical to the (macro-) inter-ests of all, liberals in fact occupy a uniquely privileged and unencumbered position. Liberals are thus structurally open to the accusation that they have been strict rationalists, narrowly figuring their advantage, all along.

One cannot escape this charge simply by claiming to stand outside ratio-nality's hegemony. When, for example, Anthony Appiah argues against seeing rationality as the whole of modernity, and urges a renewed respect for "magical views" of the sort instantiated by African culture—of which he is a product and distant representative—does he not operate exactly like a canny rationalist? The unanswerable question will always be whether rationality harbors (like capital as seen by Marx) some self-abolishing virus that dictates its own supercession, or whether (like global capitalism as it sees itself) it simply replicates itself by diverse means, never yielding an inch of territory once conquered.

I am arguing that while it is, apparently, possible to describe the attributes, behavior, or functions of rationality, the nature of rationality remains highly uncertain because one of its traits is a compulsion to mutate, to ex-ceed or disguise itself, to appropriate other modes of thought which may or may not thereby become rational. The attribution of traits to rationality can only proceed *as if* the prior question of what it is has been settled. But to proceed on this basis is to repress the evident fact that rationality constitutes not only the acme of reason as such, but also a disturbance in the field of reason. Once again, Nozick seems not so much confused as unaware of his confusion, a telling sign of which is his casual treatment of rationality and reason as synonyms, as when he speaks, at the end of a book about rationality, of "reason's origins and original functions," the

"Dignity of Reason," and the functions to which Kant "consigned reason" (180). Nozick's confusion is not his alone; others confirm a contemporary slippage between the two terms. Nicholas Rescher titles a recent book *Rationality: A Philosophical Inquiry into the Nature and the Rationale of Reason;* Paul Feyerabend bids *Farewell to Reason* when he actually means to diss and dismiss rationality; and Alan Gewirth, trying hard to give two books the same title, settles on *Reason and Morality* and *Moral Rationality.*

But it is possible to imagine a time or a circumstance in which the two terms, or the traits they designate, were far from identical. Kant recognized reason as the guarantor of respect for a categorical or noncontingent law, the solution to increasing secularism and skepticism in that it made such respect as "automatic" as the understanding of mathematical truths. To recognize the ethical law as binding on oneself was, for Kant, a mental gesture as rigorously necessary as recognizing the way in which the hypotenuse of a right triangle was calculated. And since Kant, impersonality has been a mark of the moral. The intricate lacework of distinctions Kant drew was intended to secure the internal integrity of truth, ethics, and taste and their various subcategories; but at the end of the day, reason laid claim to totality, for its apprehension of the law transcended every localism, every village prejudice, every mere custom or habit. For Kant, reason could explain everything.

And then we turn to the unedifying scene of self-glorifying, morally indifferent aggressivity that is rationality in its raw state, its strict formulation. How did it happen that reason as the kingdom of ends became synonymous with rationality as the empire of means, the site of the law identical to the lawless will to power? One possible answer has already been implied. Since Kantian reason entailed a certain element of calculative rigor, the distance between reason and a strictly calculative function (subsequently called rationality) was always already overcome, at least in principle, and reason was always vulnerable to the intrigues of its ambitious subordinate. Now, two centuries' ends later, the town having been taken, we suddenly become aware that our success in modernizing has given us possession of empty buildings, dry wells, dead telephones. Some attribute modern sterility to Kant's emphasis on reason, charging that reason's motto—"I can explain everything"—was the voice of a guilty thing surprised in the act of repressing more supple and humanistic modes of cognition. They ignore the spaciousness, complexity, and richness of Kant's conception (although Kant was, to be sure, enough of a rationalist to describe marriage as a contract between two persons giving each exclusive rights to the use of the other's genitals); they fail to recall that reason has become dessicated only as it has been reduced to rationality.

With no space between reason and rationality, we have lost the capacity we might have had to determine "the nature of rationality," which has become for some the nature of intelligence as such. As distinctions fade, we become incapable of addressing such questions as whether rationality is the crystallized essence of reason or reason's monstrosity. In order to reclaim the power to pose such questions, we must reinstitute distinctions. But where, how, between what and what?

Imagine a thing called reason, or Reason, that is so vast and complex that simply to think about it is to try to reduce it, to abstract it, to limit it, to draw internal distinctions. Make a first cut, placing on one side an acceptance of traditions, customs, conventions, institutions, the intricacies of the human heart, and context in general as factors in understanding and assessment: call this "reasonability." What's left on the other side is the kind of understanding that recognizes the force of necessity, of laws without appeal, a faculty of comparison, demarcation, differentiation, logical entailment, and computation that may be called "rationality." A master politician if not an impressive intellect, Lyndon Johnson was known for saying, "Let us reason together," not "Let us rationalize together." Reasonability is only comfortable operating on a human scale, according to more or less disorderly procedures involving intuition and "feel"; rationality gravitates to the interstellar and the subatomic, where a calculator is all that's needed.

Among reasonable people, rationality manifests itself as both an ideal and a pathology. In fact, a probing and sympathetic article on autism by Oliver Sacks sheds unexpected light on rationality. His primary example, a biologist and engineer named Temple Grandin, is exceptionally well organized, efficient, logically precise, and distinguished in her field, but has a number of obvious limitations. Music and poetry, and even the metaphors of everyday life, baffle her. Often, she finds herself lost in a world of signals and stimuli others find transparent. She cannot understand what people feel when they see natural beauty or fall in love; sublimity does not exist for her. "I never knew what they were up to," she says about *Romeo and Juliet*. In addition to "a sort of moral or intellectual intensity or purity," autistic people, Sacks concludes, have "no true concept of, or feeling for, other minds, or even of their own" (109, 107). They are deprived not of affect as such—Temple Grandin feels very strongly for animals—but of affect in relation to complex human experiences. The autistic lack above all "an implicit knowledge of social conventions and codes, of cultural presuppositions of every sort" (116). Lacking this kind of knowledge, those whose autism permits them to function in the world have to "compute" others' feelings and states of mind. Temple Grandin in fact often compares her own mind to a computer; her example suggests that rationality is, to an undetermined extent, autistic.

Grandin is fascinated by, even obsessed with, her own mind and has made a secondary career out of explaining its mysterious powers and deficiencies. And here we encounter another of rationality's instabilities: in one respect a measure of one's freedom from the distorting effects of self-consciousness in an unmediated apprehension of the truth, rationality is, in another respect, self-awareness itself, the neutral apprehension of one's own mind that alone can enable one to gauge and discount the effects of subjectivity on perception and understanding. But rationality's awareness is limited, it would appear, to the mind. In Temple Grandin's discourse, the body is opaque, inert. The indifference and even revulsion she feels toward the prospect of physical contact with humans suggests the hypothesis that rationality (at least to the extent that its nature is disclosed by autism) may reflect something like a deep cognitive embarrassment concerning the bodily, affective, and social embeddedness of the mind. The pairing with reasonability becomes especially instructive at this point, for reasonability, too, might constitute a species of embarrassment, not at embodiment or acculturation, but at the mind's nihilistic or totalitarian willfulness, its inclination to ignore others altogether and focus on the purity of its own operations. The union of the two in Reason suggests that nowhere is the mind fully in sync, free from discomfiture, wholly at ease in its operations.

In summer 1994, a sign was observed on a light pole outside the Los Angeles courthouse reading, "Dear O. J., I'm very sorry about your situation, but I'm glad that you surrendered and you're still alive. . . . Some good can come from your situation. Be strong and stay positive!" It was signed—appropriately, I contend—"R. L. J. A fan and voice of reason"; or, to be more precise, the voice of reasonability: of community, open-endedness, working things out together and over time. It is definitely not the voice of "strict" rationality. What could be in it for O. J. to go through the trial, appeals, lengthy incarceration, and possible impoverishment just so the rest of us might become slightly more skeptical of the fitness of ex-athletes to serve as role models for our children, or temporarily more aware of the evils of spousal abuse? On the other hand, the sign that appeared in the skies of Oz—"Surrender Dorothy"—spoke in the accents of rationality to creatures obsessed with their own lacks, seeking to minimize threats and promote their own system of ends. Reasonability would concede their ties to a person who had rescued them, stuffed their straw, oiled their hinges, etc., but rationality would measure the uncertain benefits of sticking by this powerless alien against the real and present danger of an infuriated witch.

Each by itself is not just incomplete but unworthy. Unadulterated reasonableness would be spineless, inconsistent, unaccountable, pious, flaccid, indifferent; pure rationality would be imperial, rigid, narcissistic, terroristic, autistic. The wonder is that these two styles or functions, so radically flawed in themselves, can collaborate in the production of Reason.

But collaborate they do, and must. For it is impossible to press our imaginings to such a point of rigor that we can isolate a pure strain of either one. At least this is the conclusion that follows from the practice of thinkers who, at the moment of truth, abruptly revert from one to the other. When a communitarian reasonability seems too flabby or indecisive to settle a hard case involving competing demands justly, its genealogical affiliation with the rigidity of Kantian Reason can be invoked ("The community is not just mush; justice and law prevail here!"). And when rationality seems too obsessed with calculating interests, advantages, and probabilities to command anyone's respect, philosophers can introduce terms such as *fundamental, enlightened, long-range,* or *deeper* in order to right the balance and restore a measure of reasonability to an operation that threatened to become fanatic or self-destructive. Thus, in a move that cements the connection between rationality and reasonability (as well as Weberian capitalism), interest *becomes* principle.

We can now understand rationality's compulsive mutations as a necessary consequence of its theoretical incoherence, its real confusion with its other. This structural imbrication is demonstrated again and again by the inability of accounts of rationality to stay rational, to avoid a moment when rationality is subjected to its other. A recent instance is provided by Philip Clayton and Steven Knapp, who argue a series of linked propositions: that "the rationality of a given claim lies in its relation to an ongoing process of collective assessment"; that rational calculation requires a self-conception, "that is, an image, however ill-defined, of the self she wants to be or become"; and that a "rationale" is "a reason that would be taken to be adequate in the right social—or, as we shall say, *intersubjective*—context" (152). Clayton and Knapp contend that a "feed-back principle" is intrinsic to rationality, which cannot be fully imagined or even properly defined without including the reasonable, which is to say, the contextual, the long-term, the ill-defined, the other-oriented, the not-strictly-rational. Their argument confirms an insight suggested at some point by all rigorous accounts, that rationality requires an inmixing, the importation into its inner fastness of the qualities of reasonability. This importation, once again, does not corrupt the nature of rationality; it *is* the nature of rationality.

Reason consists, then, of a dynamic impurity, a synonymic-antonymic oscillation between functions that are themselves imperfectly distinct. The fissure in reason keeps it from settling into predictable univocality, while its capacity to contain its differences prevents it from splintering into fragments. As compensation for theoretical inconsistency, the subject of Reason enjoys a certain mobility, the freedom to shift from one mode to another, to go from a rock to a soft place, to respond flexibly without departing from Reason. In fact, this mobility itself, rather than any specific trait associated with reasonability or rationality, constitutes the distinctive historico-conceptual power of Reason.

Given the flex in the terms, it might seem to make little difference whether you described a given action or belief as reasonable or rational. But it does, for each term marks a certain emphasis, a certain kind of claim. Even while describing reasonability, Clayton and Knapp retain the *name* of rationality in order to give the argument edge and muscle. The point is not that they have gotten it wrong, but that the choice between the two terms can only be determined by muscle; for when it comes to the reasonability-rationality complex, there can be no simple or necessary name that does not forcibly exclude, preempt, and repress the other.

If each name represses the other, are rationality and reasonability, then, each other's "unconscious"? This seems implausible. Rationality in particular seems *all* consciousness, if not all *of* consciousness. For what it's worth, Temple Grandin claims that she "does not have an unconscious": "There are no files in my memory that are repressed. . . . There are no secrets, no locked doors, nothing is hidden" (Sacks 122). As we have already seen, rationality seems semidetached from the individual human mind, as though it were characteristic not exactly of a mind, but of a kind of discipline in which the mind could participate, if it were disciplined enough. It is modern economics, the economics of competition and free markets, the economics of the rat race, that seems the proper worldly home of rationality. And rats have no unconscious.

But are rats rational? Readers of Nozick might well think so, for certain features of his account correspond to the image of rats documented in popular stories from "The Pied Piper" to *Willard,* in which they threaten to swarm over the face of the earth, taking towns, devouring everything in sight. Like the rat race, the race of rats presents a spectacle of mindless ferocity, utter determination, unstoppable sexual drive, and, in general, *appetite.* So why do we perform experiments on rats that are designed to illuminate human behavior?

One doubts that researchers who use rats (or used them in the heyday of rat behaviorism from the 1930s to the 1960s) would explain the matter in this way, but we can speculate that what makes rats singularly interesting is, in the first instance, that they make visible our own instincts, uncomplicated by any interference from outside. Rats are programmed to a uniform frenzy of egoism when they are placed in settings of scarcity. No conscience, no faculty of moderation, inhibits them from devouring each other, their young, anything in sight, if they are hungry. Carrying individual appetite to the point of species suicide, rats under stress allegorize the self-preservative *and* the death instincts. Their other contribution to behavioral science lore, their eagerness to "press the sugar button" to the point where they junk-food themselves to death, manifests the self-destructive potency of the pleasure principle. What rats lack, it would appear, is the reality principle, a prudential capacity to take the long view, to pursue their enlightened self-interest, to exchange dominant for cooperative behavior in order to produce a better result, to advance from Bentham to Mill.

As these formulations already imply, what makes rats grippingly fascinating is that their behavior exemplifies not just instinct, but rationality, or more precisely, the "strict formulation" that seems impossible to isolate in human beings. It is not the chimps and porpoises of the world in which we can recognize our rationality, but in rats. (Here the obligatory popular-culture evidentiary text would be the children's movie *The Secret of NIMH,* with its vision of hyper-rational, technologically adept rats.) The natural behavior of rats defines our hard-won modernity. As if this were not enough, the way in which rats pursue their own ends while replicating each other carries the darkest possible implications concerning the freedom and autonomy that rationality is supposed to exercise. As a template for modern humanity, rats suggest that what we consider to be free, rational behavior actually reflects self-destructive short-term ends that we do not even determine for ourselves. Might not our disgust and loathing at the sight or even the thought of rats display, then, the energy of repression we invest in order to keep from ourselves the recognition that we not only are, but have chosen to become, ratlike; that rattiness has become an evolved trait for us, and that *this* represents the essence, the pure spring of rationality, which is in turn the essence of Reason, the basis of our claim to metaphysical dignity and self-worth?

Actually, the real message of rats is more complex. So appallingly limited, rats represent in extraordinarily concentrated form both a variety of human instincts *and* rationality. Rats fine-tune Hume's theory, ventured in the *Treatise on Human Nature,* that "reason [actually rationality] is nothing but a wonderful and unintelligible instinct in our souls" (1.3.6). What rats *mean* is that instinct and rationality are not altogether incompatible, and may, at a primitive level of development, actually be identical. Studying them, we learn that while in one respect we are rational insofar as we can overcome our base instincts, in another, rationality just *is* those instincts. As Lacan says in a seminar on "Le Rat dans le Labyrinthe," "Ce n'est pas pour rien qu'on a choisi le rat" (133).

As experimental subjects, rats have been replaced by computers, which are cleaner if not cheaper. But rats may be poised for a comeback as models of how rationality can be cultivated to the point of self-destruction in a world of dwindling resources, and also of how an unlimited supply of "sugar" can destroy the organism that makes and consumes it. Research conducted with such subjects would begin with the assumption that Rational Man, Economic Man, Progressive Man is capable of pursuing instinct by other means.

Thus we are returned to the unconscious. Perhaps Temple Grandin, or some hypothetical being whose mind is all rationality and nothing else, is not exactly incapable of repression, bereft of an unconscious, but rather something altogether more strange and compelling. Perhaps the best way to characterize a mind such as hers is to say that its consciousness is limited to elements that most adults have repressed—a marked fellow-feeling for animals; a neutral and uncommitted indifference to other people except as mysteries to be solved, problems to be negotiated; a profound self-absorption; a deep need for repetition; an emotional repertoire concentrated at the poles of violent over-response and inert nonresponse. On the other hand, what most people feel consciously she does not feel at all. She has not repressed it, she simply doesn't have it in her. Only an unconscious "has no unconscious."

So rationality, in the exercise of which you can virtually feel your brain working, is staged in the field of consciousness, while its root, nucleus, or motor is unconscious. It is paradoxical. But to take the next step in these highly speculative and preliminary reflections, we must press beyond paradox to example, to an instance of rats, and *rat,* in action.

This would, of course, be Freud's "Notes upon a Case of Obsessional Neurosis," the subject of which has become celebrated for structuring his mental world, largely through puns, around the theme of rats. For the Rat Man, rats are the real: everything is rats and rats are everything. Through a kind of snag, he associates rats with his father, a gambler or *Spielratte,* who had beaten him in childhood for masturbating; with the penis, as a carrier of infection; with illicit sex, especially with prostitutes who (like rats) are associated with sewers and gutter life; with marriage (*heiraten*); with children, himself in particular, since he had also been punished as a child for having bitten someone; and with money (through "installments" or *Raten* —"In his obsessional deleria," Freud notes, "he had coined himself a regular rat currency" [70]). His obsession had not, however, crystallized until, as an adult serving in the army, he had heard from "Captain M." of a peculiarly horrible punishment in which an overturned pot containing hungry rats was placed on a man's buttocks, and, as the Rat Man recounted to Freud, " 'they . . .'—he had again got up, and was showing every sign of horror and resistance—'. . . *bored their way in* . . .'—Into his anus, I helped him out" (27). The Captain's *petit récit* made all kinds of sense to the Rat-Man-to-be, locking in the motif of punishment with those of anality, sexuality, and—by recalling an old fascination with anal intercourse, which originated in a childhood bout with worms—childhood. Freud himself actually gets *mise* in this *abyme.* When he tells his prospective client the hourly fee, the Rat Man mutters to himself, "So many florins, so many rats"; and then, during the treatment, the Rat Man repeatedly addresses him as "Captain."

But Freud was already in the picture in ways he does not guess. What, after all, does Freud do? Confronted with a suffering patient, Freud identifies a margin between the system of the patient's pathology and that of the normal world, and proceeds to occupy that space. A case study represents the record of a mediation in which the pathology becomes translated into the discourse of the norm, and the norm is deformed by the project of representing the pathology. The technical term, drawn from the case of the Rat Man itself, would be "compromise formation." Obsessional neurosis is marked by such formations, which emerge as the neurotic struggles with his obsessions. But while compromise formations characterize the disorder, they mask it as well. Freud begins his exposition by explaining that he does not fully understand the pathology, in part because he has few patients: obsessional neurotics rarely present themselves for treatment because the compromises they strike permit a marginally ordinary mundanity: they "dissimulate their condition in daily life." The illness itself must be considered a "dialect of the language of hysteria" that is "more nearly related to the forms of expression adopted by our conscious thought than is the language of hysteria" (17). Obsessives are the walking wounded, their disorder largely invisible, even to themselves. In this case, normal therapeutic technique repeats the disorder, asymptotically compromising with a disorder defined by its compromises.

Obsessional neurosis displays a number of traits that bring it even closer to the norm Freud tries to represent in his therapeutic practice. Sufferers exhibit an *"obsession for understanding"*; the Rat Man in particular "forced himself to understand the precise meaning of every syllable that was addressed to him, as though he might otherwise be missing some priceless treasure." A "doubting mania," a positive "need for uncertainty" predicated on "the untrustworthiness of memory," a pronounced tendency to *"rationalize"* one's obsessions, a withdrawal of affect, a belief in the "omnipotence of thoughts," a "regression from acting to thinking"—all these mark both the illness and, to a very great extent, the cure (48, 49).

The principle of therapy seems to be that the analyst voluntarily assumes the burden of the neurosis, entering into it in an effort to understand it as itself, while retaining a foothold in the norm. By this gesture, the analyst demonstrates that the neurosis can be brought under the control of free choice and conscious decision, and thus that it can, eventually, be deselected or chosen against. Therapy becomes a matter of substituting the freedom and flexibility of reasonable consciousness for the iron laws, the resistant autism, the rules and principles of an unconscious that is, on its own terms, strictly and uncompromisingly rational. For the analyst, the risk of this procedure lies in the necessity of submitting oneself, however provisionally, to a pathology that, as a law of its being, seeks to dictate behavior, to extend its sway. As unconsciousness is the enabling condition of the pathology's power, it must resist all efforts to expose it to the light of day, and must, in fact, constantly try to subjugate the analytical consciousness that is its enemy, enticing it to repressions and misprisions, to "indefinite or ambiguous wording" that would permit the pathology to slip away unrecognized (100). Freud himself describes the risk epigrammatically, noting that the thing to be warded off can make its way into the means of warding it off; and that when thinking thinks about sex, "the thought process itself becomes sexualized" (99).

Who wins in the case of the Rat Man? Freud declares the Rat Man cured, free (if only to lose his life in the Great War); but flaws in his own analysis suggest that certain factors remain, for him, "unconscious," and therefore that his understanding has been compromised by its object. In the cloud-particle of puns that swirl around the Rat Man, Freud misses two. The Rat Man's childhood governess, with whom he had his earliest sexual experiences, had, at the time of the analysis, married, "so that," as Freud says without comment, "to-day she is a Frau Hofrat" (22). The second is of a different order: *ratio*. The failure to imagine a *Ratten-ratio* connection—a failure repeated by Lacan in his pun-filled seminar—becomes, in the context, both symptomatic and necessary. Symptomatic in the sense that it constitutes a repression of the possibility that his own analytical methods might be implicated in his subject's pathology, and, more particularly, that he himself has become professionally obsessed not just with the Rat Man but with everything that torments the Rat Man—masturbation, sewer life, the anus, cruelty, and even payment. And necessary in that such a repression cannot be admitted if the therapy is to proceed, the patient to be cured, the interests and norms of the community to prevail, the war to be won.

In the course of the analysis, then, the Rat Man becomes more reasonable and less crazy, while Freud becomes crazier and more rational.

Together, they demonstrate, among other things, that rationality is not "inhuman," as sentimentalists about the human condition sometimes charge. It is, rather, thoroughly, even definitively human, even if it does not exhaust the human. By decree of instincts that have evolved into conflicting categorical imperatives, human beings must be rational, and other than rational. Rationality must "compromise" with its others; it must exist in an undecidable circumstance of general corruption: that is its "nature," and ours.

At the end of the century, it is necessary to understand what rationality can be made to mean, and where it can be positioned. Standing at the constantly advancing pinnacle of human evolution and accomplishment, rationality is also, we must recall, a common human endowment, the basis for the humblest, least impressive cognitive feats. The very worm in the ground ascends in wet weather and descends in dry, pursuing its interests. Politically, too, rationality bears a mixed message. In its "Nazi-like" mode, rationality is indifferent if not actively hostile to such things as rights, which it can only regard as quixotic luxuries, frills of the ethos of individualism. Such a disposition can be countered in various ways, but the way most habitual to the tradition of modernity is to insist on the autonomy and dignity of the individual, as evidenced by . . . rationality, by the inherent human capacity to recognize facts, assess circumstances, and maximize one's position by diverse means. It is only on the basis of some such common endowment that human beings can lay claim to "the rights of man," "human rights," rights that people possess independent of merit or status. Rationality is "inalienable" no matter how foolish, limited, degenerate, or primitive one is. In fact, "premodern" cultures, with all their superstitions, delusions, and errors in thinking, lasted for thousands of years, longer perhaps than we will, and in that basic respect could claim to be superior in point of rationality. This might be an argument in support of the thoroughly modern, or postmodern, injunction to "respect" the otherness of the nonmodern other, to "tolerate" or even "celebrate" its difference. But protean rationality is not so easy to suspend. Should the entire world be forced to modernize by cultivating its rationality? Of course not, we answer. But the real question takes a different form: do people have a "choice" at all? Once a distinction between rationality and something else has been formulated as a choice, the decision has been made, because free choice represents the essential circumstance of rationality, just as autonomy defines the subject of modernity generally. Perhaps this is why, in an overwhelming majority of instances, people who (think they) have a choice decide for rationality and modernity. Whether in doing so they are pursuing their enlightened, fundamental interests or just pressing the sugar button remains, of course, to be seen.

The Ideology and Ecology of the Aesthetic

No concept is more fundamental to modernity than the aesthetic, that radiant globe of material objects and attitudes ideally independent of politics, rationality, economics, desire, religion, or ethics. For as Shaftesbury, Kant, Alexander Baumgarten, Friedrich Schiller, and their successors have elaborated it, the aesthetic gathers into itself and focuses norms and notions crucial to the self-description of an enlightened culture. These include the privilege of disinterested assessment; the relative autonomy of the artifact from historical, social, or economic forces; the uncoerced liberty of the judging subject, the universalizability of subjective responses; the human capacity to imagine and create objects, and indeed a "world," that are harmonious and whole; and even what might be called the destiny of freedom to actualize itself in the world. Interestingly, however, this defining concept is itself underdefined, for "the aesthetic" ambivalently refers both to particular kinds of objects and to the attitude appropriate to judging them. What renders the definition even less precise is that neither objects nor attitude can exist by themselves: each not only depends on the other but flourishes only in a certain kind of culture, a "modern" culture capable of sustaining a "disinterested" attention to things that have no utilitarian function, no necessary connection to meanings or concepts. One of the paradoxes of modernity is that modern cultures, which hold works of "art" to be singularly useless, also hold themselves to be uniquely equipped to "appreciate" them; while premodern cultures, which invest their "aesthetic" creations with numerous cultic, religious, or variously propagandistic ends, are, by the logic of modernity, manifestly unsuited for, even unworthy of them.

The aesthetic is thus—to an extent that remains to be assessed—an ideological concept, an attribute posited by modernity of itself. A brief *tour d'horizon* of modern ideologies confirms this point. The Anglo-American discourse of liberalism, for example, typically invokes the aesthetic in the course of defending the value of freedom against encroachments from metaphysics, theory, fixed values, universals of all sorts. Where Jeremy Bentham, Thomas Malthus, Herbert Spencer, and others envisioned a "science" of society, liberals followed J. S. Mill's argument that it fell to "art" to define the ends which science could then study (*System of Logic*). An antiscientific aestheticism continues to define liberalism today. Michael Walzer begins his influential book *Spheres of Justice* with the premise that "distributive justice is not . . . an integrated science, but an art of differentiation." For modern liberalism, "art" seems to represent a principle of humane inexactitude or unpredictability, one that not only allows for a certain speculative or intuitive component in analysis, but, by extension, constitutes a warrant for a practice of free self-determination unconstrained by the rules of rationality, utility, or social convention. Also traceable to Mill, this time to his conception of liberty as the cultivation of individual flourishing, even of "originality" or "eccentricity"—"the path that merely concerns [oneself]"—such a practice even informs projects as remote in spirit from Mill's enlightened utilitarianism as Nietzsche's self-forming Overman, the capitalist romance of the "self-made man," and the aestheticized *pratique de soi* advocated by Michel Foucault (Mill, *On Liberty;* Foucault, *The Use of Pleasure*).

Kant makes a powerful claim on liberal sympathies when he distinguishes between a public realm concerned with social organization and justice and a private realm in which the aesthetic is centered. Where and how to draw this distinction constitutes an ongoing debate within liberalism between, roughly, liberals and libertarians. What's wrong with Richard Rorty's (libertarian) position, according to Anthony Cascardi, is that it concentrates all its attention on the individual, sacrificing a crucial Kantian point, that aesthetic judgment, while based on private sensations of pleasure and pain, also lays the foundation for the formation of a community through an extension to everyone of individual judgments of taste. As Cascardi puts it, Kant's point is "that the aesthetic provides the means by which these realms may be made transparent to one another while their distinct identities are simultaneously preserved" (21). Cascardi especially wants to preserve, against Rorty's insistent privatization of aesthetics, a dialectic between the individual sensual experience and what Kant calls the "supersensible substrate of mankind," with its possibility for collective judgments (*Critique of Judgment* 207-8; hereafter *CJ*). Hence Cascardi's project for an "aesthetic liberalism" which "reflects an effort to grant the shaping power of art over our identity as individuals seeking at once to ground that identity in community and to distinguish it therefrom" (22). Debates within liberalism today typically "grant the shaping power of art," and often the shaping power of Kant as well. Even Jürgen Habermas, while wary of the libidinally disruptive experience of art and hostile to the Kantian categorical imperative, may still retain an unacknowledged allegiance to Kant. Habermas's "discourse ethics," according to Cascardi, covertly presumes a supersensible substrate of humanity in urging as an ideal the notion of distortion-free rational communication, and his normative speech community is, according to Terry Eagleton, simply "an updated version of Kant's community of aesthetic judgement."[1]

This community was first updated by Schiller, who, in *On the Aesthetic Education of Man*, extended the idea of the aesthetic from the subjective to the political, proposing an "aesthetic modulation of the psyche," an "aesthetic education" that would ultimately produce an "Aesthetic State" (163). Schiller's project has always excited and troubled leftist thinkers, many of whom, including Herbert Marcuse, Ernst Bloch, Theodor Adorno, and Fredric Jameson, have sought to return to the fountainhead, the fundament of modernity, the original ciphers of freedom, through the aesthetic. As Christopher Norris points out, aesthetics has long functioned on the left as a "secularised redemptive hermeneutic," holding out the promise that society could overcome its contradictions and theory could transform itself into a discourse responsive to art's always latent emancipatory potential (*What's Wrong with Postmodernism* 17; hereafter *WWWP*). Schiller, according to some in this tradition, represents an early progressive response to industrial alienation, a necessary political reworking of Kant that, according to Cascardi, actually "anticipates the diagnoses of modernity later put forward by Marx, Weber, and Lukács" (15).

But others are not so sure, either about Schiller or about the aesthetic. Terry Eagleton concludes his recent historical inquiry into "the ideology of the aesthetic" with a notably cautious endorsement of the aesthetic, which is, he suggests, to be distrusted whenever it posits pure, autonomous values, but prized when it insists upon a vital relation between bodily or material life and the universal level on which questions of reason and justice are raised. Any such endorsements actually seem to be wrung from recalcitrant material, for as Eagleton demonstrates, the aesthetic is dialectical to the point of incoherence. While a "feminine" register of sensuous form dominates the originary work of Alexander Baumgarten, this pure spring is almost immediately fouled, first by Kant's "stark impera-

---

1. See Cascardi, "Aesthetic Liberalism" 16–18; Eagleton, *The Ideology of the Aesthetic* 405; hereafter abbreviated as *IA*. Relevant texts of Jürgen Habermas include *The Philosophical-Political Discourse of Modernity* 96 ff.; "Philosophy as Stand-in and Interpreter"; "Consciousness-Raising or Redemptive Criticism: The Contemporaneity of Walter Benjamin," in *Philosophical-Political Profiles;* and *Moral Consciousness and Communicative Action.*

tives" and then by certain aspects of Schiller's worldly reinterpretation.[2] Eagleton applauds the Schillerian (and later, the Communist) politicization of the aesthetic but depreciates its corollary, the aestheticization of politics, which has had, he says, the effect of providing imaginary reconciliations to contradictions that remain unresolved in the real world. Even for the supposed beneficiaries, however, the aesthetic was not wholly beneficial. As Eagleton notes, the aesthetic provided the emergent middle class with "a superbly versatile model of their political aspirations, exemplifying new forms of autonomy and self-determination," and theorizing a new and mysterious circumstance in which values appeared to be floating free and bodily pleasures and drives were invested with fresh significance; but the aesthetic also signified a kind of internalized repression cognate with Gramscian "hegemony" (Eagleton, *Ideology of the Aesthetic* 28; hereafter *IA*).[3] In the end, as in the beginning, Eagleton cannot sustain a single attitude toward this "markedly contradictory concept," and the book is both riveted and riven by paradox endlessly repeated. In analyses of Kant, Schiller, Hegel, Marx, Kierkegaard, Nietzsche, Freud, Benjamin, and Adorno ("two different Adornos"), Eagleton tracks the logic of "on the other hand" as it reinscribes itself, even in his own increasingly predictable argument that while the aesthetic has functioned as a language consistent with political domination, it also, once upon a time, provided the most powerful available critique of bourgeois possessive individualism and appetitive egoism, and might, if it could return to its origin or essence, reclaim its destiny of imitating a defiantly independent *Lebenswelt*.

But that, as Eagleton himself demonstrates, is a big *if*. For his own laborious slogging through a mass of historico-philosophical corruption en route to an unspoiled, delightfully feminine, and corporeal origin is, as we have just begun to see, entirely typical of efforts both on the left and on the right to save the aesthetic from its own perversions. Just as Eagle-

2. Alexander Baumgarten, *Reflections on Poetry*. For a sharply critical discussion of Eagleton's "peculiar" discussion of the gender of aesthetics, see Christine Brooke-Rose, *Stories, Theories, and Things* 275–83.

3. Eagleton's argument receives support from Meyer Abrams, who demonstrates that the eighteenth-century discourse of "taste" served a number of functions for the newly emergent bourgeoisie, none of them remarkable for their freedom from worldly concerns. Abrams notes the historically unprecedented emphasis on "the perceiver's stance" and "the contemplation model" of perception, an emphasis that foregrounded the "disinterested" (because affluent and leisured) connoisseur, as opposed to the classical emphasis on craft and production that had been so rich in the "concepts" and "ends" that Kant banished from the aesthetic. See Abrams, *Doing Things with Texts: Essays in Criticism and Critical Theory* 139.

ton returns to Baumgarten as the source and regards Kant and others as the corruption, and just as Cascardi regards Kant as the author of a liberal discourse sullied by pragmatism, still others return to Schiller as the fundament that subsequent thinkers have betrayed. The sense of corruption seems inescapable with a concept that, as Eagleton recognizes, can take "either a left or a right turn. The left turn: smash truth, cognition and morality, which are all just ideology, and live luxuriantly in the free, groundless play of your creative powers. The right turn . . . forget about theoretical analysis, cling to the sensuously particular, view society as a self-grounding organism" (*IA* 368–69).

With respect to the right turn, Eagleton notes an "unnerving affinity," through a shared contempt for the utilitarian, between the aesthetic and the kind of cynical evil concentrated in "the upper echelons of fascist organizations" (*IA* 412). Indeed, a great mass of evidence suggests that it is the right, not the left, that has found the idea of an aesthetic politics most attractive. What dismays those on the left is the conservative appeal not to the "free particulars" of the aesthetic but rather to its "transcendence," its erasure of history. When a canonical work of art is praised for containing "timeless and universal truths," or for being "as relevant today as it was when it was written, 830 years ago," or "appealing to everyone alike," one senses that the rhetoric of aesthetic praise itself occults or sublimates precisely those forces and factions that jostled that work, and not some other, into the canon in the first place. Such a hegemonic rhetoric, conservatives have discovered, can be applied to institutions, governments, authorities of all kinds. Many on the left suspect the aesthetic of being a double agent, accomplice to reaction, a mystified surrogate for political forces that operate within it in an attenuated or oblique way. The title of a recent article by the British Marxist Tony Bennett captures leftist distrust succinctly: "Really Useless 'Knowledge': A Political Critique of Aesthetics."

As Bennett well knows, conservative theoreticians from Edmund Burke to Roger Scruton have argued for the usefulness of aesthetic knowledge as a way of recapturing a renewed social grace—or, Bennett might argue, of sheltering the world of privilege ("taste") from unwelcome political distractions, and the complacently self-sufficient subject from the claims of justice and the rigors of critical reflection. "In the sentiment of beauty," Scruton writes, "we feel the purposiveness and intelligibility of everything that surrounds us, while in the sentiment of the sublime we seem to see beyond the world, to something overwhelming and inexpressible in which it is somehow grounded" ("Modern Philosophy and the Neglect of Aesthetics" 616; see also Scruton, *Aesthetic Understanding*). The seductive power of the aesthetic actually intensifies as one moves further and further right. Fascism, according to a famous comment by Walter Benjamin in 1936, meant the aestheticization of politics; and others were quick to seize the hint, analyzing the link between aesthetics and politics as one explanation for the fascination of fascism, the way in which, in it, rational discourse was superseded by fantasy, myth, spectacle, and fetish.[4] Almost as if to illustrate what Eagleton describes as the contradictoriness of the aesthetic, Scruton and others on the right have established a "right" reading of Schiller's Aesthetic State as a vision of how society might look if it could overcome the baneful antinomies of secular rationalism, achieve the ordered perfection envisioned by poets and philosophers, and mime in social terms the sublime harmony achieved by poetry through the union of language and symbol, form and content, subject and object.

Strongly centralized governments seem to have a special genius for practicing politics as a form of art. In *On the Genealogy of Morals,* Nietzsche described the first politicians as "a conqueror and master race" whose "work is an instinctive creation and imposition of forms; they are the most involuntary, unconscious artists there are. . . . They do not know what guilt, responsibility, or consideration are . . . they exemplify that terrible artists' egoism that has the look of bronze and knows itself justified to all eternity" (86–87). Nietzsche may well have been thinking of the account by his teacher Jacob Burckhardt in *The Civilization of the Renaissance in Italy* of the Renaissance city-state as a "work of art" molded by the ruthlessly effective autocrat-warrior who, with little regard for concerns of morality or justice, ordered the state according to his own interests, making of the people a mere disciplined multitude. For Burckhardt, however, the state as a work of art was a calamity, stifling every possibility for a truly healthy culture (1:22; see "The State as a Work of Art" 1:21–142). Hitler himself seems to be anticipated in Nietzsche's words, and is portrayed in those terms more explicitly, if phantasmagorically, in Leni Riefenstahl's film *The Triumph of the Will,* in which he is shown descending from the clouds.[5] Such images may seem unworthy of serious philosophical consideration, but a comparable complex appears in Ernst Jünger's novel *Die Arbeiter* (The worker), which, according to recent work by Richard Wolin and Michael Zimmerman, exerted a powerful, and hardly unphilosophical, fascination on his most famous reader, Martin Heidegger.[6] The history of fascism com-

4. Benjamin's comment occurs in "The Work of Art in the Age of Mechanical Reproduction" 241.

5. Mussolini, too, clearly felt that part of his mission was to "shape" the masses, who were "like wax in my hands." See Mussolini to Emil Ludwig in 1932, cited in Denis Mack Smith, "The Theory and Practice of Fascism" 82.

6. Richard Wolin, *The Politics of Being: The Political Thought of Martin Heidegger* 77–130; Michael Zimmerman, *Heidegger's Encounter with Modernity: Technology, Politics, Art* 46–93. For the aesthetic connection with German fascism, see Bill Kinser and Neil Kleinman,

pels a difficult recognition, that the violence of extreme reaction, racism, and even genocide represents not a total break with the Enlightenment tradition of modernity, but rather, as a political form that is instinct with the aesthetic, a recognizable variant within that tradition.

The vulnerability of modernity to corruption through the aesthetic is demonstrated once again by postmodernism, which Norris has called "a wholesale version of aesthetic ideology" (*WWWP* 24). Postmodernism can, perhaps, be considered the purest form of the aesthetic turned ideological, and perhaps not surprisingly, is a deeply fissured movement. Considering only the work of two of its most eminent apologists, Jean-François Lyotard and Jean Baudrillard, one can say that each side of the postmodern fissure realizes one of the possible ways of misreading the relations between the Kantian faculties. Describing himself as a Kantian "of the Third Critique," Lyotard seeks to stiffen the distinctions between theoretical reason, ethical understanding, and aesthetic judgment that are elaborated most decisively in the *Critique of Judgment,* where, Lyotard says, Kant finally "cures himself of the disease of knowledge and rules."[7] In his most widely known work, *The Postmodern Condition,* Lyotard claimed that the imperial violence of knowledge, in the forms of "metalanguages" and "metanarratives," could be resisted through art conceived as the site of a disruptively unique "event." The postmodern artifact clears a space for innovation, for the "unforeseeable" or "impossible" move unrestrained by obligations to represent either the objective world or its own subjective nature. Lyotard's postmodernism departs, of course, quite radically from Kant's modernism, which posits a supersensible substrate of humanity, a space in which judgment can work its synthesizing analogies between the sublime and theoretical reason on the one hand and the beautiful and ethical understanding on the other. For Lyotard, the fact that judgment operates "without criteria" means precisely the opposite, that it cannot integrate or synthesize, and cannot therefore lay claim to worldly or theoretical knowledge. The best hope for resisting the "totalitarian" implications of the collapse of "phrase regimes" such as prescription and

---

The Dream That Was No More a Dream: A Search for Aesthetic Reality in Germany, 1890–1945; also Walter Benjamin, "Theories of German Fascism: On the Collection of Essays *War and the Warrior.*" See also Alice Yeager Kaplan, *Reproductions of Banality: Fascism, Literature, and French Intellectual Life.* For helpful counsel on this material, I am indebted to Martin Jay, whose essay "The 'Aesthetic Ideology' as Ideology; Or What Does It Mean to Aestheticize Politics" is especially lucid.

7. Jean-François Lyotard, *Instructions païennes* 36. Quoted and translated in Bill Readings, *Introducing Lyotard: Art and Politics* 106.

description is, he argues, to preserve the "abyss" between them. Thus what might seem a state of conceptual paralysis in which no movement between regimes is possible actually implies to Lyotard the prospect of human progress, of a move into the future enabled by the unaccountable aesthetic event.[8]

If for Lyotard the Kantian distinctions between the faculties must be purged of their universalizing tendencies and the lines between them must be drawn ever more sharply, for Jean Baudrillard culture has reached a stage in which the distinctions have been effaced by a postmodern practice of image production that requires, and invokes, no original referent at all, existing, only in the undecidable mode of "hyperreality." For Baudrillard, postmodernity has made it impossible to distinguish between truth and true-seeming consensus judgments, "science" and "ideology," or representations and "simulacra." It is Baudrillard that Norris chiefly has in mind when he describes, and condemns, postmodernism as "a project of annulling all the terms and distinctions that Kant sought so strenuously to hold in place, and a consequent refusal to acknowledge any limits to the realm of imaginary representation" (*WWWP* 24; see also 164–93).

What annoys those who, like Norris, see in these terms and distinctions a warrant for a politically progressive critique based on the ultimate accessibility of evidence, accurate representation, the probative powers of critique, and so forth, is postmodernism's ideological flaccidity. Especially in his more recent texts, Lyotard seems eager to avoid any positive program whatsoever, cultivating instead of a politics an ethics based almost exclusively on deferral, indeterminacy, or "hesitation." For those on the left, postmodernism is especially frustrating because it envelops Marxism without realizing its aims, deploying Marxism's central categories through inversion. Postmodernism stands for materiality without substance, totality without community, homogeneity without equality, economics without class, populism without humanity, dynamism without aspiration, and liberation without justice. For those on the right, postmodernism is equally offensive, representing uniformity without direction or purpose, collec-

---

8. This is especially true in the radical case of the sublime, for the sublime in Kant's formulation represents a limit to aesthetic gratification, since by definition no form can be adequate to the sense or feeling of the sublime. Thus the sublime checks the impulse to pass beyond aesthetic form to ideas of a supersensible character on ethics and politics. For a sympathetic and intelligent exposition of Lyotard, see Readings 72–74. For critical readings, see Eagleton, *Ideology of the Aesthetic* 395–401; and Norris, *What's Wrong with Postmodernism* 7–15. Among a number of recent studies of Kant that focus on the sublime, albeit in very different ways, are Paul Crowther, *The Kantian Sublime: From Morality to Art;* and John Sallis, *Spacings: Of Reason and Imagination in Texts of Kant, Fichte, Hegel,* esp. 82–131.

tivity without nationalism or racism, control without authority, passivity without faith. A "wholesale version of the aesthetic ideology," postmodernism seems to detach itself from any ideology worthy of the name.[9] Perhaps because of its deeply in-wrought aesthetic component, it takes a comparably ambivalent position with respect to the promises of Enlightenment rationality; for it is difficult to say whether postmodernism represents the culminating historical realization of the Enlightenment tradition or its degradation.

What might be even harder to determine is how postmodernism can be the very flower of the "aesthetic ideology" when it had, not so many years earlier, been advertised as the "anti-aesthetic" (see Foster). Has postmodernism recently gone to seed, or is the aesthetic to be distinguished from its own ideology? The term "aesthetic ideology" was coined by Paul de Man in essays written near the end of his life, when he showed a new interest in ideology critique. Aesthetics, de Man argued, was in Kant a "distinctive mode of understanding," one that had a clearly defined province and relative importance, preserved through what Norris calls the "*rigorous and principled insistence* that the faculties should maintain their internal system of differentiated powers and prerogatives, and not be tempted into various forms of illusory premature synthesis" of, for example, phenomenal perception and ethical categories or theoretical reason (*WWWP* 18). De Man identifies a structural temptation in the aesthetic to the fusion and confusion of what Kant intended as an intricate network of differentiations between faculties, with the threatened result that form is simply taken for meaning, performance for cognition, perception for understanding—and, by natural-seeming extensions, aesthetic forms for the culture at large, and the culture at large for the state.

The stakes involved in these misprisions, these failures to respect boundaries, are high indeed. Ultimately, an imperial aesthetic—the "aesthetic ideology"—comes to substitute for those faculties it was intended to serve, with disastrous cognitive, political, and ethical consequences. Conceding that a comment in Joseph Goebbels's novel *Michael* to the effect that "politics are the plastic art of the state" is "a grievous misreading of Schiller's aesthetic state," de Man then adds that "the principle of this misreading does not essentially differ from the misreading which Schiller inflicted on

9. Eagleton constructs a "case for the defence of postmodernism" based on its iconoclasm, its demotic confounding of hierarchies, its subversions of closure, and its populism—then immediately, follows with a case for the prosecution based on postmodernism's hedonism and "philistine anti-historicism," its erasure of truth, and its "blank, reified technologism" (*IA* 373).

his predecessor, namely Kant."[10] Fascism is a degenerate form of a degenerate form of Kant, succeeding by a highly effective suppression of the violence required to bring about its syntheses. Thus the aesthetic makes "claims on the shape and the limits of our freedoms" that are by no means merely theoretical (*Rhetoric of Romanticism* 264). According to Norris, de Man is here both describing and pleading guilty to a philosophical wrong turn that had informed his notorious wartime journalism for the Belgian collaborationist newspaper *Le Soir*. When, in the late sixties, de Man began to publish his major critical and theoretical essays, he devoted himself to tasks that, in effect, constituted a melancholy and penitentially rigorous critique of the "monadic" or "totalizing" figures characteristic of the aesthetic ideology, distinguishing, in his later work, between Kantian "critical hermeneutics" and the grievous misreading represented by Schillerian syntheses.

This account has, for many, the double virtue of establishing the worldliness of the later de Man and going some ways toward exculpating de Man from charges of personal immorality. And indeed it is striking how de Man routinely casts even the most technical-seeming issues in moral terms, particularly in terms of seduction. In an essay on "reception aesthetics" in *The Resistance to Theory*, de Man says, for example, that "the aesthetic is, by definition, a seductive notion that appeals to the pleasure principle"; and in "Phenomenality and Materiality in Kant," he comments that "morality and the aesthetic are both disinterested, but this disinterestedness becomes necessarily polluted in aesthetic representation [by] . . . positively valorized sensual experiences."[11] Norris reproduces this moralization of the aesthetic, if not the figure of sensory "pollution," when he describes de Man's sense of the aesthetic ideology as "a permanent temptation of thought, a desire . . . to conflate the two realms of phenomenal experience and conceptual understanding" (*WWWP* 256). The history of literary thinking in particular gives ample reason for thinking the temp-

10. Paul de Man, "Kant and Schiller." In *The Aesthetic Ideology*. The quotation from Goebbels is taken from this text. For a reading of Schiller sharply at odds with de Man's, see Joseph Chytry, *The Aesthetic State: A Quest in Modern German Thought*. Chytry argues that Schiller "does not identify the moral with the aesthetic," but "fully recognizes the dangers of untrammeled aestheticism," which he sees as resulting from "an inadequate experience of beauty" (90).

11. Paul de Man, "Reading and History." In *The Resistance to Theory* 64. "Phenomenality and Materiality in Kant" 137-38. Gilles Deleuze argues forcefully, contra de Man's point, that morality for Kant is not disinterested: "*There is a single dangerous misunderstanding regarding the whole of practical Reason:* believing that Kantian morality remains indifferent to its own realization." See *Kant's Critical Philosophy: The Doctrine of the Faculties* 39.

tation to be permanent. For, as de Man and Norris point out, virtually all major schools of literary theory, such as formalism, reader-response criticism, reception theory, and, for that matter, any approach in which cognition, desire, and morality are fused or confused, succumbs to it. The list of the fallible includes not only T. S. Eliot but such mainstream scholars as H. R. Jauss, W. K. Wimsatt, M. H. Abrams, Earl Wasserman, Michael Riffaterre, Roman Jakobson—all of whom, no matter how rigorous their arguments or unimpeachable their scholarly rectitude, fall prey to the aesthetic ideology. In its ideological mutations, aesthetics yields a "knowledge" that is corrupt, but far from "useless." [12]

Against these temptations, de Man urges the ethical superiority of literature, whose rhetorical tropes and figures, irreducible to grammatical order, resist the seductions of aesthetic ideology, immersing the reader in the ways of unknowing by presenting a kind of meaning that simply cannot claim to be directly perceived (*Allegories of Reading* 17). The result is, as de Man tirelessly argued, a structural necessity of "misreading" that virtually defines the literariness of literature. It is, however, not immediately clear how this form of misreading, accurately reflecting the properties of literariness, differs from "grievous" misreadings such as Schiller's of Kant. More disquieting still is an internal difficulty. Rigorously argued, and argued on the very basis of rigor as against collapse, seduction, and desire, de Man's distinction between literature and the aesthetic remains stubbornly counterintuitive, cutting across the grain of an ancient tradition in which even Kant participated, of considering literature, especially poetry, as the art of arts, the highest aspiration and purest instance of the aesthetic. De Man is not simply distinguishing between the essence and the rind of the aesthetic; he is claiming that what had always been considered the essence is in fact the rind.

As a consequence of his earnest efforts to warn against the seduction of the aesthetic, de Man has placed himself in a double dilemma. He has tried to critique the aesthetic by removing what is, on many accounts, its very heart; and he has, by casting the problem in political and moral terms, built back into the aesthetic the very energies he is trying to banish. We should not, however, be quick to accuse de Man of avoidable error, for as we have already seen, the effort to distinguish the fundament or essence of the aesthetic from some derivative or corrupt aspect of itself is a re-

---

12. For other discussions by de Man of the aesthetic ideology, see *Blindness and Insight: Essays in the Rhetoric of Contemporary Criticism* 187–90; also *Resistance to Theory* 3–26; *Rhetoric of Romanticism* 263–90. See also Christopher Norris, *Paul de Man: Deconstruction and the Critique of the Aesthetic Ideology* 88.

current gesture. On one reading of this gesture, philosophers and critics have simply been extraordinarily subject to distraction or confusion. But on another, surely more powerful, reading, the aesthetic itself is, through a predisposition to sensory or ideological pollution, responsible for the misreadings that have plagued it, misreadings that both represent and re-present aesthetic overdetermination. Positing in the first instance an illegitimate entanglement of objects and judgments, forms and concepts, the aesthetic cannot escape entanglement with its own others such as politics and morality, and is thus itself condemned to misreading as the only adequate principle of understanding.

Indeed, since Kantian "judgment" analogizes, and thus mediates, between sensory perception and both theoretical and ethical reason, it draws the boundaries between the faculties in dotted lines, so that "pollution" may be the very essence of judgment, an entailment of its "freedom." According to Gilles Deleuze, judgment is different in kind from theoretical or ethical reason, and has the quite distinctive function of providing the system of faculties with a basis in freedom. Whereas in the first two Critiques, either theoretical reason or speculative ethical understanding "legislates" over the other, in the instance of judgment described in the third Critique there is no dominance at all; the faculties enter into an unregulated yet harmonious accord. As Deleuze puts it, "The first two Critiques set out a relationship between the faculties which is determined by one of them; the last Critique uncovers a deeper free and indeterminate accord of the faculties as the condition of the possibility of every determinate relationship" (68). Without the "free and indeterminate accord" articulated in the third Critique, the faculties would be frozen into postures of antagonism, much like those at some universities today; with such an accord, they can assume a variety of determinate relations. Thus the reason that Kant and his followers have to struggle to hold the distinctions between the faculties in place is that they do not hold themselves: unanchored by the freedom inscribed in reflective judgment, each term distinct from yet permeable to and realized in the others, the Kantian faculties invariably disappoint philosophers seeking rigorous distinctions, moralists seeking clean resistances, and aesthetes seeking art as such—those for whom "free and indeterminate" relations represent only incoherence, promiscuity, stain. Precorrupted, the faculties make but feeble protests against their own perversions.

Hence the bewildering spectacle of de Man trying to enlist Kant's aid in defending against a circumstance Kant regarded as benign, portraying as pollution what Kant defined as empowering complexity. Indeed, so significant are the differences between Kant and de Man that it may be doubted whether the latter's thought is "enlightened" at all. Certainly nothing like Kant's "motto of enlightenment"—"Have courage to use your *own* understanding!"—is to be found in de Man's work, which, on the contrary, typically dismisses as illusory any sense of individual cognitive success. For de Man, a correct or adequate reading of a text cuts across the grain of the reader's desires, negating any possible narcissistic investment in the text. Nor does de Man anywhere celebrate human freedom, a mistaken enthusiasm for which, one may infer, could only produce misreading. De Man does not, in fact, seem greatly interested in progress in human institutions. Kant begins his answer to the question "What Is Enlightenment?" by announcing that *"Enlightenment is man's emergence from his self-incurred immaturity,"* strongly implying that such an emergence is both timely and desirable—precisely the sort of buoyancy that de Man invariably calls "premature." De Man's work occupies and seeks to prolong a moment of hesitation before the satisfying leap to achieved meaning, cultivating the obdurate theoretical problems that impede a passage from form to meaning, artwork to interpretation, rhetoric to questions of meaning and value, literature to the aesthetic. A Kantian pedigree might be claimed for the delay-inducing "misreading," for Kant insisted upon the purely subjective nature of judgment, its nonreliance upon any intrinsic qualities of the object being judged. But in Kant the autonomy of judgment from the thing in itself enables a direct appeal from the individual to the universal substrate of humanity; while in de Man, such appeals are not only premature but false, for the mind can claim to be disinterested only in the coldly technical apprehension of an anti-aesthetic "text."

In Kantian terms, then, de Man's work, with its dark forebodings of "prematurity," remains "immature" with respect to enlightenment. Norris, on the other hand, manifestly wishes to preserve the Enlightenment distinctions, and to move, after a decent interval to be sure, from the "distinctive mode of understanding" of the aesthetic to political argumentation. On the basis of the freedom inscribed in the aesthetic, Norris argues, one can not only criticize what is, but envision and depict what is not, or not yet (see Norris, *Spinoza and the Origins of Modern Critical Theory*). The way to ensure the effectiveness of the critique is through the rigorous working out of distinctions, working through of arguments, close readings, interrogation of premises, etc., as guarantees against "the uncritical passage from art to the other dimensions of human experience (ethical, historical, political) [by which] the aesthetic ideology has left its disastrous imprint on the past hundred years of European life and thought" (*WWWP* 22). But the question may be put to Norris: given that the passage must be made in order for freedom to be realized in the world, what, exactly, constitutes a "critical" as opposed to an "uncritical" passage, a "mature" as opposed to a "premature" synthesis? Mere delay in the passage cannot guarantee that the destination is not reached too soon; so how do we know if, in the honest effort to be enlightened, we have not in fact been fundamentalist? How can we specify the difference between the fundament of modernity and fundamentalism per se?

Negation

We seem to be approaching a maximum of theoretical confusion. I would argue, however, that we are also approaching the most definite and precise definition of the aesthetic that has yet been ventured—precisely *as* "theoretical confusion," as the undecidability between object and subject, freedom and the repressive law, critical and uncritical passages, grievous and necessary misreadings, even art and ideology.[13] While Eagleton marks the contradictions of the concept of the aesthetic, he does not consider this more radical proposition, that the aesthetic represents "the concept" *as* contradiction. Wittgenstein seems more sensitive to this possibility when he asks, "Isn't the concept with blurred edges just what we want—especially in ethics and aesthetics?" (*Philosophical Investigations* 77; see Harpham, *Getting It Right* 18-38). Want it or not, the blurred or contradictory concept is what we have "in ethics and aesthetics," for the reason that these categories, unlike, for example, the trivium and the quadrivium, or the categories of scholastic theology—categories that purported to represent real, if ideal, entities—designate kinds of mental representation whose common origin in mind guarantees a certain blurring. In the case of the aesthetic, blurring is achieved in manifold ways, from the projective act of judgment, through the permeation of faculties, on up to the large-scale delusions of ideology. On all levels, apparently crisp distinctions are blurred by misattribution, misprision, or misnaming.

The negative form of the agents of unclarity awakens a more general point, that the aesthetic is defined by negation. Recall Kant's description of judgment as not phenomenal perception, not theoretical reason, not speculative understanding, not desire, not utility, not politics—all the things judgment is "disinterested" in or "undetermined" by. The concept of the supersensible invoked by judgment has, Kant says, no peculiar

---

13. Indeed, Eagleton notes the prominence of "confusion" in the discourse of aesthetics as early as Baumgarten. " 'Confusion' here means not 'muddle' but 'fusion,' " Eagleton notes; "in their organic interpenetration, the elements of aesthetic representation resist that discrimination into discrete units which is characteristic of conceptual thought" (*IA* 15).

realm of its own; it is "unbounded, but, also inaccessible" (*CJ* 13). The judgment of taste is "based upon a concept," but one "from which nothing can be cognized in respect of the Object, because it is in itself undeterminable and useless for knowledge" (*CJ* 208). Such judgments presuppose some *a priori* principle, "although that principle is neither a cognitive principle for understanding nor a practical principle for the will, and is thus in no way determinant *a priori*" (*CJ* 32–33). Deriving from the free play of the faculties when raised to their highest powers of self-knowledge, the "unsought" or "undesigned" subjective purposiveness of the imagination cannot be discovered by reference to any set of preestablished rules. The act of judgment itself registers no intrinsic properties of the object, and even constitutes what John Sallis has called a "withdrawal from the object" (86). Responding to this pattern of insistences with his own distinctive rhetoric, Foucault asserts that, for Kant, enlightenment or *Aufklärung* "is neither a world era to which one belongs, nor an event whose signs are perceived, nor the dawning of an accomplishment. Kant defines *Aufklärung* in an almost entirely negative way, as an *Ausgang*, an 'exit,' a 'way out'" (Foucault, "What Is Enlightenment?" 34). Lyotard, too, describes the aesthetic as a strictly negative knowledge, a way out of positive determinations of all kinds, even a way out of knowledge as such: "The position of art," he writes, "is a denial of the position of discourse." [14]

In *Getting It Right: Language, Literature, and Ethics,* I sketched out the terms of a possible rapprochement between Kant and Freud in the area of ethics. Here, I want to suggest that, in the unconscious, Freud reinvented Kantian judgment. Of course, as Freud said, the unconscious knows no negation, but even this denial of negation is phrased in negative terms. Freud did not say, "The unconscious knows only positive terms," because the essential thing is not the unconscious itself but rather its relation to consciousness, a relation that is entirely negative. "The unconscious—what a strange word!" Lacan remarks. Yet "Freud didn't find a better one, and there's no need to go back on it. The disadvantage of this word is that it is negative, which allows one to assume anything at all in the world about it, plus everything else as well. Why not? To that which goes unnoticed, the word *everywhere* applies just as well as *nowhere*. . . . It is nonetheless a very precise thing" (*Television* 5). Less precise, perhaps, than many thinkers, Lacan connects Kant and Freud, the aesthetic and the unconscious, the ethical and the psychoanalytic, through his devotion to such emblems of negation as the lost object, the algorithmic bar, the reality that cannot be spoken, the unsatisfiable desire. Disinterested in time, space, or reality

14. Jean-François Lyotard, *Discours, figure* 13. See Eagleton, *Ideology of the Aesthetic* 344–65, on Theodor Adorno's aesthetics for an extended discussion of aesthetic negativity.

in general, the Freudian unconscious replays the most salient features of Kantian judgment.

Indeed, on a number of occasions, Freud discusses "judgment," making it clear that this term, although vigorously conceived as "the intellectual action which decides the choice of motor action, which puts an end to the procrastination of thinking, and which leads over from thinking to acting," cannot bypass a certain "Kantian" or "reflective" basis in negation. For judging requires a degree of independence from repression and from the pleasure principle, and such independence is achieved only with "the creation of the symbol of negation," which enables repressed material to be admitted to consciousness and thus available for judgment, on the condition that it be denied ("Negation" 216–17). If the implications of this account of judgment were permitted to rebound, we could then speculate that enlightened thought possesses something like an "unconscious" that retards a sturdy movement toward justice and morality, making all positive determinations seem premature, arrogant, ungrounded, unjust.

It might appear from this that the history of the aesthetic constitutes the chronicle of a formidable resistance to ideology. But in fact, the aesthetic seems to have hollowed out the ideologies that have appropriated it. The form of negation in liberalism, for example, is quite literal. In a famous essay in 1970, Isaiah Berlin gave the name of "negative liberty" to the fundamental liberal right of every individual to determine his or her own ends free from coercion or intrusion from the state apparatus, the right to assume the condition of the modern artifact: free, self-referring, autonomous.[15] The fascistic version of the aesthetic ideology suppresses negative liberty but promotes such forms of negative agency as restraint, discipline, passive beholding, irrationalist acceptance. Fascism might seem to invoke positive determinations, for as Philippe Lacoue-Labarthe and Jean-Luc Nancy point out, it is typically a mythology of identity; but "identity," especially racial or national identity, is constructed on the basis of what it is not—Semitic, Gypsy, Black, Swiss, Russian, Creole, and so forth, the misleadingly definite name (e.g., Aryan, "white," African American) sublimating both external affinities and internal differences.[16] For its part, postmodernism encompasses both negative liberty, in the form of a resistance to what Lyotard calls hegemonic "metanarratives," and a detached accep-

15. Isaiah Berlin, "Two Kinds of Liberty." Berlin distinguishes between "negative liberty" and "positive liberty," a conception of the ideal that underlies "morally just public movements" and frequently takes coercive forms.

16. See Philippe Lacoue-Labarthe and Jean-Luc Nancy, "The Nazi Myth." The authors analyze Nazism as a form of "combat" in which "it will be necessary to eliminate from [the world] the nonbeing or nontype par excellence, the Jew, as well as the nonbeing or lesser being of several other inferior or degenerate types, gypsies, for example" (311).

tance of appearances. The indebtedness of postmodern theory to the third Critique is most strongly marked in its trademark phrases: judgment without criteria, images without originals, depthlessness, lack of affect. Marxist thought is most distinctively aesthetic in the negative, or dialectical, form of its arguments, in which, as Eagleton says of Adorno, "the reader has no sooner registered the one-sidedness of some proposition than the opposite is immediately proposed" (IA 342). The dialectical tic is most evident, according to Tony Bennett, in the Marxist construction of aesthetics as not-science and not-ideology, so that literature's positivity "turns out to consist of a set of negatively defined relational attributes subjected to misleading ontologisation."[17] Occasional dalliances with Schiller notwithstanding, Marxism has often posed as the dialectical opposite of aesthetics; but Marxism's own negative or dialectical construction of aesthetics raises the possibility that Marxism has borrowed its essence from the historically prior discourse of art. So despite a structural negativity that might seem to render the aesthetic an unreliable accomplice in any ideological project, the aesthetic has not only proven to be infinitely useful to such projects, but seems actually to have formed them in its own non-image.

In order for the full significance of this curious fact to emerge, it must be generalized into the hypothesis that ideology itself has "aesthetic" elements. If, for example, ideology is considered simply to be "false consciousness," then it, too, is defined negatively. And if, moreover, ideology is constructed in the manner of Adorno as "an identity between concept and phenomenon" or of Althusser, as "an imaginary relation to real conditions"; or of Eagleton as "the value system that underlies our factual statements," then it draws even closer to the aesthetic, which, as we have seen, invariably begins by establishing some co-implication of subject and object. And if, following de Man, we understand ideology as "the confusion of linguistic with natural reality," we approach the aesthetic by the only slightly different route of misnaming (Resistance to Theory 11). The homologies between aesthetics and ideology help explain why, despite the fact that the aesthetic seems to offer a structural resistance to ideology, it also seems naturally or inevitably to assume ideological form. The

17. See Bennett, Outside Literature 131–33. Nor is Kant the inventor of aesthetic negativity or aesthetic misnaming. The discourse of the beautiful, to which the discourse of the aesthetic is heir, shows the same symptoms. As Diderot remarked, Plato "shows us indeed what [beauty] is not, but tells us nothing at all about what it is." Diderot, "The Beautiful" 136. The circularity of many medieval and Renaissance meditations on beauty—was the object beautiful because pleasing, or pleasing because beautiful?—suggests an intractability that would be formalized as what I have been calling misattribution when, with Baumgarten and Kant, the discourse of the beautiful mutated into that of the aesthetic.

aesthetic names both the perversion of ideology (inutility, ahistoricity, misnaming) and the inalienable essence of ideology itself, ideology in general. The appropriately dialectical conclusion is that ideology and the aesthetic constitute each other's negation, each other's misreading; both are real imaginative constructions that (somehow) effect a passage from the subject to the object, the sensory to the conceptual, the phenomenal to the moral or political. If the aesthetic is always already ideological, so, too, is ideology always already aesthetic.

The Gulf Wars

For a true measure of the stakes involved in this passage, we must, as de Man, Derrida, Norris, Habermas, Lyotard, and theoreticians without number have told us, return to Kant, attending to the following crucial passage at the beginning of the *Critique of Judgment,* in which Kant, discussing the "two kinds of concepts," those of nature and those of freedom, acknowledges that

> between the realm of the natural concept, as the sensible, and the realm of the concept of freedom, as the supersensible, there is a gulf fixed, so that it is not possible to pass from the former to the latter (by means of the theoretical employment of reason), just as if they were so many separate worlds, the first of which is powerless to exercise influence on the second: still the latter is *meant* to influence the former—that is to say, the concept of freedom is meant to actualize in the sensible world the end proposed by its laws; and nature must consequently also be capable of being regarded in such a way that in the conformity of the law of its own form it at least harmonizes with the possibility of ends to be effectuated in it according to the laws of freedom. (*CJ* 14)

Deeply influential even among those innocent of it, this passage posits a "gulf fixed" between the material or phenomenal world and our ideas about and idealizations of that world. It claims, moreover, that both "worlds" are entitled to very particular forms of autonomy, but that the supersensible realm of freedom is bound by an inner imperative to the goal of actualization, and not only actualization but the actualization of a particular end, born of freedom; and that the sensible world itself yearns toward such actualization, or at least is "capable of being regarded" as if it did. These positions represent nothing less than modernity in the grand style. But from the same premise, of a "gulf fixed" between the determined material world and the determining world of freedom, a number of anti-Enlightenment conclusions could also follow, so that, for example, a Nietzschean or postmodern gloss on the same passage would stress the incommensurability of mind and its objects and the consequent helplessness of the intellect to achieve the worldly ends for which it appears to be destined; the arbitrariness of the dictates of Reason, which seek to enforce their program on a Nature powerless to reciprocate; the dogged resistance of Nature to freedom, its sullen enslavement to fundamentalisms of all kinds.

For virtually all participants, this gulf is the center of tension and attention, separating and linking sensory experience and judgment, private and public, particular and universal, sensible and supersensible, taste and reason, feeling and understanding. For some, the gulf is there to be conquered, overleaped, claimed; while for others, the existence of the gulf preserves a necessary separation. The Kantian passage, in short, establishes the terms of a "gulf war" between a first world, represented by the governing forces of reason, freedom, and the supersensible, and another world ruled by the forces of nature. One surprising testament to the continuing vitality of the (in many ways) curiously antiquated thought of Kant is the fact that these terms apply, by a shoddy and corrupt allegory, to the 1991 Gulf War, as constructed almost overnight by the media and by the Bush administration. The alignment of American-led coalition forces with "freedom" and "supersensible" idealism as against the armies of "interest"—mercenaries, fanatics, and slaves—fielded by Saddam Hussein seems to many in the West perfectly appropriate. What might, if it had been articulated, have seemed less natural and certainly more debatable is the consequence that follows, explicitly in Kant and implicitly in American foreign policy: that the West is "*meant*" to govern Iraq, along with all the other territories on the far side of the gulf (a list that has included in recent times Chile, Cuba, Nicaragua, El Salvador, Haiti, the Philippines, Libya, Panama, Vietnam, Laos, Saudi Arabia, Angola, and more), and that everything these countries do—their primitivism, their bizarre internecine cruelties, their fanaticism, their bigotry, their misogyny, their use of outlawed weapons, their sponsorship of terrorism, their ready embrace of genocidal war aims, even the ludicrously lurid corporeality of their official discourse—suggests that they are not only structurally amenable to such governance but require it for their own good.

This was the Gulf War the Bush administration wanted to fight, not a conflict between altogether different worlds, but rather an expanded form of riot control to preserve and stabilize a world already essentially modern. It was such a world that was projected by President Bush in a letter to Saddam Hussein dated January 9, 1991, one week before the "liberation of

Kuwait" was to begin, a letter that began, "We stand today at the brink of war between Iraq and the world" (see Sifry and Cerf, 178; hereafter *GWR*). Almost like Alice stepping through the looking-glass, Iraq had departed from "the world," from the postcolonial "family of nations," by refusing the passive role of the "sensible," refusing to be either obediently postcolonial or post–cold war. The invasion of Kuwait had toppled the old world order, whose boundaries had been drawn by the British, and deferred the realization of the "new world order" first announced in early September 1990. As President Bush put the matter in an address to the nation and/or the world on 16 January 1991, just before the bombs began to fall, it was to be "a new world order, a world where the rule of law, not the law of the jungle, governs the conduct of nations" (*GWR* 313). With the collapse of the Second World, President Bush appeared determined both to relegate Iraq, an erstwhile junior partner in the First World, to the "jungle" of the Third World, and then to eliminate that World, so there would be simply one, resolutely modern and enlightened, world, in which fundamentalism and ethnocentrism would simply have vanished in the course of the inexorable evolutionary advance of *Homo Sapiens* and the legitimate destiny of freedom, a world in which nature would submit to the rule of freedom as the law.[18]

The complex role of "freedom" in American policy, particularly in the cold war and since, cannot be overestimated and must not be misconstrued. The American sense of freedom has, of course, been shaped by many hands, including Locke, Hobbes, Paine, Madison, Jefferson, Mill, Stowe, Lincoln, Frederick Douglass, Wilson, Roosevelt, King, and others; but even granting historical and conceptual overdetermination, it is possible to isolate a distinctively Kantian strain, precisely because that strain runs beneath, or through, many of the others. In the instance of the Gulf War, freedom functioned in various ways. First, the invasion of Kuwait was treated not as the issue of a historical process but as a fresh and free-standing event that could be brought under no concept, made to serve no end (of the United States), a virtual Kantian artifact. Second, the invasion was deplored as a violation of the "freedom" hitherto enjoyed by the Kuwaitis. And third, the invasion was held to inaugurate a fully warranted progression from tyranny toward the worldly realization, or rerealization,

18. The position of Iraq with respect to the enumerated worlds is far from clear. For while most of the people lead "Third World" lives, and while, for a time, Iraq had close relations with the Soviet Union, the ideology of Saddam Hussein's Baath party is, as Elie Kedourie notes, an amalgam of discredited Western ideas—the less moderate statements of Nietzsche, the racism of H. S. Chamberlain and Alfred Rosenberg, the concept of state socialism, and exclusive nationalism. See Kedourie, *Arab Political Memoirs and Other Studies*.

of freedom, in which the heroes were the liberal project pursuers of the West, seeking redemption from ancient syndromes, and the villains were so illiberal as to be virtually non-narratable. The predominance of freedom as a rationale for policy also helps explain the war's most mystifying nonevent, the militarily odd decision not to pursue the remnants of the Iraqi military who were racing back to Baghdad after their defeat. A policy based on the freedom of Saudi Arabia or Kuwait could, with some ingenuity, or disingenuity, help explain the need for military intervention to an American public that has never believed in the worthiness of mere "interest" or "need." But despite a profound administration desire to see Saddam Hussein deposed, eliminated, removed, freedom could not sponsor an invasion of Iraq after the "liberation of Kuwait" had been accomplished. To everyone's amazement, the public rationale for the war—the freedom of Kuwait, rather than the overthrow of Hussein or even the destruction of his nuclear and chemical capacities—turns out to have been the functional rationale.

Freedom by itself is inadequate as a rationale for policy, and for what von Clausewitz calls its "continuation by other means," war, because while it seeks "actualization in the sensible world," it is powerless to specify positive ends: predicated on negation, it can be no more than the unconscious of policy. The proper telos of all cognition, according to Kant, is the exercise of practical reason, or ethics; and while judgment enables and points toward ethics, it cannot tell one how to behave. In order to be effective as action, freedom must suffer contradiction, must succumb to temptation, must be misread, perverted, corrupted, polluted with practical politics and worldly interest, so that it can acquire a countenance, or leave an enlightening trace in the pragmatics that it sponsors. Without such pollution, freedom, condemned to a virginal indeterminacy, is vulnerable to appropriation by precisely those interests least concerned with freedom, interests in need of a surrogate. Freedom unpolluted—or, more accurately, unrealized—is as indifferent to freedom as any fundamentalism.

The Gulf War provides eloquent testimony to the costs of purity. By failing to work out a positive program for peace, by deploying its armed forces with a wholly negative mission, first of "defense" and "security and stability in the region," and then of "the liberation of Kuwait," with the presumption that if obstructions were removed the peoples of the Gulf would naturally assume a free and indeterminate (i.e., pro-West) accord, the United States has succeeded in inflicting unpublicized but horrifying and militarily unnecessary misery on the Iraqi people, leaving them with less power in every sense than they had before the war; it has stalled, but also virtually guaranteed, imminent additional devastation to the Kurds, who thought they had been promised freedom in one sense and now find themselves free (i.e., cut loose) in quite another; it has redrawn boundaries that had been drawn in an utterly arbitrary and historically insensitive way in the first place; and it has restored a politically regressive monarchy in Kuwait—all while strengthening Saddam Hussein's political position within Iraq.

I am arguing that the ideological construction of the Gulf War betrays, in both senses of that term, the conceptual resources of Kant's critical philosophy. But I want, too, to assert that Hussein's Iraq has been portrayed in the West as a signal instance of what amounts to the "aesthetic ideology," its invasion of Kuwait an example of a premature or uncritical passage from one domain to another, or the seizure of power by those with no legitimate claim to it—while the West has depicted itself as the rightful executive of the laws of freedom that inform a properly enlightened aesthetic judgment, one that respected boundaries. Confused and destructive as it was, the Gulf War replayed in a different medium the intricate meditations of philosophers as they sought patiently to draw lines in the sand demarcating the realm of ideology from that of freedom. Constructed as an intra-aesthetic conflict between the pure form and its ideological corruption, the war confirmed Walter Benjamin's assertion that "all efforts to render politics aesthetic culminate in one thing: war" ("The Work of Art in the Age of Mechanical Reproduction" 241). Just as inevitable, I would argue, were the consequences of the fetishization of an inarticulate freedom, which, like Billy Budd, could only respond to challenge with violence. For the one-sided ferocity of the Gulf War represents not just the continuation of politics, nor even its failure, but also a powerlessness to specify or even to imagine positive political projects involving other nations, because such projects conflict with a version of modernity founded in, and crippled by, freedom as an absolute, an inviolable dogma: People should be (because they are already essentially) free. The rubble of Baghdad allegorizes—again, shoddily—Western rage at conceptual or ideological impotence, at its own incapacity to bring a nonmodern culture to acknowledge the superiority of the modern, the inability of smart bombs to impart enlightenment to their targets.

Such an inability implies another gulf, and another Gulf War which shadowed the first. While universal "freedom" named the justice of the American cause, it could not justify the inevitable loss of American lives because it could not be made coherent. To shepherd a rogue fragment of the world back into line so that the world could resume being what it already is, free, is not a cause Americans readily understand, much less would choose to die for. Only a palpable threat from some *other* "world," some danger to the American "way of life" or to "essential values," could make military intervention not just comprehensible but acceptable or necessary. A bridge had to be constructed, then, from freedom as a global value to freedom as a specifically American way of life. This transition was articulated with matchless efficiency by "Hollywood Huddleston, marine lance corporal" in a comment somehow obtained by President Bush and quoted in the war's eve speech: "Let's free these people so we can go home and be free again" (GWR 314). In the same speech, Bush himself attempted the same rhetorically tricky transition by speaking of the new world order as a universal and disinterested "rule of law," and then immediately opposing this global norm to a rival law, the "law of the jungle" that regulated, and failed to regulate, the desert nation of Iraq. The necessity for such a transition also drove what commentators called "the Hitler analogy" by which the Bush administration analogized from one genocidal despot seeking world domination to another. In geopolitical terms, the Hitler analogy suggests not so much a weak seam in the fabric of a free world as a more profound conflict between the self-proclaimed enlightened world and its other, a world that had rejected the primacy of the "laws of freedom" as it had rejected the colonial and neocolonial rulers who had imposed them, a world dogmatically unenlightened, seeking not to advance to new plateaus of reason but to return to some pure and sacred origin, a world that could not be brought to conceive itself as "meant to be governed" by laws alien to their interests and values, a world that in all probability would concur with Theodor Adorno and Max Horkheimer's conception of enlightenment in general as "mass deception."

Between these two gulfs—between the-modern-world-and-*its*-other, and the-modern-world-and-its-*other*—there is a gulf fixed, and the question is whether the laws of freedom, the laws implied in aesthetic judgment and realized in practical reason, are meant to govern the whole world or just the First World. If the world is not fundamentally modern or becoming modern, if the earth contains several "worlds"—a prospect raised by Kant, as we have seen—then "freedom" will necessarily be subject to recoding as advantage. Thus, from the global point of view that modernity would claim for its own, the dominance of interest over shared values would make wars highly probable. Even more injurious to our sense of "national security," wars could not claim the kind of moral legitimacy and evolutionary sanction with which the United States has historically been eager to invest them. This Clausewitzian recognition might encourage a laudable principle of candor, for if war has no transcendental rationale, then policy makers might feel themselves obliged to articulate and justify the worldly means and ends attending the translation of "freedom" into a positive practical program. But such candor would itself imply that a diacritical and politicized freedom seeking its own advantage may, without self-betrayal, harden itself into belligerence, take up a shield, become a storm, binding, and perhaps strategically blinding, itself to interests for which it serves as surrogate. In coming to countenance, freedom, the fundament of cosmopolitan enlightenment, assumes—again, from the global point of view—the form of an ethnocentrism, a "law of the jungle." The very prestige that modernity accords to freedom as a mark of its own superiority to the jungle bespeaks a localism modernity claims to transcend. For it is only in a modern world, or in that fraction of the world conscious of its modernity, that freedom as such is an unquestionable good. But what the Gulf War—or, for that matter, any war—testifies is that modernity does not blanket the globe, and that, as a consequence, fundamental values clash in the form of fundamentalisms.

So while it might appear to be enlightened simply to assert that the globe contains many worlds, that values are variable and local rather than universal and constant, and that policy ought to reflect this simple fact, such an assertion does little to mitigate the threat of war. Moreover, in the present instance, the supposed beneficiary of such wise multicultural counsel does not appear to agree. Listen to Tariq Aziz, Iraq's foreign minister, speaking on January 9, 1991: "Concerning the new world order, or the international world order, I said I have no problem with that order. And we would love to be partners in that order. But that order has to be implemented justly, and in all cases, not using that order in a single manner, in a selective manner, impose it on a certain case . . . and neglect the other issues and not show sincerity and seriousness about implementing it on other issues" (*GWR* 174). The complaint is not that the new world order is too disrespectful of difference but that it is too partial, too limited, too ethnocentric—in a word, insufficiently modern—to permit Iraq to join. The utterances of Aziz, and of Hussein himself, during the period before the war invoke precisely the same principles and values as those intoned by President Bush: peace, stability, security, defense, justice, common understanding, and liberty.[19] Iraq, it appears from the utterances of its officials, believes in enlightenment, in justice as fairness, in global citizenship as a humane and open conversation between equals. It really is a small world.

The universal acceptability of "freedom" and its collateral terms suggests

19. All these terms are taken from the comments of Saddam Hussein in the now-famous conversation with U. S. Ambassador April Glaspie on July 25, 1990. See Sifry and Cerf, *GWR* 122-33.

both that the rhetoric, at least, of modernity may indeed have blanketed the globe, but also that this rhetoric is so empty as to accommodate any practices. The enlightenment-value, as it were, of "freedom" is precisely zero. Only in alloys with force or interest can freedom serve to promote modernity, and even then the application of principle to instance remains subject to the negations and misattributions that structure any act of judgment. It is difficult to know exactly how to feel about this fact as a general proposition. Nevertheless, two kinds of commitment recommend themselves to policy makers as ways of hedging some of the more extreme deformations that befall the cause of freedom. First, positive goals as well as negative liberties must be specified so that the relevant community can judge whether these goals would serve to advance the particular form of freedom it prizes as well as the ends it actively seeks. The necessity of a determining "fundamentalist moment" that is at once the goal and the negation of freedom must be accepted, and accepted as nontragic. Second, the value of freedom, and of modernity itself, must be recognized as subject to challenge from other fundamental principles, a challenge not necessarily resolvable by what Habermas calls "the unforced force of the better argument."

By themselves, of course, these commitments, even if adopted immediately and wholeheartedly by every human being on earth, do nothing to ensure peace. On the contrary, they presuppose an undecidability about which gulf we are or ought to be negotiating, or about whether the leader of the "free world" is by rights the leader of the whole world, or whether he is merely the head of one (unusually powerful) nation among many, a nation that, like some others, has chosen to call itself "free." And this undecidability implies that the gulf war may be as unwinnable in the political and military senses as it has proven to be in the philosophical.

To a sentimentalist like me, the simple academic phrase "history and the limits of interpretation" summons up a golden memory of the early seventies, when the American academy was just discovering Continental criticism and theory. Then, just as the institution of literary criticism was beginning the self-reformation that would eventuate in the glorious if temporary tyranny over the humanities by English departments, which represented themselves as the professional home of interpretation as such, some adventuresome historians proposed that history was just a form of literature. In an early instance of what deans everywhere would soon cry up as "interdisciplinarity," these scholars, chief among whom was Hayden White, argued that narrative forms and rhetorical tropes determined the meanings of historical narratives. Paradoxically, White argued, history became modern and "objective" when it rejected the chronicle form in favor of the narrative method. Many understood from White's arguments that historians were now claiming that history was a created thing like fiction, that it came in "literary" genres, and was therefore properly subject to the kind of interpretation that constituted literary criticism. Thus—we literary types thought—was History, the very home of naive facticity, humbled before an all-conquering and newly sophisticated English.

This account is undoubtedly partial. At the time I'm referring to, I was doing graduate work in the department of English at UCLA, just a few steps away from the history department where White was teaching. Whatever disciplinary pride I may have felt was, however, tempered by a rankling envy of the excitement felt by White's students, an excitement that greatly exceeded in intensity and duration the more sober satisfactions available in the pre-theoretical, indeed virtually prehistoric, department in which I was obscurely toiling. (There, the fundamental unit of criticism seemed to be the anecdote, especially the L.A. anecdote about Henry James's discomfiture in a Santa Monica hotel, the immense cache of gin bottles discovered near Fitzgerald's house after he died, the sensational appearance of Marianne Moore in the Polo Lounge, etc.) Clearly, White's revelation constituted an extraordinary incident in the history of History. If it was paradoxical that the writing of history became modern and objective at the moment it became narrative, it was even more paradoxical that the study of history became thoroughly contemporary and up-to-date by defining itself as a branch of literature.

It was also, if only we knew it, an extraordinary opportunity for literary studies to come to some fresh understanding of its own activities in light of this expression of mutual interest on the part of some historians. Literary criticism could have taken the opportunity then and there to "historicize" itself, to shed its image as the marginal, effeminate, elitist cultivation of the nonexistent and to assume a more robust profile as history's instruction manual, the key to the treasure of the real. At the time, however, the attention of literary studies was engaged elsewhere. Distracted by the powerful new tools placed at its disposal by Continental thinking, English spurned the offer of a rapprochement from History. Not that all historians were beating down our doors begging to be initiated into the mysteries of metaphor and metonymy. While some young bloods, increasingly sensitive to the difficulty of defending traditional notions of truth or referential adequacy, and fearful that, in the incipient postmodern era, history was about to become yesterday's headlines, may have sought to make a "literary turn" on the model of the "linguistic turn" effected a few years earlier by philosophy—another fine moment for English—others were indifferent. Indeed, how eager could mature, thoroughly competent historians have been to take on a whole new set of problems, especially somebody else's? It must have seemed to most established historians as attractive a proposition as marrying someone with three troubled adolescents. In fact, White's own career as a cause célèbre in English departments and an eventual professor of the "history of consciousness"—as opposed to the history of events—suggests that one of the costs of his discovery was that he had to stop calling himself a historian. I am certain that, in some faculty club somewhere, a few emeriti are asking each other whatever happened to young White, that promising late-medievalist.

In retrospect, the hesitation many historians felt about embracing literature and literary studies looks wiser and wiser. For literary criticism was, at this time, becoming strikingly indifferent to literature and more concerned with itself. The discipline, as the elders may recall, was then leaving an era when formalist concerns dominated the agenda of literary studies, and entering an era when the reader, that ambitious agency of interpretation, would rule. Through the insistent brilliance of Stanley Fish and other "reader-response" critics, the reader was installed at the very center of literary criticism, not as the subject of the literary experience, but as the object of interest itself. It was also during this heady time that metaphoricity became the essence of literality, the text squeezed out the world, and criticism began to conceive of itself as a practice of "strong misreading," an improvisatory, spontaneous, and "creative" activity. This last notion, the free invention of Geoffrey Hartman, represents the furthest extension of interpretation's will to power, a warrant for thinking of interpretation as a fine art. Under this dispensation, interpreters felt emboldened to produce inspired readings that, regardless of their programmed fidelity to a few fixed ideas, often made a very persuasive appearance of being unconstrained by traditional scholarly protocols. "Wild" deconstruction as practiced occasionally by Derrida and more frequently by some of his students and colleagues, became the gold standard of contemporary criticism.

This, then, was the sort of marriage history might have gotten itself into. How or why it was averted on the side of history, I cannot say with authority. But it is interesting to note that during the eighties, "history" became the slogan of a disciplinary reaction within literary studies to deconstruction, reader-response theory, and to Continental philosophizing generally. In general, we can say, when literary criticism becomes uneasy or embarrassed about the fecklessness, irresponsibility, and gratuitousness of interpretation, it turns, as to a powerful father, to history. Inspired, perhaps, by the electrifying presence of Michel Foucault, a few scholars at UC Berkeley founded the journal *Representations* as a counter-Derridean American movement dedicated to promoting the "new historicism" as practiced by Stephen Greenblatt, Walter Benn Michaels, Catherine Gallagher, Michael Rogin, and others. With the arrival at UC Irvine of Derrida, J. Hillis Miller, Jean-François Lyotard, and others, the dispute became a California civil war of academe, with the Historians of the North arrayed against the Postmoderns of the South. I'm simplifying, of course, but so did many at the time. In any event the whole episode is perhaps too recent to be interesting as history, but what was, and remains, relatively unexplored is the extent to which the New Historicism defined itself not just as antipostmodern or even antiliterary in the traditional canonical sense, but specifically as anti-interpretation.

While New Historicists sometimes foregrounded their own motives or intentions, and sometimes adverted to their own intensely interesting inner lives and admirable political commitments, they did not do so in order to glory in the contingency of their interpretations. "The critic's role," reads the polemical introduction to an anthology called *The New Historicism*, "is to dismantle the dichotomy of the economic and the noneconomic, to show that the most purportedly disinterested and self-sacrificing practices, including art, aim to maximize material or symbolic profit.

Such a critic," the editor continues, "would not conduct symptomatic readings—so called for their focus on traces, margins, things left unsaid, and other tell-tale signs of all that a text represses" (Veeser xiv). The New Historicist does not, in other words, patiently scrutinize a privileged text, humbly seeking to divine its innermost meaning; he does not—to deploy the central deconstructive term—*read*. The work of New Historicists is described instead in metaphors of virile resistance to authority. Such critics, it is claimed, "challenge conventional assumptions"; they "mingle disparate periods and upset the calculus of Left and Right politics" (Veeser xv). And they do all this without recourse to anything as piffling as interpretation, in this above all remaining faithful to the presumed evidentiary force of history itself.

For interpretation, as I will shortly argue at greater length, is the disease of which "symptomatic readings" are the symptom. When Greenblatt modified his call for a "New Historicism" to a call for "Cultural Poetics," he solidified a growing antagonism to the notion of interpretation. For while "history" may be thought of as an accretion of interpretations, "poetics" is a more strictly formalist undertaking. This was, indeed, White's point, that history was a kind of poetics, the meaning of historical texts determined "unconsciously" by a system of tropes. As Louis Montrose, a New Historicist mole operating on the southern flank of southern California at UC San Diego, put it, "implicit in [cultural poetics] is a conviction that formal and historical concerns are not opposed but rather are inseparable" (17).

The inseparability of formal and historical concerns presupposed the separability of historical and interpretive concerns. The accounts given by New Historicists of both their activity and the object of their interest confirm this distinction. No longer, they say, are they interested in autonomous literary texts, a separate domain of art; rather, they see literary and nonliterary texts, or discourses, circulating freely in a gigantic cultural marketplace where exchange and negotiation are the ruling principles. Not pure art, but impure culture. And, as a corollary, not the interpretation of a freestanding artifact, but rather the assembling of cultural collages, the cultivation of marginal events, the refusal of grand narratives and deep readings. And not, definitively, the hermeneutical homage to great monuments and sublime genius, but rather a rivalry that contests the very concepts of the Great Writer and canonical literature. The constructive business of the historicist critic is not to contribute a gloss, produce the inner meaning of a text, translate its mysteries into plain English, or mediate between absent author and present audience, but to retrieve, arrange, and describe phenomena that are themselves unstable, partial, heterogeneous—in a word, uninterpretable. Addicted to action verbs, New

Historicists avoid the very word *interpretation,* which seems, from their point of view, insufficiently ballsy, especially by comparison to the others on the preferred list, a partial inventory of which is contained in Montrose's pronouncement that "the project of a new socio-historical criticism is . . . to analyze the interplay of culture-specific discursive practices. . . . By such means, versions of the Real, of History, are instantiated, deployed, reproduced; and by such means, they may also be appropriated, contested, transformed" (23).

Formal and historical concerns are inseparable because, for New Historicism, the job of "analysis" is over when the form of events, of historical sequences and assemblages, is determined. Once one has traced or renegotiated the paths of cultural exchange, the "meaning" is manifest and requires no further work to divine; or, perhaps, the meaning just *is* those paths of circulation. It is thus partially as an escape from interpretation, with its contingency and arbitrariness, its indebtedness to the individual interpreter, and its incongruous combination of passivity and will-to-power hubris, that the New Historicism defined itself. I am not, of course, saying that "history" and "interpretation" are in fact mutually exclusive, for both terms are highly labile and can designate a range of referents. I am simply pointing out that these terms were, in this particular setting, defined as an opposition. One mark of this opposition is surely the interest of history-minded critics in events that seemed to be formed, but to resist meaning, as in a sentence from Gertrude Stein: "A dog that you have never had has sighed." About this sentence, Fredric Jameson comments that it is "transparent on a level of pure sentence formation. : . . . But I would hesitate to claim that it has a meaning, and indeed Gertrude Stein is a particularly good example of a writer whose characteristic materials—household odds and ends, string, boxes, lettuce leaves, cushions, buttons—disarm modern criticism in that they neither solicit visual perception nor haunt the mind with the symbolic investment of depth psychology" ("Metacommentary" 4; hereafter M). Jameson finds the uninterpretability of Stein both an instance of a particular Modernist style and a bracing affirmation of a contemporary circumstance in which, as he begins his brilliant 1971 essay "Metacommentary" by saying, "exegesis, interpretation, commentary have fallen into disrepute" (3). To many, he reported there, interpretation had become identified with allegory as two modes whose obsolescence could no longer be denied.

The scandal of such a pronouncement to a profession that sometimes carried professional piety to the point of tracing its roots back to biblical exegesis or midrash, a profession that thought of itself as a postreligious "interpretive community" (one that, moreover, studied interpretive communities) can hardly be overestimated. But as Jameson lays out the case, the scandal had been there for some time, at least since the advent of literary Modernism, and had simply gone unrecognized by a discipline that had grown up interpreting, blithely unaware that it was outdated at birth, hopelessly premodern, already surpassed by the art that was contemporary with it, though the need to understand that art was supposed to constitute the future of the profession. The situation, he says, had only been irritated to the point of inescapability in recent years, when a hostility to interpretation as such drove both postmodern art and poststructuralist theory. But the profession of literary interpretation, Jameson implies, had been running on fumes since the beginning. The startling possibility raised by this argument is that interpretation as currently practiced is not a perennially incomplete project of infinite dimension, but a historically delimited thing. The anxious perplexity before the radiant obscurity of the object, the restless grasping after its meaning, the translation of aesthetic form into language—these are not permanent features of our interaction with art, but rather conditioned responses expressive of a particular situation. Interpretation proceeds, Jameson says, from an "ontological inferiority complex" that results in the foreclosure of the plenitude of sensation in favor of the pursuit of the disappearing traces of an ultimately final reading—a reading that, like the endlessly interpretable Godot, never comes. Thus Jameson finds himself considering not the nature of interpretation but the need for it in a particular historical climate, the keen appetite for an activity he characterizes as strange and unnatural, the contorted enthusiasm with which a culture can will itself into an "overemphasis on knowledge." This kind of historically informed reflection on interpretation itself is what he calls "metacommentary," or "genuine interpretation," the aim of which is, he says, to direct attention *away* from interpretation as such and "back to history itself" (M 5).

There is no doubt that, for Jameson, the terms *history* and *interpretation* are highly stressed, each dragging long trains behind it. Interpretation seems to be associated with the bourgeois ego, with strictly individual categories of thought and action, and consequently with ideologically generated delusions of autonomy. Whenever Jameson broaches the topic of individual subjectivity—the Jamesonian equivalent of private property for an older Marxist tradition—we get a sensation of darkness visible, as the discourse becomes inflected with religious or pararreligious affects. When he speaks contemptuously of "my *private* interpretation of an *individual* text," the target is actually the pleasure principle of the sovereign ego, and the animus is not just epistemological but moral. Whatever negates, frustrates, exceeds, or otherwise scourges the sovereign ego, on the other hand, generally wins Jameson's approval.

History entails interpretation. When we ask why we are condemned to interpret despite our "increasing repugnance" for the task, we ultimately arrive, Jameson says, at the fact that History has somehow precluded a direct apprehension of meaning, forcing us to undergo a middle passage through form. Formalism is thus "the basic mode of interpretation of those who refuse interpretation" (M 7). Notice that Jameson's historicism does not lead him to reject interpretation, only to conceive of it in a limited way as a function necessary for the time being.

The most spatial of thinkers—he declared, as a wit once said, the arrival of a new era in global capitalism when he found himself at an MLA convention in Los Angeles, unable to navigate the ins and outs of his hotel—Jameson is strongly disposed in favor of interpretable forms. But the point to be emphasized is that, according to him, *only* form is interpretable, and we should call all that is interpretable "form." Content, he argues, *"is itself already essentially and immediately meaningful,"* and need only be "restored" to a fallen world that will receive it as a token of a utopian future. The ultimate goal of interpretation—which should more properly be called hermeneutics inasmuch as the idea is not the maximal unfolding of semiotic potential as the recovery of a virtually sacred moment of origin—is, then, to get to this point where the original message or experience that had been obscured or dissimulated by some censoring mechanism, which he calls generically History, is laid bare. A proper metacommentary will, then, constitute not a rendering of the meaning of the content, which would be strictly coals to Newcastle, but rather "an explanation why the content was so distorted," a description of the mechanism of censorship itself, and an account of why it was necessary to protect people from an unmediated or undistorted experience—an account, ultimately, of the activity of History in transforming Content into Form (M 14). History is, for Jameson, the origin of interpretation inasmuch as it creates Form, and the end of interpretation in that, when you understand Form, you understand the workings of History. At this point, History and Interpretation seem to have entered into a kind of partnership; but the dominance of History suggests a general law about such marriages, that whenever you have a concordat between forces that had been or might be opposed, one of them has, perhaps covertly, swallowed the other.

Ten years later, in *The Political Unconscious* (1981), Jameson elaborated on his account of interpretation, making it more complex and apparently more substantial. The "aesthetic" text is, he argues, an ideological structure that converts social contradictions, the essentially antagonistic form of class relations, into antinomies, incompatible structures between which the individual protagonist must choose. Thus, in a work of art, the mighty but unrepresentable processes of class struggle are converted into a structure that foregrounds a moment of individual decision: politics shrinks into ethics. According to the "ideology of form," processes that are properly collective, antagonistic, and dynamic must be represented in terms that are individualistic and conducing to resolution and finally stasis. The task of interpretation is to try to thaw the frozen aesthetic form, and to restore the dynamism—the political struggles of class antagonisms—of history. The whole complex scenario casts Politics in the role of Sleeping Beauty, lovely under glass, in a kind of aestheticized coma. The Marxist interpreter is the rescuer-prince, hacking his way through the tangled vines that had grown up around the castle, finally reaching the princess—the artifact as woman—and bestowing the kiss that enables her to awaken and enter into her majority. The interpreter liberates (to continue this perhaps inexact decoding of Jameson's Ur-myth) the voice of the people and the life of the body, so that the royal tableau can be seen in the context of a total social situation involving various levels of society from nobility on down to servants and peasants. Restored to life, Princess Politics rides off with Prince Interpretation to begin a new but uneventful life in the suburbs as Mr. and Mrs. Self-Evident Content.

The point is that, ramify it how he will, Jameson once again envisions an end to interpretation in a moment when the movements of history (or politics; Jameson does not always distinguish clearly between them) are disclosed, and the reader confronts a transparent text. Interpretation is self-abolishing; its triumph is its extinction. This position was understood intuitively by literary scholars (or that minority who actually worked their way through Jameson's text) as a shot across the bow. They knew that an end to interpretation was an end to careers, to an entire way of life; and they had always, officially at least, promoted an elusive principle of "excess" in the literary work as a warrant for a literally inexhaustible activity of interpretation, to which no turn of the historical screw could ever bring an end. This is why, before either Jameson or the New Historicism, literary critics had been careful to circumscribe the historical approach by describing it as a useful background, but one that always risked imposing a reductive and falsifying uniformity on the various products of an era. They sought, in other words, to circumscribe history in the same way Jameson had circumscribed interpretation. And in the same terms: history was, they said, passive, preliminary, a valuable approach but not the thing itself. History threatened the notion of the author's history-transcending genius, and it was, in the end, the presumption of the infinitude of literary genius that necessitated the issuance of a standing search warrant for more and more interpretations.

And *this* is why, when a few imaginative historians began, a generation ago, to conceive of history as "narrative," "trope," "genre," or "fictive structure," there was general jubilation among literary critics at the prospect not exactly of a marriage, but a capitulation.

History offers another kind of affront to the institution of interpretation. Especially as Jameson describes it, history is the site of collective processes, and interpretation is not. Why is it that the very idea of a collective interpretation seems impossible? We can imagine collective understandings, collective beliefs, collective values. These we call "ideology." But if we do not call ideology an "interpretation," the reason must be that Jameson is in this respect right, that our understanding of interpretation remains stubbornly individualistic. Interpretation is individualistic, too, in its construction of the material it interprets. The biblical tradition of hermeneutics is exemplary in this respect, beginning with the stipulation that the disparate scriptural manuscripts constitute the direct utterance of the immense but unified and self-consistent mind of God—this being the necessary condition for interpreters to get to work. The important precursor texts of the modern practice of interpretation reassert what might be called the Protestant bias of interpretation. Schliermacher, to name only one such precursor, stipulates that the task of the interpreter is to reconstruct from the imperfect representations of the text the subjectivity of the author. Interpretation is plural only in the number of meanings that might be extracted from a given text. For each given interpretation, an individual interpreter confronts, interacts with, converses with, the work of an individual creator.

The true consequences of this banal formulation have, I believe, never been adequately examined. When we say that literary interpretation as we know it is constituted as a meeting of two individual minds, we make tacit but inescapable assumptions about the kind of agency that produced the text. What is the text-producing literary mind? How do—how must—we understand the subjectivity responsible for an interpretable text? It is, to be sure, a mind situated in the concrete materialities—as well as the abstract ideologies or conceptualities—of history. But the primary fact, the one that legitimates interpretation, is that the text is the product of an intending agency. This, I take it, is the point of Walter Benn Michaels's and Stephen Knapp's demonstration in the notorious 1980 article called "Against Theory," that a poem produced by accidental agency such as a receding ocean wave leaving a poetic stanza on the sand is just uninterpretable—because, they claim, it is not even language at all. But the real point of this argument lies deeper. Conscious purposiveness is clearly not enough to create an interpretable text. A four-year-old child could, after all, intend to write the words of William Carlos Williams's "Red Wheel Barrow," and an ape could intend to bang on the keyboard in a way that, as it happened, produced "Let me not to the marriage of true minds admit impediments." For all I know, perhaps even this very discourse contains some profundity. But if it does—that is, if it is interpreted that way—it will be because some reader attributed that profundity to me and my agency, not to the accidents attending mere inarticulateness or ineptitude. And if one of my readers should feel that some statement "accidentally" expressed a profound insight despite my personal obtuseness, what he would really be feeling is that if *he* wrote those words, they would be profound. It is not the words or the marks themselves that stimulate and license interpretation, but the presumption that, behind the words or marks, there is something more, a complex mental state that remains imperfectly rendered by the surface features of the text itself.

We are now in the vicinity of the "excessive" quality attributed to "great" literature. The most provocative recent text I know of to take up this traditional argument is Knapp's *Literary Interest,* which contends that subjects treated in literature are invested with a host of associations that have, from a strictly pragmatic or rational point of view, nothing to do with them. Thus the issue of regicide as treated in *Macbeth* is tangled up with the particulars of the Macbeth family romance, witch's prophecies, the ambulation of Burnam Wood, the rivalry between the man who reigns and the man whose sons reign, the strangely detachable sexuality of Lady Macbeth, the manly dread of dying without issue, the dynamics of guilt and confession, the upshot of cesarean birth, and so on. None of these affectively charged issues is necessarily connected to regicide, but regicide in *Macbeth* cannot get quit of them to stand alone. Nor, for that matter, can the particular figures strutting and fretting on the stage get quit of the fact that, for the reader, their actions raise an issue, regicide, that is much more capacious and resonant in a world-historical sense than they themselves could comprehend. Let these characters stand for the mind of the author, so that we can say, in general, that interpretable things are in some ways unaware of themselves. Interpretable texts are, we necessarily presume, produced by a mind (immured in a body, with emotions, affects, drives; and embedded in history, the moment, the family, the class, etc.) whose fullness exceeds its conscious intentions or field of immediate awareness. (This, incidentally, is why canny and critically sophisticated postmodern literature seems to paralyze interpretation: it saturates the field of the conscious and drains the field of the unconscious.) To "interpret," I claim, is to attend to the *inadequacy* of the surface features of the text as an expression of the mind of the author. Interpreting *Macbeth,* we presume, whether we know it or not, that there were more things in Shakespeare's mind than even *Macbeth* could express, things that Shakespeare *intended unintentionally,* things that only an interpretation could determine.

Note now a further entailment of the concept of interpretation, that, like the mind that produced it, the text itself is "deep." The surface or manifest level of meaning could be produced by the agency of a child, an ape, or Gertrude Stein; but the deeper, latent level of meaning bespeaks something else. As Jameson says of modern literature *tout court,* the interpretable text has an "unconscious," a dimension of itself filled with unexpressed meaning. This recognition provokes a historical hypothesis Jameson does not consider, that the very idea of interpretation arises alongside the notion of an unconscious. The modern reflection on the nature of interpretation appears at just about the time—broadly, the post-Enlightenment Romantic period—that the picture of the mind takes on a certain chiaroscuro quality. Freud's work was critical in confirming the substantiality of the unconscious, but it was equally critical in conferring a certain status on the activity of interpretation as a necessary methodology for literary and other kinds of texts. In the climate of Freud, literary modernism, the unconscious, and interpretation form a Triple Alliance. Did interpretation as a self-conscious professional activity exist before the general dissemination of Freud? Did it exist at all in its fully developed, or as I would now put it, "psychoanalytic" mode, in which the object is the articulation of elusive subsurface strata of meaning, of intentions beneath intentions, before culture became generally receptive to the idea of the unconscious and the "deep" subject?

I am not claiming that Freud had a direct exemplary effect. It is possible to interpret without approving of or even knowing directly about Freud. What I am arguing is that sustained thinking about modern literary interpretation will very likely "spontaneously" discover the unconscious simply through a reflection on its own procedures and assumptions. Nor am I trying to deny a certain continuity between modern interpretation and earlier practices of exegesis. These earlier practices proceed, however, according to certain established protocols that fix or limit the final result in a way not sanctioned by modern interpretation. Nor, finally, am I trying to minimize the legacies of those other great "initiators of discursive practices," as Foucault describes Marx and Nietzsche. But, as we have already seen, the heirs of Marx are characteristically uncomfortable with the act of interpretation as it has come to be practiced. And while Nietzsche, in the late texts *On the Genealogy of Morals* and (some sections of) *The Will to Power,* described interpretation as an act of violence, a willfully repressive smoothing over of contradictions or inconsistencies, it was Freud who actually dramatized this truth of interpretation. The claim for the primacy of Freud in this respect is, if not altogether demonstrable, at least makeable.

Freud was, of course, the only one of the three to mount extended interpretations of literary and artistic works. His reading of *Oedipus the King* as an allegory of a primitive condition of mental development, one far beneath or anterior to the entire concept of canonical art that had seemed for centuries to be the work's only proper context, was a dazzling act of intellectual penetration that set a standard of conviction, provocation, and sheer ambition that criticism does not often attain. But I believe that Freud's contribution to interpretation becomes decisive only in the case studies. For it is here, in scenes of incomparable novelistic drama (scenes that have proven to be damaging to his reputation as a therapist and scientist), that Freud's brilliance truly illuminates, in a way Nietzsche never did, the Nietzschean character of interpretation. When Freud insists to Dora that he possesses the only possible explanation of her mysterious cough in her disavowed desire for oral sex with Herr K., or when he tells the Wolf-man what he must have seen—a "primal scene" involving parental coitus *a tergo,* with white sheets, in the summertime, at a certain hour of the day—in order to have the dream he had, Freud exemplifies the violence and arbitrariness—the ruthless overriding of the apparent, manifest, and obvious—of an interpretive practice that presumes an unconscious, which is to say, of modern interpretation itself. What further distinguishes Freud from Nietzsche is that Freud denies what (late) Nietzsche affirms, and insists that he is not imposing or distorting, but simply delivering the naked truth that had been encrypted in the symptom, or the dream.

Especially significant in the present context are those moments where Freud lays down in theoretical if coded form the underlying principles of modern interpretation. I am thinking here especially of the passages in the case of the "Rat Man," where Freud relates how he instructs this miserable man on the elementary principles of psychoanalysis, including the three "great characteristics" of the unconscious. First, Freud says, every fear corresponds to a former wish which is now repressed. Second, the unconscious is the precise contrary of the conscious. And third, it is connected to "something in the nature of *sensual desires.*" Now if these are the laws of the unconscious, they must also—assuming I am right—constitute the rules of interpretation as we know it.

Of course, adjustments have to be made in order to accommodate the changed referent. And coming up with the appropriate adjustments presents a certain challenge to ingenuity. But perhaps it is not impossible to do so. With respect to the first rule, we might ask whether it is not the case that what we call an "interpretation" presumes as a general principle that certain energies in the text are "attracted" to things that are represented as objects of aversion or indifference—in other words, that things "feared" in the text in fact represent what might be seen, from another point of view, as "wishes." One might test this hypothesis by comparing something that looks like an interpretation to something that does not. *Huckleberry Finn* tracks the fortunes of a few people of no particular consequence engaged in an improbable adventure. But to say this is not to interpret the text. An "interpretation" would contend, for example, that Twain's text represents the soul of America as it struggled with the legacy of slavery, or the American quest for an unregulated freedom in "the territories," or the theme of the civil law versus a higher moral law. The large-scale themes eschewed by the language of the narrative emerge in an "interpretation," in just the same way as the proslavery arguments and attitudes Huck parrots are, on "interpretation," seen to be objects of critique. In general, the very form of "meanings" or "themes" or any of the numerous extracts or precipitates from literary works are sufficiently different in kind from the terms of the work itself that they might qualify as "fears" of the work, fears that interpretation discloses to be secret "wishes." Jameson himself confirms this point, arguing in effect that the politics "feared" by the ethics-obsessed text is its profoundest "wish." Freud's formulation is, it must be admitted, a bit dogmatic. He cannot mean that *every* fear corresponds to a former wish. Some fears are logical, rational, even universal; and, too, some textual "fears" do not harbor and betray their own inversions. But when we interpret, we mark those that do.

The sharpest and most general formulation of this principle is adduced by Freud as the second law of the unconscious, that it is the exact contrary of the conscious. Here Freud comes close to Nietzsche's theory that things take their beginnings in their antitheses, so that (presumably) an interpretation of anything would disclose its opposite at its origin. An "interpretation" purports to discover beneath the perceptible surface of the text an order of meaning that is not simply different but radically, even perfectly different, and not just in the area of wishes and fears. It is an "interpretation" to say that Joseph Conrad is obsessed with sex even in works where none seems to be present; that Napoleon was a true democrat; that Neville Chamberlain was far-sighted, but a bit of a thug. If a statement is not to some extent counterintuitive, and even apparently counterfactual, it is not an interpretation. And—up to some unspecifiable limit—the more violent the rewriting of the apparent or manifest meaning of the text, the more dramatic and effective the interpretation will be. Clearly, what counts as an interpretation will change over time, as the cultural consensus on given issues in a text produces fresh paradigms or conventions. An element of history, or timeliness, is thus built into interpretation in this sense: every interpretation presumes a prior consensus, which it honors by contesting.

The third factor, which is as controversial in literary studies as it was in the history of psychoanalysis, is *"sensual desires."* Freud revolutionized the study of the unconscious by aligning it with sex and the senses rather than with spirit or soul. But what is a sensual as opposed to a nonsensual desire? Given that the mind (whatever that may be) is always engaged in desire, given that desire is always to an undetermined extent fantasmatic—how can one draw the line? And what role do the "senses" play in the cognitive act of interpretation? (Interestingly, Kant correlates "desire" with "reason," suggesting a richer and more spacious concept of each than we have become accustomed to.) Perhaps we can make a beginning by thinking of interpretation not as a rewriting or a re-creation, but as a "stripping," a disclosure or revelation of what is, of what had been all along, beneath the "clothing" of a superficial or misguided understanding. If, following Nietzsche, you supposed that truth is a woman, then you could see how interpretation worked by a process of disrobing. One could, of course, suppose that truth is a man, an androgyne, or anything that accorded with one's desire, without altering the basic proposition that interpretive unveiling proceeds from and gratifies an interest that can be called sensual. Susan Sontag's 1964 denunciation of interpretation in favor of an "erotics of art" missed this point, that interpretation, at least under this dispensation, is essentially erotic.

If all this is correct, and interpretation unwittingly but faithfully follows an itinerary consistent with that of psychoanalysis, then the antipathy of Marxist thought to interpretation may now be explicable as a kind of disciplinary-ideological phobia, a reaction, perhaps, to the public success of Freudian thinking. (It is interesting, incidentally, that the basic principles of Freudian thought have been thoroughly assimilated by the public, while the particulars have been vigorously contested and even rejected outright by psychoanalytic thinkers today; while Marxian thinking has not enjoyed this unthinking acceptance by the larger community despite the fact that its most basic principles are generally *not* repudiated by contemporary Marxists, many of whom continue, in a spirit of qualified fidelity, to call themselves "post-Marxists.") What is especially significant, however, is the inability or unwillingness of historical or political criticism to expunge interpretation altogether. Jameson provides once again the most indicative instance, in his treatment of the unconscious. Clearly, the notion of a "political unconscious" reflects the influence of Freud; and while Jameson insists that Freud must be transcended by a properly historical, that is, Marxist hermeneutic, still the process must pass through Freud, becoming, if only for a time, Freudianized. Jameson himself acknowledges Freud's centrality in "Metacommentary," where he concedes that the very notion of a censor "implies a model not unlike the Freudian hermeneutic . . . one based on the distinction between symptom and repressed idea, between manifest and latent content, between disguise and the message disguised" (M 13).

But for a more accurate index of Jameson's attitude toward Freud— as well as the intimate relation between interpretation and the Freudian model of the mind—we must attend to the way in which Jameson confines interpretation to a particular, preliminary moment through a careful restriction of the unconscious. The formed artifact must, he concedes, be interpreted so that its political unconscious may be disclosed. But while politics *is* an unconscious, politics does not *have* an unconscious. That is, there is no question of plumbing politics or history themselves to discover the deep "textual" or "aesthetic" or "ethical" drives that have become invisible in them through a repression of style, form, inscription, or imperativity. History may be the censor that distorts the message, and it may be the censored element within the work of art; but it is not in itself crossed or structured by censorship. While Marxist discourse might accommodate Freud to the extent of borrowing the notion of the unconscious in order to get at a politics that has been "contained," it must, in order to preserve its own integrity as a discourse, also pursue its *own* "strategy of containment," neutralizing by stigmatizing interpretation once the level of the political or historical has been achieved. For many readers, it is the attack on ethics as the code of individualism that seems to dominate *The Political Unconscious;* but a deeper strategy, one that may have been invisible to Jameson himself, might have been an ambivalent attack on Freud, on psychoanalysis, on the very notion of the unconscious that appears to inform and drive the entire project. Indeed, Jameson's subsequent indifference to modernism's aesthetic of depth and his keenly responsive attention to postmodernism's aesthetic of "gleaming surfaces" and the "hysterical sublime" may be seen as a turn to a more decisive repudiation of the entire ensnarling problematic of the unconscious.

I would not be understood as a pro-Freudian anti-Marxist. For, remarkably enough, Freud himself sheltered the unconscious from interpretation. Once you drained the id dry and replaced it with ego, one of his most famous epigrams suggested, there was no further work to be done. Once you discerned the "laws of the unconscious" through what he called a "technically correct analysis," you could collect your money and summon the next patient. The unconscious, according to Freud, has—well, not "no unconscious," of course, but no antithetical other within, whose force and nature have to be interpreted into the daylight. The unconscious is itself alone, and reaching it, you've touched bottom. The gesture of containment performed by Freud on interpretation with respect to the unconscious is identical to the one Jameson makes in asserting the irreducibility of history. So one cannot simply prefer Freudian to Marxist thought on the basis that one solicits a free interpretation while the other hedges it in: both do both.

Nor, for that matter, does literary criticism or theory imagine with any pleasure an infinite interpretability. Theoretically, as I suggested earlier, literary critics are committed to interpretation in the long, even the infinitely long, term. But in practice, every interpretation implies an acceptance of finitude. Hence the remarkable fact that no school of criticism actually even advertises, much less achieves, a wide-open endorsement of the prospect of infinite semiosis, which is intuitively understood to be radically antiacademic, anticritical, and antiprofessional. And so, while interpretation is "officially" honored by all critics, it is also, in its pure ("late Nietzschean" or "Lacanian") form, the object of a universal dread. Literary criticism has accepted, in practice if not precisely in theory, the principle that some kinds of analysis will be recognized as more technically correct than others, that meaning can be stabilized to a definite if uncertain extent, and that the text is a concrete record of decisions made by the historical author at a certain point in time. Largely through the ideology (or fetish) of the material text, the institution of literary interpretation has, in practice, accepted the idea of an end to interpretation. As the most general name for such limits, history is securely installed in the interior self-understanding of literary criticism.

And so, in retrospect, it was probably inevitable that some reflective historian such as White would discover that history and literature shared a commitment to formal devices such as rhetorical figures and narrative structure. For what goes under the name of form is just the assurance, absolutely necessary for the rational study of history and literature and anything else, of an end to interpretation. Form represents a point of nullity where the text is truly unconscious in that it is no longer representative of consciousness, no longer mimetic of the probing and motile movements of consciousness: unconscious in that it is anticonscious.

Since it signals a failure of identity through the disclosure of an unconscious, interpretation must be contained, constrained, negated by any discourse that aspires to consistency or identity. Still, as a sentimentalist about many things including the decline of modernism, I find myself wanting to insist that interpretation, marking the spot or moment in which something becomes something else, also constitutes a principle of vitality, complexity, and mobility, and so must be solicited by any discourse interested in survival. Are we now in a postinterpretive era, where the rapid sequencing of jagged, exploding, ephemeral, cryptic surfaces counts for everything? Perhaps; but depth may prove to be a hard habit to shake. In the end, when we think of interpretation and its dark familiar the unconscious, we may find ourselves appropriating folk wisdom from a different context; we may simply shrug our shoulders and acknowledge, with a rueful smile, that you can't live with 'em, you can't live without 'em.

Forever, it seems, Fredric Jameson has been described as "America's leading Marxist critic." Since the appearance of the challenging and sternly magisterial *Marxism and Form* in 1971, nobody else has had a shred of a claim to this title, certainly not now, when to be the foremost Marxist might seem a bit like being the leading manufacturer of typewriters, turntables, or four-wheel roller skates. The stature of Jameson, a distinguished professor of comparative literature at Duke University, has survived the dissolution of that perennial embarrassment and drag on theory, "actually existing" socialism; it has survived, too, the general (if premature) decline of interest in Marx himself as a writer and theoretician. Jameson might even come to be regarded as the foremost, the greatest, the leading Marxist critic during the entire period of its influence in the academy. He may even be seen, some day, as having "transcended" Marxism itself. So powerful is his claim to preeminence that it is difficult to imagine it as contested, difficult even to name those struggling back in the peloton, difficult to construct the pyramid whose capstone he is. He is a singularity: Mount Jameson, thrusting up in solemn majesty from a range of modest foothills.

He has, to be sure, been linked in various ways with Edward Said, the leading exponent of colonial and postcolonial literary and cultural studies, and with Terry Eagleton, the leading British Marxist literary critic and theorist. But such a grouping immediately suggests, once again, Jameson's distinctive style of preeminence. Alone in this group of prodigiously knowledgeable, influential, and prolific "political" critics, Jameson has not been consistently identified with any particular political cause, except that of the left generally, or of the even more general idea of a "Utopian" alternative to the culture of "late capitalism." Unlike Said, he does not appear on *Nightline* to smite his enemies; nor is he possessed by anything like the furious passion that so manifestly drives Said as he battles with Zionists and others in the public press and earlier "Orientalists" in his scholarship. Jameson has his critics, but he does not characteristically respond to them by accusing them of gross and unforgivable failures of perception, nerve, honesty, competence, or morality, as Said does with immense energy and relish. Replying to Jewish scholar Robert Griffin in *Critical Inquiry* in 1989, Said declares him to be "Griffin," an "ideological simulacrum." "As you read this," Said informs his readers, "every minute there are Palestinian women and children who are being beaten with clubs or shot with plastic bullets, their houses invaded, their lives tampered with, their loved ones killed or maimed. And 'Griffin' has the gall to speak of Israel not penitently or apologetically but in the brassy, hectoring tones of war criminals like Rabin or Ariel Sharon. . . . He speaks not only as a hypocrite but, given his pages of utter rubbish, as a knave." He concludes by inviting Griffin "(if he is a human being)" to clear out of "a discussion he has degraded" ("Response" 646). With respect to the immediate political arena, nothing is more alien to Said than accommodation or compromise, nothing more natural than conflict. On the other hand, his literary judgments are characteristically nuanced. In *Culture and Imperialism,* he treats the work of Yeats, for example, as a "major international achievement of cultural decolonization" despite the poet's "arrogant if charming espousal of fascism" (230). Kipling receives a carefully measured respect as a man of highly conditioned and passive understanding but immense novelistic power. And the Conrad of *Heart of Darkness* solicits Said's interest because of a "tragic limitation" that inhibited Conrad from drawing the appropriate political conclusions from his clear understanding of the brutality and injustice of imperialism.

For Jameson, by contrast, nothing seems more natural than dialectic, nothing more alien than a nasty, abusive public *ad hominem* dispute about some contemporary issue. Marxism means, for him, chiefly a body of theoretical and critical discourse; his "interventions" are intellectual and pedagogical rather than directly activist. To read Balzac differently is, he points out, to tamper not just with the canon but with the university as an "ideological state apparatus" and, at a great distance, with the legitimacy of the superstate. Said's Third World is filled with directly inflicted suffering and intimate combat; Jameson's seems more ideal and decidedly more linguistic. The West, he argues, might learn from Third World cinema and literature how to reinvigorate its degraded language, since, in the Third World, "eloquence in the older sense, the word as such, retains a prestige and a power that it has lost in late capitalism" ("On Contemporary Marxist Theory" 120). Jameson's judgment of literature can be harshly political. He is capable of dismissing Yeats, along with Pound and Eliot, as "true reactionaries of the blackest stamp" (*Postmodernism* 312; hereafter *P*). But this is a single, almost off-handed comment, made without energy, detail, or real conviction. More characteristically, his literary criticism documents the evaporation of political content. His Conrad serves, in *The Political Unconscious,* as an instance of the masking, containment, and disappearance of politics rather than its disorderly and unresolved manifestation. Nor is Jameson especially keen to capitalize on the opportunity to score political points. In the wild debate that ensued in the discovery of Paul de Man's "wartime journalism," Jameson was not a player: initially silent, he eventually commented, in the middle of a very long essay in a very long book *(Postmodernism* [1991]), that de Man had always seemed a good liberal to him, and his "ingenious" youthful scribblings bore every trace of a young man "altogether too smart for his own good." In the same passage, he confessed to a "sneaking admiration for Heidegger's attempt at political commitment," declaring it "aesthetically preferable to apolitical liberalism (provided its ideals remain unrealized)" (257).

If Jameson is not as engaged as Said, he is not as engaging as Eagleton. We will not see a play sparkling with Jamesonian wit on the boards in the near future, on the model of Eagleton's *Saint Oscar;* nor are audiences likely to hear him preface a lecture with a song of Irish independence, or indeed any song at all. Never accused of being a winning stylist, Jameson makes no concessions to the popular taste he anatomizes; he does not josh, pun, popularize, preen, or seduce. Where Eagleton is always cutting to the chase, anecdotalizing, putting the matter in plain English, Jameson is relentless in his highmindedness. *Marxism and Form* begins with a salute to the density and obscurity of the German philosophical tradition from Hegel to Adorno as an admirable "conduct of intransigence," and a bracing "warning to the reader of the price he has to pay for genuine thinking" (xiii). And where Eagleton is invariably concerned to bring out the political valence and force of philosophical ideas, Jameson is just as invariably interested in the structural, formal, or conceptual content of political ideas. While the edges of Eagleton's politics, or at least his political rhetoric, have become markedly beveled over the years, he has from the very first given the impression of being a good fellow to have a drink with, a popular man of the crowd. Eagleton is amused by the world, and manifestly at ease in it; Jameson—is not.

Both Said and Eagleton are attuned to the present moment, and to their presence in it, and this often produces a frazzled sensitivity to the question of how, exactly, they are faring in any given forum or debate, a sensitivity that makes them seem, despite their outsized records of accomplishment, like unusually focused, productive, or convinced versions of recognizable human types. They respond to the strictly personal aspects of intellectual dispute, and for them the "personal" includes ethnic identity and affiliation. In this respect, they top out below the timber line. Jameson seems not only indifferent to controversy and insensible of criticism, but—at least in print—a stranger to envy, paranoia, gloating, vanity, irritation, or vindictiveness as well. When an interviewer tried to goad him by bringing up Eagleton's brotherly comment that it was hard to see how Jameson's Marxist reading of a minor Balzac novel in *The Political Unconscious* was going "to help shake the foundations of capitalism," Jameson simply refused to rise to the bait. "Read carefully," he replied, "Terry's question is not so much a critique addressed to my own work as such, as rather the expression of an anxiety which everyone working in the area of Marxist cultural studies must feel" ("Interview" 72). Not only do Jameson's works suggest no sense of urgency or threat, they seem to issue from a center of consciousness unconnected with, unimplicated in, any kind of neighborly community. His first books appeared starkly without dedicatees, and, with the exception of his very first, in which he thanked his dissertation advisor, without the customary list of friends and colleagues and institutions who made it all possible. He continued this practice until recently; his most recent book, *The Seeds of Time,* is dedicated to a Chinese scholar—who is named as "an old friend," and then immediately converted into a sign of "the immense heterotopia of China itself."

Jameson's charisma is based not only on the sense of personal, or impersonal, invulnerability his work communicates, but on the distinctly inhuman scale on which his arguments are constructed. His subjects, faithfully retained from book to book, are vast—History, Form, Modernity, Ideology, Collectivity, Utopia, Totality, Necessity, Freedom—and his erudition almost, it seems, without limit in its scope, if not always impeccably thorough from the specialists' point of view. His "official" field (at the beginning) was French, but his sensibility and sentences seem Germanic, and his range of reference, especially when the subject is postmodernism, global. Despite his repeated argument that "ideological commitment" is "first and foremost a matter . . . of the taking of sides in a struggle between embattled groups," it is often unclear exactly which embattled group Jameson himself has sided with (*Political Unconscious* 290; hereafter *PU*). He seems somehow too capacious for favoritism, too big to fit on one side. He reserves his most evocative and dramatic voice not for appeals for justice or revenge in this or that case, but for indictments of "History itself as one long nightmare," or of "the foreign bodies of business and profit," or, in one remarkable passage, of work itself: "The more existential versions of this dizzying and properly unthinkable, unimaginable spectacle—as in horror at the endless succession of 'dying generations,' at the ceaseless wheel of life, or at the irrevocable passage of Time itself—are themselves only disguises for this ultimately scandalous fact of mindless alienated work and of the irremediable loss and waste of human energies, a scandal to which no metaphysical categories can give a meaning" (*Syntax of History* 162; hereafter *SH*). The fact that some people are happy just to have jobs is, for Jameson, part of the scandal, considering the "alienated" character of work, its failure to deliver meaning in the same abundance as it delivers the goods. Even when Jameson takes up issues that would inspire in most people a wealth of local or personal associations, he makes them not just largely strange but strangely large. His account of the 1960s, for example, does not begin with the Kennedy presidency or the long, hot summers of urban violence in Detroit or Watts, but with "the great movement of decolonization in British and French Africa" (*SH* 180). The sixties are, for Jameson, not the era of the Supremes, Lyndon Johnson, the Beatles, Neil Armstrong, the Manson family, Ho Chi Minh, Bob Dylan, Stokely Carmichael, Jacques Derrida, Eugene McCarthy, Richard Nixon, Charles de Gaulle, Robert Kennedy, Martin Luther King, or indeed anybody else; they are a "decisive and global chapter in Croce's conception of history," an illustration of Hegel and Marcuse, and above all a phenomenal incident in the even more phenomenal history of global capitalism (*SH* 181). Jameson, one suspects, is just not interested in what most people mean by politics, or in most people as people at all, but in the "deeper content" that determines them.

One way of explaining the amorphousness of Jameson's politics might be to point out that his genre is literary, philosophical, or cultural criticism. But another, perhaps more pertinent factor might be a reaction, partly principled and partly phobic, to the whole idea of the individual who might make judgments, commitments, or decisions, the person who might take sides. Jameson adds to the French Marxist Louis Althusser's sense of history as a greyish "process without a subject" a certain tang of disgust or contempt, as when he warns against the dangers of "contamination . . . by categories of individual action," or the "taint of . . . individual experience"; or contends that "identity is not an option but a doom"; or belittles the whole idea of "my *personal* reading of an *individual* text" (*PU* 49, 294; *SH* 174). Against the grain of a massive cultural fetishization of the individual, whose history is lovingly detailed in narratives, whose image is earnestly inscribed in film, television, and advertisements, and whose interest is relentlessly courted and cultivated everywhere in contemporary culture, Jameson argues that the individual is a historical calamity.

At the heart of Jameson's commitment to collective psychic, social, and political identity is, then, a virtually somatic distaste for the idea, the ideology, of the single person. Jameson sees the individual not only as a tainted, but as a mutilated thing, a kind of bleeding amputee wailing in the darkness, keening for its lost limbs, its authentically collective being. What's wrong with capitalism? Not its injustice, crassness, indifference, or inequity, but the way in which it "maims our existence" by chopping us up into individual units. The very notion of a distinct realm of "art" reflects, for Jameson, the capitalist "reification and privatization of contemporary life," a violation of normative social existence in which the formerly integrated "individual subject" is wrenched from the precapitalist polis and banished to a life of solitary confinement in the prison-house of the merely individual. Jameson makes this fragile distinction theoretically productive by taking on the city halls of modern culture, including reason, desire, narrative, and ethics, all of which he criticizes as discourses of the maimed, methods of repressing and stigmatizing solidarity and class cohesion. "The need to transcend individualistic categories and modes of interpretation," he writes, "is in many ways the fundamental issue"; the task of our days is "transcending the 'ethical' in the direction of the political and the collective" (*PU* 60).

All of Jameson's affirmative energy converges on this radiantly unrepresentable entity, the collective. For liberal and conservative thought alike, collective life impinges on the freedom of the individual. For Jameson, on the other hand, the individual constrains the collective. Jameson rarely says much about the details of collectivity, for reasons that will emerge in a moment. But he is specific on the time, or times, proper to it. Life was collective in the deep past, and may be so again in the unspecified future. Jameson seems to understand Adorno's dictum that "society precedes the subject" not as a logical but as a historical statement. The culture of the individual—"fallen culture," as Jameson insistently puts it—obliterated an older way of life that has, nevertheless, left "spoors and traces" that may be tracked like luminous breadcrumbs leading home as we struggle toward some undefined futurity. To stress collectivity is not, then, simply to affirm a particular ethos, but to resurrect History, to reawaken "the essential *mystery* of the cultural past, which, like Tiresias drinking the blood, is momentarily returned to life and warmth and allowed once more to speak, and to deliver its long-forgotten message in surroundings utterly alien to it" (*PU* 19). Only if we recover a lost sense of totality so that we may see "the human adventure" as a single thing rather than as the sum of innumerable discontinuous private destinies can we grasp the contemporary pertinence of ancient philosophical, theological, or social disputes; only if we retell all the tales of the past as incidents in "a single great collective story" unified by the "fundamental theme—for Marxism, the collective struggle to wrest a realm of Freedom from a realm of Necessity"—will the point and coherence of history and everything in it become clear (*PU* 19).

As a concrete historical home for preindividual existence, the past thus acquires a powerful moral status, which Jameson evokes in a startling image in the 1979 essay "Marxism and Historicism," where he envisions the past not as an inert object of nostalgia, a passive object to be judged, but as "a radically different life form" that "rises up to call our own form of life into question and to pass judgment on us" (*SH* 175).

Future collectivity, in one sense the restoration of some original, forgotten, virtually extinct mode, takes no such lurid forms; indeed, it takes no form at all. It summons us as the destination toward which history ought to be tending, but which is nowhere realized or configured in the present. Jameson has taken the Marxist slogan that anybody who has a plan for the future is a reactionary, and has given this principled cluelessness the name of Utopia. This ancient concept has always been charged, for Jameson, with thoroughly contemporary, if idiosyncratic, meanings. Absent from his dissertation, which became the 1961 book *Sartre: The Origins of a Style,* Utopia began to appear in Jameson's work after the sixties, as he assimilated the writings of Ernst Bloch, and of his UC San Diego colleagues Herbert Marcuse and Louis Marin. The latter's *Utopiques: Jeux d'espaces,* which defines "the Utopian event itself" as a "revolutionary *fête,*" was, Jameson notes, "elaborated in the very eye of the hurricane during Marin's Nanterre seminar in May 1968" (*SH* 77). To this quintessentially sixties formulation Marcuse added the warning that Marxism "must risk defining freedom in such a way that people become conscious of and recognize it as something that is nowhere already in existence" ("The End of Utopia," quoted in *SH* 76). Returning to the theme of Utopia in nearly every one of his books, Jameson always stresses both its value as a revolutionary concept and its obdurate resistance to figuration, narrativization, concrete imaginings of any kind. Anything we can think of must be non-Utopian, since we do our thinking as "private" individuals. In a fallen culture, whatever is—even in our dreams—is wrong. And so while other Marxists were discomfited by actually existing socialism, Jameson had conceived a much vaster antipathy to actually existing anything.

He was, however, insisting that the future was not altogether remote, that slender wires were strung between now and then, if only we could find them. They are not in the obvious places, or in the places we might wish to spend much time looking. But if we could tolerate extended stretches of ennui, we might turn them up. For the proper literary, or preliterary form of precapitalist life was loosely connected, repetitive chains of episodic incidents, to which the only possible response for most moderns is boredom. Jameson is always interesting on the subject of modern boredom, which he sees as indicative of the distance we have traveled from the collectivist past, the affective marker of a lost capacity to invest ourselves in anything but formed narratives about individuals, but most important, as a "precious symptom of our own cultural limits" and therefore a signal that a radically different form of social organization is still possible (see *SH* 117-19). Jameson takes from Adorno and Horkheimer the principle that *all* class consciousness bears within it the kernel of the future; he accepts, too, their claim that even certain repugnant ideas such as anti-Semitism are, as he puts it, "profoundly Utopian in character" because they constitute a "repressed recognition" of the Utopian impulse. But he extends these ideas even further by arguing, in the conclusion to *The Political Unconscious,* for the Utopian character of all collectivity. Even fascist organizations qualify as Utopian on these generous grounds, as does the Klan, the White Patriot's Party, the Michigan Militia, the Nation of Islam, Aryan Nation, Dow Chemical, the PLO, the Khmer Rouge, the JDL, the Republican Party, the NRA, the studio audience of *Family Feud,* the State Legislature of Louisiana, the LAPD, the Cincinnati Bengals, Serbia, K-Mart shoppers—anything at all that exceeds and enfolds the individual. Expressions of class privilege, class arrogance, class complacency, class envy, or class hatred—all this is "in its very nature Utopian" (*PU* 2889). While, in a fragmented social life in which all groups struggle against all others, no form of class consciousness can be immediately universal; all without exception are universal in essence because, he claims, all herald the transformation of the present into the postindividual future. Only the most doggedly "ethical" perspective, he asserts, could bother itself about such questions as which kinds of class consciousness are "good" and which "evil."

I have dwelt at such length on this system of arguments and claims for three reasons. First, it has endured, with variations in emphasis, for thirty-five years; even those texts in which it does not appear do not contradict it. Second, it is extraordinary. The eminence of Jameson notwithstanding, these ideas have, as far as I know, no other serious sponsors, even among Marxists. One does not hear, in the corridors or meeting rooms of academic conferences, earnest discussions about Utopia, angry denunciations of the culture of the individual, or lamentations about the horror of work. And third, it poses an interesting question about the relation between Jameson's stature and his message. What can we say of the fact that an argument about the poverty of the individualist present as compared with the glories of an undefinable but hopefully collectivist future has produced, from the moment of its inception, virtually no effects in the academic or even the broadly intellectual community other than a mass of rewards, honors, and distinctions for Jameson himself? To reply smoothly that one's private position in the world is unconnected to one's public convictions is simply to reprise a classic "liberal" mistake that Jameson himself has condemned. On the other hand, to explain the matter by assigning message to the "base" and reputation to the "superstructure" only aggravates the question, since, for Jameson as for Marx, the superstructure has no genuine autonomy, no history of its own.

How to think about this relationship, this problem? Is it a "contradiction," or perhaps an "antinomy"? Jameson begins his new book, *The Seeds of Time* (hereafter *SofT*), the texts of the Wellek Library Lectures in Critical Theory at UC Irvine in 1991, by taking up precisely this distinction, which, for him, is far from idle or scholastic. A cleaner form, an antinomy goes nowhere: two statements stand in stark opposition and that's that. But a contradiction—ah, that's another thing altogether. Contradictions might represent two perspectives on the same object, or two moments in a process, or two merely apparently incompatible statements, which can still, with some determination, be harmonized or reconciled. In *SofT,* Jameson analyzes a series of "antinomies of postmodernity" by which contemporary thought is paralyzed, and attempts to convert them into contradictions, thawing them out, enabling them to mingle with their opposites, and making conceptual, and therefore social progress possible once again. The question of whether the conjunction of Jameson's singular and hierarchical stature and his collective values constitutes a contradiction or an antinomy, then, is really a question about whether his work can be considered kinetic, forward-looking, and politically progressive, or whether it cannot.

It may not, in other words, always be the case that contradiction is preferable to antinomy, but Jameson is committed to the contradiction for other reasons. Understanding the status of the contradiction takes us, indeed, directly into the internal gearing of his thought and provides one way of understanding its form and its history. Few other major critics are as explicit about their methodology, and few invest method with such importance. Everything, for Jameson, begins with contradiction. Sometimes he analyzes the contradiction between the world and our (necessarily ideological) thoughts or opinions about it; more typically, he discovers internal or formal contradictions in a work, a discrepancy between kinds of energy or different "modes of production." In classical Marxism, capitalism is doomed to self-destruction because of its contradictions. But in all cases, contradictions disclose an incoherence, and therefore a dynamism, an instability that suggests a movement toward a state in which the contradiction is overcome, the discrepancies harmonized. In short, contradiction propels us to the future, to necessity, and to truth.

An excellent, highly concentrated example of the Jamesonian contradiction in action can be found in his 1977 "Class and Allegory in Contemporary Mass Culture: *Dog Day Afternoon* as a Political Film." According to legend, Jameson wrote this tightly argued piece during a chaotic New Year's Eve party, off in a corner with an Olivetti on his lap; in any event, it has the force and feel of an insight that cannot be denied, party or no party. Sidney Lumet's film, he begins, seems to belong to two distinct genres. It gestures toward the neorealist or documentary presentation of social fact, but the virtuoso "splendor" of Al Pacino's performance "irreparably condemns" the film "to remain a Hollywood product." Thus we have "that unresolvable, profoundly symptomatic thing which is called a contradiction," an entity that can be "focused in two quite distinct ways" that suggest two separate moments of cultural consciousness. Form becomes content by disclosing an "uneven development," a condition in which residues of the collective past are mixed up with the psychologizing, ethicizing, aestheticizing rule of capitalism (*Signatures of the Visible* 41). Registering the signs of a frustrated class consciousness struggling for expression within "the present multinational stage of monopoly capitalism," Jameson concludes that the film is a "pre-political" work, a symptom of a cultural circumstance in which the experience of totality, "the truth of our social life as a whole," is foreclosed or precluded. But behind the contradictory form of Lumet's film, we can catch a glimpse of an "external face," a radical otherness that cannot be directly perceived, "some new, so far only dimly conceivable, collective forms which may be expected to replace the older individualistic ones" (54). What Jameson expects from the contradiction, then, is nothing less than a premonition of the postindividual, postcapitalist, and, as he has taken to saying, "postcontemporary" future; and what he expects from criticism that interrogates contradiction is a small shove in that direction.

The Church Ladies of Marxism have found Jameson's lingering at the "premonition" stage highly *convenient* because it eliminates the need for spelling out the specifics of the "radical alternative," much less for committing oneself to action in pursuit of it. Despite professing an untroubled commitment to Marxism as a theoretical discourse, Jameson has never been exactly right with the feft, as his very choice of subjects indicates. He has been consistently drawn to those figures whose relation to Marxism is aberrant, conflicted, or partial, such as Walter Benjamin, Sartre, or, Lukács. He reserves his deepest intellectual admiration for Adorno, despite Adorno's skeptical view of the Utopianism of the sixties, which Jameson describes as "a sympathy not a little tarnished by the deathless shame of having called the police into the University" (*Late Marxism* 7). And, too, he has always had an appetite for those figures who have either no relation to

Marxism or a hostile one, such as Conrad, Gissing, Balzac, or Wyndham Lewis, not to mention the artists and architects he has been discussing since the early eighties. A keen interest in the exotica of the far right runs like a streak of scarlet through Jameson's Marxism.

One of the most curious signs of this "comprehensiveness" or "inclusiveness" is a persistent friendliness toward religion, which makes a remarkable appearance at the end of *The Political Unconscious* as a "symbolic affirmation of the unity of a given tribe," a profound expression of "nostalgia for the collective and the Utopian," and an "anticipatory foreshadowing" of Marxism itself (292, 292, 285). Jameson's understanding of the future seems to be modeled on that of the book of Revelation; and his hermeneutical principles seem to be drawn from Augustine, who imagines a time when the "canopy of skins" separating heaven from earth will be drawn back, and we can enjoy a "face-to-face" intimacy with God, or Totality. And like Augustine, Jameson figures this moment as a return to an earlier condition, a restoration of a prelapsarian immediacy. The works of culture come to us, he argues in texts written during the late seventies, as signs in a virtually forgotten code, fragments of "a totality we have long since lost the organs to see" (*SH* 174). In older cultures, works carried their own interpretations, and fact and commentary were welded together, as was everything in the social gestalt. If we must now wander in the wilderness, searching for traces of a "concrete social subtext" that might serve as signs of a "concrete future"—if "thought asphyxiates" for sheer lack of concreteness—this is because some virtually theological disaster has befallen us.

Jameson does not add that this disaster came about precisely because our post-Edenic ancestors did in fact entertain a lively vision of a radical alternative, and produced modernity and capitalism as a consequence. But his argument is not, as he would say, "properly" scriptural, but more generally religious, or subreligious. What really excites Jameson about religion is not just its collectivity, and not, of course, its doctrine, but the discipline associated with the religious or monastic order. He is alive, in fact, to the possibilities for mortification wherever they may arise. One of the first Americans to promote the work of Jacques Lacan, Jameson stressed an aspect of Lacan's thought that has gone largely unnoticed by subsequent commentators. His Lacan, in both *The Political Unconscious* and in the long essay "Imaginary and Symbolic in Lacan," reprinted in *The Situation of Theory,* is not a wild new theorist of postmodern carnival, a dazzlingly unpredictable narcissist, an inventor of conceptual drolleries. He is, rather, a displaced Marxist, whose realm of the "imaginary," alienated within "the symbolic," corresponds to Jameson's deep collective past, mired in modernity; whose "Real" can be refigured as "History"; and whose vision of the "decentered subject" constitutes a call for "a renewal of Utopian thinking." But this is just the beginning. The most profound value of Lacan, for Jameson, lies hidden in Lacan's exposition of the "discourse of the analyst," which Jameson describes as "a position of articulated receptivity, of deep listening (*L'écoute*), of some attention beyond the self or the ego . . . [a means of] hearing the Other's desire. The active and theoretical passivity, the rigorous and committed self-denial, of this final subject position, which acknowledges collective desire . . . may well have lessons for cultural intellectuals as well as politicians and psychoanalysts" (*Situations of Theory* 115). The "analyst," whom Jameson morphs into the "cultural intellectual," must evacuate himself so he can hear the voice of the Other, and all the Others. A pronounced "receptivity" to ascesis informs Jameson's discussions of other thinkers as well. He appreciates de Man, we might speculate, despite the latter's indifference to every one of Jameson's preoccupations, because de Man is constantly wrestling with the "resistance to temptation" or "critical self-denial." And he quotes Paul Ricoeur at length in the conclusion to *The Political Unconscious* because Ricoeur's retrograde commitment to "categories of the individual subject" was at least based on a congenial program of purification, on a "willingness to suspect, willingness to listen: vow of rigor, vow of obedience" (quoted in *PU* 284). It is in terms of such vows that we must understand such Jamesonian epigrams as "History is necessity," "History is what hurts," and "Always historicize!," with "History" serving as a token of impersonality and rigor (*PU* 102, 102, 9). Jameson clearly has no interest in pleasure as such. He concludes a long discussion of Roland Barthes in the 1983 article "Pleasure: A Political Issue" with an earnest formula for "the proper political use of pleasure" (*SH* 73). To be properly political, pleasure must not be permitted to gorge or wallow; rather, it must be understood as "the *figure* for Utopia in general . . . [and] for the tranformation of social relations as a whole" (74).

If (mere) pleasure provokes disapproval, pain stimulates articulation. In postmodernism, he says, cultural identity is subordinated to the global system, "and lived as a constraint and a domination about which intellectuals and artists are lucid" ("On Contemporary Marxist Theory" 130). Much of Jameson's own work can be considered under the general heading of "lucidity about domination"—not only the domination of one group over another, but also the domination of other minds over his own. The extraordinary consistency of his thought, the durability of his major themes and concerns, is perhaps the most conspicuous source of his intellectual power. But another, largely unremarked, factor is his equally extraordinary plasticity. Jameson engulfs his subject like a mighty python, taking on its shape in the way that a python, having swallowed a piglet, looks like a piglet. *Late Marxism,* his book on Adorno ("my master"), is Adorno-esque not just because of its immense tracts of quotation or its generally approving tone, but also because of a certain quality in the prose. Jameson expresses the hope that his translations of Adorno might be "the occasion of forging a powerful new Germanic sentence structure in English"—his own English (ix). His book on modernity, *The Political Unconscious,* is itself modern in Jameson's own terms—oracular, prophetic, and large in scale; while *Postmodernism* is decisively postmodern, a depthless, decathected, and decentered pastiche that seems, by comparison with its predecessors, to have suffered a "waning of affect." Early and late, Jameson's work takes the form of a reduplication of its objects. In 1971, Jameson counted as a strength the malleability of dialectical thinking, which, because it depended so closely on the habitual everyday mode of thought which it is called on to transcend, could take a number of different and apparently contradictory forms (see *Marxism and Form* 370 ff.). But twenty years later, when he was widely being taken for a "postmodernist" rather than a Marxist, this malleability had come to seem an annoyance. "If I may indulge in a personal note," he says in *Postmodernism,* "it has happened to me before to have been oddly and comically identified with an object of study." The incident was the 1972 appearance of *The Prison-House of Language,* when, he recalled, some readers "addressed me as a 'foremost' spokesperson for structuralism, while the others appealed to me as an 'eminent' critic and opponent of that movement" (297). The identification of dialectical thought with its subject produces, it seems, a general uncertainty about the angle or thrust of the message—and, in Jameson's case, a general conviction of the eminence of the messenger.

This identification is surely why *The Political Unconscious* remains Jameson's greatest work: its subject is modernism, or greatness as such. Jameson's modernism is an era of giants, of Great Writers and "great souls"; it is a time of "great realisms," great "cultural monuments," "great forces of nineteenth-century history," "great theorists," the "great narrative and aesthetic dilemmas of high capitalism," and "great Proustian glimpses" of steeples: "modernism," he says bluntly, "was still a time of giants and legendary powers no longer available to us" (*P* 305). Looking backward, all this greatness must, Jameson argues, seem out of synch with the democratizing thrust of modernist technology and rationalization. Greatness is a "residual" force lingering on in a predominantly anonymous or "Fordist" mode of production, an "uneven development" that signals modernist culture's dynamic disequilibrium, in which unalienated but elitist forces coexist with alienated but egalitarian ones. *The Political Unconscious* is itself out of synch, seeming to deplore the very phenomenon of greatness, but itself inescapably great throughout. Even as late as *Postmodernism* (1991), Jameson's heart, one can tell, is still with titans such as Balzac, Flaubert, Conrad, Stein, Frank Lloyd Wright, Kafka, or Duchamp. "Despite Tolstoy," he comments, "I think we still do admire the great generals (along with their counterparts, the great artists)" (*P* 306).

The cultural formations that have replaced modernism elicit, by contrast, a temperate rhetoric of suspicious appreciation, and to move from *The Political Unconscious* to *Postmodernism* or *SofT* is to experience a sudden drop in altitude, one that, I will argue, marks a signal change in the character of Jameson's work and even forces a rethinking of the question of his stature. Now that culture is more "in phase" with itself, we have, according to Jameson, eliminated some of the most egregious forms of modernist inequality, but we have also lost the stimulus for thinking of a future radically different from the present. History has gone missing, and has taken Economics with it. In fact, Jameson defines postmodernism generally in terms of lack and negation. Postmodernism is not only depthless and without passion; it is also formless, antioracular, and antivisionary. In *SofT,* Jameson deploys his most durable visual aid, the "semiotic rectangle" borrowed from Greimas, a way of charting transformation according to which each initial term in a conceptual opposition generates its own logical negation, inversion, or cancellation, so that the terminal state is the initial state turned inside out. Thus Modernism's "innovation" and "totality" become, in our time, "replication" and "part" or "element." But perhaps most pertinently, and most generally, Jamesonian postmodernism inverts or cancels High Modernism's very positivity, its massive confidence in the substantiality and density of its own huge but coherent projects.

Reading Jameson, one begins to suspect that postmodernism does not exist, or at least that no limits can be set to it. Not just a set of high-cultural monuments, postmodernism represents the "cultural logic" of "late" or multinational capitalism. Global, popular, and decentered, postmodernism might be anything or anywhere. The "four distinct antinomies" with which *SofT* begins represent a first attempt at mapping this murky, amorphous, and indistinct thing. Jameson is admirably, even acutely sensitive to the possibility that his categories may only be private inventions or fantasies that map nothing at all. He seems close, at times, to saying that postmodernism is a cultural circumstance in which it becomes impossible to say whether discourse is determined by the object or by the subject. Instead, however, he says that since he himself is part of the Zeitgeist, his cognitive habits must be postmodern. It is, in any event, difficult to test his hypotheses by looking at postmodernism "itself"; and with such little resistance from the "object," his distinctions are, as it were, free to pursue their own projects, their own fates, their own desires. And what they desire, it seems, is to marry, to merge, to form families. Thus the four distinct antinomies form, upon mature consideration, two pairs; then those in the first pair are seen to "[fold] back into each other"; and then, within a few pages, the third and fourth do the same. The argument of *SofT*'s long first chapter takes the form of a series of demonstrations that what had been taken to be an opposition is not: postmodern time just is space, postmodern identity is difference, an unparalleled rate of change constitutes standardization, market society has become nature, homogeneity is heterogeneity, and arguments against Utopia are in fact Utopian. The thawing out of antinomies into contradictions has an entropic, Daliesque effect, like softening a wristwatch, and the political—or indeed the conceptual—payoff of this analytical softening, or *SofT*ening, becomes difficult to articulate in positive terms. In fact, all Jameson can claim for his work here is that it "is not a self-defeating exercise in futility or nihilism but is bound to have unconscious results."

For whom? Much of *SofT* reads like a "Jamesons Wake," an unfiltered dream-monologue composed of endless sentences in which all manner of odd or unsorted things float around, occasionally bobbing to the surface:

> Meanwhile, the Zeebrugge Terminal, like the helmet of an immense cosmonaut, part plastic part metal, "a cross between a ball and a cone" (*El Croquis,* 80), includes, in the same nonspecifiable way, whole former structures, such as a hotel and an office building, along with the *rose des sables* of the on- and off-ramps, as delicately interlaced as the great Figueroa grade crossing in downtown Los Angeles: allegories, perhaps, of that other intestinal necessity of the modern building about which Koolhaas has frequently complained, that of the pipes and wiring, the "services" ("it is unbelievable how a component that amounts to one third of the section of a building and may represent 50 percent of the budget is in a way inaccessible to architectural thought" [13]), whose problematic he elsewhere dramatized, as an opportunity rather than a dilemma, in his "theory" of the elevator (discussed in Part One), where the existence of such a central mechanism seemed to offer a way of concentrating everything heterogeneous and external together in a governable fashion. (138–39)

Perhaps "unconsciously," Jameson seems to be describing his own sentence, with its vast "intestinal necessities," as it creeps along through its typologies and quadrants, its "pipes and wiring" inaccessible to syntactic design, its manifest will to enclose a world "in a [barely] governable fashion." The clotted and yet strangely airy feel of a prose in which Zeebrugge, Los Angeles, Tokyo, Las Vegas, "the Congrexpo in Lille," "the Convention Center in Agadir," "the Romeo and Juliet box" ("more complex," we are assured, "than anything since Schoenberg's *Klangfarbenmelodie*"), "Venturi's Gordon Wu building at Princeton," "Rossi's Hotel Il Palazzo at Fukuoka," "the Sainsbury center of 1978"—all these things emerging momentarily, mentioned but only rarely described or pictured—coordinates with Jameson's account of postmodernism itself, which becomes once again an account of his own cognitive style. What's more, the suspicion that gathers around much of postmodern culture—is this the triumph or the failure of style?—also hangs over this book. Has Jameson really *gone over* this material? Why do the illustrations have no captions, so that one is often uncertain what one is looking at? Why is the index so reliably wrong or inadequate? Why has no kind—or unkind—editor intervened?

The most serious problem with which Jameson must grapple, however, is the fact that the unprincipled movements of capital have produced a version of "actually existing" totality more comprehensive than any that socialism, either actual or theoretical, was able to come up with. Late capital has made its way in the world through an apparently pliant responsiveness to local concerns, local values, local practices, local prejudices: it sells its totalities without insisting on totality as an abstraction. While Jameson has argued that experience should be seen as simultaneously specific and a figure for totality, multinational corporations have sought to reassure consumers that "We do it your way," so that every consumer can say, while consuming, "I did it my way," without a thought for totality. Late capitalism's totalizing strategies are, in short, effective to the extent to which they can pass themselves off as a resistance to totality itself.

Can capital's "unconscious" totality be effectively resisted, or must we all, in the end, get on board? Jameson devotes many worried pages to "Critical Regionalism," an architectural practice that represents itself as an anti-Marxist "flight from the realities of late capitalism," only to conclude that it is just more late capitalism after all. Here in New Orleans, the immediate environment offers two more effective resistances to totality and capital. The first is figured in the fate of the Piazza d'Italia, created about twenty years ago as a strange, metallic reference to ancient Roman civic architecture. Once, perhaps, a diverting commentary on public space and historical memory, it has become a contemporary pseudo-Roman ruin, littered with trash, broken glass, and syringes. A terrible place to visit, it seems to be a place where some people actually live. It resists totality, however, and has, in its current state, achieved a certain independence from late capitalism, which wants nothing to do with it and would, in fact, dearly love to demolish it. It stands now as a sign of the power of public indifference to the designs of the cultural elite. The site of the second resistance is situated just a few feet away in the open, unfinished hulk of what was to be the world's largest land-based casino. Of course, it is not the casino itself I am thinking of; casinos represent one of the most nakedly deracinated forms of late capitalism, of what Jameson might describe as "the hysterical sublime," or "the exhilaration of the gleaming surface." For that matter, gambling also provides revealing allegories of the complicity with capital of "Critical Regionalism" in the riverboat casinos that temporarily ringed the city in the late nineties. The true resistance to the interests of capital is to be found in the "disappointing" revenues of these riverboats, as well as of the "temporary" casino operated by Harrah's near the French Quarter while a "permanent" casino was being built. Throughout 1995, boats were failing, employees were being laid off, tax projections were being recalculated, and moguls were being inconvenienced, their office furniture seized by creditors. This partially amusing spectacle was climaxed in November 1995 by the sudden and spectacular bankruptcy of the temporary casino, and the abrupt cancellation of construction on the permanent one. As I write, it is bad all around, except in the city's legal profession, which has entered on a new golden age. But from the very beginning of casino gambling in New Orleans, in May 1995, a certain trend had troubled even the most hysterical, the most exhilarated: the temporary casino was attracting local African Americans, while white gamblers were taking buses to the casinos on the Mississippi coast. A combination of spontaneous self-segregation and a structurally depressed economy is now on the very brink of accomplishing what liberal moralists could not—throwing the scoundrels out, sucking the blood of the bloodsuckers, preserving, without really intending to, the fragile "character" of the city. Call it Uncritical Regionalism.

How should we think of "late Jameson"? There are two possibilities. The first can be charted with the aid of the semiotic rectangle itself. *Marxism and Form* and *Prison-House*—we might say—betray a pair of interests, in literary form and the classless Utopian society. From here we pass through *The Political Unconscious* and end up, at least for now, with the replacement of literature by "culture" more broadly defined, and with the dominance of capitalism over Utopia. Another way of thinking of Jameson's decade-long meditation on postmodernism would be as a final, dramatic sacrifice, a willed surrender of his work's greatness out of a scholarly respect for the character of his subject. Jameson has fashioned a critical style appropriate to postmodernity, and has, in the process, surrendered his "modernist" status as charismatic Master. It is not just difficult but inappropriate to be a prophet in a world that bestows the mantle of "greatness" on the Figueroa grade crossing in downtown Los Angeles. Jameson has, we might say, renounced renunciation, and the magnitude-effect that accompanied it; he has surrendered the pain that made his work so bracing, the outraged sense of the intolerable injustice of domination that had previously occasioned his lucidity. In so doing, he has become—it goes without saying— our preeminent postmodern theorist.

With the appearance of Robert F. Barsky's book *Noam Chomsky: A Life of Dissent* (1997), we have, it seems, entered the major phase of the cultural and academic activity of "remembering Chomsky." The project has been a long time germinating in Chomsky's home discipline of linguistics. Indeed, Chomsky had barely revolutionized this field when some of his students and colleagues, only a little younger than he, began to depict him as a superannuated tyrant, both domineering and out of touch; and the effort to usher in a post-Chomsky world has provided linguists of the last thirty years with a mission every bit as daunting and invigorating as the effort to deny that the world had become Chomskyan had been for linguistics ten years before that. Both of these efforts have exhausted themselves, as Randy Allen Harris demonstrated in his 1993 book *The Linguistics Wars,* a chronicle of the discipline in this century that centers on Chomsky's always-contested and always-reaffirmed preeminence. Veterans of the struggle during the sixties and seventies have now become chroniclers themselves; witness Robin Lakoff's 1989 "The Way We Were," a mellow and witty retrospective of those stormy days when trashing Chomsky was the only reputable occupation for a self-respecting linguist. The major players in that highly entertaining drama are now, for the most part, otherwise engaged, while Chomsky himself slogs on, still doing linguistics, still refining the theory, still making discoveries, still training students and sending them out into a disciplinary world that is curiously both post-Chomsky and all Chomsky.

Barsky's book represents an antithesis to Harris's book (which he primly criticizes for its "soap-opera style") in several respects. To Harris's book, brilliantly comprehensive in its grasp of historical fact and conceptual detail, and engagingly written to boot, Barsky has responded aggressively with a tome that is sloppy, underresearched, and deeply uninformative. After reading it, you have the strange feeling of knowing *less* than you had when you began, because while you may have had a bluffer's knowledge of a few buzzwords before, the treatment of the corresponding concepts in

Barsky is so murky or skimpy that you begin to doubt even the trusty old clichés. Thus you finish Barsky with a weakened grip on discovery procedures, evaluation procedures, deep structure, syntactic autonomy, phrase structure rules, semantic interpretation rules, transformation, principles-and-parameters, and generative grammar; you finish with no insight at all into generative semantics or government-and-binding, or the issue between Chomsky and Foucault in their one encounter, or the history of Chomsky's concern with East Timor; nor will you find out what is contained in Chomsky's path-breaking work, *Aspects of the Theory of Syntax*. You will learn that Chomsky fell out with his teachers Zellig Harris and Nelson Goodman, but will not be told why; nor why Chomsky would choose to defend the principle of academic freedom in a preface to a book by Robert Faurisson that called the Holocaust into question. The reader interested in Chomsky's politics would be better served by Milan Rai's 1995 book *Chomsky's Politics*. And even on Chomsky's personal history, Barsky is far from comprehensive. Notoriously diffident about such matters, Chomsky has actually been *more* forthcoming than Barsky, giving a long interview to James Peck that serves as the introduction to *The Chomsky Reader* (1987), and a frequent source for Barsky.

In one important respect, however, *Noam Chomsky: A Life of Dissent* provides a genuine antithesis to *The Linguistics Wars*. Harris is sufficiently independent to have provoked angry criticism from many of those he discusses, including Chomsky, while Barsky, who dedicates his book to his subject, tells it like Chomsky sees it. In fact, he lets Chomsky tell it himself, quoting at great length from the many letters Chomsky sent him, letters Barsky is so proud of having received that he includes a photograph of them, with the "Dear Robert" salutation clearly legible. These letters deserve a prominent place, for they often represent the full extent of Barsky's research. Indeed, so omnipresent is Chomsky's voice, so utterly does Chomsky triumph over odds, enemies, falsehood, and mendacity, that a more candid title page might have read *"Noam Chomsky: A Life of Da Saint*. In his own words (with Robert Barsky)."

One area on which everyone including Chomsky is in perfect accord is Chomsky's specialness. Harris describes him as "a hero of Homeric proportions, belonging solidly in the pantheon of our century's finest minds, with all the powers and qualities thereof." "Staggeringly smart," dwarfing without effort or interest even the most brilliant minds around him, almost unbelievably productive, totally dedicated to a wide variety of causes, a "born leader" who shapes his field by sheer force of will so that language just is what Chomsky says it is, and "—the quintessential heroic trait—he is fearless in battle" (*Linguistics Wars* 54; hereafter *LW*). Of course, it's lonely at the top, and Chomsky traumatized the field he revolution-ized, but many of Harris's readers must have been amazed to read Chom-sky's own assessment that "as I look back over my own relation to the field, at every point it has been completely isolated, or almost completely isolated" (259). It is often proudly claimed by Chomsky's supporters that his brilliance detaches him from all ideologies, orthodoxies, parties, and pieties. As Peck says in *The Chomsky Reader*, "his laserlike rationality is so radical, as others' thinking is not, because of its intense anti-ideological ethos" (*CR* ix–x). The argument is that sheer rationality, when carried to a Chomskyan extreme, virtually enforces isolation inasmuch as most people simply live out their fantasies, or rather, the fantasies they are spoonfed by their ideological masters. Perhaps; but the interview given to Peck is not just extreme but devoted to its extremity as a principle, or fetish. "I always felt completely out of tune with almost everything around me," Chomsky comments about his youth; "I was always on the side of the losers"; "ever since I had any political awareness, I've felt either alone or part of a tiny minority"; "[my early work in linguistics] was simply not recognized as re-lated to that field"; "elite intellectuals often simply cannot perceive that one could have the opinions that I do hold"; "intellectuals just look at me with blank stares of incomprehension," etc. (see *CR* 13–18, 35).

This sense of his own magnificent difference as a solitary crusader for the truth has fortified him in perilous places. Places such as MIT, with its Department of Defense millions. A tireless critic of the DOD, Chomsky is not, apparently, amused by a fact that others consider ironic, that his in-stitution is supported by it; and, moreover, that "the overwhelmingly pre-dominant funding source for transformational grammar," as Harris points out, is "the U. S. military"; and not just transformational grammar in gen-eral, but the MIT linguistics department in particular; and not just the de-partment, but even Chomsky himself, one of whose papers (like virtually all others, Harris reports, from the MIT linguistics faculty in the sixties) carries an acknowledgment that reads, "This work was supported in part by the U. S. Army Signal Corps, the Air Force Office of Scientific Research, and the Office of Naval Research" (*LW* 218, 273n). Chomsky, whose pro-tests, as Barsky records them, have been limited to suggesting that MIT set up, in the interests of candor, a "Department of Death," clearly feels un-compromised, whistling serenely through the minefield, singleminded in his dedication to scientific truth and social justice. Chomsky's objection to Harris's book reflects not a disagreement over specifics but a determined repudiation of the very proposition that he has been engaged in any sort of power struggle, any battles, any "political" controversies within linguis-tics: he has, he asserts, simply been doing linguistics, and the stuff Harris fills his three hundred pages with is just corrupt postmodernist history, which is to say, fantasy. Interestingly, this very personal sense of a protective distinctness echoes in his linguistics itself, which begins with the principle of the "autonomy of syntax," which itself derives from a principle of "modularity," according to which the mind is not just a complex and unsorted mass of interrelated functions but is highly compartmentalized, a network of "highly special structures" or "mental organs," the most stupendous of which is responsible for the way in which we—as Chomsky puts it in a curious phrase—"grow a language" (*LW* 67). And Chomsky has always worked on what Harris calls a "rather narrow, almost individual, set of linguistic problems" (*LW* 199). Language *is* Chomsky, it seems, in more senses than one.

Harris consolidated an image that had been coming into focus for many years, of Chomsky as a scowling and overpowering patriarch, the head of a dysfunctional professional family where the discipline was as harsh as it was unpredictable, an inviting target for generational revolt by the countercultural generative semanticists of the sixties and seventies. Barsky's final verbless sentence is clearly a retrospective, third-generation reappraisal: "Noam Chomsky, sixty-eight years old, Institute Professor, linguist, philosopher, grandfather, champion of ordinary people" (*NC* 217). Thus the singular Chomsky is situated within a number of collectivities, but, many readers might feel, at the cost of his edge. (Moreover, the "grandfather" is a bit abrupt inasmuch as no mention had been made of any of the children marrying.) But it is precisely here, I want to suggest, that Barsky becomes interesting. Within the anodyne image of the scarred and grisly old hero down on the floor with the grandkids—an image, say, of Brando as the aged Don Corleone, romping in the garden, adorable for a moment before the big one hits—is another image that inhabits the book like an anamorphotic smear. Read aslant, Barsky actually provides a series of deeply revealing clues to the peculiar kind of distinction that is Chomsky's. Standing as it were off to the side of Barsky's portrait of Chomsky as Holbeinian Ambassador, one perceives in the smudge of Barsky's discourse not a death's head but a child. It is, in fact, an image of Chomsky himself, at the age of ten.

At this time, Chomsky was, by his own account, a thoroughly happy child, the son of brilliant Jewish parents in Philadelphia, the father an accomplished Semitic philologist and the mother, also a teacher, a sought-after speaker on "scholarly and communal subjects," as Barsky ambiguously puts it. Chomsky himself was attending an experimental school which encouraged ungraded individual creativity, and was reading historical linguistics, newspapers, and much else on his own. The family was politically aware, left-libertarian in its leanings, pro-Roosevelt, Zionist. And so when young Noam read of the fall of the Spanish anarchist uprising in Barcelona in 1937, he was, unlike most of his classmates, in a position to write an editorial for the school newspaper, his first published article. I have not seen this article, but Chomsky has spoken frequently of Barcelona as a signal event in his life, and wrote about it at great length in one of his better-known essays, "Objectivity and Liberal Scholarship" (1968; reprinted in *Chomsky Reader*). What impressed him, he makes clear, was that the Barcelona uprising represented a genuine popular movement, the sudden emergence of a wholly egalitarian and self-determining society in the midst of the war, a radical transformation of the structure of society that, as Orwell depicts it in *Homage to Catalonia,* which Chomsky read eagerly, extended from various gestures of collectivization, the burning of churches, the elimination of tipping and private cars, the proliferation of graffiti, on down to the wearing of workers' clothing and forms of address—"Comrade." This moment of high revolutionary enthusiasm lasted just a few months before Franco's forces crushed the movement in Barcelona and elsewhere. Some, including Eric Hobsbawm, attribute the failure of social revolution in Spain to the "moral gymnastics" of the anarchists themselves, but, in a complex and remarkably detailed argument, Chomsky points to the opportunistic and hypocritical unwillingness of Western democracies to support the genuine freedom of Barcelona against the fascism of Franco. Thirty years after the event, Chomsky still heard an urgent contemporary message issuing from Barcelona.

Coming near the beginning of his career as a political activist, this essay actually predicts the future of Chomskyan interventions as a series of doomed, heroic, "moral" failures. But the essay resonates as well in his linguistics, which was by 1968 a twenty-year undertaking. Barcelona could be taken as a kind of social "module," a specialized system with distinct properties. One of Chomsky's primary early sources on Barcelona was the anarchist Rudolf Rocker, who had published *The Tragedy of Spain* in 1937, the same year he also published *Nationalism and Culture,* in which he described Wilhelm von Humboldt as a prominent representative of natural rights, an early opponent of the authoritarian state. Humboldt was also deeply interested in a general linguistics based on what Chomsky would come to call "Cartesian common sense," the belief that human nature is essentially reasonable, various, and creative, and must be permitted the harmonious development of its diverse and innate powers, the evidence for which is the awakening of language in the human mind. Through Rocker's writings, the young Chomsky would have been able to intuit the essential unity of politics and language, when both are seen from an anarchist point of view—the view, as it were, from Barcelona.

It is the argument emerging from this point of view that will constitute Chomsky's enduring legacy. While the political struggles in which he has been engaged will fade from—have already faded from—memory, and the mighty work he has done in linguistics is constantly evolving, taking on quite far-reaching modifications, he has, over the last thirty years, devoted himself to articulating a powerful synthetic statement, prosecuted with incomparable detail and philosophical depth. In general, he claims that his politics and his linguistics are separate enterprises, but he has, on occasion, brought the two together in a way that defines and illuminates both as aspects of a single argument.

The most luminous statement of this argument is the brief, brilliant, action-packed *Cartesian Linguistics,* a work of intellectual history generically unlike his other works, but which in other respects epitomizes them. The timing is especially crucial. Written a couple of years earlier but published while Chomsky was on sabbatical at Berkeley in 1966, the book stands in a central position in Chomsky's career, following his first, spectacular burst of revolutionary linguistics—just a year after *Aspects of the Theory of Syntax*—and preceding his major political statements. Moreover, the book was received by linguists and philosophers as an effort to occupy a middle ground between his own previous "syntactic fundamentalism," as Harris puts it, and the position of those who were arguing for the interdependence of syntax and semantics. When, for example, Chomsky commented in *Cartesian Linguistics* that "deep structure" was something "purely mental, that conveys the semantic content of the sentence," he seemed, to his elated colleagues and students who read these words back at MIT, to be renouncing his isolation and joining them in focusing on semantics (35). They discovered their mistake when Chomsky returned and immediately launched a series of lectures directed against the emphasis on semantics. But whatever the book says or implies about technical linguistics, the book stands as an unusually powerful, condensed, and capacious statement of the argument that, I am claiming, will represent Chomsky's enduring legacy.

Packing in some elements from before 1966 and some that emerged only later, the argument is the following: that the fact that children learn to speak and understand language with no effort, based on fragmentary, unsystematic, widely various, and degenerate data, and learn the same things as all other children in their linguistic environment, compels the inference that language is a genetic endowment, "universal by biological necessity"; that the mind is not, as the empiricist tradition would have it, a tabula rasa, but is rather a highly structured apparatus that includes the form of language and the disposition to use it as part of its start-up kit; that language learning involves primarily a "filling-in" of an innate structure, a structure that defines a hardwired "human nature" (making linguistics a part of "cognitive psychology"); that the fact that we can deploy a "universal grammar" in the forms stipulated by our particular natural language in order to produce an infinite string of sentences we have never before heard, in response to other sentences we have never heard, suggests that human nature is fundamentally "creative"; and, moreover, that human creativity thus understood flourishes best in a political environment free from "external" manipulation, an environment that fosters opportunities for individual expression and collective realization on the basis of a presumption of human solidarity or "species character"; and that states of affairs in which coercion and exploitation are permitted to exist violate not just the moral or legal codes, but the genetic code as well.

On the basis of the child's amazing linguistic powers, Chomsky draws rigorous inferences concerning both human nature and the optimal forms of society and government, based on what Kant described as "man's inclination and duty to *think freely*." His argument cuts across numerous disciplines including mathematics (not marked in the above précis), political theory, contemporary affairs, history, intellectual history, psychology, and philosophy. Information obtained through tireless research and the Freedom of Information Act has been as relevant to the construction of the case as has scientific research and theoretical reasoning. And yet it is possible to see as the crucible of this majestic and well-nigh global argument the moment when the young Philly boy, living in a politically aware household devoted to the study of language, heard of the fall of Barcelona, far away; when, for him, "Barcelona" became conceivable as a module of purity, freedom, and creativity under fierce attack from the various self-interested factions and forces around it because of its fidelity to "universal" principles. At this moment, whose nearest kin in intellectual history may be the moment when Gibbon saw a procession of monks passing through what had been, in ancient times, the temple of Jupiter, and instantly conceived of *The Fall of the Roman Empire,* the deeply serious, isolated boy becomes articulate, entering the world, beginning a "revolution" that has outlasted Castro's, armed with an image of language as a Barcelona of the mind. As Barsky points out in a comment that suggests more than he intends, Chomsky is fond, when explaining his positions, of such phrases as "even a ten year old could understand such a notion" (17). And indeed, there is a constant pressure in Chomsky to achieve this level of transparency, a perfectly pellucid proposition in which the truth stands forth from the obfuscations, confusions, and false complexities that had blocked our vision. Has he changed over the years? Peck asks him. "Not really, I think, in any fundamental way. I've learned a lot . . . but I cannot honestly say that my beliefs or attitudes have changed in any significant ways" (*CR* 55).

One reason Barcelona may have crystallized the young Chomsky may have been that, as described by Orwell and Rocker, the city itself, during that brief period of revolutionary glory, was *like a child,* or rather, like the sort of child that Chomsky must have been. Distinct from the various "adult" ideologies that surrounded it, alone in its fierce purity, Barcelona 1936–37 could have been seen by an imaginative youth as a civic echo, a heroic enlargement of himself; the comparison locks in with Barcelona's defeat and absorption into the corrupted world, a fate that the child will undergo as well. But the moment of fidelity to universal principles is, I am arguing, preserved by Chomsky in the amber of language. Chomsky turned linguistics inside out by changing its day-to-day enterprise from classification and description to the search for principles of regularity that would give access to the human mind itself. In Chomsky's paradigm, the child suddenly assumes a privileged position by exercising a faculty—one that, recent research indicates, begins to wither at about the age of eleven, making subsequent language learning incomparably more difficult. Previous linguistics, especially in the United States, had focused, in an anthropological spirit, on native American languages when it did not attend, in a Peircean or Saussurean spirit, to the system of signs. In both cases, society was the implied frame of reference, as it was for the generative semanticists. For Chomsky, by stark contrast, it is the unsocialized child, the primary instance not of minds but of mind—Mind itself—who is the privileged site of a rich conceptual structure waiting to be awakened by experience. One could argue, with appropriate hesitations and qualifications, that in both his political and his scientific work, Chomsky argues essentially for the presexual purity of the child; that the essential truth he discloses in his political work and wards off in his scientific insistence on modularity is that corruption or the threat of corruption is everywhere, even where you least expect them. Take, for example, the government or the media—or, more paradigmatically, the parents, who merely *appear* to be friendly and available nurturers but who, every single night, enter a different world altogether, a tainted and impure kind of existence which the child cannot, and would not, enter.

One of the aspects of the Chomskyan revolution that fascinates Harris is the social milieu of the discipline; and one of the fascinating aspects of that milieu in the present context is the Catalonian ethos of the early years especially, as Chomsky created around himself the aura of Barcelona in Cambridge. There was, for example, the modularity of the enterprise, with very nearly all of the people doing transformational grammar centered at the Research Laboratory of Electronics at MIT, which was, for a time, a well-funded revolutionary cell, highly conscious of being a subversive and embattled anomaly, a tiny tribe of righteousness among a throng of foes, "fighting for survival in a hostile world," as Robin Lakoff wrote years later (967–68). The implied intergenerational conflict peculiar to Chomsky's embattled early years revisited the discipline some years later, when young rebels—data-happy generative semanticists who celebrated anomalies and theory-destroying exceptions, and whose examples tended to focus on "Nixon" loitering around men's rooms—rose up against him; but, while they may have been counterculturalists in some ways, they could not successfully claim a monopoly on the purity of youth. For one thing, Chomsky was, while a few years older than most of them, waging the battle of the young against the Vietnam war far more vigorously and effectively than any of them. For another, it was Chomsky who went to Berkeley while they stayed at MIT; and for another, it was *Cartesian Linguistics* that stood as the decisive articulation of the "childhood" of rationalist linguistics, not their own highly technical researches; and for another, it was Chomsky who insisted on the "autonomy of syntax," the purity of the module, while they argued for a promiscuous intermingling of syntax and semantics. The rebels occupied the position of the late-sixties postadolescent; the position of the child remained Chomsky's.

The marginal presence of Robin Lakoff and a few other women not-withstanding, the entire field, especially during the sixties and seventies, had the structure, and many of the social graces, of a boys' club. When an opponent complained about Chomsky's behavior, he said that Chomsky "fights dirty," as though he bit ears. George Lakoff concluded one paper, "Nyahh, nyahh!" (see *CR* 203). And, more interestingly and revealingly, Harris reports Chomsky's view that linguistics is an "underdeveloped field," an immature and even "semi-existent" discourse whose current "infantilism" will gradually wither away as the discipline grows up (*LW* 255). But surely part of the reason linguistics is the way it is—and it may be more like other disciplines than Chomsky implies—is the powerful sense of cabal and conspiracy that seems to cling to Chomsky and those around him. One is struck, reading Chomsky on politics, by the extreme specificity of his accounts, coupled with the powerful sweep of the analysis. Chomsky's general understanding of the world, one could say, is that of a network of self-interested groups, the "ruling elite," bent on exercising as much power and influence as they can, spreading ideological illusions everywhere, plotting not the overthrow, but far more often the preservation and extension of government, all playing in their own ways at being Master of the Universe; and, against these, the tiny cells of resistance, the beleaguered pockets of truth to which Chomsky has always been attracted, from his early interest in small, mostly Zionist groups (as Barsky notes in perhaps his most interesting contribution) to the all-day classes at Penn with Zellig Harris (which constituted most of Chomsky's undergraduate education), to the Research Laboratory in Electronics, on down to the present.

And, both within this milieu and against it, stands the lonely, proud, uncorrupted outsider, a dangerous figure whose corrosive and pitiless intelligence discloses the truth others would deny. Harris attributes Chomsky's sense of his alienated position within his profession to arrogance and delusion. But it is, in a far more direct sense, a continuance of an early mindset, that of the prodigiously gifted, fiercely logical, independent, and imaginative child. Chomsky has occasionally been compared to the patriarchal Freud, but he is actually a prepubescent Stephen Daedalus.

To all these elements—the acute sense of isolation, the claim of uncorrupted purity, the sense of belonging to an oppressed minority, the application of conspiracy as a template for both political and scholarly activity, the claim to be in possession of universal rules and principles—must be added a certain distinctive tonality, to which Barsky has provided the clue. Retrieving a 1992 audiotape from "Alternative Radio," Barsky quotes an interview in which Chomsky casts his mind back to a moment in high school, a football game, when he stopped himself in mid-cheer, asking, "Why am I cheering for my high school football team? I don't know any of these people. They don't know me. I don't care about them. I hate the high school" (22). Support for the squad, which he sees as the germ of ideological coercion, has troubled Chomsky ever since, but not always for the same reason. When he raised the issue in Peck's 1987 interview, it was by way of defending the notion of "Cartesian common sense." Here it was the unbuttoned garrulity he heard on radio sports talk shows while driving around town. "People know a tremendous amount," he told Peck; "they know all sorts of complicated details and enter into far-reaching discussion about whether the coach made the right decision yesterday and so on." They are unintimidated by the supposed authority figures, and their independence of mind suggests that they could do great things if they applied themselves to the "areas that really matter to human life" rather than to this "fantasy world" (*CR* 33). The passionate expertise of the fan suggests in this instance not unthinking jingoism but rather squandered intelligence.

In both cases, however, Chomsky's own position is the same, that of the isolated, bespectacled, proud, bewildered, contemptuous, unathletic boy in the midst of a frenzied pep rally, the pep rally of modern culture. One gathers that, for Chomsky, a lively interest in sports represents an identifying mark, like the slightly pointed ear or the unusual twitch of the brow that signals the alien trying to pass as an ordinary human. One imagines him wincing involuntarily as a hitherto trusted student or colleague lets fly with some unguarded comment on the Patriots' running game—which, to be sure, has historically been unworthy of thought—or the great, all-court hustle of John "Hondo" Havlicek. "Even at MIT," he thinks to himself, his eyes narrowing.

The issue of sports raises the question of the character of Chomsky's identification with the "ordinary people" Barsky says he "champions." Certainly Chomsky is no ordinary person; his immense distinction, his gifts, his interests, his industry, his travel schedule set him apart from the general run—even the general run of A-team academics. It is difficult to imagine the details of Chomsky's interactions with what he calls the "unemployed working class, activists of one or another sort, those considered to be 'riff-raff'"—"the kind of people," he says, that "I like and take seriously" (*NC* 215). How sustained and reciprocal are these relations, anyway? On the other hand, however, Chomsky has been eloquent in his disidentification with many of those with whom he does have certain things in common. He is one of the hardest arguers of fine points around, and Harris notes, in addition to Chomsky's generosity and compassion, his unusual capacity for spleen and invective. His comments on many of his colleagues have a remarkable clarity, a bracing cleanness of line. It is unlikely, however, that his targets appreciate his stylistic brilliance. His astonishing 1971 destruction of B. F. Skinner—still a great read—invoked, as an "almost perfect world" from the behaviorist point of view, "a well-run concentration camp with inmates spying on one another and the gas ovens smoking in the distance. . . . [We could] enhance the total reinforcement and improve the culture," Chomsky continued, "by devising a still more intense threat, say, by introducing occasional screams, or by flashing pictures of hideous torture as we describe the crematoria to our fellow citizens. The culture might survive, perhaps for a thousand years" ("Psychology and Ideology," in *CR* 178). (Chomsky concedes, however, that such a reading of Skinner, while possible, would overlook "a fundamental property of Skinner's science, namely, its vacuity.") Replying to Steven Lukes, who had criticized his comments on Pol Pot, Chomsky charges that Lukes had become "an apologist for the worst slaughter relative to population since the Holocaust," that he appealed to an intellectual community whose inability to "comprehend this kind of trivial, simple, reasoning" suggests a "level of indoctrination vastly beyond what one finds in totalitarian states" (*NC* 188). Another prominent Jewish, Boston-based public intellectual, Alan Dershowitz, is depicted as at best a brother from another planet, "a complete liar, as well as a Stalinist-style thug . . . on a crazed jihad" (*NC* 171). Hans Aarsleff, a critic of *Cartesian Linguistics,* prompts an expression of omnidirectional disgust for the breed: "I've never bothered to respond, because . . . my contempt for the intellectual world reaches such heights that I have no interest in pursuing them in their gutters" (*NC* 105). Beyond candor, such comments cement Chomsky's deeply felt solitude, reinforcing his self-image—as far as Lukes, Dershowitz, and Aarsleff are concerned—as a creature of a fundamentally different kind from those around him, a difference, I have argued, whose type is that experienced by a child of a certain sort living in a world dominated by adults.

Just as pronounced and even more interesting is Chomsky's aggressive indifference to those whom he might have been expected to influence the deepest, those "postmodern" literary critics and theorists for whom "language" has been the central concept. Chomsky has little use for "theory" as a scholarly enterprise, commenting about the Frankfurt School theorists that "the ideas that seem useful also seem pretty simple, and I don't understand what all the verbiage is for" (*NC* 25). He is equally dismissive of Derrida and Lacan; but he has wavered on the latter (with whom he once dined, through the mediation of Roman Jakobson), writing to Barsky in 1995 that Lacan "at least should be read," apparently forgetting a 1989 interview published in *Radical Philosophy* in which he said that "my frank opinion is that [Lacan] was a conscious charlatan, and was simply playing games with the Paris intellectual community to see how much absurdity he could produce and still be taken seriously" ("An Interview" 32). Chomsky has a low regard for Paris intellectuals anyway, inasmuch as "almost no one in France has ever had any idea of what my political or academic work is about." Given their "standard infantilism," their "highly parochial and remarkably illiterate culture," in fact, Chomsky went so far as to "almost never [give] political talks in France" (*NC* 196). A Bulgarian living in Paris, Julia Kristeva seems to have picked up the local microbe: "Kristeva I met once. She came to my office to see me about 20 years ago, then some kind of raving Maoist, as I recall. I was never tempted to read further" (*NC* 195). And when he does read, he does not always understand. "Maybe I'm missing something, perhaps a lot. . . . Maybe I'm missing a gene [or a hormone]. I seem to be able to understand other difficult things, but virtually nothing here. . . . It could be that some entirely new form of human intelligence has arisen, beyond those known before, and those who lack the appropriate gene (evidently, me) just can't see it" (*NC* 198). Foucault, with whom he had a single encounter on Dutch television in 1971 (the transcript of which, in a little-known publication called *Reflexive Waters,* tactfully deletes Foucault's enthusiastic references to the drugs he was currently taking), is given the most generous assessment as a thinker who—after the layers and layers of obfuscation are peeled away—actually says something.

It messes you up to hear one of the great minds currently sojourning on earth pronouncing incomprehensible the very stuff you've retailed to undergraduates for twenty years. But Chomsky's modesty conceals a determined near-miss, one that, moreover, seems to be matched on the other side. Chomsky is notorious for complaining that he is ignored (even while he is, according to a recent *Arts and Humanities Citation Index,* the most-cited living person—but what sort of list is it, anyway, that lists Cicero as one of the top ten in history?), but in the field of literary criticism, ignorance of Chomsky seems to be endemic, and not just in Paris. At times, the proximity of Chomsky's thinking to that of literary theorists is tantalizing, as when Chomsky proposed a "trace theory" in 1973, the same year that the translation of Derrida's *Speech and Phenomena* appeared, with its neo-Heideggerian talk of graphematic "traces." In fact, each seems to be imperfectly aware of the other, barely conscious that the other represents a powerful challenge to which their own work, alas, only implicitly responds. Derrida's critique of the "metaphysics of presence" in all its guises seems, for example, to be an indirect attack on Chomsky's mentalism, his confident and determined approach to the secrets of the mind and the structure of human nature itself—but the issue is never joined. And while Derrida begins *Of Grammatology* by announcing a philosophical "science of writing" based on the premise that "writing *comprehends* language," he never takes extended account of the man who has made language scientific, thereby bringing it into the domain of philosophy. Nor does Chomsky—whose work invariably begins with sounds, who sees no need at all to have a theory of writing—seem overly concerned with Derrida. Of course, a shared capacity for scornful invective notwithstanding, there are stylistic differences. Camille Paglia describes Chomsky as "sanctimonious" and "nebbishy," while Derrida has, even by Paglia's lofty standards, a cosmopolitan elegance (she simply thinks he's an irrelevant idiot, a "Gloomy Gus one-trick pony") (Paglia, *Vamps and Tramps* 495; *Sex, Art, and American Culture* 241). Derrida's often-elusive, neither-right-nor-left political stance confounds those who believe in clarity and emphasis; and his rhetoric— with its wildly unpredictable affect, by turns freewheeling, pun-obsessed, inventive, intensely emotional, mournful, cryptic, droll, meandering, melancholic—does not seem to have impressed Chomsky as it has many others. Still, the fact that Chomsky positions himself squarely within the phonocentric tradition Derrida critiques, but has nowhere joined the issue is highly frustrating.

Just as striking, but perhaps less frustrating considering the possible outcome of dialogue, is the silence on the question of Chomsky by those interested in "performance." For Chomsky, too, is interested in performance, which provides him with all the evidence for his theories. Perhaps the problem is that most "performance theorists" are also invested in the neo-Foucauldian argument about the "discursive construction of the subject," and this argument finds no echo in Chomsky. Contemporary performance theorists speak of "hyper-representation," while Chomsky talks about mind. They speak about aesthetic performance, phenomenology, theatricality; they take Marxism, feminism, and Freudianism seriously; they practice literary and cultural criticism. Chomsky . . . does not. Performance has become a virtual field of "research" by those interested in issues of gender and sexuality; and, among many of these, the hidden "masculinist" agency of rationality itself is taken as a given. What better way, they ask, to assert yourself in the world than by claiming "neutrality" or "reason" for your (in fact male) arguments? But reason, for Chomsky, is not performed, nor is it associated in any serious way with a given sex or gender. It is won through hard work, and, when it does its work, it invariably works against those who advance their interests by illegitimate means.

We can take up the mystifying issue of the willed ignorance of Chomsky—that is, Chomsky's willed ignorance and the ignorance of him by others—in terms of three concepts which are important to both Chomsky and those engaged in "theory," but, in the manner in which they are formulated by contemporary theoreticians, are simply and absolutely unacceptable to Chomsky, as are his formulations to them.

The first is the unconscious. The capacity for language on which Chomsky has staked his career is unconscious, and, in this respect, crucially different from the "innate ideas" posited by Leibniz and Descartes, whom Chomsky claims as predecessors. But Chomsky's unconscious is not precisely Freud's, being structural rather than dynamic. The Chomskyan unconscious provides a form that language acquisition in a given environment then fills in; it does not have a separate agenda from consciousness, but underlies and enables it. And Chomsky envisions nothing like the endless opportunities for communication—and the consequent opportunities for subversion, sublimation, transcendence, translation, illness, or embarrassment—between the two systems that are so prominent a feature of Freud's account. In Chomsky, there is timelessness and an absence of negation, but no surge of desire, no symptomatology, no obsession with sex or the body—quite the opposite—no substitution of psychic for external reality, no regressive "death instinct," no analogue to the ambivalent "preconscious." Chomsky's unconscious is as it were written from within latency; it is biological, but not bodily. Freud is, of course, deeply interested in the role played by language in the unconscious, but his interest is chiefly drawn to such disturbances as schizophrenia, in which words become objects themselves, and subject to the same distortions and condensations as dream-thoughts. In fact, Chomsky's sometime opinion of Lacan as trash-theory notwithstanding, his unconscious corresponds rather more closely to the Lacanian Real, the unsymbolizable because wholly unacceptable kernel of desire that generates a fantasy, indeed, but one that virtually constitutes "reality." Similarly, Chomsky's unconscious never achieves consciousness—science can only guess at it—and it is, through language, very largely responsible for structuring "reality." The decisive difference is that Lacan's own discourse attempts to mime that of the unconscious, while Chomsky's attempts to describe its form in scientific terms.

Despite Chomsky's political interests, his unconscious is not "political." Indeed, the nonrelation of Chomsky and Jameson is one of the darker holes of contemporary intellectual history. What's the problem here? Why do two of the most eminent intellectuals in the country—men of roughly the same generation, with comparable stature, compatible politics, and highly developed interest in language—have virtually nothing to say to, or even about, each other? Why do the indexes to Jameson's books include "*Civilization and Its Discontents,*" "Chrestien de Troyes," "*Chinatown* (Polanski)," and "Clash, the"—but not "Chomsky"? Certainly there are political differences in that Chomsky's anarchism and militant individualism do not square with Jameson's dreamvisions of a utopian collectivism; but surely, one might feel, the left is big enough to accommodate these differences. One might, but Chomsky probably does not; nor, with his acute ingrained sense of the operation of small power elites and self-interested conspiratorial groups, would he have any response but indignant incomprehension at Jameson's notion that all class consciousness, which Jameson describes as "ideological in the strongest sense," is "in its very nature Utopian." I will return to the concept of ideology below and focus here on the factor that, for Jameson, produces ideology in the weakest sense, in the process rendering politics "unconscious": ethics. For Jameson, ethics is the ideological form taken by a politics that for whatever reason cannot manifest itself as such. Thus, for example, a given opposition whose natural or authentic form is political struggle will be coded as an ethical opposition between good and evil. Chomsky, by contrast, believes that ethical principles guide, or ought to guide, politics, and that both are highly conscious activities, the more conscious the better. An "unconscious" politics is, for Chomsky, simply a sloppy or unrealized politics. All the real action occurs on the conscious level, and if people are unconscious of reality, it is because they are simply unaware, probably because some powerful group has conspired to conceal the truth. For Chomsky, as he put it in *American Power and the New Mandarins,* "it is the responsibility of intellectuals to speak the truth and to expose lies," adding, with mystified annoyance, that this obvious truth is missed by "the modern intellectual" (*CR* 60). Jameson counts as one such intellectual. His discourse is far more sophisticated, far more theoretical than Chomsky's—and far more abstract, to the point where the word *political* seems, from a Chomskyan point of view, virtually a misnomer.

The second subject on which Chomsky and contemporary sages refuse to communicate is that of power. Here the intimate enemy would, of course, be Foucault, whose "hegemonic" theory of power would, one might expect, be deeply repugnant to Chomsky. According to Foucault's most suggestive formulations, power is not modeled on the "repressive hypothesis" in which a superior force issues from a dominant center and compels the compliance of subordinates. Rather, he says, it circulates everywhere, meeting a "resistance" that is just more power. We all participate in power, whose center is everywhere and limit is nowhere; thus, we are all complicit in the construction of a society in which no one is exempt from processes of regularization, normalization, and discipline. The consequence is that "resistance" can claim no moral superiority to "power," for they are simply different names for the same thing. We do not, Foucault insisted in the defining exchange during his debate with an amazed Chomsky, engage in political struggle to advance the cause of justice; we do it to win.

Chomsky, of course, made no concessions in arguing the precise opposite. But it is instructive to examine the understanding of power in general that underlies both their positions. At first glance, one might feel that Chomsky would have no use for Foucault's highly suspicious rhetoric of complexity, that he believes that what Foucault dismisses as the outmoded repressive hypothesis is in fact the most adequate account of power—with a trap door to allow for the free rational mind. But in fact this is not the case. For Chomsky believes, as the title of one of his books suggests, in the "manufacture of consent." He believes, that is, that with the assistance of the media, governmental and corporate agencies can effectively disseminate lies and contradictions that do not square with observable reality, and can by this means bring large numbers of people to a degraded condition of ideologically induced delusion in which they consent to demonstrably false propositions. This broad-shouldered, meat-and-potatoes macro-argument actually entails, however, theoretical delicacies that approach those of Foucault—as Chomsky's soft words about Foucault, alone among Parisians in having something, however slight, to say, seem to concede.

For the manufacture of consent produces, when successful, a powerful sense of free will. If the journalist has at some deep level signed on to the overall program of the state, then he may well believe that freedom rings, that he is at liberty to tell the truth, that the state does not censor. It is the deep level of assent that Chomsky focuses on, pointing out that those who disagree with the basic propositions (that the United States is an imperial power, that democratic states routinely commit acts of base violence, that corporations care only about their profits, etc.) are relegated to the status of a "broad spectrum of opinion"; their view, while perhaps represented in some small measure, is not picked up and carried forward as genuine "news," the form of the ongoing story. For that vast majority who consent to the essential program, the experience of freedom is genuine. Hardworking investigative reporters get up and go to work each morning convinced that they're discovering and purveying the truth, publishing even those stories that discredit (at a superficial level, Chomsky would say) the official version of things. But in fact, they're operating within a model established at a deep level, below their capacity or desire to interrogate. The phenomenological experience of freedom and autonomy on the part of journalists, teachers, intellectuals, or popularly elected officials actually secures the larger-scale wishes of the ruling elite. From a certain point of view, then, the distinction between wholesale and retail is fudged; everybody is "freely" producing the consent that is actually desired only by a very few, power *appears* to be shared and circulating, it's all around, where you least suspect it; everything—hullo! What's this? –Michel! What brings you here?

The radical distinction between Chomsky and Foucault, in other words, may ultimately be pretty fragile. This fragility is recorded in a fascinating way in one of the very few texts written by a contemporary critical theorist that takes Chomsky seriously, Christopher Norris's *Uncritical Theory* (1992). Norris rehearses the Chomsky-Foucault debate, comparing their general positions, and declares Chomsky the winner and still champion, a man whose arguments are not only "completely at odds with Foucault," but also clearly superior "to any reader whose mind remains open to persuasion on rational grounds" (110). It is, in fact, difficult to side with the cynical Foucault in this particular debate (especially since the photos accompanying the text show him at his most ghoulish), but what is truly interesting about Norris's argument is the unsettling way in which it underscores an unexpected but persistent common argument. Thus, after setting up the debate as a clash of titans from wholly opposed camps, Norris finds himself making sotto voce concessions: "Of course there are points on which Foucault and Chomsky can make common cause despite their far-reaching disagreements. . . . Now of course there is a sense—and

Chomsky concedes as much—in which dissident truth-claims are always *to some extent* bound up with existing forms of power/knowledge. . . . Now of course this passage [from Chomsky] could be read as supporting one of Foucault's major theses. . . . As I remarked above, there is a measure of agreement between Foucault's and Chomsky's positions. . . . [Chomsky's model] comes, on the face of it, fairly close to Foucault's way of thinking. . . . Again, one could argue that this leaves Chomsky in a position of broad agreement with Foucault . . ." (see *Uncritical Theory* 112–15).

Norris finds himself on oiled glass, laboring to establish some clear difference that any rational person would recognize. Most often, however, it is degree rather than difference that he appeals to. We might recognize the force of the postmodernist position, he says, and still not "go all the way with Nietzsche's amoralist pronouncement that truth is nothing more than a particular kind of lie," or "push this argument all the way to Baudrillard's desperate conclusion," or "go all the way down to the point where any notion of journalistic truth or honesty would appear just a species of naïve illusion" (see *UT* 111–14). Norris does not render a verdict on the naïveté implicit in Chomsky's relation to Faurisson. But he does blame Foucault for adopting a position that "leaves no room for genuine debate," with all truth-value drained from assertions. The question that remains after reading Norris, however, is whether there *is* much "room" for debate between Foucault and Chomsky on the question of power.

On the third subject of failed dialogue, ideology, Chomsky's position is not too close for comfort, but rather too traditional for contemporary relevance. Ideology, *chez* Chomsky, is "a mask for self-interest" ("Objectivity and Liberal Scholarship," in *CR* 83). Someone in a position to do so puts out a set of claims that look neutral and descriptive, but in fact serve his or her own ends, producing "false consciousness" or misrecognition of the truth in the minds of those influenced. Against this stand the methodological safeguards of science: keen and unbiased observation, accurate description of particulars, rigorously drawn inferences. By definition, science cannot serve, propagate, or tolerate ideology, because science can have no self-interest—hence, perhaps, Chomsky's curious accounts of the disciplinary battles raging around him, battles that have virtually defined and in some cases destroyed the careers of many others but have left him, he suggests, strangely indifferent and unaffected, as if he, a scientist, simply has no stake in such uninteresting squabbles. Chomsky cannot, therefore, conceive of Jameson's "strong sense" of ideology as a general intellectual/attitudinal structure that determines a group's apprehension of reality, for the only legitimate apprehension of reality is scientific, that is, free of attitude, of point of view. Nor, *a fortiori,* could Chomsky grasp

Žižek's proposition that reality is only accessible to us as a dream structured by an obscene, wholly "inadmissable" desire. "In vain do we try to break out of the ideological dream by 'opening our eyes and trying to see reality as it is,'" Žižek writes (*Sublime Object of Ideology* 48). When we do so—or rather, when we think we have done so—we have only succeeded in wrapping even more, and even tighter, coils of ideology around ourselves. Then why write? Chomsky might ask. Terry Eagleton begins his book *Ideology* with sixteen definitions of ideology, only one of which—"false ideas which help to legitimate a dominant political power"—finds any support in Chomsky (1-2). All the rest ("that which offers a position for a subject," "forms of thought motivated by social interest," "the conjuncture of discourse and power," "the process whereby social life is converted to a natural reality," etc.) seem, from a Chomskyan perspective, weak, evasive, merely distracting, or plainly and perniciously false.

There must be an inverse relation between force and nuance, rhetorical power and theoretical sophistication. The assurance with which Chomsky holds to his single, rather primitive account of ideology invigorates his writing to an almost alarming degree. "The results are nil," he writes of Skinner's quarter-century of work, whose specifically ideological and anti-scientific pursuit of behaviorism stimulates Chomsky to rhetorical peaks few can match. "It remains impossible for Skinner to formulate the relevant notions in his terms, let alone investigate them. What is more, no nontrivial scientific hypotheses with supporting evidence have been produced to substantiate the extravagant claims to which he is addicted. Furthermore, this record of failure was predictable from the start. . . . My impression is, in fact, that [Skinner's] claims are becoming more extreme and more strident as the inability to support them and the reasons for this failure become increasingly obvious" (*CR* 170). And Chomsky is barely halfway through. He might, in fact, have profitably stopped at that point, because he immediately proceeds to a distinction between persuasion and control that suggests a real crudity of thought, an inability to detect gradations of force in the formation of belief, judgment, or opinion. "Persuasion," he declares bluntly, "is no form of control at all" (*CR* 171). One can be persuaded that one has been persuaded when one has really been controlled, but Chomsky seems determinedly unaware of this possibility, which, incidentally, defines—according to several of Eagleton's definitions—the operations of ideology.

It is as if Chomsky is missing a word or a concept here, and his thinking has become, as a consequence, stiffnecked. That word might, in fact, be *hegemony*, a term applied both to the unconscious and to power as well as to ideology. The term entered Western academic discourse on the publication in 1970 of an English translation of the *Prison Notebooks* of the Italian antifascist Antonio Gramsci, a political prisoner under Mussolini who rapidly became a hero of the theoretical left. Gramsci deployed the term as a name for the "organic" relationship that properly bound the leaders of opinion and the class whose interests they represented. In this sense, the word functioned as a name for the desired affinity between leaders and led, and a warning against excessive theoretical abstraction. But, in an interesting ambivalence, Gramsci also used the word to designate the kind of "consent" that, in Chomsky's terms, was relentlessly "manufactured" by the ruling elite, the willing participation of the people in their own domination. In this second sense, hegemony might indicate, more darkly, a condition in which people have "forgotten" the acts of violence or coercion that founded their liberal social order—a condition, in other words, in which a general amnesia has befallen the polis such that the distinction between persuasion and control has been functionally obliterated because, from different points of view, people are both free and unfree.

Gramsci sees no real limits to the extent to which people can be persuaded that they have been persuaded while in fact they have been controlled. People are, Gramsci argues, essentially malleable, unencumbered by a fixed and immutable "human nature," a chimera which, he argues, Marxist science has proven to be nothing more or other than "the totality of historically determined social relations." Chomsky attacks this comment as just another example of the collaboration of Marxism and empiricism in the production of an ideological fantasy, but never takes up the issue of hegemony (*CR* 196). Nor does he, to my knowledge, have anything to say about the work of the most widely known contemporary exponent of hegemony, Ernesto Laclau; and here the silence is, once again, deeply intriguing.

On the surface, the two seem to be virtually eggs from the same basket—both left-libertarians interested in what Laclau calls, in *Hegemony and Socialist Strategy*, "radical democracy," both concerned with language, both arguing from the nature of language to the form of a just society. But—once again—there is a bar, or perhaps a flaming sword, that blocks dialogue. For Laclau, language is defined by Saussure, whose account of the arbitrariness of the sign, the internal split within the sign, the sign system, and the social system that keeps it all running in an orderly and systematic way constitutes the kind of "scientific" knowledge that grounds theory in a body of known fact. From this body of fact, Laclau derives a complex theory of the "unfixity" of every individual, class, or social identity, which are all relational and contingent, achieved not through the expression of some stable essence but rather through "articulatory practices" emerging in a fluid and ever-changing social medium. From Saussure's understanding of the sign system as "differences without positivity," Laclau moves "beyond the positivity of the social" to an account of discursively produced social "positions" whose provisionality provides the essence of "radical democracy." For in Laclau's view (and that of Chantal Mouffe, his coauthor), it is only if we see identity as "unsutured" and structurally "antagonistic"—linguistic through and through—that we will be able to grasp the necessity of creating a social order that is structurally dynamic, receptive to an open-ended future. And, Laclau further contends, it is this openness, condensed into the concept of the "empty signifier," that represents the essence of democracy (see *Emancipations*). The similarity to Chomsky's basic mode of argument, which moves from a description of facts about language to prescriptions about the social order, masks a deeper antipathy. For Chomsky believes that if people really were subject to fluctuations to this degree, if there were no "positive" human nature beyond the reach of articulation, then people could not protest—or, at least, their protests would have no conceptual weight—when the ruling powers articulated them in whatever direction suited them. It is only the positivity of language, and thus of human being, that grounds a resistance to oppression. Only if we think of ourselves as organisms in the natural world, with a nature disclosed by the phenomenon of language, will we be able to infer not just a capacity but a right and even a duty to think freely. The determined, even aggressive argument for infinite malleability seems, to Chomsky, an instance of intellectual treason and political suicide, not to mention a sign of profound ignorance about language.

In a very general sense, there are two obstacles to dialogue with Chomsky. Especially in his political work, Chomsky sustains a belief in a knowable world of fact that is so powerful that a "literary" person must sense, however dimly, a deep threat to the universe of infinite possibility, with "real life" always permeable to fantasy, that he or she inhabits as a condition of professional life. Chomsky has spoken of the way in which, because of de facto censorship and disinformation, people are prevented from obtaining a total grasp of any given situation. People may, for example, know one or two stories of the F.B.I.'s wickedness, but they don't comprehend the totality; and this disempowering fragmentariness defines part of Chomsky's mission, to render the total picture with its overall pattern. We could call this the *Men in Black* premise, recalling the film in which a secret force tries to protect society from the knowledge of the widespread presence of aliens, so that people can continue to lead their deluded but untroubled and productive lives. Chomsky, too, believes that if people knew the whole truth, their lives would be shattered, but argues that it is the entire apparatus of the ruling powers, not just a few agents, that conspires to keep people ignorant as a way of keeping them passive and ensuring the continuance of privilege. But especially in a time of peace and prosperity, however merely apparent or local those may be, people do not crave such blinding moral clarity. They cherish the very pettiness and unimportance of their lives, their sports teams and clothing catalogs, their habits and addictions, their fantasies and fictions; they resist entering into the closed world—the *noir* universe—of total knowledge.

Chomsky's linguistic work presents a symmetrical difficulty. As Harris shows in very considerable detail, Chomsky's "revolution" is ongoing: the initial theory involving phrase structure rules, transformational rules, deep structure, and so on, has been subject to a continual process of refinement and revision, leading, in the early nineties, to a new paradigm altogether. Transformations have been transformed out of existence; deep structure has been deep-sixed, and the entire picture has been radically recomposed. It seems that language can be reconceptualized, as if it were an "arbitrary" sign, even an "empty signifier" that could bear any set of attributes, answer to any call. Chomsky, Harris suggests, should be considered "a great and restless artist—like Picasso, with his postimpressionist period, his blue period, his rose period, his cubist period" (*LW* 233). In short, Chomsky's ongoing linguistic work presents, at least to the mildly informed outsider, the alarming possibility of theoretical infinity, a freeplay unburdened by resistant fact and driven by the sense of invention rather than discovery. And this, too, is repellent to "theorists" who, despite their general ignorance and rejection of science, and their desire to live in an expanding universe, still retain a belief in measurable progress toward the goal of an adequate description.

But in the end, the reason that contemporary thinkers seem to be just as hard at work "forgetting Chomsky" as they are remembering him is that despite a wealth of common issues, common values, and a common emphasis on language, he speaks, and speaks of, a fundamentally different language. Indeed, the hoped-for dialogue never occurs in large measure *because* of the common investment in language. For the word *language* simply does not refer to the same thing for Chomsky as it does for the others. They begin with Saussure, and perhaps Peirce and Wittgenstein, all of whose accounts of language face outward, toward the middle distance of system and society, while Chomsky faces both inward toward biology and mind and *way* outward toward universality. Contemporary theorists seem predisposed to a positive evaluation of such diverse concepts as contingency, freeplay, materiality, ungroundedness, arbitrariness, systematicity, and order; Chomsky dwells on the granite slab of mental necessity, but his understanding of linguistic performance stresses its perfect "creative" unpredictability. So utter and fundamental is the difference that it must seem to all concerned that the other side has—*ignored language.* There may be no way of overcoming this genuinely radical difference. But, properly considered, the difference itself may yield a different, if not a deeper, truth about "the nature of language" than anybody has yet grasped.

Commenting in 1987 on the last books of Northrop Frye, Geoffrey Hartman proposed that advanced age should be considered a style, a "schematic" or "skeletal" reduction of the author's essential message, its leanest and most structurally lucid articulation. Some of Hartman's own more seasoned colleagues can be interestingly considered in this light. Harold Bloom, a crucial intellectual ally of Hartman's at one time, has, especially with his book *The Western Canon*, become the human incarnation of a body of texts he had already memorized. Since the 1986 *Memoires for Paul de Man*, Jacques Derrida has become increasingly preoccupied with spectres, ghosts, memories—the funereal in general. He is getting on; but in his very earliest works, Derrida had invoked the "dead letter" of the text as the decisive agent in the undoing of Western metaphysics, the "carrier of death" into the heart of the myth of living presence. Eventually, one could argue, Derrida abandoned his distracting concerns with language and philosophy and settled down to talk about death itself. For Paul de Man, the case has been made that his later work on the false seductions of the "aesthetic ideology" constituted a complex rectification of the distortions and moral confusion of his "wartime journalism"; but one could also maintain that the journalism actually engaged all the major themes of his mature work, with the added frill of collaboration, which he later shed as inessential to the project.

Hartman's new book *The Fateful Question of Culture* may represent the most distilled form to date of a remarkably various scholarly project now steadily approaching the half-century mark. It is not, to be sure, altogether obvious that this is the case. For to those who recall classical Hartman—the distinguished Romanticist, the philosophically acute deconstructer, the exuberantly scandalous advocate of critical creativity—the new book is, at first glance, nothing like. It is morally earnest, rigorously unplayful, concerned with civic virtue and personal morality. And, with chapters on Wordsworth, the concept of culture, the Holocaust, the question of public discourse, the book is heterodox to the point where it may not seem like a single argument at all, more a scattering of bones than a proper skeleton. But given Hartman's advancing years—he was born in 1929—we may well ask: is this what he's been about all along? If so, what is the essential structure of concern; what kind of creature is indicated by these bones? To approach these questions, we must read Hartman in an archeological spirit, under the sign of return—the sign which, as it happens, hovers like an evening star over the beginning of his first book, *The Unmediated Vision,* where he draws attention to Wordsworth's account, in "Tintern Abbey," of his fateful second visit to the Wye Valley: "Once again / Do I behold these steep and lofty cliffs . . . ." To assemble the entirety, to reconstruct the entire beast, we must proceed as if *The Fateful Question of Culture* were such a return, a beholding or re-beholding of things once glimpsed but not, perhaps, fully grasped.

The book's high and sometimes windy argument concerns the contradictions of culture. In one of its phases, culture represents a human aggregation rooted in place, in nature, in ethnicity, in customs, in nationality, a model of collective identity that answers to the feeling of being an insubstantial outsider to life. Culture is "an embodiment to satisfy a ghostly hunger" of the kind that besets us moderns, with our heavy investments in abstraction, cosmopolitanism, rationalism, and individualism (*Fateful Question of Culture* 38; hereafter *FQ*). Culture is above all a form of identity. Groups typically assert their own distinctiveness by making claims about their culture, not about their political or social structures, which, however worthy, are too secular and disenchanted to provide a sense of grounding. Culture not only grounds; in a sense, it *is* ground: it seems to promise an identity born of the earth, and retains, Hartman argues, a suggestion of agriculture. Buying into this aspect of culture is, however, like playing air guitar; for culture is itself a phantom "as devouring as a vampire," an abstraction sometimes strategically allied with a commodified high culture that represents itself not as *a* culture but as culture per se (38). The split in the concept of culture between earth and wind repeats itself within the intellectuals who most eagerly embrace this concept, for they are at once the only ones capable of demystifying culture's pretensions and "deracinated airheads" (216).

As a ghostly embodiment, "culture" is its own negation, its own worst nightmare. But it can create nightmares for others, too. Circulating within the concept of culture is the cult, unnatural but powerfully cohesive and ambiguously religious. Whether as agriculture or as cult, the emphasis in culture always falls on authenticity and purity. Wherever purification projects arise, some account of culture is generally nearby. The Holocaust was, Hartman argues, an extreme but representative form of culture-consciousness, originating in a spirit of "populist ecstasy" as a *Kulturkampf* and proceeding to genocide. Hartman's acute sensitivity to the violence that can attend cultural arguments sets him decisively apart from other contemporary culture-theorists, who, collectively, endorse culture's authenticity while ignoring its will to reduce difference in the name of unity, its genocidal potential. According to the contemporary consensus, or "myth," as Walter Benn Michaels once bluntly described it, what you do, or ought to do, or ought to want to do, can be read straight off from what you are. If you "belong" to a given culture, then your identity, your values, and your character follow. What's missing in this anodyne argument, Hartman would contend, are the downside potentialities.

Another note missing from the contemporary chorus concerns the cultural function of aesthetics. Against an anti-aesthetic tide, Hartman argues that art can play a public role in shaping cultural discourse and consciousness, that it can help to define and refine the dialect of the tribe, and indeed the tribe itself. While Heidegger's various silences, avoidances, and evasions had a coarsening cultural effect, Hartman says, the discourse of art could work in the opposite direction, enabling people to overcome the distance separating them from others and from themselves: "And *is it not here*," he asks with unusual emphasis, "*that art, which generically combines aesthetic distance and emotional participation, finds its value?*" (FQ 122)

The question is answered with a single word: Wordsworth. In Wordsworth, Hartman discovers a sensibility attuned to the ghostliness of the post-Enlightenment ethos, but one who did not turn, in response, to exclusion, violence, or noisy proclamations of national identity. Rather, Hartman demonstrates, we find in Wordsworth a powerful new conception of culture based on sympathy not only with nature, but with wanderers, vagrants, the lost bits of the community, which Wordsworth prized as the most distinct and authentic voices available, invaluable mentors in the growth of a poet's, and a culture's, mind. Profoundly English, Wordsworth yet reminds us that the literary canon can serve not just as a vanity mirror for nationalists, but as a common collective endowment, even an "immune system" against identitarian viruses. Hartman virtually attributes to Wordsworth the fact that England did not suffer a Reign of Terror, and did not inflict itself on other nations in the manner of Napoleonic France.

A proper culture of criticism, Hartman argues, might profitably take as its project the transmission of the accomplishments represented by the canon, teaching principally the unity-in-heterogeneity of these accomplishments and not their utility as markers of cultural identity or signs of the nation's greatness. Hartman is skeptical of contemporary "multiculturalism," which seems to him undertheorized, sentimental, violence-prone, and forgetful of the key fact, that "it was created in the *wake* of an older idea of culture, by the latter's heroic, historical struggles for land or against the land" (*FQ* 185). Multiculturalism has misplaced nature, work, and deep time. And so the task for us is not so much to edit the idea of culture so that only the affirmative side is left, but to remember everything, nature and work included, in the hope that the good will outweigh the bad. We must try to preserve the sense of grounding while avoiding provincial and exclusionary fantasies; or as Hartman puts it, we must try "to complete the French Revolution without becoming despotic" (179). The question for us now, he says, "is whether culture can diminish aggression and tilt the balance toward love" (14).

So it's come to this, the career begun in 1954 and continued through more than twenty books since. What strikes—even pokes—the contemporary eye in Hartman's new argument are his radically unfashionable emphasis on nature; an equally uncongenial reminder of the constant potential for violence in one branch, at least, of the family of "culture"; and a manifestly retro assertion of an emancipatory function for the aesthetic. But even more arresting, in this apparently discordant and even disorderly text, is the repetitive, probing movement of Hartman's thought as it picks over and over a nested set of concerns, including literary history, literary criticism, literature, philosophy, public language, the memory and meaning of the Holocaust, and, at the very bottom of the nest, identity itself. The scattered bones of these diverse concerns are yet haunted by the rest of the argument so patiently evolved over the course of Hartman's other books, and acquire their true countenance and full dimension from that argument, just as the essential message of those other books achieves, we are hypothesizing, its most crystallized and essential expression here. An account of the totality must be speculative, for no single text could possess both form and substance of the whole. But there is a totality, I would argue, discernible most readily in certain "incoherent" moments in which the surface of a given text is disturbed by the pressures of forces that exceed the subject at hand, and even the expressive powers of language itself.

One of the most ripened of such moments in the Hartman oeuvre is the preface to *Beyond Formalism,* a collection of essays published in 1970, just before his traumatizing encounter with Derrida but well into the friendship with Bloom, to whom the book is dedicated. This four-page text begins by asking, "What, after all, is *criticism?*" (ix). The banal question entails, Hartman notes, "theoretical difficulties," especially those associated with history. Now, with Derrida waiting in the wings and de Man's *Blindness and Insight* just published, theoretical difficulties were about to become the order of the day. But those difficulties were to take linguistic and not historical form, and in that respect Hartman was out of synch. Nor was his abrupt, fractured answer to the question of criticism destined to become a consensus position: "Corpses of ideas, a self-dissolving or purgative series of reflections" (ix). This cryptic fragment still disturbs for its gratuitous evocativeness, which seems to point in some other direction than criticism, even to respond to some other question.

That would be the question of life and death, and their parareligious combination. Criticism, Hartman suggests, is a record of the scourging of the responsive mind by the literary text. The critical mind, according to Hartman, is cleansed and wintry, mortified of concepts by the scourging power of sensory particulars. A graveyard of ideas, criticism is haunted by ghosts, which are, as we can already begin to see, Hartman's most durable figure, the anchor of an entire system of images that metastasize and metaphorize almost without limit. Art itself, he says in *Beyond Formalism*, is something that "does not have real body, and yet is," and therefore "must be a species of ghost" (103).

Art kills. That, at least, is what readers may conclude from the following, richly obscure sentence, in which Wordsworth's attack on habit is folded into an ascetic understanding of the agency of art: "The natural positivity of the mind is engaged only to be chastened, as the literary work . . . teases the reader out of thought" ("Preface" to *Beyond Formalism* ix; hereafter *BF*). The critical mind is thwarted on the way to a desire, humbled before a force that is, paradoxically, strictly negative in its operation. By "natural positivity," Hartman seems to mean a tendency to settle things, to achieve a determined final solution, a tendency to conceptualization checked only, it appears, by the corrosive effects of literature, which purges the mind of its own detritus. And so art kills—the death instinct itself: the mind "naturally" seeks its own death by investing in concepts, and must be redeemed for life by art.

Once, Hartman believed in a pure perception, or, to recall the title of his first, remarkably precocious book, in an "unmediated vision." There, in 1954, Hartman spoke in the accents of a German Romantic about a return to knowledge through a second naiveté, about the "pure immediacy of perception," the "creative power in the senses," and their capacity to shape "real, immediate interpretations" (*Unmediated Vision* 154; hereafter *UV*). "Words," he said there, "do not answer to words" (a pronouncement he would reverse almost exactly in the 1984 essay "The Culture of Criticism," where he would assert that "the return to things is always really a return to a text") (*UV* 128; "Culture of Criticism" 382). But by 1970, when he was writing the preface to *Beyond Formalism*, Hartman had abandoned this youthful creed, and was emphasizing not the embodied reader, but literature's own "flight from literariness," a kind of kamikaze instinct to self-immolation that structures the work of art from within (ix). Now, it is not the reader but the text itself that tries to go "beyond formalism" in a quest Hartman acknowledges to be hopeless, a quest to achieve a direct intuition of reality. The critical recognition of the limits of formalism merely accedes to this fact about literature and tries to find a way to live with it, and with the endless mediation that results from a lack of grounding. We cannot, Hartman says, hope to "intuit things directly," and must resign ourselves to myths, dreams, "consciousness of consciousness" (ix). What was once the middle is now the end—an endless middle.

Ascesis always has a payback; and if we give up on the senses and on formalism, Hartman says, we get in return an enriched understanding of "art's role in the life of the artist, his culture, and the human community" ("Preface" ix). We read through literature to culture, which is conceived in ghostly terms that endure even in *The Fateful Question of Culture,* as does the keen sense of the danger of purity. "Oneness makes war," Hartman says in the preface, quoting D. H. Lawrence (xii). But perhaps the preface's most memorable moment, the one that most decisively transcends the occasion, is an account of the purifying "journey" of criticism, which is said to pass through "a deeply negative moment: solipsism or despair, self-emptying or the brooding dark." An extravagant way, it seems, to describe literary criticism, but Hartman does not stop there, proceeding to ask whether this "zero point" is best conceived as a "cataclysm like the Black Death, Protestantism, the French Revolution, the German 'Kahlschlag.'" "Such questions," he blandly concludes this disturbingly overheated passage, "arise in every wholistic consideration of art" (x–xi).

Introducing a collection of essays with a brief preface, Hartman finds himself telling another kind of story altogether, describing criticism as a Way of Privation, a Middle Passage. Hartman stands, at this moment, at a fascinating juncture in his career, a radical middle in which he can no longer believe in embodiment but cannot yet fully embrace the mediation of language. The idea of the middle is beginning to command his attention and even respect, but not yet his love. Take for example the discussion in *Beyond Formalism* of Blanchot, whose novels evoke a "curious middle world, or rather middle void." Blanchot, Hartman argues, can only discover "the sphere of his liberty" in a "new and hard concept of mediation, which defines man purely by the quality of the void in him." The artist, Hartman concludes with a trace of bitterness, "bears the curse of mediacy" (108).

Indeed, we all bear this curse. In what is surely the most influential essay in *Beyond Formalism,* "The Voice of the Shuttle: Language from the Point of

View of Literature," Hartman describes middles with an obsessive evocativeness, as a fragile domain of aesthetic freedom, the very site of meaning, and more. "So far," he begins an often-quoted passage, "all we know is that figures of speech may be characterized by overdetermined ends and indeterminate middles," and that this indeterminacy "allows, if it does not actually compel, interpretation" (*BF* 339). After a dazzlingly improvisatory performance (that includes a passing reference to middles as "ghosts of departed quantities"), he abruptly declares that "human life, like a poetical figure, is an indeterminate middle between overspecified poles always threatening to collapse it. . . . Art narrates that middle region and charts it like a purgatory, for only if it exists can life exist" (*BF* 347). Especially in "periods of condensation" when life is pushed up against the poles, art becomes precious: "Is there any authentic way," Hartman asks, "of inserting a middle strong enough to satisfy a now extremist imagination?" (*BF* 347, 348). There might be, if we knew more precisely what those poles were, and what that middle actually contained or might contain. But the passage, far from resolving the problem of poetic language, is itself a "figure of speech": it clearly reflects some trauma, some intimate experience of "overdetermination," but remains resolutely "indeterminate."

This understanding of figurality distinguishes Hartman decisively from the "boa deconstructers" and "skywriters," as he called them, with whom he was often grouped. For de Man, rhetoric was a dimension of literary language; for Derrida, metaphor represented an antirealist component of language as such, even the rigorous language of philosophy; for Hillis Miller, tropes constituted cognitive impasses, abysses, or absurdities that marked the disappearance of God, or, later, of epistemological assurance. In this crowd, Hartman stands alone in his insistence that the subject at issue was "human life," especially "culture," alone in his effort to broaden rather than to restrict or cripple the scope of criticism.

Still, as the lighthearted characterization of his colleagues suggests, Hartman seemed to enjoy himself tremendously during the decade of deconstruction, which concluded with the death of de Man in 1983. *The Fate of Reading* (1975), and especially *Criticism in the Wilderness* (1980) and *Saving the Text* (1981), an exuberant response to Derrida's *Glas,* represent Hartman in a decidedly buoyant mood as he celebrated first "the joyous franchise of art," and then, beginning in the mid-seventies, the equally joyous franchise of criticism, in particular the "happy discipline" of deconstruction ("Culture of Criticism" 382). What deconstruction gave Hartman was not only a sobering awareness of the difficulty of moving beyond formalism, the obduracy of the mechanisms of tropes and figures, but also a quickened sense of the positive possibilities of mediation. During this time, the middle became a playground, a scene of gratification. In "The Voice of the Shuttle" (1969), interpretation was simply a scene of opportunity, like "a football game. You spot a hole and you go through"; but five years later, in *The Fate of Reading,* a new tonality appeared, in which "interpretation is a feast, not a fast. It imposes an obligatory excess" (*BF* 351; *Fate of Reading* 14; hereafter *FR*). Now, interpretation is a performance of desire, and critical writing an ambivalent *homage* not precisely to the maternal breast but to "the doublebreasted book" (*FR* 19). The gap that had once signified a chastening and a privation, a cleansing escape from concepts, had come, by the mid-seventies, to signify the astonishing miracle of life itself in the face of the forces of closure.

But while the mood is light, the stakes are unexpectedly high, as Hartman insistently implicates literary criticism in a project of a very different kind than the mere explication of texts. Moreover, the old spooks linger, albeit in new sheets. Now it is not art alone that is ghostly, but the critic as well: "the book begins to question the questioner, its *qui vive* challenges him to prove he's not a ghost" (*FR* 190). The spectre of insubstantiality or unreality both empowers and haunts the scene of criticism at this heady moment, during which the governing idea seems to be: that which is not alive cannot be killed, and has therefore achieved a kind of immunity. This, at least, is how we might read Hartman's commentary on Valéry in *The Fate of Reading,* where the whole point of poetic language is said to be the postponement of closure, the prolongation of the middle, the cultivation of the "negative capability" of "linguistic process." An antiformalist energy in Valéry is said to disclose a triumphant vitalism, a capacity for infinitude within poetic language that represents good news for humans: "The ascesis of style is made to exert itself on a recognizably sensuous content which survives it" (233). Survival is the point: this message emerges into the clearing only occasionally, but when it does, the effect is startling, especially in the context of then-prevailing "theory." In a move no skywriter could have made, Hartman concludes the essay on Valéry by invoking the poet's postwar context, with its "manic" rhythms: "The sting, in real life, is a massive need for intoxicants, raising perpetually the threshold of stimulation, and so shortening, and perhaps injuring, the very *durée* of thought" (246). Gripping as "thought" may be to think about, it is only a sign that something more important—"real life"—is going on.

Throughout the seventies, Hartman deploys a pun-obsessed and relentlessly witty discourse in the service of a thematics of threat, death, wounding, and spectrality. Even the famous scandal, the libertine claim that criticism should be considered a rival rather than a loyal servant to literature, is far from frivolous or merely irreverent in its motivation. One of the most provocative claims to emerge from the "theory" movement, this argument was taken up by many who failed to grasp its real aim. An institutional mood determined in part by Saussure, but also, at a deeper level, by such factors as the cold war and inflation, valued assertions of the unreality or instability of language as gestures of recognition toward the ultimate truth of things—which was to say, the ultimate unknowability of the truth, even the ultimate nonexistence of truth. The "Yale School" was seen as endorsing and theorizing this recognition by emphasizing the illusory or merely conventional character of reference, the pervasive "indeterminacy" of language, the "arbitrariness" of the sign, the "metaphoricity" even of philosophical or scientific discourse. But a return to Hartman's late-seventies text, "Literary Commentary as Literature," reveals other motivations. Hartman does not concern himself, in the first instance, with "language," but with Georg Lukács's discussion of the essay, which, according to Hartman, can be considered an "intellectual poem," as unpredictable, unstable, and potentially nonreferential as the literature on which it comments. Informal, supple, and lacking scholarly armature, the essay gets itself mixed up with its object in much the same way that "books or habits of reading *penetrate* our lives" (*Criticism in the Wilderness* 203; hereafter *CW*). The mutual permeability of books and life grounds the argument, not some putative feature of language.

This sense of a general vulnerability to encroachment also provides the context for Hartman's enthusiasm for deconstruction. The innovation represented by Derrida's *Glas,* which juxtaposes and in a sense equalizes a philosophical text by Hegel and a literary text by Genet, is that it raises "the specter of texts so tangled, contaminated, displaced, deceptive that the idea of a single or original author fades, like virginity itself" (*CW* 204). For others, the author was said to have died or faded before the superior force of the "autonomy of discourse" or the "infinity of language." But for Hartman, it is the heteronomy of discourse, the inability of any bit of language to seal itself off from others, or from life, that entails not precisely the death but the defloration of the author, his/her confusion with others.

In Hartman's earlier work, it was first the senses and then art that held open the life-prolonging and creative middle; but now, art has come to represent closure, and criticism occupies the middle, enlisting Hartman's sympathies as the victim of "Aesthetics," or, as he puts it, "Xthetics, where X signifies something excluded, something X-ed from a previous system and now redeemed" (*CW* 212–13). But Hartman seems uncertain during this time (roughly from the late sixties to the mid-eighties) about what functions should be assigned to what. On some occasions, the work of art is said to shrug off idealizing theories; on others, such as the 1984 "The Interpreter's Freud," the primary text (of the dream) and the secondary text (of the scientific metalanguage that would describe the dream) are said to criss-cross, effecting a "transactive" exchange of properties that compromises the purity of each. What remains constant, however, is the basic scenario, in which some would-be totalitarian power meets and is defeated by a resistance from some insubordinate erstwhile underling, the belated outsider. Generally respectful toward Bloom, Hartman draws the line at only one point in Bloom's account of the "anxiety of influence": the confusion of "priority" with "authority" implied in the claim that the strong poet, i.e., Milton, sets the agenda for those who follow. Firstness, Hartman insists in *The Fate of Reading,* does not imply rightness, much less destiny (see *FR* 49).

Another 1984 essay signals a transition from the concern with criticism to the concern with culture that dominates Hartman's latest work. Deeply impressive and deeply conflicted, "The Culture of Criticism" argues, once again, for a practice of criticism resistant to totalities and "methodically suspicious of the limits imposed on imaginative activity by officially sanctioned modes of speaking and writing" (373). This critical practice must issue from a philosophically sophisticated, methodologically rigorous, linguistically sensitive "culture of criticism"; its antagonist is . . . culture. The culture of the elite produces an encoded form of condescension that is often coordinate with nationalism and other forms of brutality or arrogance; the culture of the bourgeoisie produces an equally encoded hostility to art, a false pretension to naturalness. A properly philosophical culture of criticism will point the way, Hartman claims, "beyond culture" and its various prejudices, complacencies, and misrepresentations. This is not just another Hartmanian play on words; rather, he seems at this point to lack a word, or to be one idea short. This slip of the pun returns, as we will see, to haunt *The Fateful Question of Culture.* But before trying to guess the missing word, I would like to try to understand why it is missing, why Hartman must use the same word for the wound and the cure.

Wordsworth provides the essential clue. Over the years, Wordsworth has provided the raw material for Hartman to work out whatever problems occupied him at the moment; and for this reason, the essays collected in *The Unremarkable Wordsworth* (1987) are far more indicative as snapshots of Hartman's evolving thought than the formidable performance of *Wordsworth's Poetry* (1962). What unifies these essays is not only their subject, but their subtext, which declares itself unmistakably in a 1975 essay on Michael Riffaterre's analysis of a Wordsworth poem. The ostensible topic is "structural analysis" as a methodology, but the real project is nothing other than an elaborate articulation and defense of the concept of the ghost. When Riffaterre analyzes "Yew-Trees," the impersonality of the poet's voice in that poem harmonizes, Hartman notes, with the impersonality that structural analysis itself aspires to, and so the structural critic may be predisposed to think that the speaking subject simply does not exist in this poem. But the truth, Hartman argues, is subtler: what really matters "is Wordsworth's inward grounding of an idea of ghostliness that motivates elision of self-reference" (*Unremarkable Wordsworth* 133; hereafter *UW*). "Listening" to the silence of the yew-trees, Wordsworth is made articulate, Hartman says, but not exactly as himself. He speaks, rather, as a tree, from which certain of the poem's lines appear to issue. In the presence of the trees, the speaker is "phantomized," and the reader, too, finds himself ghosted, the burden of selfhood lifted by immersion in the language of the poem. "The thought ghosts of the poet become ghost thoughts" of the reader, echoes of the poem in the reader's mind that "[give] it a home" (135, 136).

Thus structural analysis is slotted into the place reserved in Hartman's thought for totalization, closure, death—while, curiously enough, ghosts of the poet and the reader assume the burden of life, even of immortality. But Hartman is not done with Wordsworth's tree, which he translates into a figure of variousness, a question mark implanted into the midst of certitude. "Yew-Trees" begins, Hartman points out, with the contemplation of "This solitary Tree!," a singleton that reminds the poet of others:

> But worthier still of note
> Are those fraternal Four of Borrowdale,
> Joined in one solemn and capacious grove;
> Huge trunks! And each particular trunk a growth
> Of intertwisted fibres serpentine
> Up-coiling, and inveterately convolved;
> Nor uninformed with Phantasy . . . .

The solid wood of one tree splinters, like the brooms of the sorcerer's apprentice, into multiplicity and phantasms, yielding, Hartman says, a new kind of "Yewnity," which he proposes as "a model for analysis imitating the branchings of tree or flower from a deeply nurtured, perhaps covert, point" (*UR* 139). The arboreal voice "left" in nature that first arrested the poet Wordsworth, suggesting the possibility of an emancipation of speech from speaker and thus a ghostly afterlife of speech, also arrests the critic Hartman, suggesting a model for a criticism sensitive to ghosts, internal echoes, voices coming from nowhere—a criticism that would construct homes for wandering utterances. Intimations of immortality come from the mediation of language, and not, as Riffaterre argued, from "sensation."

And so, Hartman concludes, Wordsworth is not a recorder of nature but a conjurer of spirits; and "nature poetry" such as his is "the most ghostly poetry ever written: one in which speech itself is near to fading out, like echo, or the voice of genius that dies with the tree it inhabits" (150). Hartman even detects in Wordsworth a certain "resentment of nature," and a profound interest only with "what is permanent in man," chiefly (the ghost of) language (27).

In all his work on Wordsworth, Hartman remarks on equivocation, indeterminacy, ambivalence, mediation; the point of his analyses is persistently to undo what has been done, to derealize and phantomize that which was thought to be substantial. Hartman's addiction to puns reflects not just verbal high spirits, but a persistent gothicism, a settled conviction that words generally are the primary form in which ghosts inhabit the world, that words are the most immediate and generalized form both of ghosts and of the haunted houses inhabited by the spirits of other words, of scriptural or Miltonic echoes, as well as an unmasterable quantity of phonic echoes. So committed is Hartman to this scenario that it sometimes seems, reading through *The Unremarkable Wordsworth,* that Wordsworth is not the true object of discourse at all, but simply a useful occasion for an argument about the ubiquity of ghosts.

Ghosts complicate everything, adding—or is it subtracting?—a dimension of the invisible if not imperceptible; they are a factor of impurity. But as committed and insistent as the assertion of ghostliness is, it would be misleading to characterize Hartman's work as merely an antipurity crusade, for this would be to miss the positive movement of sympathy that determines both Wordsworth and Hartman's understanding of Wordsworth. It would miss, for example, the compassionate interest that Wordsworth takes in the marginal people of the Cumbrian countryside. As Hartman notes, Wordsworth had an extraordinarily responsive eye and ear for itinerant peddlers, homeless women, destitute shepherds, blind beggars, wild boys, mad mothers, cripples in the quarry, paralytic men—the random unattached people he met on his walks, whose "unconsummated spirit," as Hartman puts it, haunted the poet and stirred him into creation. As Hartman points out in *The Fateful Question of Culture,* this responsiveness signals not only an increase in poetic realism but also an advance in cultural morality, a widened and deepened sensibility. The ability to empathize and communicate with others in circumstances different from one's own supplements, Hartman contends, the official Enlightenment motto, *Sapere Aude*—dare to know—with another: dare to feel. In "Wordsworth and Goethe in Literary History," Hartman delineates a difference of national styles between a culture of knowledge and a culture of feeling.

Goethe represents, he says, a markedly German mastery of a "demonic" spirit of creation: "What a supremely confident maker!" Wordsworth is cast in an altogether different mold, and represents a tradition "deeply uncertain of the 'character' or 'identity' of the poet" (*FR* 195). Impressed by Goethe, Hartman still identifies himself—and criticism, and the optimal culture—with Wordsworth.

Perhaps, however, it would be more exact to say that Hartman identifies himself in the first instance with Wordsworth's conversational partners. In the introduction to *The Unremarkable Wordsworth,* he recalls the experience of being obliged to read Wordsworth in "high school in England." Wordsworth "reflected back," Hartman says, "my own sense of nature: rural nature, but more generally a world that felt as ancient and immemorial as 'rocks, and stones, and trees,' that encompassed, inanimate yet animating, the mind in its earth-walks" (*UW* xxv). How could a high school student in wartime England come by such a sense of nature? Hartman had left Germany at the age of nine, the beneficiary, with other Jewish children, of a Children's Transport funded by one of the Rothschilds. He arrived in England a refugee orphan. I imagine a stunned and silent boy, marked by the accent of the enemy, trying to assemble the scattered pieces of his life in a new country, more at home with books, or alone on long walks in the countryside, than on the playing fields, his past an intolerably vivid dream, his future and even his identity gray and uncertain. I see him in a drafty, poorly lit room, opening the book of Wordsworth's poetry and encountering there a man who actually stopped to speak with wanderers and outcasts, who dared to feel for such as he. Amazingly to the boy, this hospitable shade was represented as the living voice of English culture, the most recently deceased author in the curriculum. To the boy's starved and traumatized sensibilities, Wordsworth must have seemed a desperately welcome and welcoming figure, a ghost who understood ghosts, and maybe even refugees, who knew about thoughts that lay too deep for tears. "Wordsworth opened himself to my understanding," Hartman says in *The Longest Shadow* (1996), "as soon as I read him" (16). The boy positioned himself, perhaps, in Wordsworth's poetry as the maimed figures who suddenly speak because they have an ear in the poet. The chill was taken off the air, and gradually, with the end of the war and the passage of time, the boy, damaged but resilient and resourceful beyond measure, silently marked his unspeakable losses and began, with the powerful sponsorship of the Laureate, to chart a path for himself, imagining a new connectedness in this land, even an anchor in nature itself.

And so, years later, this boy, now a distinguished scholar writing in full knowledge of the Holocaust he had and had not escaped, professes to his fellow scholars his judgment that "Wordsworth is preeminently the poet of 'dark passages' that lead from immature ecstasy to socialization," a thinker who pursues the "theme of the growth of a mind, capable of re-generating itself and perhaps society"; and, too, that Wordsworth's poetry "has the strength to absorb thoughts that might unbalance the mind"; and, further, that Wordsworth "summons [a] voice out of the silence of a nature-buried past" (*UW* xxvii, 153, 60).

But was it not his own voice that, like the yew-tree's, was summoned by the poet of childhood and late adolescence? And if so, was it not sum-moned out of a *culture*-buried past? For many liberal Jews today, the es-sence of Jewishness is not race but Jewish culture, including religion. But in the polemical terms of the German culture wars of the 1930s, Jews were a race incapable of culture; they were "earth-centered," lacking in idealism, parasitic on a German culture they polluted. Extremists, such as Supreme Party Judge Walther Buch, held that "the Jew is not a human being. He is an appearance of putrescence"; moderates such as Hitler described Jews as an impurity in the nation, an impediment to the realization of the national cultural imperative (36-37). "To be German," Hitler had written in *Mein Kampf*, "is to be clear"; and racial homogeneity was one crucial component of that clarity. In Wordsworth, Hartman discovered a differ-ent evaluation of the leftovers from culture, a different sense of culture altogether, and, in "nature," even a different principle from culture itself. At the beginning, he was himself a radical outsider to the culture and the nature of England. But through what he would learn from Schiller to call "aesthetic education" at the feet of Wordsworth, he became capable of imagining otherwise, of growing as it were from the outside in, to the point where, in a triumphant act not of assimilation but of appropriation, he would become capable of writing that "we"—a cultural, rather than a racial grouping—are neglecting "our" heritage through insufficient at-tention to Wordsworth: "How seriously," he asks, "are we taking our own tradition, especially its poetry?" (*UW* xxvi).

Wordsworth may be an ornament of the cultural tradition of English-speaking countries, but as Hartman's own experience testifies, culture con-strued in aesthetic terms may be possessed even by the utterly dispos-sessed; it is not restricted to natives, or confined to native grounds. "An organic relation to place is what I lacked and would never recover," he says in *The Longest Shadow* (19). But a "scholar" or "critic" stands apart from his object of scrutiny, and if that object is the cultural tradition, then culture itself must hold a place open for those who are not altogether "inside" it. Indeed, not being inside can become a project with political impli-cations and consequences, an opportunity for agency and self-assertion.

In this spirit, Hartman contends that the relation of culture to criticism ought to simulate what "Wordsworth, describing the interaction of nature and mind, called 'mutual domination' or 'interchangeable supremacy'" (*CW* 259).

This prescription occurs in a late-seventies essay on "the recognition scene of criticism," a term applicable to Hartman's criticism as a whole, which may, I have been suggesting, be read as a remarkably diverse, ingenious, and extensive series of such scenes, wherein Hartman discovers "cultural" spaces and roles for himself. Every critic does this, of course, but Hartman's criticism reveals an unsuspected cultural dimension of critical positionality, a model of how one might make one's way in a post-Holocaust diasporic world, finding one's welcome where one can, attaching oneself to those edges of the culture where externality is a positive requirement. In this respect one can learn more about the legacy of the Holocaust by reading Hartman on Wordsworth than by reading Hartman on the legacy of the Holocaust. With his recent writings about the significance, the problem, the memory of the Holocaust in *The Fateful Question of Culture* and *The Longest Shadow,* Hartman has become less, not more autobiographical.

What I am really trying to identify in Hartman's work is not, however, a particular degree of self-referentiality, but rather the difference in kind that distinguishes a major thinker from a minor one, terms whose very crudity answers to a commonly felt but not easily described sense of inequality. The text of the major thinker, I would suggest, is legible as a record of obsessions, passions, and nonnegotiable perhaps because of unconscious commitments. Texts discussed by a major critic are pretexts for the working of his or her ongoing project: the need to articulate precedes and exceeds the ostensible but contingent subject, so that the major thinker's work is personal, dyed or banded with the mark of identity. At the same time, such a thinker in the field of literary criticism is defined by a superior capacity for self-overcoming, a stronger passivity in the face of the work of art, a power of impotence that encourages, as it were, the work to disclose its secrets, imprinting itself on the critic's sensibility, which retains the image while remaining itself—in the way that, for example, a poet might ventriloquize the voices of the voiceless, redeeming their authenticity, and making of them great poetry. Critics less powerfully powerless than Hartman declare their minority by producing texts that are legible either as repackaged fixations or as neutral or neutered records of the will to objective truth. In the first case, the critic's sensibility is a hard slate scratched but not altered by the work; in the second, a passive or liquid medium with no density or shape of its own. The greater critic is determined by the larger forces of history and by unexorcised personal demons—by what is not and cannot be fully conscious; the lesser, by such things as doctrine, desire, fashion, consensus, and will. Unhappily, one cannot choose which kind one is going to be, or even which kind one is.

But by this crude measure, Hartman is, beyond dispute, a major critic. And one sign of his stature is that he is incapable of giving up on culture despite his intimate experience of its nazistic dimension. Wordsworth, and the reading and criticism of Wordsworth, remains the cure for the cursed ground of the Holocaust, and the context for the activity of literary criticism remains the overarching problem of culture. And so, what seems an unruly juxtaposition in *The Fateful Question of Culture* of the fraternal four—the criticism of Wordsworth, the scholarly meditation on the Holocaust, the literary history of modernity, and the history of the idea of culture—simply clarifies the intertwisted fibers, nor uninformed with Phantasy, that has determined Hartman's enterprise from the outset.

Why, we may ask, does a distinguished elder of the academy retain the prickly problematic of culture? What contemporary relevance do these ancient, murderous ghosts have for us as we sit facing the various screens that mediate our lives? The answer may not be immediately forthcoming from those screens, but retaining the idea of culture could be one way of structuring a debate, for example, on Zionism. If we see Israel as the space of a Jewish culture, rather than, say, as the ancient ground of the Jewish race, then coexistence seems almost conceivable. If "culture" is capable of sponsoring genocide, it is still less inherently belligerent than "race" or "nation." Hartman's most profoundly wishful thinking on culture stresses nonviolence, inclusion, multiplicity, a Wordsworthian harmonizing of discordant elements rather than the sinister unification of voices. The cultural work of criticism, he says, consists in the gentle probing of an "older speech," a discourse that "respects the other's idiom while extending it tenderly" (*FQ* 190). Still, we might ask, if one of culture's hands is dripping with blood, why bother celebrating the tenderness of the other? Why not stop promoting the concept of culture altogether?

Here we return to the "missing word" noted earlier. I call it missing because I think that I can see Hartman almost purposefully missing it. He speaks, near the end of his book, of a contemporary confusion of culture with nature, and of the use of "culture" to designate a collective and destined form of identity, both of which violate, he argues, the "creative and unpredictable potential" of culture properly understood. And then, he says: "It is here that critique can begin, for now the concept of 'society' . . . pulls away from that of 'culture'" (*FQ* 178). And then—he returns to culture. The missing word signals a missed opportunity to challenge culture from the outside, to oppose to it another concept that lacks, perhaps, culture's singular power to convert longing into belonging, but lacks, too, its eager responsiveness to purification programs.

As I noted in the first chapter, the term *society* initially had a specific meaning of companionship or fellowship, a conscious organization or relationship, but has developed in addition to this a more general sense referring to the common life shared by all. This simplicity and inclusiveness stand in pointed contrast to "culture," which is, Raymond Williams says, "one of the two or three most complicated words in the English language" (*Keywords* 87). Like Hartman, Williams notes a kinship between agriculture and culture, and attributes to this association one of the fibers of the term's meaning, the conscious and self-interested tending of nature to produce desired results. While many in Wordsworth's time held "society" to be mechanistic and inorganic, the term as Williams defines it actually corresponds closely to Hartman's sense of Wordsworth in that it denotes a diverse polity, an ethical and civil structure held together by ties of voluntary association based on shared interests and values. In "society," the emphasis is on the conscious gesture of affiliation, not on the "dark inscrutable workmanship" of nature forging the links of culture. Perhaps, from Hartman's point of view, this is precisely the problem: "society" produces no corpses, neither of bodies nor of ideas; it summons up no ghosts. A benign but a comparatively shallow principle of human aggregation, "society" suffers from a poverty of dynamism, an inability to satisfy a ghostly hunger for substantial identity. The question is whether, in rejecting the Holocaust and all its ideological cognates, we sacrifice energy and identity as such.

Hartman did not care for the works of the elderly Frye. But neither did he care much for Frye's earlier works, which were, he said in an essay called "Ghostlier Demarcations," obsessed with form and dismissive of temporality. The same cannot be said of Hartman, who was temporal when temporal wasn't cool, when form and structure were all. Now Hartman is himself the "older speech" soliciting dialogue with the next generation. Those who would preserve and extend his thought must enter into a "mutual domination" in which their thinking is worked by his, a confusion of names that mimes the gesture of identification and loss of self by which Hartman had once dreamt his way out of one world and into another, a world of words, and Wordsworth, and all the others, by that means assuming the burdens and claiming the possibilities of culture, society, profession, self.

It is, in fact, not possible to speak about the moral view revealed within [*The Golden Bowl*] without speaking at the same time of the created text, which exemplifies and expresses the responses of an imagination that means to care for and to put itself there for us. . . . I claim that the views uncovered in this text derive their power from the way in which they emerge as the ruminations of such a high and fine mind concerning the tangled mysteries of these imaginary lives.—Martha Nussbaum, *Love's Knowledge* 141

With his remarkable sensitivity to the moods of academe, Woody Allen creates, in *Crimes and Misdemeanors* (1989), a venerable philosopher, Professor Levy, whose message to the world, captured on videotape by Allen, a documentary filmmaker, is to reject philosophy, which seems capable only of imagining harsh, judging deities and depressingly unattainable ideals. Better seek the good, the wise professor advises, in the details of daily life, the minor affections of the home, the solace of love. If philosophy refuses to provide consolations, we can and should turn to the untheorized comforts of human affection.

To be sure, Professor Levy adds a disturbing codicil in his last, hastily scrawled text: "I'm going out the window." But this final alienating gesture notwithstanding, he manages to capture a contemporary feeling that philosophy is a wounding discourse, a cold and steely instrument for making sharp distinctions in a spirit of surgical indifference, even antipathy, to the warm-blooded and inconstant human beings it presumes to represent, judge, and regulate. Moral philosophy seems especially sere; the "absolutism," the formal rigidity, the extreme affective poverty of its account of the imperatives that properly inform a rational human life represent to many a perverse understanding of life, one determined by nothing more or other than philosophical sadism. And narcissism, too: philosophy, the Levys of the world charge, is interested only in itself, its own rule-generating activity. It is indifferent to the body, affection, desire, imagination, culture, politics, the unconscious—to everything that constitutes a rich, fulfilled, and worthy life. Enjoining respect for the law, philosophy fails to respect the people required to follow it, and fails in such a thoroughgoing and consistent way as to constitute a kind of hate speech directed at life itself. The great prestige of abstract rationality, enshrined since Kant as the "philosophical" style par excellence, has created a permanent incentive for a humanist backlash. And so, ever since Marx at least—witness, for example, Nietzsche, Kierkegaard, Heidegger, Wittgenstein, Sartre, Derrida, Rorty, Cavell, Bernard Williams—the gesture of going "beyond the limits of philosophy," to borrow Williams's phrase, has become installed as a philosophical convention, even almost a requirement. To be a modern philosopher is to repudiate philosophical modernity, even if that only means attempting to recapture, like many of those listed above, the philosophical glory that was Greece.

An ambitious philosopher in the grip of this mood might not rest with critique, but might try to develop a set of principles that are responsive to real life. Such a philosopher might be inspired by one of the forgotten cultural attainments of the ancient world, the Lesbian Rule, described by Aristotle as a flexible strip of metal "that bends to the shape of the stone and is not fixed"—a model, Martha Nussbaum says, for those qualities that moral rules should possess, including "responsiveness and yielding flexibility, a rightness of tone and a sureness of touch that no general account could adequately capture" (*Love's Knowledge* 72, hereafter *LK;* see *Nichomachean Ethics* 1137b 30–32). Nussbaum's attempt to articulate a new morality, developed over the course of three impressively crowded and large-souled volumes written during a remarkable burst of productivity from the early 1980s to the early 1990s (*The Fragility of Goodness: Luck and Ethics in Greek Tragedy and Philosophy* [1986; hereafter *FG], Love's Knowledge: Essays on Philosophy and Literature* [1990], and *The Therapy of Desire: Theory and Practice in Hellenistic Ethics* [1994; hereafter *TD*]) is consistent with many others in its claim that philosophy took a series of wrong and unnecessary turns, submitting itself to Christianity, Kant, and linguistic analysis. Still, she argues, if we take just one more turn, we can proceed straight ahead once again, along the (responsive, yielding, flexible) true path, which she finds set forth, in the first instance, by Aristotle. This is a less representative argument, but it is, I will begin by suggesting, the very idiosyncrasy of Nussbaum's work that most tellingly discloses the real character, as well as the prospects, of modern antirationalism.

Many thinkers today reject rationalism particularly for its pretension to an ahistorical grasp of timeless and global principles. Nussbaum is not one of these. She has no interest in moral principles bent in the shape of some group's particular experience. The Lesbian Rule does not apply only to lesbians; nor, as we shall see, is Nussbaum's a specifically feminist morality, or a group-specific morality of any kind. Indeed, while her work is grounded in classical philosophy, she insists on a "fundamental commitment to reason" that we associate with the grandest universalizing aspirations of the Enlightenment, and consistently operates not only with an acute sense of local detail but also with a defiantly unrestricted sense of scale (*TD* 5). Especially in the central volume of the trilogy, *Love's Knowledge,* she typically manages this leap from the highly particular to the universal by deriving moral principles directly from literary texts, a reading practice that represents a direct attack on modern literary criticism as well as philosophy. Unlike most other philosophers who claim to take literature seriously—Arthur Danto, Alexander Nehamas, Hilary Putnam, Rorty, Bernard Williams, Stanley Hauerwas, and Alasdair MacIntyre, to name only a few of the most eminent—Nussbaum manifestly loves novels. While these others often sound, in their literary enthusiasms, like philosophers on a weekend, momentarily relaxing their rigor to make a humane and cosmopolitan gesture of hospitality toward a discourse that their deepest convictions tell them is at most a rich source of examples awaiting illumination by philosophy, Nussbaum is clearly a passionate reader who regards novels as having high moral significance. She is most appreciative of those iconoclastic thinkers in whatever tradition who, like Lucretius, deploy the power of "narrative understanding" to illuminate philosophical concepts and to register the actualities of human life (*TD* 508). A philosopher who does not question the value and priority of the philosophical inquiry into the conditions of a worthy life, Nussbaum sustains a commitment to literature so sustained, detailed, and intense as to subject philosophy to a searching disciplinary skepticism. Her own markedly "literary" style, with its sinuous argumentative line, its rising line of tension and complication, its cultivation of affect and suggestiveness, its supple and sensitive tracing of the delicate evolution of perception and understanding in a narrative sequence—all these create a singular discourse that both challenges philosophy at its stylistic basis and exposes itself by relinquishing the epistemological high ground.

Nussbaum may promote and exemplify sensitivity, affect, the humility of the spectator, but her argument is assured to the point of pugnacity. What she contends is that the stylistic differences between philosophy and literature amount to a moral difference. Philosophy's high degree of refinement and specialization blinds it to the real character of morality. Many of Nussbaum's characteristically expansive formulations about novels suggest, by contrast, an untroubled relation with morality. "The novelist's task," she writes, "*is* a moral task" at every level (*LK* 163). First, the novelist's "loving and nonjudgmental attention to the characters is paradigmatic of an element in love toward which one should aim in life itself" (334). The novel is a "school for moral sentiments" not just because its characters can model our lives, which they do, but also because the narration encourages and develops in readers just the kind of sensitivity to the fluctuating minutiae of daily life, the precise character of the contingent moment, that philosophy discourages on principle (240). Novels possess, moreover, "certain ethical commitments (to particularity, to the moral relevance of surprise) just in virtue of their form," which qualifies them as works of Aristotelian moral philosophy (190). Thus, in a gesture as breathtakingly inclusive as Fredric Jameson's assertion that *all* collective identifications, even racist, homophobic, ethnic, or nationalistic ones, augur a classless utopia, Nussbaum asserts that the activity of reading novels— even, apparently, the novels of de Sade, Dreiser, Kosinski, Anne Rice, Dostoevsky, Swift, Jacqueline Susann, and Stephen King—"is a valuable part of moral development" in which we "quite naturally assume the viewpoint of an affectionate and responsive social creature, who looks at all the scene before him with fond and sympathetic attention" (346). The experience of reading is nothing less than "a moral activity in its own right, a cultivation of imagination for moral activity in life, and a test for correctness of real-life judgment and response" (339).

From the artist's initial perception and imagination, to novelistic representation, to readerly apprehension and understanding, novels constitute a structure of continuities between morality and aesthetics. We are what we perceive, what we write, and what we read. And so when we read traditional philosophy, with its "plainness and hardness," as Iris Murdoch puts it, we become ourselves plain and hard, defensive and controlling, "aiming to leave no flank undefended and no mystery undispelled" (Murdoch quoted in *LK* 251, 282). Inasmuch as responsive and sensitive reading is not just a good thing to do, but, for Nussbaum, the paradigmatic moral act, philosophy could even be said to have damaging ethical consequences for its readers. If, therefore, philosophy would provide the kind of "wisdom about ourselves" and practical guidance that people crave and deserve, it must "turn to literature"; it must become "more literary, more closely allied to stories, and more respectful of mystery and open-endedness" (290, 284).

From the point of view of recent literary criticism, so many crimes and misdemeanors, not to mention heresies and fallacies, are committed in these dicta of Nussbaum's that it seems almost cruel to enumerate them. Perhaps only Nussbaum's status as a disciplinary outsider has prevented readers from dismissing her as incompetent on the face of it. Her discussions of novels could not be used as a model in any graduate school, for they read, in certain respects, as if they were written many decades ago, before the discovery of the evils of the "aesthetic ideology," in a distant time when a gullible populace believed that novelists were not just talented wordsmiths but moral geniuses whose powers of superior penetration and expression gave them a singular authority concerning the human condition; or that literature was invented to provide moral guidance to a troubled and confused populace; or that the very greatest literature yielded timeless insights into the human soul; or that, while authors were demigods, literary characters were just like us, and we could read about them as if they were real people and our immediate contemporaries—even, in a sense, ourselves.

Nussbaum's argument can usefully be compared to that of Murdoch who, in a well-known essay, "Against Dryness: A Polemical Sketch" (1961), also advocated a turn from philosophy to literature. Murdoch's interests bear a superficial resemblance to Nussbaum's in that both argue for literature's superior representation of the density and complexity of the world, and both insist that morality is, as Murdoch says (quoting Simone Weil), "a matter of attention, not of will." But Murdoch's view of that world, and of literature, is utterly different from Nussbaum's. "We need to return," Murdoch says, "from the self-centred concept of sincerity to the other-centred concept of truth. We are not isolated free choosers, monarchs of all we survey, but benighted creatures sunk in a reality whose nature we are constantly and overwhelmingly tempted to deform by fantasy." Where Nussbaum speaks confidently about how we may become good by perceiving aright, Murdoch speaks of the difficulty of knowing anything at all; and where Nussbaum is confident that literature is morally beneficial, Murdoch is upset that modern literature does not contain sufficiently persuasive pictures of evil. And, finally, where Nussbaum holds that novels are moral agents by virtue of their form, Murdoch contends that "form itself can be a temptation, making the work of art into a small myth which is a self-contained and indeed self-satisfied individual" (49). By contrast with Murdoch's dark and brooding conservatism, Nussbaum's vision is progressive to the point of jubilation.

By comparison with contemporary literary theory and criticism, however, Nussbaum's understanding of literature is deeply regressive. Aware of the differences, Nussbaum weighs in with charges of her own, that literary criticism and especially literary theory have turned away from literature, and have confusedly cultivated a stylistic and more than stylistic dryness and abstraction, miming philosophy's antiliterary dessication. Embarrassed by the moralizing criticism of an earlier generation, contemporary professionals have banished any consideration of the ancient question of how one should live, with such dubious success that, in contemporary literary theory, "the ethical vanishes more or less altogether"; so that, today, any approach to literature that emphasizes morality is going to have to struggle against wind and tide, and may even appear to be going backwards, as Nussbaum proudly does (*LK* 170).

A contrarian literary critic, Nussbaum is also a defiantly aberrant philosopher. Fully credentialed and trained in classical philosophy, she yet worries questions that simply do not seem amenable to a properly philosophical analysis. I am not referring to her defenses of the philosophical dignity of emotion or friendship, arguments that have, as she points out, precedents deep in the philosophical tradition. Nor do I refer to her general insistence that philosophy should try to surpass, or bypass, mere rationality in the pursuit of a more comprehensive understanding of the totality of life; for such arguments, too, have a long philosophical pedigree. I refer, rather, to the (at first sight) strange distinctions she draws, or rather, to her strange way with distinctions.

Take for example the discussion in *The Therapy of Desire* concerning a moral (and erotic) imperative to "attend to the humanity of those we love" —as though one could attend to something else, or that the humanity of those we do not love is less worthy of attention (*TD* 189). Or the meditation near the end of *Love's Knowledge* on the precise distance that "life" should stand from "life." One of the moral benefits of novel reading, Nussbaum says, is that it inculcates an "active sense of life," preparing us "for a life that is lived at one remove from life, a life that gains fineness and clarity by warding off certain risks and dangers" (162, 188). But, she warns, one can be too fine, too clear, like the women of James's fictional town of Woollett, Massachusetts, of whom Nussbaum says, "that's just it: they triumph over life, they don't *live*" (179). Such women apparently stand *more* than "one remove" from life—but how many; and how many are appropriate? Working up this question, Nussbaum dishes out wise counsel with both hands, recommending that while we *should* try to extend our capacities, we should *not* try to "leave behind altogether the constitutive conditions of our humanity, and to seek for a life that is really the sort of life of another sort of being"; we should *not,* that is, aspire to "depart from human life altogether" (379, 380). Instead, we should make "the fundamental choice to live as human" (390). "What is recommended," she concludes in a discourse without any parallel in the world of contemporary academic philosophizing, is "a delicate and always flexible balancing act" between "internal" and "external" forms of excellence, even though, she concedes, "it is not easy . . . to say where a line is drawn" (381). Not easy at all; for how could anyone ever aspire to live an *inhuman* life, the life of some other kind (*what* other? a robot? an angel? a gopher?) of being? What do these terms and phrases—common enough, perhaps, in pop psychology or ordinary social discourse—mean in philosophical terms? Can they ever be made rigorous or theoretically legible? Her frequent leaps from argumentation to advice also mark her text as singular, as when she says, vis-à-vis Seneca's *Medea,* that "when two important values, such as passion and the love of children, collide by chance in a life dedicated to both, there may be no avoiding some harm to someone" (*TD* 474).

At such moments, Nussbaum seems to be only superficially a philosopher, and, at a deeper level, a kind of academic Abby; the "Abbification," or better, the Abbdication or even Abbduction, of philosophy, we could call it, by way of indicating for the first time a certain crisis of genre that her work provokes.

And yet she preserves in surprising fashion certain features of professional philosophical discourse. So disarmingly personal at some moments, favoring the reader with anecdotes and recollections about friends, trips, her childhood, her daughter, men she has loved, the unique "properties" of her "current lover," Nussbaum is also astonishingly willing to prescribe the law in the old style. Not, perhaps, as rare in the world of philosophy as one might wish, such willingness is still brought to a high polish by Nussbaum, as in the following, altogether characteristic passage.

> Morality essentially involves thinking of oneself as one person among others, bound by ties of friendship and sympathy to those others. These ties, in turn, involve, essentially, two further things. First, they require us to look around us, taking thought, so to speak, for all that we can see. And they involve, too, general social conversation, the giving and receiving of justifications and reasons. Therefore, they require that we permit ourselves and our actions to be *seen.* These practices both express our concern for our fellow beings and bind them to us in a network of mutual concern. The presence of these features in the spectator explains why assuming, in thought, the spectator's position can be a way of assuming the moral point of view. We have built into the account of the spectator the most essential features of our moral humanity. (*TD* 345)

As I have argued elsewhere, moral discourse is defined in part by a strategic silence, a tendency to tautology—you ought to because you ought to—whenever the subject of the ground of the moral law arises (*Getting It Right* 18–27). Nussbaum's silence on this question is particularly massive, her presumption in declaring, in descriptively neutral tones, what morality "involves" and "requires" almost flamboyantly ungrounded. In this respect she does not opt out of philosophy, but tries to beat it at its own game.

In general, I will argue, Nussbaum's silences are unusually eloquent, and constitute a more reliable guide to the true power and interest of her work than do her unconventional premises or methodology: "X"—a determined absence—marks the spot. In order to understand, and even to apprehend, Nussbaum's project, we must, I am suggesting, try to grasp the invisible force that drives and structures it. We must ask what seems to motivate and center her project beyond the presumed goal of telling the truth about morality, philosophy, and literature; what seems to elude the project's articulation; what is withheld from the surface of the text, and why. We must finally ask what the text *is* and *does,* apart from simply articulating a series of positions and arguments. And we might begin with the hypothesis that Nussbaum's powerful idiosyncrasies proceed not simply from a dissident spirit or defective training, but from a tension in the project that renders its own cause inarticulable.

Perhaps the most obvious tension, and one of the more curious silences, concerns gender. On the subject of sexual difference, Nussbaum is actually less silent than coy. Male philosophers may have dedicated their books to their fathers and grandfathers without mentioning their mothers and grandmothers—reversing Nussbaum's dedication to *Love's Knowledge*—but no man, to my knowledge, has given a major philosophical work a title that announces in such unmistakable terms a sexual point of origin. Of course, titles such as *A Theory of Justice, Being and Nothingness, The Claim of Reason, The Theory of Communicative Action, The Order of Things,* or *The Nature of Rationality* may, to the sensitized eye, represent nothing so transparently as the dubious neutrality of the alpha male philosopher, and that would, in fact, constitute part of Nussbaum's point. Still, she does not claim to offer a specifically female, much less a feminist, alternative or supplement to the male-dominated tradition she often criticizes. Hers is, rather, a prescriptive account of how one should live, male or female, in whatever circumstances one finds oneself—how one should live as "human."

Nevertheless, *Love's Knowledge* presents morality as woman's work. The women of Woollett notwithstanding, the kind of "living" Nussbaum espouses corresponds pretty closely with the aptitudes and orientations conventionally and traditionally attributed to women of the sentimental portion of the first-world middle class. It is not, in this tradition, conventional for men to say, as Nussbaum does, that "the tender susceptible heart is morally finer than a firm one" (*LK* 237). Nor is it altogether common for men, or indeed for anyone, to affirm that "love" is the "dominant passion" not only of the novel but of "social democracy" (391). The careful attention paid to emotional or affective nuances, the respect for the rush of untheorized sensibility, the insistence on the superiority of perception to action, all suggest the priorities of the local Browning Society, or a parody of a Carol Gilligan test group, a model of womanhood that feminism of all periods has wrestled with as with an intimate enemy. The dangers presented by such a model emerge in the work of an extreme case like the feminist philosopher mentioned in the second chapter of this book, Virginia Held, who unhesitatingly—and, some would say, unthinkingly—seeks to replace the rigorously abstract tests of motive and universalizability, the schemata of neo-Kantian ethics, by the virtues associated with "caring." For Held, the experience of adult childrearing women, especially those who care for the elderly, the infirm, and children, has a greater claim on society's respect than the formal principles Kant proposes as tests of moral quality (see *Feminist Morality* 30 ff.). Held sees as crucial to her project a resistance, in the name of locality, affect, and embodiment, to the very thought—the mere thought—of universalization. Only a chimerical "agent as such," that ideally unfeeling, unemotional, singular atom of reflective experience that one finds (and, she argues, finds only) in a certain strain of male philosophizing could find Kantian neutrality appealing or worthy. And as there are no such agents, the superiority of the "feminist" account of morality is clear. Nussbaum is far more difficult to place, for she is a "difference" feminist without being explicitly feminist at all; indeed, on the relatively rare occasions on which she discusses feminism, she quarrels with "difference" feminists who feel, for example, that women do not value, and should not be judged by, reason to the same extent as men. Nussbaum discriminates between reason and objectivity themselves and the abuses or perversions of them that sometimes occur; and she defends, for example, the capacity of women to operate as women in the discourse of philosophy without resorting to irrationalism (see "Feminists and Philosophy"). As a crystalline example of the form such work might take, we could turn to an imagined debate, occurring late in *The Therapy of Desire,* in which the arguments of an "Aristotelian"—for some reason designated a "she"—are played off (victoriously) against those of a male "Stoic" (chap. 12). Nussbaum is actually neither feminist nor antifeminist, but something more deeply paradoxical, an essentialist who claims for the essence she delineates a "human," rather than a specifically female, provenance and applicability. Hers is a sexed world . . . without sex.

The nonfeminist feminine difference Nussbaum etches is perhaps most subtly but decisively marked in the position accorded to the "silent inner work of perception," which she touts not as an alternative to decision and action, but as a form of decision and action in itself, a form, in fact, finer in its nature than the grosser forms fetishized by traditional philosophical morality—and, it is implied, superior as well to the scarcely cognitive and excessively proximate activity Held describes as caring (LK 93). Nussbaum makes enormous claims for the act of "seeing a complex and concrete reality in a highly lucid and richly responsive way," which she accounts both "a created work of art" and a "moral achievement," just as "obtuseness is a moral failing," and perhaps an aesthetic mess as well (152, 155, 153, 156). Inferred from Aristotle (a controversial genealogy, inasmuch as Aristotle defines ethics as a subset of politics), perception comes, over the course of Nussbaum's work, to occupy something like the position accorded to Reason by Kant, the master category within which others must nestle, the source of the overriding imperatives that define the virtues. On the slender pillar of perception, an entire worldview is reared, a way of seeing that implies a certain subjective position, a relation to others, and even general principles of conduct. To perceive rightly, for Nussbaum, is not just a precondition of virtue, but a virtue in itself. Only a sense of one's own possession of virtue, secured by accurate perception, could embolden a philosopher to move from closely observed textual moments directly to global laws, as Nussbaum does when she declares that a novel by Henry James "suggests" that "all daughters should treat their fathers with the same level of sensitivity to the father's concrete character and situation . . . that Maggie displays here" (167).

How—the cautious literary critic or philosopher might ask—does this follow? How does a fictional character's perhaps admirable sensitivity to her fictional father imply a universal rule for daughters? How are "levels" of sensitivity measured? Why harp only on daughters; do they have a special obligation to be sensitive—and then only to fathers? And what does "sensitivity" mean, not only for James or for his characters, but for those who would bear this lesson away? The term is so undefined, so capacious, that it effectively excludes nothing—one can "sensitively," but mercilessly, detail another's flaws or shortcomings—and yet, for Nussbaum, it is enough, because it has been "perceived" in James. The value, status, and definition of perception are, like moral principles generally, subjects of stipulation, not argument.

But the entailments of perception are considerable, and potentially controversial. They include the implications that the morally optimal position is slightly, but not wholly, removed from the tumultuous scene of action; that the obligation to perceive aright precedes and determines whatever other, more interventionist or activist obligations one might have; and that "principles" as formal guides to conduct are not the lighthouses they were once thought to be, but rather partners in a "loving dialogue" with perception (*LK* 155). Most important, they include a reciprocal obligation to *be perceptible,* which means not only to be engaged in the act of perception, but to be publicly available for inspection for others, rather than furtive, secretive, or duplicitous. One must not, in Nussbaum's moral world, have hidden passions, invisible secrets that would block accurate perception by others; one must situate oneself within the field of view in order that others may act virtuously. The overriding law of perception even determines, one may infer, the particular character of Nussbaum's account of literature as a verbal structure that exhibits, elicits, and tests the perceptual—rather than, say, the interpretive—powers of author, narrator, character, and reader. Her treatment of literature as a virtually visible entity has a curious affinity with the protocols of "ethical" reading described in J. Hillis Miller's *Ethics of Reading.* Miller describes an ethical imperative to "*read,*" to suspend all efforts to achieve interpretive closure and to dwell in the (sharply perceived) aporias of the text. Unlike Nussbaum, Miller is deeply impressed by Kant, has no serious interest in readerly emotions, and, above all, has no respect whatsoever for the proposition, sacred to Nussbaum, that literature is continuous with life. But they share an antipathy they define as ethical to the closeted secrets of the text, to those encrypted, unfolding interiorities that are the typical object of the recoding or translation operations by which the mind of the author, the narrator, or character is "analyzed," by which the literary text is converted into terms and contexts not its own, made to bear meanings with implications for the conduct of life.

Is perception the pure good Nussbaum describes? She demonstrates little interest in the Foucauldian Panopticon as a model for moral perception, and writes critically, when she writes at all, about Foucault. But her stipulation that one must see and be seen renders "moral" what Foucault describes as "normalizing" or "disciplining," even punitive, and we may well ask whether the imperative of perception, even in its most benign or Jamesian instances, harbors a regulatory or carceral kernel. Does perception-as-law confirm or disconfirm Nietzsche's argument that morality is just sublimated punishment? Can perception be placed at the service of violence, as Angelo Dundee seemed to contend when, broadcasting a heavyweight championship bout in the mid-eighties, he commented that "Weaver's jab is more *perceptive* than Dokes's"? Can it serve the cause of exploitation, as in de Sade's probing attention to detail? These are not questions Nussbaum considers; she *perceives* perception, we might say, but she does not *interpret* it.

Her silence on such questions seems, in the context of her insistent raising of them, a sign of the "tension in the project" we are looking for, an overdetermined void that betrays a definite will to know some things and not to know others. It is a stance one might characterize as passive-aggressive, so definite and assured are Nussbaum's arguments on the virtue of perceptual and other forms of passivity. For Nussbaum, "passivity" names a praiseworthy receptivity, a kind of prerequisite for proper reading, which requires a "surrender, a "primary act of *assent*," a "falling and learning to fall," a "trusting and loving activity" in which "we allow ourselves to be touched by the text" (*LK* 237, 282). Reading is, in this respect, like love, which, Nussbaum asserts, "simply *happens* to us" (336). Once again, we face a crisis of genre. For some complex reason deeply rooted in the history of sexuality, the act of reading literature has, to the disgust of most, but clearly not all, professors, long been associated in the popular mind with the act, or rather, non-act, of being seduced. Transferred from the literary text to the professor, seduction can be a programmed classroom (or office-hour) occurrence, as "The Teaching Company" has recognized. This enterprising outfit begins its advertisement in the *New York Review of Books* for video disks of "SuperStar Teachers" by declaring without visible embarrassment that "art seduces. And who"—they challenge the reader—"is a better cupid for the literary romance than a professor who loves what he does?" The professorial pleasure-machine in question is not in fact Nussbaum but a colleague of hers at Brown, Arnold Weinstein. And of course Nussbaum did not write the copy, which, however, represents something like a mass-market version of her elevation of swooning to a point of high philosophical and moral principle. When Nussbaum praises a Jamesian character's "willingness to be passive, surrendering the invulnerable agency of the Kantian self," she speaks to the regressive desire to be seduced—by a text, a professor, or, lacking these, a videotaped lecture (180).

What we are beginning to identify is an energy within Nussbaum's sustained philosophical exhortation to be conscious and moral that is not, itself, either conscious or moral. This energy comes more sharply into focus when one compares Nussbaum's passivity with that of another philosopher, Emmanuel Levinas, who indeed seems at times almost purposely to contrast his view with Nussbaum's. Levinas speaks not of the passivity one must have in order to perceive and therefore to know, but rather of "a passivity still more passive than that of receptivity in knowing" ("God and Philosophy" 186). And while his passivity has ethical credentials, Levinas does not connect it to perception, nor does he entertain the possibility of a morality of perception. In fact, his account of knowledge as a kind of afterthought to ethics is altogether alien to Nussbaum.

But perhaps the most telling difference is that, for Levinas, passivity constitutes the essential ethical posture toward the Other, before whom we have an infinite obligation. The other is untouched by our obligation, for the relationship is theoretically nonreciprocal, except inasmuch as we constitute the Other for the Other and so could—if we chose to work out the implications of the system for ourselves—expect to receive the same abjection from the Other as he or she receives from us. For Nussbaum, by glaring contrast, a cognitive-moral passivity does not proceed from any obligation to the Other, but rather from an imperative we experience as an inner necessity. The entire issue lies within, and the visible Other is simply a test, an opportunity, an object: while perception must perceive something, and must be properly passive if it would be, to borrow a Jamesian phrase she admires, "finely aware and richly responsible," the responsibility, for Nussbaum, is entirely to the perceiving subject him- or herself. If, as Nussbaum suggests, the best model for "moral attention" is "our attention to works of art," then those to whom we attend figure, in our inner moral drama, only as texts (*LK* 149). And if novel reading, with its bonds between reader, character, and author, models the moral community, then we can see immediately the immense difference Nussbaum imagines between the alert and living reader, the center of the whole scene of action, and the others, who can only be speculations, inferences, derivations, constructs, but not full subjects. It becomes necessary to conclude that, according to Nussbaum, we do not labor to perceive because of any benefit the perceived derives from our efforts. Indeed, acute perception may well work to the disadvantage of the perceived—the detailing of flaws and shortcomings mentioned earlier. At most, the perceived person derives the negative benefit of a relative autonomy from the perceiver, purchased at the cost of distance. But the true ground of the imperative to perceive seems to be the fact that, as creatures capable of perception, we are obligated to exercise our capacities to the fullest: we can, therefore we must. Needless to say, Levinas would scarcely regard this as an "ethical" argument at all.

This difference about the site of responsibility helps account for an even more deeply revealing difference: that erotic love is good for Levinas as a kind of gateway drug to the family, the "instant of eroticism" promptly yielding its place to the "infinity of paternity," and—up to a certain point—bad for Nussbaum (*Totality and Infinity* 306). One of the readerly mysteries presented by *Love's Knowledge*, as well as *The Therapy of Desire*, concerns the fluctuating moral status of "love," especially erotic love. In roughly the first half of the book, erotic love is persistently presented as an ethical problem. To love with sexual desire, Nussbaum points out, occludes clear perception. Inward-turning, consumed by private passion, jealous, mysterious, obsessed, implicitly demanding that people avert their gaze, lovers remove themselves from the optical community, throwing off its coils of friendship and sympathy. Blind to most others, the lover would strike others blind as well. A morality of perception legislates against this kind of love, and even works against an overintense familial love (*LK* 151–55). Thus the Jamesian father and daughter mentioned earlier must, Nussbaum says, renounce certain claims on each other in order to perceive the other aright. Erotic lovers lie under an even heavier obligation because their manner of loving is far more destructive. One of the moral bonuses of novel reading is, in fact, that it produces this perceptual renunciation painlessly, distancing us from "blinding personal passions" that lead outside of straight moral judgment, without requiring the surrender of anything we really care about (240). The very "stance of the novelist" is, Nussbaum claims, "linked with a refusal of passionate love" (194). The moral could not be clearer: inspired by the novel and by the novelist, we must renounce erotic love if we would be good.

So why is the book called *Love's Knowledge?* Here we peer into the navel of the dream. What Nussbaum refers to as her "project"—an interrogation of how one should live that proceeds by "an explicitly organized and theoretically justified enterprise that goes on the borderline (or by refusing to acknowledge that there is one) between philosophy and literature"—actually moves through three imperfectly differentiated phases, argued serially with only a minimal attempt to harmonize them (*LK* 289). In the essays constituting stage one, as Nussbaum explains in an introductory essay written after the other essays had been composed (but, confusingly enough, appearing before them in the book), she did not question Aristotle's thinking on the primacy and comprehensiveness of ethics—or Henry James's, which she held to be essentially the same as Aristotle's. In stage two, she says, she began to be aware of a possible conflict between love and morality, a conflict Aristotle would have resolved unhesitatingly in favor of morality. In the second phase, Nussbaum conceives of a kind of horizon to morality that invites speculation about what may lie "beyond" it. That something turns out to be love, which is now seen to be in tension with morality, even subversive of it, something to be renounced. This position does not, however, survive the onslaught of stage three, in which Nussbaum discovers the messy, complex, disorderly state of love as the fullest realization of human potentiality. In her most enthusiastic stage-three moments, Nussbaum declares not just that erotic love and morality, while different, can support and inform one another, but that the moral life is only the threshold to the erotic one.

Other philosophers have taken on the subject of love in recent years, but their efforts underscore the distinctiveness of Nussbaum's third stage. In *The Broken Middle*, Gillian Rose explores, by way of a meditation on Augustine, Hannah Arendt, Kierkegaard, and Hegel, the relation of love to "violence" and "the state," and concludes, in an argument notable for its conceptual and rhetorical density, that love cannot be thought either together or apart from these two, and must be regarded as being in a condition of "diremption" from them both (*Broken Middle* 232–38; hereafter *BM*). Levinas's account of love, while disputed by Rose for its unrealistic view of "love outside the state," shares with Rose's the quality of philosophical disembodiment in its explicit rejection of mere "concupiscence" (*BM* 264; Levinas, "Ethics as First Philosophy" 85.) Later Nussbaum, the philosopher encountered in the last few essays in *Love's Knowledge* and in *The Therapy of Desire*, has no problem with concupiscence: hers is no theoretical experience of love, no account of love's "relation" to this or that concept or principle, but a fibrous evocation of the actual frictive movements of flesh and fantasy. In Nussbaum's supercharged stage three, the judicious Jamesian spectator is left choking in the dust of the horses of passion, a "vanishing mediator" that, by promoting renunciation as a general proposition, eventually fosters the renunciation of itself.

Coming upon stage three, we confront another crisis of genre: is *Love's Knowledge* a work of philosophy, a self-aware, serial exposition of carefully linked and progressive arguments that are ultimately consistent with each other; or is it a narrative, a series of arguments that are logically distinct, related to each other as stages of an evolutionary process? If the former, then we would, as readers, be challenged to discern the design of the totality, each moment of which would contain all the others in a structure that, its gradual exposition notwithstanding, existed in a single logical moment. If the latter, we would be required to chart the progress of the text as an initial situation (Aristotle knows everything), followed by a rising line of complication (or maybe not; maybe emotion, if not erotic love, has moral status), approaching a recognition (erotic love may well have a status comparable to morality), a reversal (indeed, it may be beyond morality in a positive sense), and a dénouement (morality is but a propaedeutic for the more kinetic sympathy of erotic love). We could even tentatively assign a subgenre to the narrative: comedy, a comedy of marriage and transcendence.

In order to determine the kind of knowledge Nussbaum has created in this book, we must examine much more closely the "love" that provides that knowledge. And this leads us to the penultimate chapter, on Dickens's *David Copperfield*, called "Steerforth's Arm: Love and the Moral Point of View." Here, Nussbaum begins with striking indirection, with an anecdote about a trip to England with her fourteen-year-old daughter, who "fell in love with James Steerforth," the older boy—and later, the young man—who befriends David. At first critical of her daughter's moral and aesthetic taste, Nussbaum eventually decides, as a conciliatory gesture, to read the book and, to her astonishment, finds herself suddenly swept away with erotic energy. Sitting on the beach, book in hand, she feels a sudden "wind in my face and an excitement in my heart, a sensuous delight in the fresh presence of each thing that seemed to be connected, somehow, with the vividness of the chapters, with the power, above all, of Steerforth's presence." And now, her forty-year-old heart soars, "rushing into the eager volatility of desire" (*LK* 335). And she is momentarily confused, her moral and aesthetic convictions confounded. For as she has already argued, erotic passion represents an insult to the very morality that she has been at such pains to articulate. And why should she throw over her morality just for a common character in a common Dickens novel—she, the mature philosophical admirer of Aristotle, Proust, and James?

The well-nigh ecstatic essay that follows is, once again, difficult to categorize. Modeled on Mann's *Death in Venice,* down to the seedy and garish beach town (Yarmouth, not Venice), it registers to the maximum possible degree the extramoral erotic appeal of (especially popular-vulgar) literary texts, and seems nearly literary itself, even to the point of sentimental overwriting and suspect reconciliations: the essay concludes with a conception of "a world in which general sympathy, erotic moonlight, and active generous loyalty live together in conversation" (*LK* 363). And yet, every effort is made to represent the philosopher's ecstasy as consistent with philosophical principle: there is morality, Nussbaum argues, "*in the willingness to enter into that world of love, loving Steerforth without judgment*" (359). Clearly, some transcendent point, some pure ultimate has been reached here; but how?

It is important to note that the philosopher has not simply been blasted out of her meditative repose by the sight of a man. She is, rather, closely attending to, even repeating, her daughter's attraction to a fictional character: what she calls her "desire" is provoked not precisely by "Steerforth's presence" but by her reading of a novel recommended by her daughter, who, in a kind of adolescent girlish confusion, had "fallen in love" with Steerforth, just as David, in a moment of boyish confusion, does in the novel. The whole sequence is mimetic, and begins with Steerforth, whom Nussbaum identifies as "in a sense the author of this novel, the creator of its erotic charm" (*LK* 357). In his symbolic role as the representative of the author, Steerforth stands as the displaced center of the entire system, a black hole of infinite attraction that sucks in other characters, readers, and even readers' mothers.

In this crushing reduction of everything to everything else, morality is both utterly compromised and exhausted—and yet rejuvenated, as if it had not been defeated by a superior force, but had merely handed off the baton, even regaining its own childhood by relinquishing its claim to supremacy, allowing that it had all along been confused with love and the imagination. In fact, morality is reconceived in this late chapter virtually as a *form* of childhood, requiring a "childlike imagination" and a "childlike attention to and memory for the particularities of the world" (*LK* 362, 360). Indeed, one of the most striking and peculiar features of Nussbaum's argument in *Love's Knowledge* is the prominent role played by childhood, especially adult-child pairings. The first instance, to which I shall return in a moment, occurs in the third chapter, and then again in the thirteenth, on the *Phaedrus;* the second is the Verver father and daughter, and the third, Copperfield and James Steerforth. All, but especially the first and last, are made to stand for love itself, love in general.

Unusual in the discourse of moral philosophy, this kind of alertness to the erotic potentiality of childhood or early adolescence becomes even more powerfully strange and compelling in *Love's Knowledge* in that it is unmarked as such. In a book dedicated to sensitivity, accurate perception, and right naming, Nussbaum never considers the role David's age and sex might play in his "love" for James Steerforth. Indeed, she bluntly identifies the love she herself feels for Steerforth with David's love—and, presumably, with the love her daughter feels for him as well. Nussbaum does not blush to name this love erotic, although there is no human being in the vicinity. More interestingly still, her "erotic" relation to the fictional young man Steerforth is equated with that of the lad David's, without any notation of the fact that, if David has an "erotic" relation to Steerforth, it takes the form of homosexual pederasty. Nor does she attend to the same species of fact in her discussion of the *Phaedrus,* where she points out that "a certain type of philosophical activity may be called into being by, and in turn express and nourish, the energy and beneficence and subtle insight of happy love," and that "intense erotic love of a particular person" has cognitive and moral value (*LK* 329, 122). To read Nussbaum on Plato is to forget, for a moment, that the "particular person" is a boy, whose parents fear and whose schoolmates snicker at the hungry approach of the smitten man; it is to set aside for a moment the fact that the whole point of the "philosophy" of the *Phaedrus* is not only, as Nussbaum insists, to describe a productive and progressive love based on an admiration of "character and values," a winged ascent "toward truth and knowledge," but also and primarily to contrive a speech that will win the wary and reluctant boy by degrees to consent to sex; and to ignore the fact that Plato's text is "literary" not so much in its capacity to enter into the mind of others, but in its remarkably vivid narrative depiction of varieties of seduction, including Socrates's of the impressionable Phaedrus himself (see *LK* 324-44; *TD* 443). (Indeed, according to Dante, vernacular literature answered the same need, given a heterosexual inflection. "The first poet to begin writing in the vernacular," Dante says in the *Vita Nuova*, "was moved to do so by a desire to make his words understandable to ladies who found Latin verses difficult to comprehend. . . . Composition in the vernacular was from the beginning intended for treating of love" [chap. 25].)

All these things Nussbaum seems determined to ignore; determined, that is, not to speak the name of the love that dare not speak its own. At one point, as she reports, Steerforth asks David to call him "Daisy," as he already calls David. "Why so I can, if I choose," David responds. Nussbaum notes the flirty quality of the exchange, but directs her comments away from the issue of sex and toward another thing altogether, "the novelist's power to give names to things, to transform evil to good, guilt to innocence—or to move altogether beyond that distinction, if he so chooses" (*LK* 357). In the haze of moonglow, homoeroticism is generalized into eroticism as such, the sexual is drained into the lexical. Unless we want to believe that Nussbaum is altogether insensitive to plain facts that many others have recognized, we must believe that she has recognized these facts, but has misfiled or misnamed them, preferring for some reason an evasive and generalized account to a specific one. In fact, the most immediate explanation is that Nussbaum understands in some way the unacceptability of the very image that excites her, that seems to her the very fountainhead of philosophy itself, but has found a way to preserve the precious image by smearing gel on the lens, sacrificing the particulars in order to elude the censors. But so prominent is the *Phaedrus* in Nussbaum's understanding of classical philosophy, and so aggressive are her claims in the Dickens chapter, that we must posit as the very primal scene of her philosophical-literary imagination an image of a *coitus a tergo,* a disavowed and sublimated homosexual pederastic embrace. At the beating—indeed, throbbing—heart of her "project" is this gripping image, positioned on the compromised borderline between philosophy and literature.

What can the textual representation of this embrace possibly signify for the female, but not explicitly feminist, moral philosopher? A very great deal; for, we realize suddenly, such a representation locks in all the key terms. As an image of human beings rather than a concept, it elicits an affective response that calls philosophy into question and suggests literature; as an image, perhaps, of love, it raises the dangerous issue of an intense and extramoral relationship that suggests both the threat to morality of erotic love and the possibility of a limit to morality itself; as an image of males, it must remain, for the woman, something to be perceived rather than experienced directly; and as an image of males, it elicits from the woman at most an imaginative identification in which the possibility of erotic satisfaction is, as it were, pre-renounced, regardless of the intensity of the sense of "Steerforth's presence." Virtually all the programmatic elements of "the project" can be read off the relationship of a woman to the image of the man-boy coupling.

The project did not, of course, develop in this way, and is never presented in such form. Nussbaum's silence on the questions here raised makes it, in fact, difficult to assess her position on the particular sexual and moral issues presented by homosexual pederasty. This position is, perhaps, "philosophical" in its lofty unconcern with detail, but it is definitely not "classical." As Michel Foucault labored to establish, these issues were a constant preoccupation in Greece and Rome; Lucian's *Amores,* to take one example, meditates anxiously on the difficulty of "giving a status and justification to sexual relations between men and boys," with "an ironic ending that reminds the reader of those precise acts that the invocations of friendship, virtue, and pedagogy all attempt to smooth over" (*Ethics* 92). Nor can Nussbaum claim to be strictly contemporary, speaking from a perspective so enlightened that it would be ill-mannered and, truly, irrelevant to inquire into "precise acts," inasmuch as the contemporary academic ethos seems dedicated to naming even fugitive or temporary impulses as bluntly homoerotic, the object of a cosmopolitan tolerance, even celebration.

So what *is* the nature of Nussbaum's interest in Daisies? Why is the imagination of the mature female philosopher so riveted by man-boy eroticism? To answer these questions, we need to take a detour out of *Love's Knowledge* to *The Therapy of Desire,* to essays written in the mid-to-late eighties, when *Love's Knowledge* was also being shaped. In these essays, we encounter a new argument based on Lucretius's attack on love's misguided cognitive structure. According to Lucretius (Nussbaum says), lovers, in their "squeezing, grasping, biting" frenzy, are strangely uncertain what they are doing. They canvas the body of the other, "weakened," Lucretius says, "by a hidden wound." "It is no wonder," Nussbaum glosses this passage, "that they cannot decide. For the aim that becomes evident from their behavior, the aim that they are actually pursuing in their actions, is one so strange that they could not own it consciously without convicting themselves of absurdity." What they want is not friendship, companionship, marriage, but rather "union or fusion"; in the most extreme stage of confusion, the lover wants to "eat the other sexually, feeding on that other mind and body and having it completely" (*TD* 173, 174). An example of "inappropriate, immoderate love" might be Seneca's *Medea,* which suggests that "love itself is a dangerous hole in the self, through which it is almost impossible that the world will not strike a painful and debilitating blow. The passionate life is a life of continued gaping openness to violation, a life in which pieces of the self are groping out into the world and pieces of the world are dangerously making their way into the insides of the self" (*TD* 441, 442). Against this lurid image, Nussbaum offers a more moderate and normative picture. "What the lover wants," she says, in one of those unrestricted statements that grow suddenly out of a reading of particular texts, "is to be extremely close to the person he or she loves, to be close enough to perceive and respond to every moment and every perceptible sign." We—we normals—don't want to fuse or to ingest; we want to *know*, to obtain "the sort of knowledge that consists in awareness and acknowledgment of every perceptible portion of that person's activity" (*TD* 188). We bite, grasp, squeeze each other because we are hungry for information, not because we wish to make the other, in a literal sense, our own. To deny the very separateness that excites us constitutes a "corruption of perception." True love sees and values the other for what she/he truly is. It does not, like Medea, fixate on "angry jealousies" (*TD* 478).

Medea is certainly a reprehensible figure. But behind this banal point is a simply amazing premise, that the play concerns love at all, that Medea's hysterical and incredible claim that the epic proportions of her frantically murderous career had proceeded from "love" of Jason, that the play constitutes a commentary on love as we understand the term, that we can learn from her about the dangers of going a bit over the top in our affections, that we should be warned by her example that the "best kind of personal love" involves "a tenderness and gentleness that are only rarely to be seen in Medea's fierce passion" (the lady, we are reminded, is "without gentleness") (*TD* 441, 479). To be sure, Medea does not display tenderness when she persuades Pelias's daughters to slit their father's throat by convincing them that he would thereby be made young again, or when she murders her children, one at a time. But why, exactly, does Nussbaum mainstream Medea as a representative woman; and why are Jason and Medea selected as one of the most extended examples of love in the Nussbaum oeuvre that takes a heterosexual "couple" as its instance? Why is this play chosen to provide insight into love?

Perhaps what Nussbaum responds to is Medea's defiance of the patriarchy, a first instance of a woman making her way through sheer "greatness of spirit" in the classical world (an instance that would require, once again, the gelling-over of the particular corpses she trails behind her) (*TD* 446). But we must also be alive to an even more intriguing possibility, that Nussbaum is as deeply interested in Jason as she is in Medea. In fact, in the terms of Nussbaum's argument, it is Jason rather than his wife who occupies the position of the woman, the object of a possessive love that refuses to acknowledge the other's humanity. This refusal, Nussbaum argues, has been traditionally directed at woman, and was enabled by the "total denial, by whole societies and groups, of the reality of female pleasure" (189). As the undeterred seeker of justice, Medea may inspire modern women; but as the dehumanized, unpleasured object of love, Jason signifies the historical reality of womanhood.

This historical reality was not, apparently, firmly in place in the classical world. Medea, we suspect, insisted on her share of pleasure. And as Nussbaum points out in a crucial footnote in *Therapy,* several classical texts argue that male-female intercourse was to be preferred to male-male intercourse on the grounds that, in the former, mutual gratification was more likely (*TD* 184). In Xenophon, Ovid, and Lucian, the younger of two males is held to occupy what most writers of all subsequent ages, except, perhaps, the most recent, regard as the female (or, we may say, Jasonian) position, in which pleasure is not expected or even desired. Exclusion from the domain of pleasure thus links the various objects—women, boys, husbands of immoderate women—of a self-interested and exploitative species of a presumptively but not exclusively male lust. This exclusion is the very point of the identifications on which Nussbaum's work is centered, identifications based on a recognition of commonality between the late-twentieth-century female philosopher and the classical tradition, love and reasoned discourse, literature and philosophy.

Nussbaum does not distinguish between the provocation experienced by Socrates and his successors and any that she experiences herself. But everything about her project derives from a crucial difference. The philosophy of the *Phaedrus* is immured in the cynical rhetoric of the devious, desirous adult who seduces by disavowing a keenly felt desire. Philosophy thus begins in an apparent indifference to love, a point seconded by Nietzsche, who offers as a friendly amendment the argument that philosophical "disinterestedness" is only a cover for a celibate terror of sex. Heraclitus, Plato, Descartes, Spinoza, Leibniz, Kant, Schopenhauer (he might have added Kierkegaard)—none of them, he said, could even be imagined as married. The Kantian account of aesthetic disinterestedness in particular earns Nietzsche's contempt as a virtually deliberate attempt to evade the actual experience of beauty, with its disorderly and quasi-erotic excitations: "a lack of any refined first-hand experience," Nietzsche says of Kant's aesthetic, "reposes in the shape of a fat worm of error" (*Genealogy of Morals* 3.6.104). The amendment is friendly only if what Nietzsche— who, of course, is another member of the philosophical bachelor's club—

registers as a lack of desire may also be considered a strategic denial whose genealogy goes back to the *Phaedrus:* the birth of philosophy from the spirit of cynicism, we could say; the fat worm of error from the fat worm of lust.

But Nussbaum's philosophical position is crucially different from that of either Socrates or Nietzsche. Determined to be neither a traditional philosopher nor a philosopher's wife, Nussbaum makes her entry into the scene of philosophy through an alternative route, an identification with the unpleasured younger one, the one driven by deprivation to sober speculations on the meaning of life. Her female if not feminist interest in "moral philosophy" as a renunciation of erotic love is perhaps best understood as a reflex of this identification with the intensely desired but dehumanized lad, the outcast from pleasure, the passive one who finds him- or herself with time to think and much to think about. The unusual intensity of Nussbaum's interest in literature may appear, in this context, as an assertion of a subversive female perspective from within the primal scene of philosophy, an insistence on the submerged affective component.

The whole truth is even more complex. Literature, too, has its male and female; and they are as distinct, and as inseparable, as those of philosophy. In order to articulate the difference, we might turn to the passage concerning Henry James that I have placed at the head of this essay, in which Nussbaum speaks, in terms she might well apply to her own project, of "the responses of an imagination that means to care for and to put itself there for us." We can, I would suggest, posit a distinction within this phrase between the dominating and implicitly male imagination that "means to put itself *there,*" to make an assertion, a claim, to impose itself on its characters and narration as well as on us the readers; and the pliant and implicitly female imagination that means to "put itself there *for us,*" exposing itself to our needs and designs, our individual and unregulated reading of her text. In the first instance, then, Nussbaum locates a place where a woman might stand within the discourse of classical philosophy based on an identification with the desired but exploited lads of the ancient world. This standpoint enables her to be, like others before her, stimulated by "love" into philosophizing. In the beginning, the friendship-based "Aristotelian" philosophizing that she promotes retains a fear of sexual pleasure, especially the aggressive, non-passive ("Medean") pursuit of such pleasure, as being inconsistent with morality. But the very act of philosophizing, we can speculate, generates a sense of power and entitlement comparable to that experienced by male philosophers, as it was by their progenitor, the older lover of boys. And through this discovered identification, Nussbaum works her way around to an assertion that pleasure is even higher than morality.

An initial identification as a woman with the exploited lad ends up producing an argument even more "manly" in its bold claim to pleasure than that of the cynically "disinterested" philosophers of the male tradition.

Everywhere we look, we meet the madness of love. But we also encounter, in various forms, the "fundamental commitment to reason" that Nussbaum locates in the practice of the Greeks, and claims as an ideal of her own. We misunderstand this commitment if we regard it as a devotion to abstraction and formalism, to a severe verbal mathematics. We must instead try to grasp the *fundamental,* even *fundamentalist,* nature of the commitment, and the *fundament* of reason itself as it discloses itself in "the tangled mysteries of these imagined lives." The foundational impurity of reason is brilliantly exemplified by the continuing generic crisis that characterizes Nussbaum's work, with its philosophical seriousness, its impressive scholarly apparatus, its ambitious "project"—coupled with its deep commitment to literary affect and indirection, its unreflective willingness to advise and prescribe, and its earnest advocacy of commonplace clichés about art, love, life, aesthetic "sensitivity," "humanity," erotic "moonglow," all of which seem to issue not from the Greek Academy, much less the contemporary academy, but from some secret club at, say, Bryn Mawr College around 1910. This, perhaps, is what "classical" culture really teaches us, that reason, like the color white, contains all its opposites, including the violent, the horrifying, the lurid, the cheap, the inhuman, the vulgar, the sentimental, the erotic. Those thinkers today who would prescribe as the remedy for the ills of modernity an ever more diligent application of self-aware reason, until we reach the point where mind and society are thoroughly emancipated from prejudice, desire, and irrationality, fail to understand why we never reach the desired state, why more reason is always needed. In vain do we try to distill a purified and progressive reason from its antitheses. The more fundamental our commitment to this project—the greater, that is, our commitment to the fundament of reason—the less likely it is to succeed.

Can a work be overread? Can it be so thoroughly picked over by generations of readers that it is replete with its own interpretations, drained of contemporary pertinence, debarred from a future? If so, one such text might be Kant's brief essay "An Answer to the Question: 'What Is Enlightenment?'" Its main claim, that people should think for themselves rather than simply accepting the doctrines they inherit and inhabit, seems so obvious today that it is difficult to imagine it as ever having been controversial, and therefore difficult to see why anyone should return to Kant for instruction on this point. Even worse, when one does return to Kant, one finds that the summons to reason is nested in other notions that have become scandalous. Summarized in the notorious injunction to "argue as much as you like, but obey," a chilling emphasis on civil order is backed up by ominous references to the "numerous and well disciplined armies" that properly secure the stability of a disputatious culture. Moreover, Kant's fawning deference to his sovereign seems a relic of a predemocratic era, a mark of what he himself characterized as "immaturity," a political and intellectual position from which we can learn nothing. In short, Kant's essay is both contemporary to the point of banality, and immured in its own relatively unenlightened context.

But if this little essay has lost its power to inspire, perhaps it retains other, undiscovered powers. Let us begin with a hypothesis: Kant's "answer to the question" of enlightenment, I will suggest, expresses not only the reigning cliché in the self-description of the modern intellectual, especially literary intellectuals—that they think for themselves and are answerable to no one —but also, in its forthright compact with the authorities, a blurted confession that today's intellectuals would make if only they had the insight and the honesty. In effect, Kant says that enlightened critique is acceptable or even possible only when it occurs within a politico-conceptual space demarcated and secured by the police. Thus constrained, "free" thought must be nothing more than an agreed-upon game with a conservative program that remains hidden despite its manifest success. This program, I will begin by proposing, is a truth denied by many but disproven by none.

One who has certainly tried to disprove it is Edward Said, whose recent book, *Representations of the Intellectual,* sketches out a portrait of the activist thinker meant to confound what he sees as a dangerous and cowardly conception of the intellectual as a mere entrepreneur, someone who reflects on and is reflected in a postmodern culture with no "outside," and therefore no true politics. Indeed, Said's own career as an outsider, an iconoclastic and committed public intellectual, could be taken as a model for the kind of fiercely independent intellectual activity he advocates. The true intellectual, Said argues, is able to "speak the truth to power" because he or she is an "exile," an "amateur," unimplicated in its structures of security and so unintimidated by its threats. Only from the margins, Said insists, can one perform one's duty as an intellectual, in part because one's duty is to represent and advocate the interests of the marginalized, the dispossessed, the underrepresented. It is implicitly on behalf of these people that the intellectual undertakes to attack class privilege or social injustice and, in general, to interfere with the untroubled self-regard of the dominant group. Necessarily, the intellectual is a loner, a singular if not exactly friendless individual heedless of the personal consequences of his activities. As should already be apparent, Said's book can be read not just as an attack on postmodernism, but as a crystallization of certain tendencies in cultural Modernism. Said is seeking, one might argue, to purify Kant by liberating the intellect from the false securities offered by armies and patrons; he is trying to complete Kant's work by emancipating the injunction to use your own reason from the crippling burden of obedience.

His account labors, however, under a couple of burdens of its own making. The first is the burden of inconsistency. In one bewildering passage, Said seems to take two opposed views virtually at once, claiming first that real intellectuals try "to uphold a single standard for human affairs," and then adding, as if it were a clarification, that "there are no rules by which intellectuals can know what to say or do"—so the intellectual is both a stern partisan of the unwavering law and a figure of anarchy (*Representations of the Intellectual* xiii, xiv; hereafter *R*). In another instance, Said argues for partisanship and passionate commitment over disinterestedness—but then, a few pages later, urges a "universalist" perspective that "forbids calling one side innocent, the other evil" (*R* 44). Throughout, Said argues, with no discernible sense of the problems involved, that the intellectual must be both affiliated and independent, a cross between Gramsci and Tiresias, Sartre and St. Simon Stylites. In such moments, which are frequent, he seems to be approaching a kind of twist, a paradox in his conception of the intellectual, but not to have worked through it, or even perhaps to have apprehended it.

The argument's second burden is even more difficult to negotiate: it is Said's own eminence. Can Said be serious when he speaks of cultivating "one's rare opportunities to speak," or when he assures his audience that being an intellectual is "a lonely condition," or that the intellectual ought to risk personal security as the cost of truth (*R* xvii)? These are, after all, the Reith Lectures, broadcast over the BBC and reprinted for the mass market to an audience long familiar with their author as one of the most recognizable and distinguished public intellectuals in the world. What risks has Professor Said run? Or rather, what proof can he offer that anything has been risked, given the cascade of honors that has descended upon him? And given his eminence, how, precisely, does Said stand "on the side of" the weak and oppressed? When everything one touches turns to gold, when all one's courageous acts redound to one's personal credit and secure one's eminence, when—to put the matter in the most offensive way possible—one makes a decent tenured living doing this, how can one claim to stand in the danger zone? The unasked question is whether one's public and professional stature modulates or inflects in any way not just one's ideas or judgments, but also what might be called, with productive ambiguity, one's *position,* which is to say one's actual (as opposed to claimed) affiliations. Has Said truly identified the nature of the risk run by the eminent intellectual; or is he facing down a nonexistent enemy, pretending or ventriloquizing a circumstance of dispossession he does not experience, his back turned to another enemy whose subtler subversion he does not suspect?

Here we confront a third burden, which takes the form not of inconsistency but of uniformity. Said is speaking to and for intellectuals and their fans. One reason his account seems to intellectuals such a *welcome* statement is, I submit, that it accords beautifully with the fonder and more traditional self-conceptions of such people. The fact that his book is seen as "stimulating" rather than, say, "controversial" as it seems to want to be flags the possibility that some fugitive principle of self-regard, whose enjoyment the intellectual spoils, has found its way into the group of intellectuals themselves as they rehearse their own most heroic attributes. Since Kant, these attributes have gathered, especially among those on the left, into a pose of narcissistic oppositionality. When we—that is, professional intellectuals—hear that the mission of the intellectual is to disturb or disrupt, to risk ostracism, to be "embarrassing, contrary, even unpleasant" (*R* 12), do we not feel a decidedly pleasant *frisson?* Do we not say to ourselves, and not for the first time, "Yes, that's me—a royal pain"?

The issue at this point is the relation of the intellectual to the site of real power—the power to determine actual policy, actual legislation, actual priorities, actual goals, actual action in a democratic culture, which is to say a culture in which the majority rules and the rules must serve the majority as well as protect the minorities so that they may, if they choose, try to influence or even become the majority. When they define themselves as both amateurs and partisans, dead-set "against the prevailing norms" as Said puts it, intellectuals fashion *themselves* a minority; they protect *themselves* not from injustice but from the responsibilities and uncertainties of authority, toward which they sustain a strictly negative relation. Absent a compelling or immediately obvious reason to do so, the Saidian intellectual—in fact a bourgeois professional—imagines himself undefined by profession or class. He imagines himself, moreover, as a person who chooses to affiliate with those who do not have the power to choose their affiliations, the disempowered and dispossessed; and who chooses *not* to affiliate with those who do have the power to choose their affiliations, those who enjoy power in general. The true risk such an intellectual runs is that oppositional negation may become not just a position or an attitude, but a form, a style, a haven, and ultimately a low-security prison. To be against power and prevailing norms, to resist worldly temptations, to refuse accommodation, to operate without rules or guarantees— how can one do all this, and do anything at all? An element of fantasy and what might be called poetic invention seems to be at work here. It is not just that the agency of the intellectual seems unreal, but that the very idea of the intellectual is modeled on fiction, a discourse produced by experts in "negative capability" or the "extinction of personality," by people who stand at a reflective distance from the power center and who, as a consequence, nothing affirmeth, at least nothing of immediate consequence.

In Said's final essay, the problem exfoliates anecdotally. Here, Said recounts his fifteen-year relationship with an unnamed Iranian acquaintance. A sophisticated intellectual, this man had found himself forced to make a series of painful choices, beginning with a wary but dedicated support for the Ayatollah's theocracy, which eventually rewarded his service with persecution. The toughest call of all, however, was the Gulf War, which Said's friend saw as a conflict between fascism and imperialism, in which he chose—out of battle-hardened principle—the latter. Dismayed, Said declares this decision "unnecessary": "I was surprised," he writes, "that none of the formulators of this, in my opinion, unnecessarily attenuated pair of choices had grasped that it would have been quite possible and indeed desirable on both intellectual and political grounds to reject both fascism and imperialism" (*R* 105).

Said is surprised, that is, that nobody had thought of the intellectual's way out, which is not to choose at all, but to complain about the choices, or perhaps to construct another set of choices, more easily decided than the original ones. His friend had reluctantly signed on to service in a government run by fanatics; but might there not, Said asks, be "some more discreet—but no less serious and involved—way of joining up without suffering the pain of later betrayal and disillusionment?" (*R* 105). Might there not, in short, be some way of joining up by not joining up? "Not being a joiner or party member by nature," he says in sentences that sound almost confessional, "I had never formally enlisted in service. I had certainly become used to being peripheral, outside the circle of power, and perhaps because I had no talent for a position inside that charmed circle, I rationalized the virtues of outsiderhood." His role in the politics of the Middle East was confined to being an "independent member of the Palestinian parliament in exile," a group that made no effort to formulate policy, but only "to resist Israeli policies." Said himself "refused all offers that were made to me to occupy official positions; I never joined any party or faction." While he refused to "collaborate" with Jews or American supporters of Israel, he "never endorsed" the policies of Arab states either (107–8). Clearly, what finally separates Said from his friend is precisely this, that, caught in a snarl of history and forced to choose between imperfect alternatives, his friend had risked, and suffered, disillusionment and betrayal and worse; whereas Said had been fortunate enough to be able to resist everything without the anxieties and disappointments that beset joiners.

While Said is too capacious and singular a figure to be typical of any group or movement, many scholars and critics—especially leftist, minoritarian, postcolonial, cultural-studies types who are concerned not only with political but with broadly social issues or issues of identity—look to him as model and guide. For all these, social and political marginality is simply presumed: a certain "critical" distance from what Lacan calls the Master Signifier, taking a step back from actuality into possibility, is a prerequisite for both the classical philosopher and the contemporary intellectual. Calling the center into question constitutes, indeed, the central and unquestioned project of an entire class of intellectual work today, and it is this project, rather than the character of individuals, that I am trying to assess. One mark of this project is an emphasis on theory: the margin is the place, it seems, for that superior form of intelligence capable of formulating general principles from the ground-level swirl of phenomena. It is also, as Said would undoubtedly agree, the very site of independent judgment, of that acute or unexpected angle of vision that penetrates through conventional thinking to the core of things. Intelligence as such seems to flourish more freely, to shine more brightly, when it is distanced from the scene of action, when it pitches its tents on the alternative terrain of scientific knowledge so that it can be, in a certain sense, irresponsible or unresponsible, so it can operate without concern for the worldly consequences of its operations, consequences that might force compromises or even denials of theoretical necessities. A certain "otherness," a "nowhere" quality, appears to be built into the very nature of modern critical thought.

But this otherness can take various forms, and what I am drawing attention to is the tendency of contemporary thinkers to think *about* otherness *from the point of view of* the other. What might be called the *thought of the Other* has effectively displaced traditional paradigms and fertilized whole fields of inquiry, especially those in which questions of identity are at stake. To measure the contributions and to mark the limits of this thought we can consider one of the most influential and productive research projects in recent years, Homi Bhabha's interrogation of the relation between colonizers and the colonized. Imposing Christianity and Eurocentrism all over the globe, the great colonial powers also, Bhabha argues in *The Location of Culture,* exposed themselves to the continual possibility of counter-appropriation, deflection, parody, mockery insinuating themselves into the very gestures of deference. In the colonial circumstance, the presumption of effective hegemony was continually compromised by the uncontainable possibility of inauthenticity: a virus of "sly civility" infected the discourse of the colonized and threatened the ease of the colonizer; and the ponderous, oppressive, insecure center was made constantly vulnerable to the supple and insidious agency of the margin.

Unexpected and illuminating as it is, this argument is just the beginning. From the claim that the margin is a freer and somehow more intelligent position than the center, Bhabha proceeds to the further claim that the margin is actually more central than the center. The dutiful but insincere subaltern utterance, Bhabha points out, is "split" in that the "content" of the utterance is at variance with "the structure of its positionality." Although emerging on the periphery of power, this split indicates "the general conditions of language," the splitting of *all* utterances: rightly apprehended, the margins, and the margins alone, display the hidden law of the center, a secret division that structures, and *de*centers everything. The margin becomes, as Bhabha puts it, a "paradigmatic place of departure" for a study of identity and utterance in general (*Location of Culture* 21; hereafter *LC*). With the discovery of decentering as the rule rather than the exception, we have arrived, Bhabha suggests, at a conception that could found a progressive rethinking of all identity as hybrid, open, ambivalent, discontinuous, in-between. And it is this second claim that constitutes the real point. If the margin were merely more interesting than the center, that would be curious but politically neutral. If, however, the law of the margin could be shown to regulate the entire field, including the center—where, because of repression, it could not "appear"—then a certain dominant configuration of forces would be overturned and the world would become open to new kinds of agency. It would become possible to think, for example, not just of the "foreign" language of the colonized, but of the "foreignness of languages," all languages. The playing field would be leveled at last.

And the leveling agent would be theory. There is no surer sign of the marginality of Bhabha's discourse on marginality than the extraordinary prestige it accords to theory. For Bhabha, the political potential of criticism is realized when the condition of the margin is applied as a template to the entire field—by reconceiving the realia of subaltern identity as the basis for a theory of identity *tout court*. Bhabha fully understands that the general project of theory—in particular the theory of cultural difference—has worked to "foreclose on the Other" by depicting it as a "good object of knowledge, the docile body of difference" (*LC* 31). Still, he insists that theory can and must be reclaimed as a matter of political principle. In a postrealist age, theory arises from the ashes of ontology. "I want to take my stand," he says, "on the shifting margins of cultural displacement—that confounds any profound or 'authentic' sense of a 'national' culture or an 'organic' intellectual" (*LC* 21).

I cannot claim to be culturally displaced, but the place where I live, Louisiana, is rapidly disappearing into the Gulf of Mexico, and the river that gives my city, New Orleans, its distinctive character as "the River City" constantly threatens to shift course abruptly somewhere upriver, which would make us "the River-Bed City." These disquieting facts give me, perhaps, some sensitivity to shifting margins, enough at least to know that they are hard to stand on for persons, buildings, and cities alike. And this is the problem. Identity as hybridity, as in-betweenness, liminality, other-than-itself—these notions, while issuing from a "committed theoretical perspective," are emancipatory in a strictly theoretical sense, a sense that Said (saluted by Bhabha for his "pioneering *oeuvre*") might fault for being insufficiently committed. Said might wonder, as I do, what the "commitment to theory" (the title of Bhabha's essay) actually entails. "Committed to what?" Bhabha asks proleptically; "at this stage in the argument, I do not want to identify any specific 'object' of political allegiance—the Third World, the working class, the feminist struggle." All these, while "crucial," do not enlist the commitment of "intellectuals who are committed to progressive political change in the direction of a socialist society" (*LC* 21). More urgent—at this stage in the argument—is the theoretical project.

So urgent, so complex, so interesting is this project that it eclipses all possible "objects of political allegiance." The question of what is to be done gives way, in Bhabha, to the question of "the force of writing, its metaphoricity and its rhetorical discourse, as a productive matrix which defines the 'social' and makes it available as an objective of and for, action" (*LC* 23). Social praxis is thus humbled before its grounding circumstance and enabling condition; and theory, or "ideological intervention," acquires political credentials as the partner of praxis, existing with it "side by side." But this begs a series of questions. Isn't theory sufficiently distinct from praxis that its pursuance must come at the expense of its partner? Could it not be said that the insistence on theory is a way of keeping all options open, and all hands clean, even while promising that some positive determination—strictly in keeping with "socialist" commitments, of course—will arrive some day, not today? Is not praxis here *itself* foreclosed as a docile body of difference, a good object of knowledge? If theory makes the social realm "available" as an objective of action, why do intellectuals hold so little power? Why are all the ropes in the hands of theoretical naifs or primitives?

The cost of marginality, for Bhabha, may well be the verso of its analytical power: the principled unwillingness, for the present moment, to specify, to decide, to particularize, to commit oneself to a recognizably political statement becomes, without transformation, an inability to do so. Having opened up the field of identity, having deconstructed a false and nonnecessary structure, having exposed the agency of writing, Bhabha seems unable to spell out ways of reclosing the field in a new, more positive and productive configuration. The emancipation from the Master Signifier has not, at least not yet, produced any new determination of the postcolonial subject or polity. Everything is, for the moment, suspended, weightless, in a protracted state of indecision. Bhabha is able to imagine and desire forms of freedom, especially in the mode of "freedom from," but relatively uninterested, it seems, in the project of imagining a "freedom to," in any but the most general sense. "Socialism" functions in this context as a general oppositionality, the prospect of whose realization generates a vague sense of jubilation that could only be spoiled by the declaration of an allegiance to a particular candidate, strategy, piece of legislation, political party, initiative. The point in the present context is that marginality may be the site of insight; but it may also be the place, or nonplace, of those who are simply out of it. Today, intellectuals, most of whom are weirdly secure in a world where volatility is the rule, a world that has not made a commitment to theory, are, in general, out of it.

What the colonized Other is for Bhabha, the lesbian is for Judith Butler. Both exist not just on the margin but in the even more radically equivocal conceptual space that is neither center nor margin. For Bhabha, this is the space of uncertain motivations and overdetermined meanings; for Butler, it is the space of drag. The otherness of woman *to* man is preliminary to the otherness *between* woman and man, and nothing brings out this second otherness more efficiently than transvestism or cross-dressing. If, as Joan Rivière argued in an article cited by Butler in *Gender Trouble,* "woman" could be seen in terms of "masquerade," then cross-dressing could represent an ultimate womanliness. But Butler ratchets this possibility up to a theoretical maximum in the same way as Bhabha, by proposing that transvestism, as an instance of performed parody, constitutes the secret truth of all gender identity. In an argument by now well known, Butler says that identity is constituted by a series of selections made from a menu of choices available in the culture. We select, in the manner of the parodic transvestite, those gestures by which we wish to be known and to know ourselves, and through our purposive identifications, an identity emerges. Not even "sex," which supposedly represents a biological ground of identity, yields an ontology; for sex, she claims, is retroactively constructed, an effect rather than a cause of gender identification. Rather than beginning with the idea of a biologically grounded identity determining the public expressions of gender, then, Butler begins with those public expressions and works "backwards" to biology. In short, the very notion of a natural psychosexual center is treated as an illusion created by a repression of the truth as disclosed by the transvestite.

For Butler, freedom and creative agency exist only on the margin. While one must in fact imitate and parodically repeat in order to have an identity at all, one may in effect control one's destiny by doing so consciously, a gesture heretofore available only to the disempowered and ostracized few who, like Said's intellectuals, risk everything to speak the truth to power. One would not wish to argue that necessity is more desirable than freedom, but we must note what has been sacrificed in the name of freedom. There is, for example, no audience in Butler, no real society. *Gender Trouble* does not trouble itself about the complex negotiations and interactions with the community in which gender performance occurs, and its silence on this score mirrors its denial of an interior core of necessity. What is bracketed on both ends is the kind of force that would direct, determine, structure a performance—or an "identity"—even against the conscious willing of the performer. Criticizing Foucault for dreaming of "sex before the law," a bucolic limbo of unconstructed pleasures, Butler herself dreams of sex before drive and before culture—of sex before the unconscious. For most people—those whose gender accords pretty well with their biological sex and with the conventional positionalities, and for all those who experience sex and gender in the mode of an unwilled and compelling urge or need—the freedom she uncovers and champions must therefore be both unexpected and unwanted, since it answers to no powerful desire.

Butler's is, in other words, a model of identity derived from neurotics (for whom it's all in the head) and fops (for whom style makes the [wo]man). The consequence is that this interesting view from the margins must remain marginal, for it excludes from consideration the fundamental experience of necessity, of a drive or desire that is "in you more than yourself." I have appropriated this phrase from Slavoj Žižek's description of ideology in order to signal my awareness that the centering desire I am describing may be redescribed as an ideological mechanism . It is Žižek's point in *The Sublime Object of Ideology* that ideology operates with maximum effectiveness at precisely those moments when we think we have escaped it; it is my point here that ideology operates universally, as the naturalizing or "centering" agent in psychic or cultural formations. It centers the center, engendering the sense that the way things are is the way they have to be; and it centers the margin, too. We do well to remind ourselves that it is most often on the edges of cultural formations that the rhetoric of freedom is experienced as a bludgeon rather than a blessing, a tool of the oppressive right, for whom difference is nothing but a mistaken choice, a perverse "lifestyle."

If, for Bhabha, a commitment to the margin as the paradigmatic point of departure takes the form of a commitment to theory, and thus a deferral of praxis, for Butler the problem is slightly different. It is that a commitment to the margin understates for strategic reasons the psychocultural experience of centeredness and centering—the experience or sense of necessity—as a factor in any identity whatsoever. Both these problems, of deferral and denial, beset a certain strain of "left" political theory, the best possible example of which, for my purposes, is Laclau and Mouffe's influential *Hegemony and Socialist Strategy*. As they define it, "hegemony" implies not just the fragility but the virtual nonexistence of the center. A Gramscian "war of position," which they recast as a systemic but crucially less substantial and more linguistic "antagonism," regulates the entire political scene and not just the disorderly fringes, where it has traditionally been felt most acutely. As a general principle, antagonism implies the dissolution of positivity, presence, unity, objectivity, nonlinguistic ontology, literal meaning—of a nonsubverted center of any kind, anywhere. "Unfixity," they write, "has become the condition of every social identity" (*Hegemony and Socialist Strategy* 85).

The expected political benefit of such an "antifoundationalist" account hardly needs to be specified at this point: it is that unfixity means emancipation and the opportunity for agency and intervention into the social realm. One can almost imagine that Laclau and Mouffe's "radical and plural democracy" had been dispensed from the same supply depot, some vast Plurality Central, as Bhabha's Third Space and Butler's drag outfits. But it is of course not a center but a periphery, founded on the premise that freedom, interest, agency, and creativity are only possible on the crumbling but dynamic edges of culture, institutions, norms, dominant configurations of all sorts. And, I would contend, what they call a "post-Marxist" emphasis on fluidity, multiplicity, unsuturedness may actually inhibit a genuine and positive conception of a just society, or what political philosophers, with grand indiscrimination, sometimes call human flourishing. In such a conception Laclau and Mouffe are simply not interested; their imagining of liberty does not extend this far inward, but lingers on the edges. They offer no way of deciding hard cases where interests clash, no way of ranking interests, no principle of decision; nor do they conceive of such principles of resolution in any but oppressive terms. To the extent to which they urge such traditional values as "openness," or "participation," they remain committed to form rather than content, and thus are liberals rather than radicals.

I have considered only a few examples, and these not at length; but each one can stand for a class, and together they summon up an ethos. It is not a specifically postmodern ethos, although postmodernity (whose presiding spirits are perhaps Jean-François Lyotard's stranded Martiniquans, mistreated by French law and yet unable to secure justice because the only courts available to them are French) is congenial to it. But the presumptions and intellectual habits to which I am drawing attention originated in the very roots of modern critical thinking and now extend beyond postmodernity to postcolonial studies, gender studies, some versions of feminism, post-Marxist political theory, on out to the governing presumptions about intellectual work, especially literary intellectual work, today. It spreads, as it were, from the power-phobia of the classic left to the analysis of social, psychoanalytic, and gender identity. Within this ethos, the place of privilege is occupied by the cognitive virtues of subversive insight and critical analysis, which are typically opposed to what is represented as the reactionary arrogance of the hegemonic class. Obsessed with power and force, contemporary critical theorists of the kind I'm describing cannot seem to imagine what it would be like actually to possess or exercise them; for them, power and virtue are natural antagonists. Thinkers in this mode see power either as an instrument of specific oppression, beaming out from a center in the manner of Foucault's Panopticon, or as a circum-ambient force of local coercions, to be resisted in the manner outlined in

Foucault's *History of Sexuality*. In the first model, power is elsewhere; in the second, it is here, but not possessed by "us."

Surely, one would think, there must be exceptions. As, for example, the work of Christopher Norris, a towering figure in contemporary critical theory who has boldly proclaimed the vitality of the Enlightenment heritage as the cornerstone of a leftist critique of postmodernist antirationalism. If many on the left seem to take a skeptical heretic's pride in remaining outside the mainstream of an essentially conservative political culture, Norris does not; he speaks from the center of a theoretical and ethical rule based on reason and accurate representation that empowers the critic to make positive judgments and statements about the real world. While Laclau and Mouffe might cheerfully offload "the discourse of the universal and its implicit assumption of a privileged point of access to 'the truth'" as an obstacle to achieving radical democracy, Norris insists that only the truth will set us free. And while many sustain a noncommittal commitment to theory, Norris urges the overriding importance of the political as such.

Nowhere are these commitments more aggressively pursued than in *Uncritical Theory: Postmodernism, Intellectuals, and the Gulf War,* a book inspired, if that's the word for it, by the flaccid urbanity of the "intellectual" response to the Gulf War. The immediate insult, an anticipatory article by Jean Baudrillard suggesting that the proliferation of images generated by the media that would cover the war would so block the reality of the situation that the Gulf War would never "happen"—followed in due course by another piece after the war claiming that it did not in fact happen— epitomized for Norris virtually every moral and intellectual shortcoming of postmodern intellectualism. Go along with the epistemological arguments of Lyotard and his ilk, Norris declares, and you will play yourself off the field by removing any grounds you might have for deciding between better and worse arguments, true and false statements, right and wrong actions. Reject the distinctions made available by enlightened thought, and you cannot protest when reason is infected by morality, or when politics becomes aestheticized. You cannot, for example, raise your voice even in the event of a hugely destructive war, justified with demonstrably false statements and flawed premises. The general silence of postmodern intellectuals when the Gulf War did break out in fact confirmed Baudrillard in one respect: for them, at least, the war did not exist.

As a bracing counterbalance to the examples set by Baudrillard, Lyotard, Fish, and Rorty, Norris offers such contemporary heroes as Chomsky, Habermas, and, conveniently for me, Said, whose book *Orientalism* mounts, Norris says, a powerful argument for rejecting shoddy and biased scholarship about the Middle East coming from the imperial nations in the nineteenth century. What impresses Norris is that Said proceeds in a spirit of *"getting things right,"* a curiously powerful phrase that implies a faith that bad research—myths, pseudohistories, propaganda, revisionism—can be checked and rejected in favor of a *"better* knowledge" of fact and a *"better* grasp" of the ideological issues (*Uncritical Theory* 141). Such knowledge, Norris suggests, would contradict clichés about Arabs as "irrational, despotic, shiftless, violently unpredictable, etc." But Said is perhaps not, after all, the best possible example here, for *Orientalism* is very much the product of an "intellectual," being designed to drive out bad knowledge without assuming responsibility for replacing it with better. Said is passionately engaged, and committed to the premise that Western perceptions are systematically and mendaciously skewed; but having shown that, he lets his victims fall of their own weight, if in fact they do fall. (Which is not always the case: the discussion of Sir Richard Burton emphasizes Burton's vast knowledge of customs, languages, and history.) Nowhere does Said propose a truer or more accurate account: reading *Orientalism,* you might conclude that the West has long been systematically prejudiced against Arabs, but you will not arise armed with a nonprejudicial understanding of the positive truth about the Orient.

In fact, in one of his most impressive pieces of journalism, written during the Gulf War, Said offered his own version of Orientalism, noticing "the general air of mediocrity and corruption that hangs over" the Arab world, whose most talented artists and brilliant intellectuals are "not only unacknowledged legislators [but] have been hounded into alienated opposition." "We cannot simply accuse the West of Orientalism and racism," Said argued (while acknowledging that "I am particularly vulnerable on this point"), "and go on doing little about providing an alternative." But what alternative is there, we might ask, if the Arab world today really is dominated by self-pity, corruption, despotism, conformism, anti-intellectualism? At this point, Said reverted to vague talk of "opening lines of communication." Still, by registering the need for a positive alternative— an account that would, without compromising the truth, "join up" with the interests of the Arab world—Said marked the limitations of the "alienated opposition" of the exilic perspective that he would define two years later as the special glory of the intellectual ("On Linkage, Language, and Identity" 443–45).

Said's implication that much of the Arab world today conforms to the traditional slanders about it throws into sharper relief the project of *Orientalism,* which articulates a historically legitimate grievance against misrepresentation without providing a corrective. Norris, I have argued, overestimates the positivity of that book; but the real question is whether he also overestimates the positivity of enlightened critique generally. Take his own arguments about the Gulf War. While Norris points to specific facts about the drawing of boundary lines, the true history of American commercial and political interests in the Middle East, the actual responsibility for reported oil spills, accurate body counts, and so forth, the burden of his argument is negative and critical: he asserts that the United States was not justified in making war on Iraq, and that the war it fought was not the war it said it was fighting. He does not take the side of Iraq, or of Kuwait's ruling class. A partisan of truth and justice, he maintains a virtually Swiss neutrality with respect to the actual military conflict. One of the most committed defenses of critical commitment in recent years, *Uncritical Theory* is noncommittal on the question of what ought to be done in a situation where all options are imperfect, if not equally so. Keeping the idea of truth and reason pure, enlightened critique is reluctant, perhaps even powerless, to prescribe actions that must necessarily bear the smudges of compromise, interest, and destructive force.

As the phrasing of the last sentence suggests, I am not truly criticizing Norris, with virtually all of whose stated commitments and arguments about and against the Gulf War I agree, and only wish I had expressed with such lucidity, force, and detail. I want, rather, to foreground the "intellectual" component in his project, a commitment to theory that inflects the very form of his judgments and statements by restricting them to negative formulations. Negation is such a force in Norris's discourse that it structures his most basic and fundamental point, which is, broadly, that we should *not* abandon Enlightenment distinctions and premises. Norris is against postmodernism, against aesthetic ideology, against U.S. action in the Gulf War, against "end of ideology" thinking. But he is silent on the question of what—Kuwait having been invaded—one ought to do or even to have done. In the midst of the crisis, critique falls silent, exhausted by the task of identifying erroneous premises, false statements, and inadequate understanding.

Norris presents, then, a striking example not of an escape from the margins, but of a marginalism of the center, one that might make us despair of ever getting out of the ghetto. Perhaps Derrida, whose cause Norris has tirelessly championed, could help us out. As Norris has argued, Derrida's work, although delicately positioned on the "margins of philosophy," in fact represents a faithful continuation of Enlightenment thought, a defense against the disease of postmodernism rather than, as is commonly thought, the disease itself. It is interesting, therefore, briefly to compare Derrida's treatment of reason with Norris's, with a view to determining its relation to what I have been calling centrality. In "The Principle of Reason: The University in the Eyes of Its Pupils," Derrida outlines the principles of "basic" or "fundamental" research that would not simply study things according to the unquestioned principle of reason, but would study that principle itself. Since nothing grounds itself, the principle or ground of reason cannot, he suggests, be reasonable; it must be nonreasonable if not antireasonable. This nonreasonable ground of reason becomes visible, Derrida says, in Heidegger's conception of knowledge in terms of the representation of an object to a subject. Hidden in this banal-sounding formula is a will to mastery, even a certain rapacity, that operates covertly within reason. Exposing this will to mastery to the light of day constitutes the first task of the new "basic" research, which would resist and subvert the kind of "oriented" research programs in which the ends—generally techno-military in nature—are specified in advance. This distinction between fundamental and oriented research is crucial to modern knowledge, defining the difference between the "essential and noble ends of reason that give rise to a fundamental science versus the incidental and empirical ends which can be systematized only in terms of technical schemas and necessities." But, alas, it cannot be made, or made good. It is, Derrida states bluntly, "impossible to distinguish between these two sets of aims"; and to pretend that we can do so, to claim that reason can be purified of ends, only invites the self-deception of "serving unrecognized ends" (12). Thus the intellectual program that Derrida conceives as the most comprehensive and urgent task of contemporary thought "requires *both* the principle of reason and what is beyond the principle of reason, the *arkhe* and an-archy" (18–19). More paradoxically and epigrammatically: "Beware of ends; but what would a university be without ends?" (19).

When he is being this way, Derrida must be a trial to Norris. For Derrida here accepts—or seems to, one can never be sure—the inevitability of "orientation" in the full knowledge of its affinities with despotism, militarism, irrationality, all manner of corruption. With Derrida, we have one foot, but only one, standing firmly on the solid rock of reason, with the other plunged into the mud of unreason. And mud it is. For Derrida, orientation can only be the object of suspicion, can only represent contamination. If the argument doesn't seem to go anywhere, if we seem, in fact, to end at some logical point before the place we started from, this is because Derrida cultivates what he calls a "negative wisdom" as the essence of the university's project, and of his own. We are still, in Derrida, undoing rather than doing, subverting rather than shaping, acceding to ends rather than determining them, asking questions rather than answering them. We are still, in short, on the edge of things, on the outside looking in.

If there were a visual symbol of the cognitive style I am describing, it might be the Romanian flag, displayed at the overthrow of Ceauşescu in 1989. As Žižek recounts this incident in *Tarrying with the Negative,* the red star had been cut out so that the flag had "nothing but a hole in its center" (1). This evacuation of the locus of power represents, for Žižek, the very object of modern critical philosophy, which is to "render visible" the " 'produced,' artificial, contingent character" of the Master Signifier. For only if the Master Signifier is seen as "nothing" can thought truly be free. Žižek presumes, rather than argues, that the intellectual is most effective when he or she "stays in the hole," maintaining a critical distance from the center of power (2). But this is a prescription for purity rather than effectiveness. Indeed, as the people of Romania—who believed that the hole was truly empty and that they were free at last, only to discover that they were in fact "serving unrecognized ends"—could instruct us, it is a prescription for radical ineffectuality. To be truly effective, to contribute to the production of positive and predictable consequences, an intellectual would have to embrace, to an undetermined extent, another principle, whose symbol Žižek discovers, but relegates to an inconsequential footnote. This symbol is a "monument" at the university campus in Mexico City, composed of a jagged ring of concrete encircling a "formless black undulating surface of lava." This unmonumental monument, this monument to unmonumentality, suggests a different project, "Mexican" rather than "Romanian," in which thought seeks not the laws of its own freedom but the full-frontal apprehension and even a sober and unillusioned embrace of what is theoretically unassimilable, irreducible to thought. With this project, contemporary academic-critical thinking has virtually nothing to do.

Why does critical thinking in the West today incline more to Romania than to Mexico; why does it prefer sky to earth, empty holes to lava masses; why does it busy itself with preliminaries?

If we can manage a mighty leap from the micrological and academic to the political and historical, perhaps the distinction taken up in earlier chapters between ethics and its near-synonym morality can help us formulate a preliminary answer. The persistence of this disorderly distinction in the discourse of ethics signals, I believe, a collective and obdurate intuition of a certain theory-frustrating dialogism structuring the field of ethics (or ethics-morality) that cannot be wished or argued away. One symptom of this equivocality is the endless debate among philosophers about whether the imperatives of ethics are transhistorical, acontextual, and transcendent, or contingent, local, and group-specific. The only possible answer, I believe, is that they are both. Unsystematic empirical research in the real world suggests that, in order to be widely considered honorable, action must meet a double criterion; it has to be persuasively represented as *good* in an unrestricted or transcendent sense, and also as good *for us* and *according to us*. It is, in other words, possible to map the distinction between morality and ethics onto the distinction between the good in itself and the good for us.

This apparently genial and accommodating case cuts across the grain of those who, like Bernard Williams, stress the difference between ethics and the "peculiar system" of morality. For Williams, we may recall from earlier discussions, morality is a kind of blunt conceptual instrument that stresses the idea of law, relies on blame, overrates rationality, and draws an inappropriately bright line between obligation and inclination. Williams is distressed by the ruthlessness, absolutism, and even irrationality of morality as it crushes all opposition in its drive to judgment, decision, and closure. Ethics, by contrast, is (almost) another kind of thing altogether, a practice of judgment involving a nuanced assessment and negotiation of social norms, cultural habits, and community values—a practice that extends "beyond the limits of philosophy." What baffles and annoys Williams is that while we would all plainly be "better off" without the concept of morality, it remains as "the outlook, or, incoherently, part of the outlook, of almost all of us."

Williams's distress flags the limitation of his argument. What he does not see is that ethics without morality is precisely as likely and as desirable as a community without genuine friction or difference. In a complex, conflictual community, people need some way of deciding hard cases, some rule that overrides the confusion of customs, habits, norms, some principle that legitimates action even in the absence of clear rules or unanimous consensus. "Morality" is a very good name for this way, this rule, this principle. Without morality as Williams defined it, people would have nothing to appeal to on those occasions where they bucked the consensus. Without morality, one could never be a hero, just a dissenter, a loner, an oddball. Without morality, one could never, in good conscience, decide a case involving approximately equal alternatives, much less act on or defend one's decision in a spirit of what J. Budziszewski has recently called "true tolerance." In short, while Williams is highly sensitive to the antiphilosophical disorder created within the discourse of ethics by morality, he is oblivious to the worldly necessity of morality. It is Williams himself who is reluctant to venture beyond the limits of philosophy.

The precise definitions we give to "ethics" and "morality"—two historically inconstant terms—are less important than the fact that two kinds of imperatives are seen to be operative within the general concept of right action; for this is the one historically constant feature of post-Enlightenment ethical thinking. It is certainly the feature that leads beyond philosophy, for philosophical thinking, while exceptionally sensitive to it, is constitutionally incapable of understanding it. Philosophy is incapable, that is, of grasping the integrity of a system that entails a certain programmed self-negation. As a mode of thought and reflection, philosophy may also be prejudiced against what Williams calls morality, which necessarily involves a certain brutal and illiberal exclusion, a fanatic drive to closure, an unrepentant elimination even of honorable choices in favor of the one best choice. Ethical philosophy since Kant has been predicated on "respect for the law" as a principle of disinterestedness, and so has been inhospitable to morality's highly interested disrespect for all choices other than the one it determines to be best. What the morality system (however defined) really signifies is the absolute impossibility of making a general theory of right action into a coherent and consistent system at all.

Most intellectual workers wish to assume, or believe they have already assumed, the character of their subject. I do not just mean that African American scholars study African American culture, gay or lesbian scholars study gay or lesbian issues, and Dickensians feel Dickensian. As the author of one book on the grotesque and another about saintly ascetics, I am unwilling to push this case too hard, but I believe that people study ethics because they feel themselves to be rational and good—that is, up to the subject. To them, the assertion that the deck of ethics contains a joker could hardly be considered good news, especially if the joker is one of the fifty-two. But the ethical-moral complex has the virtue of suggesting the limitations inherent to the intellectual's marginality as well as the most productive way out of those limitations.

The deepest point to emerge from the "peculiar system" of morality is this: within the larger field of ethics is nested a discrepant principle, another kind of imperative, a different law. The good in itself and the good for us—to take one form of this internal distinction—are dynamically interactive, constantly engaged in negotiation. "Ethics" represents not the ideal triumph of an unopposed law, but the very scene of compromise. The law, the properly and uniquely ethical law, is that there is no law, no single principle that can, all by itself, determine the right judgment, decision, or act. When we think or act with a concern for ethics, we do not simply edit out conflicting impulses or values, or magically align ourselves with the Way. Rather, we submit, often, to be sure, without realizing we are doing so and perhaps even while we are denying it, to multiplicity, impurity, indecision—and to the necessity, ultimately, of making what must be to a certain extent arbitrary and willful decisions. We consent to live in the shadows.

Now the appeal of the margin to the intellectual is clear. The margin is the site of theoretical consistency, for identity organized in clear and distinct ideas ("unfixity," "hybridity," "imitation," etc.) and for a secure— exclusively critical—relationship to the powers that be. Advertised as the ethical position, the margin is actually in flight from ethics, which is centered in the center where conflicting imperatives meet and mingle. It is only when one accepts responsibility—especially the responsibility for making decisions that affect a plural totality—that one appreciates the true difficulty of decision. For responsible action, as all who are in a position of responsibility understand in their bones, exposes one not just to unjustified attacks but, what is harder, to justified attacks, attacks typically launched from the margin, where intellectuals congregate to celebrate their uncompromised rectitude. As the example of Said suggests, intellectuals prize above all their autonomy and independence, which they characterize in terms of disobedience to repressive power. It was Kant's subtle genius to recognize the kernel of obedience that lay at the heart of autonomy.

I am not advocating the abandonment of enlightened critique, nor am I suggesting that enlightened individuals have a monopoly on docility. One only needs to consult Robert von Hallberg's book on East German writers and intellectuals, *Literary Intellectuals and the Dissolution of the State,* to be reminded of the dangers of intellectual conformism within institutions. Rather, I am probing the limitations of marginal thinking, and urging thinkers today not to discover some more effective means of resisting power or normative configurations but to begin forming some other, more familiar, confident, and productive relations with them. If thinkers today would leave the ghetto, they must, I argue, strive to overcome not their lower but their higher natures; they must surrender their fastidiousness, their desire to be blameless; they must come up with more effective ways to join up with some positive set of interests than by not joining up. To do this, thinkers must acknowledge that a pluralist democracy requires the maintenance of numerous and well-disciplined armies of various kinds, with their terrible capacity for devastation; they must concede that they live in a world of norms and centers as well as edges and margins, a world in which principles must occasionally be enforced by force, a world that sometimes demands to know the answers to such questions as: whose side are you on? what must be done? which action is best? which principles and whose rights should prevail? and, who are you?

What is needed is not—I wish to be clear on this point—a new boldness on the part of intellectuals in prescribing to the world as philosopher-kings or -queens, but rather a more general willingness to "imagine the center," to see things from the point of view of a democratic and plural polity that needs on occasion to act as if it were a single integrated entity, to grasp the moment of identity and normativity that secures and dignifies culture's differences. To do this, one would have to be willing to live with that dimension of worldly life irreducible to theory and incommensurate with strict principle, willing to choose among flawed alternatives. Intellectuals who would imagine the center must be prepared to suspend for a time both their fascination and their revulsion with centrality; they must learn to regard power and identity as dangerous but necessary allies, snarling guard dogs that might turn on them at any moment no matter how well they are treated.

Kant, I believe, actually envisioned this role for the intellectual, although his endorsement was tentative, as befitted his circumstance as a subject of his prince. It may happen, Kant says, that people impose on themselves a law that inhibits their own enlightenment. But they would be justified in doing so only for "a specified short period . . . pending, as it were, a better solution," at which time, "by a general consent (if not unanimously), a proposal could be submitted to the crown" (57). Leading this consensus would undoubtedly be the intellectuals, "men of learning," as Kant puts it, with access to the print media. It is—and here Kant is at his very subtlest—the prince, and not the intellectuals, who ought to be confined to the margins. His only concern is "to stop anyone forcibly hindering others from working as best they can to define and promote their salvation." He should not generate the ideas that move people forward to a "better solution"; in fact, "it detracts from his majesty if he interferes in these affairs" (58). The enlightened prince ought to clear out, Kant felt, leaving the center to the intellectuals as the leaders of public opinion, articulating the policies and principles of enlightened public discourse. In this "general consent" led by the responsible intellectual, then, Kant actually envisioned a way of escaping his own dilemma, the intellectual's complicity with authority.

But perhaps a more compelling, because more contemporary, example might be necessary. For this I turn to a speech given in May 1996 by Václav Havel in which he positioned Europe in a particular historico-metaphysical moment, and offered, with the specificity of one accustomed to governance, an immediate project. Beginning with the statement that Europe has traditionally been defined by "shared values," Havel urged his audience to affirm a new political structure in which the whole of Europe, including such countries as the Czech Republic, would be included as equal partners. The European Union, he insisted, "should formulate a clear and detailed policy of gradual enlargement that not only contains a timetable but also explains the logic of that timetable." I cite this bracingly specific moment because it so markedly contrasts with the species of intellectualism I have been discussing. As a Czech, Havel is one who, with respect to Europe, really is on the margins. Still, while speaking the truth to power, he is concerned for the identity of the totality: as he argues, "if democrats do not soon begin to reconstruct Europe as a single political entity, others will start structuring it in their own way, and the democrats will have nothing left but their tears" (41). One of the many things that makes Havel so inspiring a figure is that he has discovered a way of being an intellectual that includes such projects as running a nation, and even a continent. He has, in short, learned to imagine the center.

Admittedly, Havel's talk of "shared values," "solidarity," and "universalism," does not inspire everyone. At the end of his talk, he urged Europeans to "follow the example of Him in whom it has believed for two thousand years, and in whose name it has committed so much evil." Are Jews, Gypsies, secular humanists, Muslims, Hindus, atheists, and the metaphysically challenged, then, not truly Europeans; are they outcast from the universe of the universal; is this universe the property of missionaries and crusaders? One would like clarification. But this problematic patch underscores the element of risk that accompanies all attempts to imagine the center. I do not have an answer to this problem, and have in fact argued that there is no general answer. If, however, anyone who reads these words should discover a way of formulating principles that actually guide action in specific contexts, and carry with them no downside risk, I urge them to call me, collect, any time of the day or night.

On second thought, e-mail me.

References

Abrams, M. H. *Doing Things with Texts: Essays in Criticism and Critical Theory.* Edited by Michael Fischer. New York: Norton, 1989.

Adorno, Theodor W., and Max Horkheimer. *Dialectic of Enlightenment.* Translated by John Cumming. New York: Continuum Books, 1987.

Althusser, Louis. *For Marx.* New York: Vintage, 1970.

Altmann, Alexander. *Moses Mendelssohn: A Biographical Study.* Birmingham: University of Alabama Press, 1973.

Appiah, Kwame Anthony. "The Postcolonial and the Postmodern." In *In My Father's House: Africa in the Philosophy of Culture,* 137–57. New York: Oxford University Press, 1992.

Aristotle. *The Nichomachean Ethics.* In *The Ethics of Aristotle,* edited by J. A. K. Thomson. Harmondsworth: Penguin Books, 1967.

Austin, J. L. *How to Do Things with Words.* London: Oxford University Press, 1976.

Bakhtin, M. M. *Toward a Philosophy of the Act.* Translated by Vadim Liapunov. Austin: University of Texas Press, 1993.

Barsky, Robert. *Noam Chomsky: A Life of Dissent.* Cambridge, Mass.: MIT Press, 1997.

Barthes, Roland. "What Is Criticism?" Translated by Richard Howard. In *Debating Texts: Readings in Twentieth-Century Literary Theory and Method,* edited by Rick Rylance. 82–85. Buffalo and Toronto: University of Toronto Press, 1987. Orig. pub., 1964.

Baumgarten, Alexander. *Reflections on Poetry.* Translated by K. Aschenbrenner and W. B. Holther. Berkeley: University of California Press, 1954.

Beiser, Frederick. *Enlightenment, Revolution, and Romanticism: The Genesis of Modern German Political Thought, 1790–1800.* Cambridge, Mass.: Harvard University Press, 1992.

———. *The Fate of Reason: German Philosophy from Kant to Fichte.* Cambridge, Mass.: Harvard University Press, 1987.

Benjamin, Walter. "Theories of German Fascism: On the Collection of Essays *War and Warrior.*" Edited by Ernst Jünger." *New German Critique* 17 (spring 1979): 120–28.

———. "The Work of Art in the Age of Mechanical Reproduction." In *Illuminations,* edited by Hannah Arendt and translated by Harry Zohn, 217–52. New York: Schocken Books, 1968.

Bennett, Tony. "Really Useless 'Knowledge': A Political Critique of Aesthetics." In *Outside Literature,* 143–66. London: Routledge, 1990.

Berlin, Sir Isaiah. "On the Pursuit of the Ideal." *New York Review of Books* 35 (17 March 1988): 11–18.

———. "Two Kinds of Liberty." In *Four Essays on Liberty,* 118–72. New York: Oxford University Press, 1970.

Bhabha, Homi K. *The Location of Culture*. London: Routledge, 1994.

Blumenberg, Hans. *The Legitimacy of the Modern Age*. Translated by Robert M. Wallace. Cambridge, Mass.: Harvard University Press, 1983.

Brooke-Rose, Christine. *Stories, Theories and Things*. Cambridge: Cambridge University Press, 1991.

Brooks, Peter. *Reading for the Plot: Design and Intention in Narrative*. New York: Vintage Books, 1985.

Buch, Walter. "The Jew Is Outside the Law." In *Nazi Culture: Intellectual, Cultural, and Social Life in the Third Reich*, edited by George L. Moss, 336-37. New York: Grosset and Dunlap, 1966.

Budziszewski, J. *True Tolerance: Liberalism and the Necessity of Judgment*. New Brunswick: Transaction, 1992.

Burckhardt, Jacob. *The Civilization of the Renaissance in Italy*. 2 vols. New York: Harper & Brothers, 1958.

Burman, Edward. *The Inquisition: The Hammer of Heresy*. Wellingborough, Eng.: Aquarian Press, 1984.

Butler, Judith. *Gender Trouble: Feminism and the Subversion of Identity*. New York: Routledge, 1990.

Campbell, Richard. *Truth and Historicity*. Oxford: Oxford University Press, 1992.

Caputo, John D. *Radical Hermeneutics: Repetition, Deconstruction, and the Hermeneutic Project*. Bloomington: Indiana University Press, 1987.

Cascardi, Anthony. "Aesthetic Liberalism: Kant and the Ethics of Modernity." *Revue Internationale de Philosophie* 45 (January 1991): 10-23.

Cassirer, Ernst. *The Philosophy of the Enlightenment*. Translated by Fritz C. A. Koelln and James P. Pettegrove. Boston: 1964.

Chase, Cynthia. "The Witty Butcher's Wife: Freud, Lacan, and the Conversion of Resistance to Theory." *Modern Language Notes* 102 (December 1987): 989-1013.

Chomsky, Noam. *American Power and the New Mandarins*. New York: Pantheon, 1969.

———. *Aspects of the Theory of Syntax*. Cambridge, Mass.: MIT Press, 1965.

———. *Cartesian Linguistics: A Chapter in the History of Rationalist Thought*. Lanham, Md.: University Press of America, 1966.

———. *The Chomsky Reader*. Edited by James Peck. New York: Pantheon Books, 1987. (Includes "Interview" with Chomsky, "The Responsibility of Intellectuals," "Objectivity and Liberal Scholarship," "The Manufacture of Consent," "Psychology and Ideology" [1971 essay on Skinner], and "Equality: Language Development, Human Intelligence, and Social Organization.")

———. "An Interview." *Radical Philosophy* 53 (autumn 1989): 30-39.

———. *Language and Responsibility*. Based on conversations with Mitsou Ronat. Translated by John Viertel. New York: Pantheon Books, 1979.

———. *Reflections on Language*. New York: Pantheon Books, 1975.

Chomsky, Noam, and Michel Foucault. "Human Nature: Justice versus Power." In *Reflexive Water: The Basic Concerns of Mankind*, edited by Fons Elders, 137-97. N.p.: Condor Books, 1974. Discussion occurred in 1971.

Chytry, Joseph. *The Aesthetic State: A Quest in Modern German Thought*. Berkeley: University of California Press, 1989.

Clausen, Christopher. "Moral Inversion and Critical Argument." *Georgia Review* 42 (spring 1988): 9-22.

Clayton, Philip, and Steven Knapp. "Ethics and Rationality." *American Philosophical Quarterly* 30 (April 1993): 151–62.

Crews, Frederick. "In the Big House of Theory." *New York Review of Books* 29 May 1986: 36–42.

———. "The Parting of the Twains." *New York Review of Books* 20 July 1989: 39–44.

Crowther, Paul. *The Kantian Sublime: From Morality to Art.* Oxford: Clarendon Press, 1989.

Culler, Jonathan. "Meaning and Convention: Derrida and Austin." *New Literary History* 13 (1981): 15–30.

———. *Structuralist Poetics: Structuralism, Linguistics, and the Study of Literature.* Ithaca, N.Y.: Cornell University Press, 1975.

Dante Alighieri. *Vita Nuova.* In *The Portable Dante,* translated and edited by Mark Musa, 587–649. New York: Penguin Books, 1995.

Das, Veena. "Subaltern as Perspective." In *Subaltern Studies VI: Writings on South Asian History and Society,* edited by Ranajit Guha, 310–24. Delhi: Oxford University Press, 1989.

Davidson, Arnold I. "Archeology, Genealogy, Ethics." In Hoy 221–34.

Deleuze, Gilles. *Kant's Critical Philosophy: The Doctrine of the Faculties.* Translated by Hugh Tomlinson and Barbara Habberjam. Minneapolis: University of Minnesota Press, 1984.

de Maistre, Count Joseph. *Letters on the Spanish Inquisition.* Translated and edited by T. J. O'Flaherty. Delmar, N.Y.: Scholars' Facsimiles and Reprints, 1977.

de Man, Paul. *Allegories of Reading: Figural Language in Rousseau, Nietzsche, Rilke, and Proust.* New Haven: Yale University Press, 1979.

———. *Blindness and Insight: Essays in the Rhetoric of Contemporary Criticism,* 2nd ed. Theory and History of Literature, vol. 7. Minneapolis: University of Minnesota Press, 1983.

———. "Foreword" to Carol Jacobs, *The Dissimulating Harmony: The Image of Interpretation in Nietzsche, Rilke, Artaud, and Benjamin,* vii–xiii. Baltimore: Johns Hopkins University Press, 1978.

———. "Kant and Schiller." In *The Aesthetic Ideology,* edited by Andrzej Warminski, 129–62. Theory and History of Literature 65. Minneapolis: University of Minnesota Press, 1996.

———. "Phenomenality and Materiality in Kant." *In Hermeneutics: Questions and Prospects,* edited by Gary Shapiro and Alan Sica, 121–44. Amherst: University of Massachusetts Press, 1984.

———. "Reading and History." In *Resistance to Theory,* 54–72. Minneapolis: University of Minnesota Press, 1986.

———. *The Rhetoric of Romanticism.* New York: Columbia University Press, 1984.

Derrida, Jacques. "Afterword: Toward an Ethic of Discussion." In *Limited Inc,* 111–60.

———. "Biodegradables: Seven Diary Fragments." Translated by Peggy Kamuf. *Critical Inquiry* 15 (summer 1989): 812–73.

———. " 'Eating Well,' or the Calculation of the Subject: An Interview with Jacques Derrida." In *Who Comes after the Subject?,* edited by Eduardo Cadava, Peter Connor, and Jean-luc Nancy, 96–119. New York: Routledge, 1991.

———. *Of Grammatology.* Translated by Gayatri Chakravorty Spivak. Baltimore: Johns Hopkins University Press, 1976.

———. "Interpretations at War: Kant, the Jew, the German." *New Literary History* 22 (winter 1991): 39–95.

———. "Like the Sound of the Sea Deep within a Shell: Paul de Man's War." In *Memoires for Paul de Man,* 155–263. Revised edition, translated by Cecile Lindsay, Jonathan Culler, Eduardo Cadava, and Peggy Kamuf. New York: Columbia University Press, 1989.

——. *Limited Inc.* Evanston, Ill.: Northwestern University Press, 1988.

——. *The Post Card: From Socrates to Freud and Beyond.* Translated by Alan Bass. Chicago: University of Chicago Press, 1987.

——. "The Principle of Reason: The University in the Eyes of Its Pupils." *Diacritics* (fall 1983): 3–20.

——. *Speech and Phenomena; and Other Essays on Husserl's Theory of Signs.* Translated by David B. Allison. Evanston, Ill.: Northwestern University Press, 1973.

Diderot, Denis. "The Beautiful." In *Aesthetic Theories: Studies in the Philosophy of Art,* edited by Karl Aschenbrenner and Arnold Isenbert, 129–47. Englewood Cliffs, N. J.: Prentice-Hall, 1965.

Dreyfus, Hubert, and Paul Rabinow. "What Is Maturity? Habermas and Foucault on 'What Is Enlightenment?'" In Hoy 109–21.

duBois, Page. *Torture and Truth.* New York: Routledge, 1991.

Eagleton, Terry. "The Emptying of a Former Self." *Times Literary Supplement,* 26 May–1 June 1989: 573–74.

——. *Exiles and Emigrés: Studies in Modern Literature.* New York: Shocken, 1970.

——. *Ideology: An Introduction.* London: Verso, 1991.

——. *The Ideology of the Aesthetic.* Oxford: Basil Blackwell, 1990.

——. *Literary Theory: An Introduction.* Minneapolis: University of Minnesota Press, 1983.

——. "Two Approaches in the Sociology of Literature." *Critical Inquiry* 14 (spring 1988): 469–90.

Eichenbaum, Boris. "The Theory of the 'Formal Method.'" In *Russian Formalist Criticism: Four Essays,* edited by Lee T. Lemon and Marion Rees, 99–139. Lincoln: University of Nebraska Press, 1965.

El-Dakhakhny, Mohammed. "Mandela: Gadhafi a 'brother leader.'" *New Orleans Times-Picayune* 24 October 1997: A18.

Eze, Emmanuel Chukwudi, ed. *Race and the Enlightenment: A Reader.* Cambridge, Mass.: Blackwell, 1997.

Fallows, James. "How the World Works." *Atlantic Monthly,* December 1993: 62–74.

Fanon, Frantz. *Black Skin, White Masks.* London: Pluto, 1986.

Ferguson, Frances. "Forum." *PMLA* 112, no. 5 (October 1997): 1125–26.

Feyerabend, Paul. *Farewell to Reason.* London: Verso, 1987.

Fish, Stanley. "Literature in the Reader: Affective Stylistics." In *Is There a Text in This Class? The Authority of Interpretive Communities,* 21–67. Cambridge, Mass.: Harvard University Press, 1980.

——. "With the Compliments of the Author: Reflections on Austin and Derrida." In *Doing What Comes Naturally: Change, Rhetoric, and the Practice of Theory in Literary and Legal Studies,* 37–67. Oxford: Clarendon Press, 1989.

Foster, Hal, ed. *The Anti-Aesthetic: Essays on Postmodern Culture.* Port Townsend, Wash.: Bay Press, 1983.

Foucault, Michel. "The Art of Telling the Truth." In Kritzman 86–95.

——. *Discipline and Punish: The Birth of the Prison.* Translated by Alan Sheridan. New York: Vintage, 1977.

——. "The Ethic of Care for the Self as a Practice of Freedom." Interview with Raul Fornet-Betancourt, Helmut Becker, and Alfredo Gomez-Müller (20 January 1983). In *The Final Foucault,* edited by James Bernauer and David Rasmussen, 1–20. Cambridge, Mass.: MIT Press, 1987.

——. *Foucault Live.* Translated by J. Johnstone and S. Lotringer. New York: Semiotexte, 1989.

——. "La Maison des fous." In *Les criminels de paix,* edited by Franco Basgalia and Franca Basgalia Ongaro, translated by Bernard de Fréminville, 145-60. Paris, 1980.

——. "Nietzsche, Genealogy, History." In Rabinow 76-100.

——. "Qu'est-ce que la critique?" *Bulletin de la Société française de Philosophie* 84 (April-June 1990): 35-63.

——. "The Return of Morality." In Kritzman 242-54.

——. *The Use of Pleasure,* vol. 2 of *The History of Sexuality.* Translated by Robert Hurley. New York: Vintage, 1985.

——. "What Is Enlightenment?" Translated by Catherine Porter. In Rabinow, 32-50.

Freud, Sigmund. *General Psychological Theory: Papers on Metapsychology.* Edited by Philip Rieff. New York: Collier Books, 1963.

——. "Negation." In *General Psychological Theory* 213-17.

——. "Notes upon a Case of Obsessional Neurosis." In *Three Case Histories,* edited by Philip Rieff, 15-102. New York: Collier Books, 1963.

——. "The Unconscious." In *General Psychological Theory* 116-50.

Gay, Peter, ed. *The Enlightenment: A Comprehensive Anthology.* New York: Simon & Schuster, 1973.

Gewirth, Alan. *Moral Rationality.* Lawrence, Kan.: Dept. of Philosophy, University of Kansas, 1972.

——. *Reason and Morality.* Chicago: University of Chicago Press, 1978.

Gorman, David. Review of Christopher Norris, *Derrida.* In *Philosophy and Literature* 13 (April 1989): 204-5.

Gramsci, Antonio. *Selections from The Prison Notebooks.* Edited and translated by Quintin Hoare and Geoffrey Nowell Smith. New York: International Publishers, 1971.

Greenblatt, Stephen. "Forum." *PMLA* 112 (October 1997): 5.

——. "Towards a Poetics of Culture." In Veeser, *The New Historicism,* 1-14.

Habermas, Jürgen. "Consciousness-Raising or Redemptive Criticism: The Contemporaneity of Walter Benjamin." In *Philosophical-Political Profiles,* translated by Frederick Lawrence, 129-63. Cambridge, Mass.: MIT Press, 1983.

——. "Excursus: On Leveling the Genre Distinction between Philosophy and Literature." In *The Philosophical Discourse of Modernity: Twelve Lectures,* translated by Frederick G. Lawrence, 185-210. Cambridge, Mass.: MIT Press, 1990.

——. *Moral Consciousness and Communicative Action.* Translated by Christian Lenhardt and Shierry Weber Nicholsen. Cambridge, Mass.: MIT Press, 1990.

——. "Philosophy as Stand-in and Interpreter." In *After Philosophy: End or Transformation?,* ed. Kenneth Baynes, James Bohman, and Thomas McCarthy, 296-315. Cambridge, Mass.: MIT Press, 1987.

——. "Taking Aim at the Heart of the Present: On Foucault's Lecture on Kant's *What Is Enlightenment?*" In *The New Conservatism: Cultural Criticism and the Historians' Debate,* translated and edited by Shierry Weber Nicholson, 173-79. Cambridge, Mass.: MIT Press, 1989.

Hacking, Ian. "What's Best." *London Review of Books* 27 January 1994: 17-18.

——. Reply to Nozick, *London Review of Books* 27 January 1994: 4.

——. "Self-Improvement." In Hoy 235-40.

Hallberg, Robert von. *Literary Intellectuals and the Dissolution of the State: Professionalism and Conformity in the GDR.* Chicago: University of Chicago Press, 1996.

Hampshire, Stuart. *Morality and Conflict.* Cambridge, Mass.: Harvard University Press, 1983.

Hand, Séan, ed. *The Levinas Reader.* Oxford: Blackwell, 1989.

Hare, R. M. *Freedom and Reason.* Oxford: Clarendon Press, 1963.

Harpham, Geoffrey Galt. *The Ascetic Imperative in Culture and Criticism.* Chicago: University of Chicago Press, 1987.

———. *Getting It Right: Language, Literature, and Ethics.* Chicago: University of Chicago Press, 1992.

Harris, Randy Allen. *The Linguistics Wars.* New York: Oxford University Press, 1993.

Hartman, Geoffrey H. *Beyond Formalism: Literary Essays, 1958-1970.* New Haven: Yale University Press, 1970.

———. *Criticism in the Wilderness: The Study of Literature Today.* New Haven: Yale University Press, 1980.

———. "The Culture of Criticism." *PMLA* 99.3 (May 1984): 371-97.

———. *The Fate of Reading and Other Essays.* Chicago: University of Chicago Press, 1975.

———. *The Fateful Question of Culture.* New York: Columbia University Press, 1997.

———. "Ghostlier Demarcations: The Sweet Science of Northrop Frye." In *Beyond Formalism* 24-41.

———. "Literary Commentary as Literature." In *Criticism in the Wilderness* 189-213.

———. *The Longest Shadow: In the Aftermath of the Holocaust.* Bloomington: Indiana University Press, 1996.

———. *Saving the Text: Literature, Derrida, Philosophy.* Baltimore: Johns Hopkins University Press, 1981.

———. *The Unmediated Vision: An Interpretation of Wordsworth, Hopkins, Rilke, and Valéry.* New York: Harcourt, Brace & World, 1966.

———. *The Unremarkable Wordsworth.* Minneapolis: University of Minnesota Press, 1964.

———. "Wordsworth and Goethe in Literary History." In *The Fate of Reading* 179-97.

———. *Wordsworth's Poetry, 1787-1814.* New Haven: Yale University Press, 1964.

Havel, Václav. "The Hope for Europe." *New York Review of Books* 20 June 1996: 38-41.

Hegel, G. W. F. *The Philosophy of Law.* In *Hegel Selections,* edited by J. Loewenberg, 443-68. New York: Scribner's, 1957.

Heine, Heinrich. *Concerning the History of Religion and Philosophy in Germany.* In *Selected Works,* translated and edited by Helen M. Mustard. New York: Scribner's, 1973.

Held, Virginia. *Feminist Morality: Transforming Culture, Society, and Politics.* Chicago: University of Chicago Press, 1993.

Herbert, Christopher. *Culture and Anomie.* Chicago: University of Chicago Press, 1991.

Hoy, David C., ed. *Foucault: A Critical Reader.* Cambridge, Mass.: Basil Blackwell, 1991.

Hudson, W. D., ed. *The Is-Ought Question.* New York: St. Martin's Press, 1969.

Humboldt, Wilhelm von. *The Limits of State Action.* London: Cambridge University Press, 1969.

Hume, David. *A Treatise of Human Nature.* In *Hume's Ethical Writings: Selections from David Hume,* edited by Alasdair MacIntyre. Notre Dame, Ind.: University of Notre Dame Press, 1965.

Irigaray, Luce. *An Ethics of Sexual Difference.* Translated by Carolyn Burke and Gillian C. Gill. Ithaca, N.Y.: Cornell University Press, 1993.

———. *Speculum of the Other Woman.* Translated by Gillian C. Gill. Ithaca, N.Y.: Cornell University Press, 1985.

Jameson, Fredric. *Fables of Aggression: Wyndham Lewis, the Modernist as Fascist.* Berkeley: University of California Press, 1979.

——. "Interview." *Diacritics* 12 (fall 1982): 72–91.

——. *Late Marxism: Adorno, or, the Persistence of the Dialectic.* London: Verso, 1990.

——. *Marxism and Form.* Princeton: Princeton University Press, 1971.

——. "Marxism and Historicism." In *The Syntax of History* 148–77.

——. "Metacommentary." In *Situations of Theory,* vol. 1 of *Ideologies of Theory: Essays 1971–86.* 2 vols. Theory and History of Literature, vol. 48. Minneapolis: University of Minnesota Press, 1988.

——. "On Contemporary Marxist Theory: An Interview with Fredric Jameson." *Alif* 10 (1990): 114–31.

——. "Pleasure: A Political Issue." In *The Syntax of History* 61–74.

——. *The Political Unconscious: Narrative as a Socially Symbolic Act.* Ithaca, N.Y.: Cornell University Press, 1981.

——. *Postmodernism, or, the Cultural Logic of Late Capitalism.* London: Verso, 1991.

——. *The Prison-House of Language: A Critical Account of Structuralism and Russian Formalism.* Princeton: Princeton University Press, 1972.

——. "Regarding Postmodernism—A Conversation with Fredric Jameson." With Anders Stephanson. In *Universal Abandon? The Politics of Postmodernism,* edited by Andrew Ross, 3–30. Minneapolis: University of Minnesota Press, 1988.

——. *Sartre: The Origins of a Style.* New Haven: Yale University Press, 1961.

——. *The Seeds of Time.* New York: Columbia University Press, 1994.

——. *Signatures of the Visible.* London: Routledge, 1992. (Includes "Class and Allegory in Contemporary Mass Culture: *Dog Day Afternoon* as a Political Film" 35–54.)

——. *The Situations of Theory.* Vol. 1 of *Ideologies of Theory: Essays 1971–86.* 2 vols. Theory and History of Literature, vol. 48. Minneapolis: University of Minnesota Press, 1988.

——. *The Syntax of History,* vol. 2 of *Ideologies of Theory: Essays 1971–86.* 2 vols. Theory and History of Literature, vol. 49. Minneapolis: University of Minnesota Press, 1988.

Janicaud, Dominique. *Powers of the Rational: Science, Technology, and the Future of Thought.* Bloomington: Indiana University Press, 1994.

Jay, Martin. "The 'Aesthetic Ideology' as Ideology; Or What Does It Mean to Aestheticize Politics." In Jay, *Force Fields,* 71–83. New York: Routledge, 1993.

——. *Marxism and Totality: The Adventures of a Concept from Lukács to Habermas.* Berkeley: University of California Press, 1984.

Johnson, Barbara. "Mallarmé and Austin." In *The Critical Difference: Essays in the Contemporary Rhetoric of Reading,* 52–66. Baltimore: Johns Hopkins University Press, 1980.

Kain, Philip J. *Marx and Ethics.* Oxford: Clarendon Press, 1988.

Kamen, Henry. *Inquisition and Society in Spain in the Sixteenth and Seventeenth Centuries.* Bloomington: University of Indiana Press, 1985.

Kant, Immanuel. "An Answer to the Question: What Is Enlightenment?" In Reiss 54–60.

——. "The Contest of Faculties." In Reiss 177–90.

——. *Critique of Judgment.* Translated by James Creed Meredith. New York: Oxford University Press, 1928.

——. "Metaphysical Foundations of Morals." In *The Philosophy of Kant: Immanuel Kant's Moral and Political Writings,* edited by Carl J. Friedrich, 140–208. New York: Modern Library, 1977.

——. "On a Supposed Right to Lie because of Philanthropic Concerns." In *Grounding for the*

Metaphysics of Morals, translated by James W. Ellington, 63–67. Indianapolis: Hacker Publishing Co., 1993.

Kaplan, Alice Yeager. *Reproductions of Banality: Fascism, Literature, and French Intellectual Life.* Minneapolis: University of Minnesota Press, 1986.

Kedourie, Elie. *Arab Political Memoirs and Other Studies.* London: Frank Cass, 1974.

Kerrigan, William, ed. *Pragmatism's Freud: The Moral Disposition of Psychoanalysis.* Baltimore: Johns Hopkins University Press, 1983.

Kinser, Bill, and Neil Kleinman. *The Dream That Was No More a Dream: A Search for Aesthetic Reality in Germany, 1890–1945.* New York: Harper & Row, 1969.

Knapp, Stephen. *Literary Interest: The Limits of Anti-Formalism.* Cambridge, Mass.: Harvard University Press, 1993.

Knapp, Stephen, and Walter Benn Michaels. "Against Theory." In *Against Theory: Literary Studies and the New Pragmatism,* edited by W. J. T. Mitchell, 3–32. Chicago: University of Chicago Press, 1985.

Kristeva, Julia. *Desire in Language: A Semiotic Approach to Literature and Art.* Edited by Leon S. Roudiez, translated by Thomas Gora, Alice Jardine, and Leon S. Roudiez. New York: Columbia University Press, 1980.

Kritzman, Lawrence, ed. *Michel Foucault—Politics, Philosophy, Culture: Interviews and Other Writings, 1977–84.* New York: Routledge, 1990.

Lacan, Jacques. *The Ethics of Psychoanalysis, 1959–60.* Translated by Alan Sheridan. New York: W. W. Norton, 1978.

——. "Kant avec Sade." In *Écrits,* 765–90. Paris: Editions de Seuil, 1966.

——. "Le Rat dans la Labyrinthe." In *Encore: Le Seminaire de Jacques Lacan,* book 20, edited by Jacques-Alain Miller, 125–33. Paris: Editions de Seuil, 1975.

——. *Television: A Challenge to the Psychoanalytic Establishment.* Edited by Joan Copjec. Translated by Denis Hollier, Rosalind Kraus, and Anette Michelson. New York: Norton, 1990.

Laclau, Ernesto. *Emancipations.* London, New York: Verso, 1996.

Laclau, Ernesto, and Chantal Mouffe. *Hegemony and Socialist Strategy: Towards a Radical Democratic Politics.* London: Verso, 1985.

Lacoue-Labarthe, Phillippe, and Jean-Luc Nancy. "The Nazi Myth." Translated by Brian Holmes. *Critical Inquiry* 16 (summer 1990): 291–312.

Lakoff, Robin Tolmach. "The Way We Were; or, the Real Actual Truth about Generative Semantics." *Journal of Pragmatics* 13 (December 1989): 939–88.

Lentricchia, Frank. *Criticism and Social Change.* Chicago: University of Chicago Press, 1983.

Levinas, Emmanuel. "Ethics as First Philosophy." In Hand, 75–87.

——. "God and Philosophy." In Hand, 166–89.

——. *Totality and Infinity: An Essay on Exteriority.* Translated by Alphonso Lingis. Pittsburgh: Duquesne University Press, 1969.

Llorente, D. Juan Antonio. *A Critical History of the Inquisition of Spain.* Williamstown, Mass.: J. Lilburne, 1967.

Lukács, Georg. *History and Class Consciousness: Studies in Marxist Dialectics.* Translated by Rodney Livingston. Cambridge, Mass.: MIT Press, 1971.

——. *The Theory of the Novel.* Translated by Anna Bostock. Cambridge, Mass.: MIT Press, 1971.

Lyotard, Jean-François. *The Differend: Phrases in Dispute.* Translated by Georges Van Den Abbeele. Minneapolis: University of Minnesota Press, 1988.

———. *Discours, figure*. Paris: Klincksieck, 1971.

———. *Instructions païennes*. Paris: Galilee, 1977.

———. *The Postmodern Condition: A Report on Knowledge*. Translated by Geoff Bennington and Brian Massumi. Minneapolis: University of Minnesota Press, 1984.

Lyotard, Jean-François, and Jean-Loup Thébaud, *Just Gaming*. Translated by Wlad Godzich. *Theory and History of Literature*, vol. 20. Minneapolis: University of Minnesota Press, 1985.

MacIntyre, Alasdair. *After Virtue: A Study in Moral Theory*. Notre Dame, Ind.: University of Notre Dame Press, 2nd ed., 1984.

Mackie, John. *Ethics: Inventing Right and Wrong*. New York: Penguin, 1977.

———. *Hume's Moral Theory*. Boston: Routledge & Kegan Paul, 1980.

Martin, Wallace. *Recent Theories of Narrative*. Ithaca, N.Y.: Cornell University Press, 1986.

Mill, J. S. *On Liberty*. Harmondsworth: Penguin, 1984.

———. *A System of Logic*. London: Longmans, Green & Co., 1911.

Miller, J. Hillis. *The Ethics of Reading: Kant, de Man, Eliot, Trollope, James, and Benjamin*. New York: Columbia University Press, 1987.

Miller, James. *The Passion of Michel Foucault*. New York: Simon & Schuster, 1993.

Monter, William. *Frontiers of Heresy: The Spanish Inquisition from the Basque Lands to Sicily*. New York: Cambridge University Press, 1990.

Montrose, Louis. "The Politics and Poetics of Culture." In Veeser, *The New Historicism*, 15–36.

Murdoch, Iris. "Against Dryness: A Polemical Sketch." In *Revisions: Changing Perspectives in Moral Philosophy*, edited by Stanley Hauerwas and Alasdair MacIntyre, 43–50. Notre Dame, Ind.: University of Notre Dame Press, 1961.

Nandy, Ashis. *The Intimate Enemy*. Delhi: Oxford University Press, 1983.

Nietzsche, Friedrich. "A Critical Backward Glance." In *The Birth of Tragedy* and *On the Genealogy of Morals,* translated by Francis Golffing, 3–15. Garden City, N.Y.: Doubleday Anchor Books, 1956.

———. *On the Genealogy of Morals*. In *On the Genealogy of Morals* and *Ecce Homo*, edited by Walter Kaufmann, translated by Walter Kaufmann and R. J. Hollingdale, 15–166. New York: Random House, 1969.

Norris, Christopher. *Paul de Man: Deconstruction and the Critique of the Aesthetic Ideology*. New York: Columbia University Press, 1988.

———. *Spinoza and the Origins of Modern Critical Theory*. Oxford: Basil Blackwell, 1991.

———. *Uncritical Theory: Postmodernism, Intellectuals, and the Gulf War*. London: Lawrence & Wishart, 1992.

———. " 'What Is Enlightenment?' Foucault on Kant." In *The Truth about Postmodernism*, 29–69. Oxford: Blackwell, 1993.

———. *What's Wrong with Postmodernism: Critical Theory and the Ends of Philosophy*. New York: Harvester Wheatsheaf, 1990.

Nozick, Robert. *The Nature of Rationality*. Princeton: Princeton University Press, 1993.

———. *Philosophical Explanations*. Cambridge, Mass.: Belknap Press of Harvard University Press, 1981.

———. Reply to Hacking. *London Review of Books* 10 March, 1994: 4–5.

Nussbaum, Martha C. "Feminists and Philosophy." In *New York Review of Books* 20 October 1994: 59–63.

———. *The Fragility of Goodness*. Cambridge: Cambridge University Press, 1986.

——. *Love's Knowledge: Essays on Philosophy and Literature.* New York: Oxford University Press, 1990.

——. *The Therapy of Desire: Theory and Practice in Hellenistic Ethics.* Princeton: Princeton University Press, 1994.

Ogden, C. K., and I. A. Richards. *The Meaning of Meaning.* London: K. Paul, Trench, Trubner, 1945.

Paglia, Camille. *Sex, Art, and American Culture: Essays.* New York: Vintage Books, 1992.

——. *Vamps and Tramps: New Essays.* New York: Vintage Books, 1994.

Plato. *The Phaedrus.* In *Phaedrus and The Seventh and Eighth Letters.* Translated by Walter Hamilton. Harmondsworth: Penguin, 1981.

Pratt, Mary Louise. "The Ideology of Speech-act Theory." *Centrum* 1 (1981): 5–18.

Rabinow, Paul, ed. *The Foucault Reader.* New York: Pantheon, 1984.

Rai, Milan. *Chomsky's Politics.* London: Verso, 1995.

Rawls, John. *A Theory of Justice.* Cambridge, Mass.: Harvard University Press, 1971.

Readings, Bill. *Introducing Lyotard: Art and Politics.* London: Routledge, 1991.

Reiss, Hans, ed. *Kant. Political Writings.* Translated by H. B. Nesbit. Cambridge: Cambridge University Press, 1991.

Rescher, Nicholas. *Rationality: A Philosophical Inquiry into the Nature and the Rationale of Reason.* Oxford: Clarendon Press, 1988.

Ricoeur, Paul. "Narrative Time." In *On Narrative,* edited by W. J. T. Mitchell. Chicago: University of Chicago Press, 1981.

——. *Time and Narrative.* Translated by Kathleen McLaughlin and David Pellauer. 3 vols. Chicago: University of Chicago Press, 1984–88.

Rocker, Rudolf. *Nationalism and Culture.* London: Freedom Press, 1937.

——. *The Tragedy of Spain.* New York: Sublime Freie Arbeiter Stimme, 1937.

Rorty, Richard. *Contingency, Irony, and Solidarity.* Cambridge: Cambridge University Press, 1989.

——. "Deconstruction and Circumvention." *Critical Inquiry* 11 (September 1984): 1–23.

Rose, Gillian. *The Broken Middle: Out of our Ancient Society.* Cambridge, Mass.: Blackwell, 1992.

Sacks, Oliver. "An Anthropologist on Mars." *New Yorker* 27 December 1993/ January 1994: 105–25.

Said, Edward. *Culture and Imperialism.* New York: Alfred A. Knopf, 1993.

——. "On Linkage, Language, and Identity." In Sifry and Cerf 439–46.

——. *Orientalism.* New York: Pantheon, 1978.

——. *Representations of the Intellectual.* New York: Vintage Books, 1996.

——. "Response." *Critical Inquiry* 15 (spring 1989): 634–46.

Sallis, John. *Spacings: Of Reason and Imagination in Texts of Kant, Fichte, Hegel.* Chicago: University of Chicago Press, 1987.

Sartre, Jean-Paul. "Why Write?" In *'What Is Literature?' and Other Essays,* 48–69. Cambridge, Mass.: Harvard University Press, 1988.

Scarry, Elaine. *The Body in Pain: The Making and Unmaking of the World.* New York: Oxford University Press, 1985.

Schama, Simon. *Landscape and Memory.* New York: A. A. Knopf, 1995.

Schiller, Friedrich. *On the Aesthetic Education of Man in a Series of Letters.* Translated and edited by Elizabeth M. Wilkinson and L. A. Willoughby. Oxford: Clarendon Press, 1967.

Schmidt, James, ed. *What Is Enlightenment? Eighteenth-Century Answers and Twentieth-Century Questions.* Berkeley: University of California Press, 1996.

Scruton, Roger. *Aesthetic Understanding.* London: Methuen, 1983.

——. "Modern Philosophy and the Neglect of Aesthetics." *Times Literary Supplement* 5 June 1987: 604, 616–17.

Searle, John. "Reiterating the Differences: A Reply to Derrida." *Glyph* 2 (1977): 199–208.

——. *Speech Acts: An Essay in the Philosophy of Language.* Cambridge: Cambridge University Press, 1970.

——. "The World Turned Upside Down." Review of Jonathan Culler, *On Deconstruction: Theory and Criticism after Structuralism. New York Review of Books* 27 October 1983: 76–79.

Sedgwick, Eve Kosofsky. *The Epistemology of the Closet.* Berkeley: University of California Press, 1990.

Sidgwick, Henry. *Methods of Ethics.* 7th ed. Chicago: University of Chicago Press, 1907.

Sifry, Micha, and Christopher Cerf, eds. *The Gulf War Reader: History, Documents, Opinions.* New York: Random House, 1991.

Smith, Denis Mack. "The Theory and Pratice of Fascism." In *Fascism: An Anthology,* edited by Nathaniel Greene. New York: Crowell, 1968.

Spivak, Gayatri Chakravorty. "Revolutions That As Yet Have No Model." *Diacritics* 10 (winter 1980): 29–49.

Steiner, George. *Extraterritorial: Papers on Literature and the Language Revolution.* New York: Atheneum, 1971.

Stewart, Susan. "The Marquis de Meese." *Critical Inquiry* 15 (autumn 1988): 162–92.

Stone, Lawrence. "An Exchange with Michel Foucault." *New York Review of Books* 31 March 1983: 43.

Todorov, Tzvetan. *On Human Diversity: Nationalism, Racism, and Exoticism in French Thought.* Translated by Catherine Porter. Cambridge, Mass.: Harvard University Press, 1993.

Tolstoi, Leo. "What Is Art?" In *Critical Theory since Plato,* edited by Hazard Adams, 708–20. San Diego and New York: Harcourt Brace Jovanovich, 1971.

Tuberville, A. S. *The Spanish Inquisition.* Hamden, Conn.: Archon Books, 1968.

Veeser, H. Aram, ed. *The New Historicism.* New York: Routledge, 1989.

Walzer, Michael. "The Politics of Michel Foucault." In Hoy 51–68.

——. *Spheres of Justice.* New York: Basic Books, 1983.

Weber, Max. *The Protestant Ethic and the Spirit of Capitalism.* Translated by Talcott Parsons. London: Unwin University Books, 1930.

Weber, Samuel. "It." *Glyph* 4 (1978): 1–31.

White, Hayden. *Metahistory: The Historical Imagination in Nineteenth-Century Europe.* Baltimore: Johns Hopkins University Press, 1973.

——. "The Value of Narrativity in the Representation of Reality." In *The Content of the Form: Narrative Discourse and Historical Representation,* 1–25. Baltimore: Johns Hopkins University Press, 1988.

Williams, Bernard. *Ethics and the Limits of Philosophy.* Cambridge, Mass.: Harvard University Press, 1985.

Williams, Raymond. "Base and Superstructure in Marxist Cultural Theory." In *Debating Texts: Readings in Twentieth-Century Theory and Method,* edited by Rich Rylance, 204–16. Toronto: University of Toronto Press, 1987: 204–16.

———. *Keywords: A Vocabulary of Culture and Society*. New York: Oxford University Press, 1976.

———. *Marxism and Literature*. Oxford: Oxford University Press, 1977.

Wimsatt, W. K., and Monroe Beardsley. "The Intentional Fallacy." In Wimsatt, *The Verbal Icon*, 3-12. Lexington: University of Kentucky Press, 1954.

Wittgenstein, Ludwig. *Philosophical Investigations*. Translated by G. E. M. Anscombe. New York: Macmillan, 1953.

Wolin, Richard. *The Politics of Being: The Political Thought of Martin Heidegger*. New York: Columbia University Press, 1990.

Zimmerman, Michael. *Heidegger's Encounter with Modernity: Technology, Politics, Art*. Bloomington: Indiana University Press, 1990.

Žižek, Slavoj. *Enjoy Your Symptom! Jacques Lacan in Hollywood and Out*. London: Routledge, 1992.

———. *The Sublime Object of Ideology*. London: Verso, 1989.

———. *Tarrying with the Negative: Kant, Hegel, and the Critique of Ideology*. Durham, N.C.: Duke University Press, 1993.

Index

homosexuality, 238; on Kant, 67-71, 73, 75-77; Christopher Norris on, 68, 78-82; on power, 85, 92, 253-54; and Spanish Inquisition, 84-85

Frederick the Great, 71, 83

Freud, Sigmund, 47; Chomsky compared to, 193-94; and interpretation, 155-60; on negation, 134-35; on the "Rat Man" (*Notes on a Case of Obsessional Neurosis*), 116-18

Frye, Northrop: Geoffrey Hartman on, 203, 219

Gay, Peter, 68n.

Genette, Gérard, 36

Gewirth, Alan, 110

Ghadafi, Moammar, 28

Goebbels, Joseph, 128

Goldmann, Lucien, 9

Goodman, Nelson, 181

Gould, Steven Jay, 11

Graff, Gerald, 52, 54

Gramsci, Antonio, 123, 199

Grandin, Temple, 111-12, 114, 116

Great Gatsby, The (F. Scott Fitzgerald), 16

Greenblatt, Stephen, 1, 96n., 148

Griffin, Robert, 163

Gulf War, 78, 246, 254-56; and aesthetic freedom, 136-44

Habermas, Jürgen, 25, 67, 70, 81n., 144; on art, 121-22, 144; on Foucault, 79-80

Hacking, Ian: on Foucault and Kant, 76; on Robert Nozick, 100-101

Hampshire, Stuart, 19, 27

Hare, R. M., 40

Harpham, Geoffrey Galt, 97n., 134, 226

Harris, Randy Allen (*Linguistics Wars*), 180-85, 187, 189-90, 201

Harris, Zellig, 181, 189

Hartman, Geoffrey: on aesthetic education, 205, 216; on criticism, 147, 206-12; on culture, 4, 14-16, 204-6, 212-16, 218-19; on Freud, 211-12; on Frye, 203, 219; and ghosts, 207, 210, 213-16; on Goethe,

214-15; and Holocaust, 215-16; as major thinker, 217-18; on middles, 208-9; on Valéry, 210; on Wordsworth, 204, 212-17; *Beyond Formalism*, 206-9; *Fateful Question of Culture*, 4, 14-16, 203-8, 218; *The Fate of Reading*, 210; *The Longest Shadow*, 215-17; *The Unremarkable Wordsworth*, 212-17

Havel, Vaclav, 262-63

Havlicek, John "Hondo," 190

Hegel, G. W. F., xi-xii

Hegemony, 198-200

Heidegger, Martin, 51, 94, 125, 205, 257

Heine, Heinrich, 74

Held, Virginia: and feminist morality, 30-32

Herbert, Christopher, 13

Hernandez, Melchior, 93-95

Hitler, Adolf: on Jews, 216

"Hitler analogy," the, 142

Hobsbawm, Eric, 184

Hopkins, Anthony (*The Remains of the Day*), 104

Horkheimer, T., 75, 77, 169

Huckleberry Finn (Mark Twain), 157

Hume, David: on *is-ought* distinction, 38-42; on rationality and instinct, 115

Hussein, Saddam, 138-41, 143

Ideology, 81-82, 197-200; aesthetics and, 120-28, 135-37; form and, 152

Ignatius of Loyola, 87

Inquisition, Spanish, 82-97; construction of truth in, 93-98; and Enlightenment, 83-85, 91; and modernity, 85-89; political rationale of, 90-92; position of *conversos* in, 92-95; and power-knowledge complex, 94-98; and "relaxation," 94-95; superiority to Enlightenment of, 89-90. *See also* De Maistre, Joseph; Foucault, Michel; Hernandez, Melchior; Kant, Immanuel

Interpretation: and Freudian unconscious, 155-60; and historicism, 147-49; and history, 147-53

Irigaray, Luce, 18-19; on ethics, 24

James, Henry, 229, 241
Jameson, Fredric, 10, 162–79; and Adorno, 167, 169, 171, 174; and antinomy, 170–71, 175–76; on Barthes, 173; and Chomsky, 194–95, 197; on class consciousness, 169, 223; on collective identity, 166–68; and contradiction, 170–71, 175–76; on Critical Regionalism, 177–78; on de Man, 164, 173; and Terry Eagleton, 162–65; on ethics, 18–20, 96n.; greatness of, 174–75; and Greimas, 175; on interpretation, 149–53, 158–60; on Lacan, 172–73; and modernism, 149–50, 174–75; and politics, 163–66; and postmodernism, 170, 175–79; on religion, 172–73; and Said, 162–65; and utopia, 168–69, 172, 176; "Class and Allegory," 171; *Marxism and Form*, 164, 168; "Metacommentary," 149–52, 158–59; *Political Unconscious*, 165, 168, 174; *Postmodernism*, 174; *Seeds of Time*, 170, 175–78
Janicaud, Dominique, 102
Jay, Martin, 74
Jews, 73, 81–82, 218; and Spanish Inquisition, 83–95
Johnson, Lyndon, 111

Kain, Philip J., 24
Kamen, Henry (*Inquisition and Society in Spain*), 83–85, 87n., 88, 92, 95
Kant, Immanuel, 83, 99, 158, 186; on aesthetics, 120–23, 126–43; on ethics, x–xii, 20–25, 56, 229–30; and fascism, 129; "Fourth Critique" of, 75; and rationality, 99, 110; "terrorism" of, 74; "An Answer to the Question," 67–80, 91, 242, 260, 262; *Religion within the Limits of Reason Alone*, 72; "On a Supposed Right to Lie," 33–34. *See also* Enlightenment; Foucault, Michel; Norris, Christopher; Rationality; Reason
Kedourie, Elie, 139n.
Kipling, Rudyard, 163
Knapp, Stephen, 113–14; "Against Theory," 45, 153–54; *Literary Interest*, 154
Kristeva, Julia, 10, 24, 30–31
Kuhn, T. S., 50

Lacan, Jacques, 10, 20, 71, 76, 78, 247; and Chomsky, 191, 194; and ethics, 24; Jameson on, 172–73; "Le Rat dans le Labyrinthe," 116
Laclau, Ernesto: and Chomsky, 199–200; *Hegemony and Socialist Strategy*, 252–53
Lacoue-Labarthe, Philippe, 135
Lakoff, George, 188
Lakoff, Robin, 180, 188
Lawrence, D. H., 208
Leavis, F. R., 6, 46
Lentricchia, Frank: on de Man, 62–64; *Criticism and Social Change*, 62–65
Lesbian Rule (Aristotle), 221
Levinas, Emmanuel, 10, 25
Lewontin, R. C., 11
Liberalism, 109, 120–21, 135
Literature: and culture, 5–6, 14–17; and ethics, 32–37; and society, 14–17; and space, 4–6; and stillness, 2–3
Llorente, D. Juan Antonio (*Critical History of the Inquisition in Spain*), 83–84, 87–89, 93–95
Locke, John, 74n.
Lucian, 238
Lucretius, 222, 238
Lukács, Georg, 3, 9
Lukes, Steven, 190
Lyotard, Jean-François, 25, 38, 70n., 76, 78, 96n., 253; *Postmodern Condition*, 126–27

Macbeth (William Shakespeare), 154–55
MacIntyre, Alasdair, 19, 25–26, 33, 40
Mandela, Nelson, 28
Marcuse, Herbert, 168
Marin, Louis, 168
Martin, Wallace, 35
Marx, Karl, 62; on ethics, 24, 43
Marxism: and the aesthetic, 127–28, 136. *See also* Jameson, Fredric
Medea, 226, 239–40
Meese Commission, the, 45–46
Men in Black, 200
Mendelssohn, Moses, 73
Mexico, 258
Michaels, Walter Benn: "Against Theory," 45, 153–54

Michener, James, 4
Mill, J. S., 121
Miller, James, 67, 98
Miller, J. Hillis, 21, 230
Modernism, 244. *See also* Enlightenment; Inquisition, Spanish; Jameson, Fredric; Rationality
Modernity: and the aesthetic, 120-44; and construction of Gulf War, 138-44. *See also* Enlightenment
Monter, William, 86
Montrose, Louis, 148
Morality: and ethics, 29-30, 258-60; and rationality, 110
Mouffe, Chantal, 200, 252-53
Murdoch, Iris, 33, 223-24

Nancy, Jean-Luc, 135
Nandy, Ashis, 102
Napoleon Bonaparte, 87, 157
New Historicism, 147-49
Nietzsche, Friedrich, 121, 125; on ethics, xii, 20, 40-41; and interpretation, 155-58
Norris, Christopher, 91, 132, 196-97, 257; on aesthetic ideology, 126-27, 129-30; on Chomsky, 78-80; on Enlightenment, 78-82; on Foucault, 68; on the Gulf War, 254-56; on postmodernism, 79, 122; on Said, 80
Nozick, Robert, 39, 41-42; *The Nature of Rationality*, 100-119
Nussbaum, Martha, 26, 22ɪ-47; and childhood, 236-37; on *David Copperfield*, 234-36; and erotic love, 232-41; as feminist, 227-28; on Foucault, 230; and homosexual pederasty, 237; on Henry James, 229, 241; and Emmanuel Levinas, 231-32; on literary theory, 33, 224-25; and literature, 222-24, 234-38, 241; on morality of reading, 222-24; on narrative understanding, 222; and passivity, 231-32; on perception, 229-32; on *Phaedrus*, 236-37, 240-41; on reason, 242; on Seneca, 238-40; *Love's Knowledge*, 33, 225, 227-28, 232-38; *Therapy of Desire*, 225-26, 238-40

Oklahoma!, 4, 13
Orwell, George, 184, 187
Ought. See Ethics

Paglia, Camille, 192
Peck, James, 181-82, 186
Phaedrus (Plato), 236-37, 240-41
Picasso, Pablo, 201
Plato, 136n. See also *Phaedrus*
Plot: and ethics, 35-37, 42-43
Poe, Edgar Allan, 8, 9
Portrait of the Artist as a Young Man, A (James Joyce), 6
Postmodernism, 78, 244, 253; and aesthetic ideology, 126-28; and ethics, 24-25. *See also* Baudrillard, Jean; Jameson, Fredric; Lyotard, Jean-François; Modernism; Norris, Christopher
Pragmatism's Freud (Joseph Kerrigan), 24
Prince, Gerald, 35, 36

Rabinow, Paul, 68, 70
Rai, Milan, 181
Ransome, John Crowe, 46
Rationality, 99-119; and animality, 101-2; and autism, 111-12; autonomy of, 101-3; complexity of, 106-8; indifference to ends of, 104-5; Kantian account of, 99; and liberalism, 109; and morality, 110; the nonrational and, 106-9; and rats, 114-19; and reason, 109-14; and reasonability, 111-13
Rawls, John, 34, 105
Reason, 110-14, 242. *See also* Rationality
"Relaxation." *See* Inquisition, Spanish
Rescher, Nicholas, 110
Ricoeur, Paul, 36
Riefenstahl, Leni, 125
Riffaterre, Michael, 212-13
Rivière, Joan, 251
Robespierre, M.-F.-M.-I., 74
Rocker, Rudolf, 184, 187
Romania, 258
Rorty, Richard, 26, 33, 54, 67, 78, 121
Rose, Gillian, 234
Russian formalism, 7, 35

Geoffrey Galt Harpham is Professor of English at Tulane University. He is the author of *One of Us: The Mastery of Joseph Conrad*
(1996); *Getting It Right: Language, Literature, and Ethics* (1992);
The Ascetic Imperative in Culture and Criticism (1987); and *On the
Grotesque: Strategies of Contradiction in Art and Literature* (1982).

Library of Congress Cataloging-in-Publication Data
Harpham, Geoffrey Galt.
Shadows of ethics: criticism and the just society / Geoffrey Galt
Harpham.
p.   cm.
Includes bibliographical references and index.
ISBN 0-8223-2300-1 (alk. paper). — ISBN 0-8223-2320-6 (paper :
alk. paper)
1. Ethics, Modern.   2. Criticism.   I. Title.
BJ46.H37   1999
170—dc21
                                                          98-55943
                                                               CIP